THE HISTORY OF HORNSEA
From the Earliest Times to the Year 2005

by

STEPHEN HARRISON

BLACKTHORN PRESS

Blackthorn Press, Blackthorn House
Middleton Rd, Pickering YO18 8AL
United Kingdom

www.blackthornpress.com

ISBN 0 9546300 5 X

© Stephen Harrison

Printed and bound by Antony Rowe Ltd, Eastbourne

CONTENTS

LIST OF FIGURES

LIST OF TABLES

LIST OF PLATES

[The historian] loves the past for its own sake and tries to live in it, tries to live over again the lost life of yesterday, turning it back as one would turn back the pages of a book to re-read what has gone before; and he seeks to see the past as a far-country and to think himself into a different world.

Herbert Butterfield, *The Historical Novel: An Essay* (1924), p.7

(W)e should no be deceived into thinking that this heritage is an acquisition, a possession that grows and solidifies; rather, it is an unstable assemblage of faults, fissures and heterogeneous layers that threaten the fragile inheritor from within or underneath ... The search for descent is not the erecting of foundations: on the contrary it disturbs what was previously considered immobile; it fragments what was thought unified; it shows the heterogeneity of what was considered consistent with itself.

Michel Foucault, 'Nietzsche, Genealogy, History' (1982), p.82

PREFACE

The past is a complex of riddles asking to be solved, whose progressive elucidation is a series of victories over chaos.

The first comprehensive histories of Hornsea were written in the nineteenth century. In 1840 the topographical and antiquarian writer George Poulson (1783-1853), drawing heavily on the earlier (unpublished) researches of the Reverend William Dade (c.1740-90),[1] published his extended parish essay, which was incorporated in his two-volume work *The History and Antiquities of the Seigniory of Holderness in the East Riding of the County of York*. Poulson's twenty-seven page essay (pp.314-40 in volume 1) provided the framework followed by all but the most recent of subsequent studies into Hornsea's past. Seven years later (and in turn drawing heavily on Poulson) Edward Bedell (1799-1849) produced the first book-length study, *An Account of Hornsea in Holderness in the East Riding of Yorkshire*; the following year a second, expanded edition was issued. As Bedell was a Hornsea resident for some years, his slender volume (just 130 octavo pages in the first edition, 154 same size pages in the second) benefits from his close association with the place and first-hand knowledge; it is particularly useful for the years 1800-48, less so for earlier times. The historiography of the town then entered a prolonged period of stasis. In the early years of the twentieth century the waspish Hull Museums curator Thomas Sheppard (1876-1945) wrote on aspects of Hornsea's past, particularly geology, prehistoric artefacts, coastal erosion and the mere; some of these articles, or material based on them, appeared in his 1912 publication *The Lost Towns of the Yorkshire Coast*; others are scattered across the pages of various journals and local newspapers (see bibliography for details). It was not until 1974 that a 'modern' history (from the *Domesday Book* to 1900) appeared: that of J.E. Hobson (*A Sketch of Hornsea*; revised edition published in 2002 by Hornsea Museum). Others have followed in more recent times, focussing on particular aspects of the town's

---

[1] In 1783 Dade issued the prospectus *Proposals for the History and Antiquities of Holderness*. This work was to be published in one folio volume, with copper plate illustrations, at a subscription of 2gns. Publication was dependent on raising 240 subscriptions. Presumably this was achieved since portions of the work were printed at York in 1784 (but not issued). Ill health intervened and the project remained uncompleted at the time of Dade's death on 2 August 1790. Following his death, the manuscripts were handed to Poulson, who rearranged the material, added considerably to it, and published it in under his own name in 1840 and 1841, as (to give it its full title) the two-volume *History and Antiquities of the Seigniory of Holderness, in the East Riding of the County of York, including the Abbies of Meaux and Swine, with the Priories of Nunkeeling and Burstall; compiled from authentic charters, records, and the unpublished manuscripts of the Rev. William Dade, remaining in the library of Burton Constable.*

past. Of particular note are the contributions of Mike Sewell, who, at intervals since the 1990s, has published booklets and three collections of essays on aspects of the town's history and its environs. Especially noteworthy is his 1996 biography of the self-aggrandising Joseph Armytage Wade (*Joseph Armytage Wade, 1817-1896, "The King of Hornsea"*). This short study is important not only for charting the course of Wade's life and, at times, turbulent career, but also for the light it sheds on politics in the town during the second half of the nineteenth century. In 2002 the first cogent and fully referenced account of Hornsea from the middle ages to 1997 appeared in the long-awaited Victoria County History volume *The Middle and North Divisions of Holderness* Wapentake (pp.273-95). In many respects all previous studies have been selective in their approach: none, for example, have ventured into the long millennia of prehistory or the early historic centuries. Whilst this present work follows in their footsteps and – hopefully – builds on their foundations, it is the first to take a comprehensive long view of the town's past.

In the seventeenth century the Lincolnshire historian Abraham de la Pryme (1671-1704; who also made the occasional foray into the East Riding) wrote:

> … it is impossible that everything removable should of a sudden be put in any book. Every age sees something more than another, and every year almost some monuments are digg'd up out of the earth some where or other that was not discovered before, so that it is impossible that such a book as it should be perfect …

The point is this: in many circles it is no longer considered desirable or even realistic for one individual to produce a 'definitive' account of the history of … wherever. The history of Hornsea, like the history of any other place, is not a single monolithic entity on which all will be agreed. It is more in the way of a debate between the present generation and its predecessors, the product of which can support a dialogue (or argument) with future generations. The present generation arranges the evidence it has inherited in such a way that it forms a satisfactory narrative for today's society; but the past is always changing, throwing up new scraps of information that need to be accommodated. Our dealings with the past are like an eternal game of cards between the present and the past: you never know which card will prove significant the next time round.

Clearly, this is *a* history of Hornsea, not *the* history. What follows skirts as much as it probes, introducing sets of reflections that are meant to illuminate suggestively more than they aim to provide definitive detail. Others would have written it very differently, with different emphases. No person can claim an equally detailed knowledge of all branches of history or of the sources for writing them. Where my own knowledge was weakest I have sought the advice of others more learned in that field. In a sense this book is a team effort. Whilst I accept full authorial responsibility for selection, emphasis, interpretation, omission and errors of fact, many people have assisted – knowingly or unknowingly – in its making.

First and foremost I owe much to my friend Dr Stewart Walker. His advice, the countless and incisive discussions we have had and his friendship have provided impetus at crucial stages in the production of this book. Much of what follows has been discussed with him and I gratefully acknowledge his help in matters of fact and interpretation, for pointing out new observables and making new points. Thank you Stewart. It goes without saying that he cannot be held responsible for any errors or omissions.

Along the way, many other debts of gratitude have been incurred. The list is extensive. Over many years my long-suffering adult education students have helped me explore the history of Hornsea and surrounding area. In particular, the enormously enjoyable Friday morning classes in the library stand out in my memory, the discussions proving especially formative to my understanding and appreciation of Hornsea's more recent past. Those who attended my occasional lectures in, and guided walks around, the town have helped in more ways than they can imagine. Their stimulating discussions and pertinent observations, local knowledge and reminiscences, have touched many parts of what follows. I am most grateful to all of them. I cannot mention by name all the curators, librarians, archivists and administrators who have kindly provided help and services and must limit myself to thanking: British Library, London; Borthwick Institute of Historical Research, University of York; Brynmor Jones Library, University of Hull; East Riding of Yorkshire Library Service and, in particular, the local studies staffs at Bridlington and Beverley; East Riding of Yorkshire Archives, Beverley; House of Commons Library, London; Hull City Local Studies Library; Hull and East Riding Museum; Humber archaeology Partnership Sites and Monuments Record Office, Hull; The North Holderness Museum of Village Life, Hornsea; Prehistoric Society, London; Public Record Office, London; Royal Air Force Museum, Hendon; York City Library; and the Yorkshire Archaeological Society. I would further wish to extend my thanks to the following individuals who helped with ideas, useful criticism, answers to tiresome questions, and for their unfailingly courteous hospitality: Felicity Browne, Frank Hobson, Janet Jefferson, John and Beryl Kilby, Helen Kirk, Pam Martin, Geoff Simmons, Michael Simpson, Peter Smith, Jenny Stanley, Ian and Polly Worsdale, and Ian Wright. I must also thank my daughter and grandson, Abigail and Dylan, for a perfect summer's day spent at Hornsea, when we, too, became 'excursionists' for a few memorable hours. And we were lucky: the sun did shine ... all day!

At various times Michael Davies, Alan Dickinson, Louise James, Dr David Peacock, and Peter Smythe read individual chapters. Their comments and suggestions have been greatly appreciated. The entirety was read and commented on by David Peacock and Gill Scott, both of whom also proofread the manuscript. Gill Scott, to whom this book is dedicated, compiled the index at short notice.

The book is better than it would have been had I not incurred these debts of gratitude. It goes without saying – but I will say it all the same – that they are collectively absolved from all remaining errors. That responsibility is of course my own.

Finally, a particular thank you to my ever-patient publisher, Alan Avery, who has waited far too long for this offering to materialise. I hope, Alan, you consider the wait justified.

Despite its flaws of balance, coverage and focus, I hope that this book offers something new, something interesting and even, perhaps, something provocative. I also hope that it provides an accessible synthesis of the history of Hornsea, which may enthuse others to delve more deeply into some of the themes discussed in the following pages. It is, essentially, a work in progress; a particular viewpoint produced at a particular moment in time. Much remains to be done.

Stephen Harrison
Orkney
September 2005

CHRONOLOGY

Term	Minimum date	Maximum date
Palaeolithic	**500,000 BC**	**10,000 BC**
Lower Palaeolithic	500,000 BC	150,000 BC
Middle Palaeolithic	150,000 BC	40,000 BC
Upper Palaeolithic	40,000 BC	10,000 BC
Mesolithic	**10,000 BC**	**4,000 BC**
Early Mesolithic	10,000 BC	7,000 BC
Late Mesolithic	7,000 BC	4,000 BC
Neolithic	**4,000 BC**	**2,200 BC**
Early Neolithic	4,000 BC	3,000 BC
Middle Neolithic	3,500 BC	2,700 BC
Late Neolithic	3,000 BC	2,200 BC
Bronze Age	**2,500 BC**	**700 BC**
Early Bronze Age	2,500 BC	1,500 BC
Middle Bronze Age	1,600 BC	1,000 BC
Late Bronze Age	1,000 BC	700 BC
Iron Age	**800 BC**	**43 AD**
Early Iron Age	800 BC	400 BC
Middle Iron Age	400 BC	100 BC
Late Iron Age	100 BC	43 AD
Roman	43 AD	410 AD
Early Medieval	410 AD	1066 AD
Medieval	1066 AD	1540 AD
Post-Medieval	1540 AD	1901 AD
Modern	1901 AD	Present

A NOTE ON WEIGHTS, MEASURES AND MONEY

The weights, measures and monetary values used in this book are the ones contemporaries used. These may be summarised as:

Money:

4 farthings	=	1d (penny)
12d (pence)	=	1s (shilling)
1s	=	5p
20s (shillings)	=	£1 (pound)
21s (shillings)	=	1 guinea

Weight:

16oz (ounces)	=	1lb (pound)
1lb	=	0.45 kilograms
14lb (pounds)	=	1 stone
1 stone	=	6.35 kilograms
2 stones	=	1qr (quarter)
1qr	=	12.70 kilograms
4qr (quarters)	=	1cwt (hundredweight)
1cwt	=	50.80 kilograms
20cwt	=	1 ton
1 ton	=	1.02 tonnes

Volume:

2 pints	=	1 quart
1 quart	=	1.14 litres
4 quarts	=	1 gallon
1 gallon	=	4.55 litres
2 gallons	=	1 peck
1 peck	=	9.09 litres
4 pecks	=	1 bushel
1 bushel	=	36.40 litres
8 bushels	=	1qr (quarter)
1 quarter	=	2.91 hectolitres

Distance:

12in (inches)	=	1ft (foot)
1ft	=	0.305 metres
3ft (feet)	=	1yd (yard)
1yd	=	0.91 metres
22yds (yards)	=	1 chain
1 chain	=	20.12 metres
10 chains	=	1 furlong
1 furlong	=	201.17 metres
8 furlongs	=	1 mile
1 mile	=	1.61 kilometres

Area:

30¼ sq yds	=	1 perch
1 perch	=	25.29 sq metres

40 perches = 1 rood = 1210 sq yds = 1011.56 sq metres
4 roods = 1 acre = 4840 sq yds = 0.405 hectares

CHAPTER 1

A SENSE OF PLACE

Introduction

Hornsea is an unremarkable town in East Yorkshire, in Holderness, in the far east of the county where the land abruptly reaches the sea in low crumbling red-brown cliffs. A liminal place, a 'place on the margins', where land and sea meet. A romantically alluring location. It lies beside the windswept North Sea and since the nineteenth century has been a popular seaside resort, though nowadays past its best. Only with the coming of the railway in the second half of the nineteenth century did it make the transition from sleepy village, shocked out of its centuries-old slumber, to bustling holiday destination for the urban lower and middle classes desperate to leave behind their claustrophobic existences for – fleetingly – a couple of weeks of hard-won escapism each year. The railway offered exciting opportunities and horizons, connections to the wider world that was Victorian Britain. In its wake, a tide of development surged over Hornsea: hotels, boarding houses, promenade, pier, pleasure gardens, and more. In its heyday, around the turn of the century, tourists flocked to Hornsea, like iron filings drawn to a magnet. By the 1940s the glory days were more or less over, replaced by something less grand, more mundane. A line had been drawn. Things would never be the same again. Progress. Today, the townscape offers constant reminders of those years, faded grandeur slowly slipping into the mists of time. But much has gone: the pier and the railway, to name only two. Much has changed. The tourists still come. Once visited, many return year after year. An affiliation with place, a sense of 'belonging', something secure, stable and familiar in an ever-changing world; well-trodden pathways; even a place of retirement. Instead of hotels, boarding houses and villas rented by the week, holidaymakers are catered for in sprawling caravan parks on the outskirts or a mile or two away. Bring your own or hire a 'static' with all the conveniences of home: a home-from-home holiday. Many prefer to visit just for the day, drawn by the mere, beach, or *Hornsea Freeport*, that hub of consumerism on the site of the former Hornsea Pottery. In the past there was plenty to do in Hornsea; now, for many, it is a convenient base for explorations further afield, a place to feed, water and sleep. The attractions are elsewhere.

Hornsea presents two faces to the world. A place of oppositions. A manic space. The contrast between summer and winter is as great today as it was a hundred and more years ago. The summer months – the 'season' – see the streets thronged, the shops, stalls, amusement arcades and beaches vibrating with activity and colour. The town belongs to the holidaymakers.

1

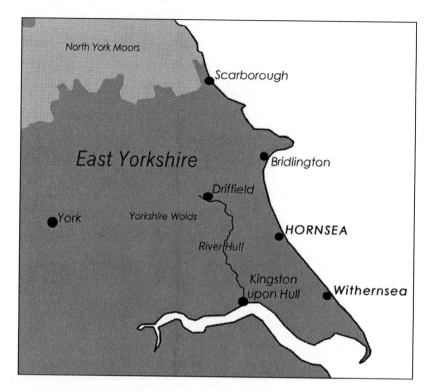

Figure 1. Hornsea Location Map.

Families, couples, groups. A carnival-like atmosphere envelops the place. For the visitor the usual constraints on behaviour are suspended and replaced by ribaldry, drink-fuelled raucousness, ice cream, and fish and chips eaten with fingers in the streets. A surreal place where fiction and reality merge. Tension between resident and visitor; contested space. The winter is different. Grey and melancholic. The streets are empty except for the local shopper. The bleak wind-scoured beaches deserted except for determined dog-walkers and plaintive, mewing gulls. Cafes and stalls closed, silent and boarded up, salt-and sand-laden gales stripping away the paint. Out of season, a town belonging to the permanent residents.

Overall though, Hornsea is situated in a deeply agricultural landscape, witnessing the quiet, largely anonymous doings of countless men and women over thousands of years, forged from a complex interplay of people and land over several millennia. Beyond the town and seaside distractions, the parish is still dominated by an organised patchwork of arable and pasture, just as it was over three millennia ago when early farmers laid out the first rough grid of fields. It is a place where town and country and seaside dissolve into each other. A constellation of meanings. A trove of memories.

The area is pleasant, its history almost totally undistinguished. Not much of any significance ever seems to have happened here. No famous person has been born, lived or done anything here. In essence, Hornsea is *ordinary*, no different from countless other towns and villages scattered across the face of England. Yet, at the same time, it is unique, a product of local

2

conditions and forces, of ceaseless interactions between people and their environment. It is this opposition that gives Hornsea meaning and character. A sense of place. What follows, then, is a biography of people and landscape, of generation piled upon generation of human endeavour in all its forms – created by webs of social, economic, political and cultural relations – in the making of place; an attempt to interpret for others what they may see in the streets and fields, the history that lies behind the scenes of everyday existence.

This book is about Hornsea's particular past, the ten or twelve thousand years – or between 400 and 500 generations – that separate the present from the mesolithic.[1] Footsteps echoing through the ages. A long procession of shadows, sometimes in focus, more often not. It is about how land and society have altered in step with one another; changes in environment, use, ownership and perception. It is a narrative of permanence and flux, of change and continuity; a geography of people and place through time; an exploration of the layers of life, the depths, the highs, interlocking and inter-related; about the way people thought about themselves, their mentalities, their assumptions, values and taboos. The past is a web woven of all that has gone before, a symphony with each moment, each year, each age adding a new bar to the score. An opus of meanings and histories.

The signature of prehistoric and early historic communities is slight hereabouts. However, the entire cultural sequence is present: mesolithic, neolithic, bronze age, iron age, Roman, Anglo-Saxon and Viking. The evidence is fragmentary, for some periods, a montage of disparate, disjointed moments: a few flint tools or scraps of pottery brought to the surface during autumnal and winter ploughings; or the brief appearance of indistinct patterns caught by the aerial photographer in growing corn at opportune moments. For other periods, it is more plentiful, 'connected' and capable of reconstruction. However, the overall outline is reasonably assured.

During the middle ages, Hornsea, because of its powerful monastic proprietors (St Mary's Abbey at York), always had the edge over other settlements in the area and developed into a thriving market centre (where the weekly market was an important locus for the redistribution of surplus agricultural produce and the work of rural artisans), a supplier of services and minor industrial production centre, all of which greatly impacted on the surrounding countryside. Along with the thirty or so other market centres in medieval East Yorkshire the place acted as a 'transformer', linking the local hinterland into the wider trade and communications circuit. Hornsea was at the centre of things, a presence in the landscape of Holderness during the medieval period.

The religious and political upheavals, those deep and righteous intolerances and intemperate extremisms of the sixteenth and seventeenth centuries, had little direct impact on Hornsea, geographically isolated from the

---

[1] Throughout this book most traditional chronological periods, other than those using proper nouns, have been deliberately placed in lower case letters, to attempt to soften their often-arbitrary nature. This reflects current concerns within archaeology to place less emphasis on period boundaries, which are in many cases perceived as constructs of archaeological methodologies. Not only are changes between periods not clear-cut, but the people who inhabited them in the past would not themselves have recognised such distinctions during their lifetimes.

mainstream as it was, beyond the sweeping away of the monastic landlords and their replacement by secular proprietors. Although Protestantism provided the new ethic and framework for life, the country hereabouts was deeply conservative and Catholicism, never far from the surface, remained a dominant and persistent presence. Old traditions died hard, more especially since many of the more prominent local families continued with their allegiance to the measureless diversity of saints, mysticism, miracles and pilgrimages. Four-hundred-and-fifty years later, Catholicism is still a significant presence in this land.

The inhabitants of Hornsea felt the chill wind of the English Civil War in the seventeenth century, but the storm never broke over their lives. Choices were made, allegiances defined and re-defined. A minority fought on one side or the other. Skirmishes took place when the paths of Royalists and Parliamentarians crossed, but none impacted on the overall course and outcome of the conflict. For the majority living in this area, ambivalence was the predominant emotion.

Hornsea came into its own during the nineteenth century, making the transition from village to seaside resort as a result of the coming of the railway and the vision of the somewhat awkward and belligerent Joseph Armytage Wade, the self-styled 'King of Hornsea.' The rail link with Hull was, however, initially for other purposes. The development of the resort came as something of an afterthought, more organic, *ad hoc*, less contrived. Joseph Armytage Wade, who lived in Hornsea but whose main business interests were in Hull, was – with some qualifications – responsible for both.

The latter could not have happened without the former. Hornsea acquired a rail link in the early 1860s. Following this, development was sustained and the place successfully made the transition from village to popular east coast seaside resort, drawing urban middle class visitors, mainly from Hull, the West Riding and the north Midlands. By the outbreak of the Second World War Hornsea had declined as a seaside resort, day-trippers taking the place of residential holidaymakers. The place adjusted to changed circumstances and adapted in different ways to meet the new challenges of the later twentieth century. In this Hornsea has been largely successful.

This then is the biography. Hornsea as subject and object. A set of spatial stories inspired by a desire to 'know' the past, to 'tell it as it was,' and, if possible, to 'explain' it. In a wider sense the (hi)story of Hornsea is the (hi)story of ourselves.

New land, new beginning

Holderness, that 'silent and somewhat desolate area' immortalised by Winifred Holtby in her 1937 novel *South Riding*, is a triangular shaped country of low-lying, intractable boulder clay, covering approximately 160,000 acres. A land haunted and isolated in its swirling mists. A flat land. A land of superstition and folklore. To the farmer it is 'strong' land or 'loving' land (because it clings to the boots); to many visitors it is largely drab, featureless and uninteresting; and to the resident it is tranquil, almost 'backward', far from the hustle and bustle and pressures of city living. But it is also a land of great subtlety and an extraordinary variety of textures, of

4

wide panoramic views and huge skies, of cold winds and steely calm, of nestling orange brick and pantile villages and scattered farmsteads; a landscape composed of an intricate skein of apparently confusing, narrow and abruptly twisting spidery lanes, winding as old roads are usually expected to do and seemingly going nowhere, stands of broadleaf woodland, and a grid of steep-sided drainage ditches, and church towers rising majestically out of the flatlands to dominate the scene. A place of infinite variety, with enough detail to absorb the eye for hours. Like East Anglia, but only less well known, it is a place of few topographical constraints, where land, sky and water meet in a capricious patterning of light and shade. A languid countryside. Its apex is to be found in the north at Sewerby, in the lee of Flamborough Head. From there it broadens out, hugging the chalklands of the Yorkshire Wolds in the west, is lapped by the estuary of the River Humber in the south, and, in the east, it terminates abruptly in a low line of straggling, indented sea cliffs. From apex to base Holderness is thirty-five miles long and from Wolds to sea it is twenty miles at its broadest. The coastline is a graceful, sweeping curve from Bridlington in the north to Spurn Point in the south, where it ends in a narrow, two-mile long unstable finger of land, mainly sand dunes, jutting out into the turbulent mouth of the River Humber. For centuries Spurn Point has acted as a guide to seafarers on this otherwise featureless coast and must have been a convenient first landfall for countless visitors, invaders and settlers alike, as in Richard II's time, when Henry Bolingbroke landed here at the head of an army to make his bid for the English throne.

In the scheme of things, Holderness is a new land, less than 20,000 years old – little more than a blink of the eye in geologic time. In a sense, it is also a land out of time and place. A million and more years ago the area was sea, and the cliff line was far to the west, formed by the eastern slope of the Yorkshire Wolds. Had they existed, villages such as Carnaby, Haisthorpe, Burton Agnes, Nafferton, Lockington and southwards down to Hessle would have been beside the seaside. Then the northern hemisphere was gripped by a succession of Ice Ages; the land became hidden and depressed under a thick mantle of ice. The climate cooled dramatically and, periodically, great tongues of ice – enormous glaciers, often up to half or even three-quarters of a mile in height – crept southwards from the Polar region across much of northern Europe, scouring, scraping and remoulding the landscape with eager and remorseless energy. A slow, frozen tide lapping and breaking on land, throwing up shining cliffs and glittering peaks. Over the last million years or so, a time known to geologists as the *Pleistocene*, there have been at least four Ice Ages, each lasting about 100,000 years. They were interspersed with warmer, inter-glacial periods, when the ice retreated northward. It was a time of advance and retreat, a slow dance choreographed by nature.

The erosive force of the glaciers was awesome. As they moved inexorably across the earth, submerging even mountain ranges in their path, grinding their way ever southward, they picked up, and carried forward, vast quantities of debris. Like giant bulldozers, they scooped up everything in their way, not only loose material but also blocks of parent rock prised from the surfaces over which they travelled. The eroded material – unsorted, scratched and rounded – was carried forward by the moving ice and, when the ice melted, re-deposited at varying distances from the original sources. Stones of

5

all sizes transported in this way are called 'erratics' and from their character and distribution it is possible to determine the source rocks and the directional trends of the main glaciers.

The pathways taken by the ice blankets can be tracked in the rock-strewn surfaces of arable fields the length and breadth of Holderness. Recently a walk across half-a-dozen fields ploughed fields around both Hornsea and Withernsea produced this roll-call of geologic and geographic origins:

- Rhomb porphyry from Scandinavia.
- Carboniferous sandstones from the Pennines and north-west England.
- Limestones from the Pennines and north-west England.
- Purple-red sandstone from the Pennines.
- Basalts, dolerites and andesites from the Lake District.
- Quartz and quartzite pebbles from the Cheviots in Northumberland.
- Porphyrite and quartz porphyry from the Central Lowlands of Scotland.
- Pink granite from south-west Scotland.
- Chalk and flint from the Yorkshire Wolds, from just a few miles to the north and west.

These erratics are incorporated in a matrix of fine clay, also scooped up, carried forward and then deposited by the melting ice sheets. Up to a maximum thickness of 30m, this *boulder clay* varies from place to place: it may be stiff or sandy, almost stone-less or so stony as to be gravel within a clayey matrix, and it may be variable in colour – reddish-brown, purple or a dark leaden hue. For the most part, a deep and heavy, well watered soil. Indeed, the impermeable boulder clay, trapping water on the surface and in its structure, gave Holderness a watery character of its own, a place of dank airs, in the past physically separating it from the rest of the county. Up until the great drainage works of the later eighteenth and nineteenth centuries, the water was ineradicable, turning every untended corner and undredged dyke into a lush tangle of rushes and teasel.

In addition to the clay, sands and gravels, deposited by meltwaters at the end of the last Ice Age, occur either as isolated, irregularly shaped hillocks or as more continuous linear spreads. The ridge linking Hornsea to the Leven-Brandesburton area is one such example. Here large-scale commercial extraction has occurred during the course of the twentieth century, leading to some important archaeological discoveries, particularly of mesolithic artefacts (see below, chapter 2).

After the ice

The last Ice Age – the Devensian – started approximately 115,000 years ago and was characterised by at least four glacial advances interspersed by shorter episodes of ice retreat. The late Devensian glaciation built up around 30,000 years ago and reached its maximum extent about 18,000 years ago. During this time, the physical geography of northern and western Europe was radically different. Sea levels were around 45m lower than they are today.

6

The southern North Sea was dry land; Britain was part of Europe and much of the English Channel was a land bridge.

Around 16,000 years ago, the ice began to retreat, finally leaving East Yorkshire about 13,000 years ago. The thaw proceeded in fits and starts, with rapid deglaciation and then an abrupt millennium-long cold snap about 12,000 years ago. Thereafter the warming continued, ushering in modern climatic conditions in northern Europe.

When the ice retreated from East Yorkshire, a new land – Holderness – was exposed: a land composed of material that had been scooped up by the glaciers during their various advances and then left behind as the thaw set in. In time, the region became available for human exploitation. However, the transformations that took place before the arrival of the first communities were long in the making. In the immediate aftermath of deglaciation, Holderness was an open, undulating, windswept place. The surface hollows, left by stranded blocks of melting ice, became lakes or meres of greater or lesser extent. In time, these open expanses of freshwater became rich and diverse habitats, exploited by communities down to fairly recent times. Many were drained during the middle ages, yet more during the agricultural improvements of the eighteenth and nineteenth centuries. Today, Hornsea Mere is the sole surviving member of this once large family.

The gradual warming (the pre-Boreal and Boreal) brought about a whole series of changes to the natural world. Forests developed and these in

Phase	Dates	Climate	Tree cover	Fauna
Pre-Boreal	10,250-9,800 years before present	• Warm and wet	• Birch • Pine • Willow	• Wild pigs • Roe deer • Red deer • Reindeer • Wild horse • Bear
Boreal	9,800-7,000 years before present	• Rapid amelioration • Warm and dry • Temperatures rising – c.7.2° C per 100 years	• Mixed oak forest • Pine and hazel especially common	• Red deer • Wild pig • Beaver • Elk • Auroch
Atlantic	7,000-5,000 years before present	• Warm and wet • Climatic optimum when temperatures were highest	• Mixed oak forest predominated	• Auroch • Elk • Red deer • Roe deer • Wild pig • Dog

Table 1. Post-glacial environmental changes.

7

turn were colonised by the new post-glacial fauna. The post-glacial vegetational history of Holderness is reasonably assured. Analysis of peat and sediment cores from various locations around the region allows for a reconstruction of the general pattern. These environmental transformations are broadly summarised in Table 1.

The physical geography of Europe also changed dramatically. The melting ice saw a corresponding rise in sea levels. Around 9,100 years ago the sea level may have lain at about –35m. Some six hundred or so years later the Straits of Dover were breached, the North Sea Plain flooded and Britain became an island. Finally, by 7,000 years ago the coastline had stabilised at roughly its present position, although continuing episodes of transgression, regression and human reclamation create a complex, ever-changing picture. Also, the height of the landmasses in relation to sea levels changed. Relieved of the downward pressure caused by the great weight of ice, the land simply bounced back – a process that is still continuing. Locally, the effects of these processes can be seen on the foreshore at Withernsea, when parts of Noah's Wood, a submerged forest, are occasionally exposed at low tide. A tangle of oak, birch, pine and other tree stumps and broken branches.

A land in retreat

Hornsea has not always been at the seaside. From the beginning, after the ice returned to water and sea levels rose, the soft boulder clay of Holderness was ceaselessly gnawed by hungry waves, its land carried away by longshore currents and re-deposited as silt in the Humber or along the coast of Lincolnshire. The sea reclaiming its own. In Roman times, the coast was a two- or three-hour walk to the east, beyond the horizon. By 1600 it was within sight, sound and smell. Two hundred and fifty years later, the embryonic seaside resort was in process of formation: promenades, new roads, hotels and boarding houses overlooked the sea. On the edge. A full-stop to the flat poetry of Holderness.

Since prehistory, communities in this land have watched powerlessly as nature had her way, people and settlements shuffling ever back from the relentless surge of the sea. A land and people in retreat. With the rise of the modern age, various coastal protection schemes have come and gone over the last one hundred years, none ultimately successful. Nature still rules.

Over the last 2,000 years alone, it is estimated that a strip of land at least three-and-a-half miles wide from Bridlington to Spurn Point has succumbed to the restless onslaught of the sea, making it the fastest eroding coastline in the world: some 70,000 acres or 110 square miles have disappeared. The process continues. It is instructive to walk along the beach today to witness erosion in action at first hand: the jagged-edged cliffs, fissured with crevasses, dropping away in an uninviting tumble of sticky boulder clay; mud flows, clay turned viscous by water, oozing out over the coarse-grained sandy foreshore, advancing like so many tongues of glacial ice; and unstable nearly-detached vertiginous stacks tottering in precarious solitude, threatening to dissolve with the coming of each high tide. A world in disintegration; a world swallowed by each land-hungry rising tide and winter storm. Turn eastwards, look out over the sea and remember: where there was once land stretching towards the horizon, nothing now but sky and clouds, water and waves, and echoes of long-gone communities. [2]

Yet, the bald statistics and here-and-now visual observations of loss mask variety: different rates at different places at different times. For the last one-hundred-and-fifty years or so, an accumulation of Ordnance Survey maps, measurements and observations provides a reliable database from which rates of erosion can be calculated, not only in average terms but for specific locations along the coastline. It will be more relevant to discuss coastal erosion as it relates to Hornsea at appropriate points throughout the text, thereby situating it in specific historical contexts. Here, some general comments will be sufficient for present purposes. Along the entire coast, erosion is variable. South of Hornsea the rate of erosion is greatest, reaching up to 3m per year. Two factors are responsible for this: firstly, the orientation of the coastline is such that there is little protection from the full fury of large waves which occur during north-easterly gales; and, secondly, because the eroded material is transported southwards by longshore drift currents, beaches are narrower and have limited ability to dissipate wave energy. Erosion to the north of Hornsea is less, between 1m and 2m per year. This is due primarily to the protection afforded by Flamborough Head.

But wave action is not the only cause of erosion. Paradoxically the greater loss occurs as a result of processes acting on the landward side. In dry weather cracks appear in the clay surface in front of the cliff edge. Groundwater seepage then widens these fissures and causes the land around the cracks to become unstable, eventually resulting in those areas breaking away and slipping down the cliff face on to the beach. Mudflows running down the cliff face are another feature of this process.

In 1858 a visitor to Hornsea's Marine Hotel provided the following account of coastal erosion in the vicinity of the hotel:

> [T]he wasting process is carried on by other means than the sea. I saw threads of water running down the cliffs, produced by yesterday's rain, and not without astonishment at the great deposits of mud they deposit at the base, forming in places a narrow viscous stream, creeping in a raised channel across the sand, or confused pastry heaps dotted with pools of pasty ochre. Mr Coniton, the proprietor of the hotel, told me that he believed that the rain had more influence than the sea in causing the waste of the land, and he showed me the means he employed to protect his territory from one and the other. To prevent the loss by rain, which he estimates, where no precautions are taken, at a foot a year, he at first sloped his cliff at such an angle that the water runs easily down and with scarcely appreciable mischief. Then, to protect the base, he had driven rows of piles through the sand to the clay beneath, and there, checking the natural drift of the sand, to the southward, preserve the under

---

[2] Since 1066, around twenty-seven settlements have been lost to coastal erosion in Holderness, from Wilsthorpe in the north to Old Kilnsea in the south; continuing erosion clearly has important implications not only to present-day cliff-edge communities, but also for the preservation of archaeological sites.

9

stratum. Where no such barrier exists, the waves in a winter storm sweep all the sand clean off, and lay bare the clay, and tumbling upon it with mighty shocks, sometimes wear it down a foot in the course of a tide. By this lowering of the base, the saturated soil above, deprived of support, topples over leaving a huge gap which only facilitates further encroachments; and in the course of a few tides the fallen mass is drifted away to enlarge the shoals in the estuary of the Humber.

The writer of the above description highlighted the problem caused by protecting only short stretches of coast. He went on to say:

> Mr Coniton entered into possession fifteen years ago, and, in all that time, so effectual are the safeguards, has lost none of his land. The edge, he says, has not receded, and, to show what might be, he points to his neighbour's field, which has shrunk away some yards to the rear.

Hornsea Mere

Ode to Hornsea Mere

Beside thee born, I love thee still,
And near thee oft my fancy strays,
Recalling every well-known rill
That to thy store its tribute pays.

Thy islands green, thy sedgy shore,
And swans that grace thy waters blue,
With Wilkinson's time-keeping oar,
I think on still with memory true.

In childhood by thy banks to stray,
And pluck the wild mint flowering there,
I've joyous passed the summer day,
Nor dreamt of such a thing as care.

In winter when thy frozen face
Compelled the aquatic tribes to roam,
I won in many a skating race,
And big with conquest sought my home.

Nor envious I of Cæsar's fame,
Or laurels gained by Charles the Swede;
Each conquered and each gained a name,
And so did I – 'tis fortunes meed.

But fled are all those halcyon days;
Thy infant waves, unmark'd by me,
May flow – while far thy poet strays,

Yet of he'll tune his lyre to thee.

And tho' in numbers rude he sings,
Aspiring not to polished lays,
With trembling hand he'll touch the strings,
And hymn the tales of other days.

Paul Gray, undated (earlier nineteenth century)

Plate1. Hornsea Mere and town, with the coastline beyond, viewed from the west.
(Photograph: Stephen Harrison)

Although he did not have the benefit of the aerial camera, Edward
Bedell's firsthand description of this scene in the 1840s (printed in his *An
Account of Hornsea, in Holderness, in the East Riding of Yorkshire*, 1848) is
still apposite:

> The Mere, or "Marre," as for several centuries it used to be written,
> and is still called by the country people, is about a mile and a half
> long from east to west, being the most extensive piece of water in
> Yorkshire. It is nearly surrounded by rising grounds, which do not,
> however, in any part of the parish of Hornsea reach a height of more
> than about from 60 to 80 feet above the sea. Along the face of these
> grounds, on each side of the mere and of the little valley eastward of
> it down to the sea, a rather steep bank, 8 or 10 feet high, may be
> traced, which forcibly suggests the idea of the action of water at a
> considerably higher level than the present mere. There are two or
> three islands, and two of these and the western parts of the mere are
> well clothed with trees. Taken altogether, the actual features of the
> village and mere, with the sea in the back ground, afford materials
> for a description literally correct, which might lead the reader to
> picture a scene of unusual beauty; but it must be admitted that though

11

there is much that is pleasing to the eye, and very great "capability," yet the general aspect of the place is perhaps more tame than might be expected from the combination of wood, water, islands, and rising grounds, which exist there.

Today there is much in this view that would have been familiar to Bedell when he was living in, and writing about, Hornsea. Bedell was something of a conservative and traditionalist: his use of the word 'tame' in the above account is a reference back to the tremendous changes (and, in his view, disruption to the old order) wrought by the parliamentary enclosure of the parish in the first years of the nineteenth century.

Measuring approximately 2¼ miles east-west by 1 mile north-south, the mere – a site of special scientific interest (SSSI) under Section 28 of the Wildlife and Countryside Act 1981 – is the largest expanse of freshwater in Yorkshire; a sheet of bright glinting water amongst farmland. In 1700 it covered 468 acres, in 1809, 361 acres, and in 1890, 324 acres; nowadays it is around 300 acres. Progressive shrinkage is the dominant trend, not only in recent times but in the past also. Once it was much larger: traces of multiple, parallel, former shorelines can be seen near the former village of Southorpe, to the south, and on the higher ground to the north of the Hornsea-Seaton road; a shallow, now generally dry depression to the west of Wassand Hall is probably also an indication of its former size. Today the depth of water is between 5 ft and 7 ft only; in the past, judging from the fossilised former shorelines, it was considerably deeper. The broad expanse of open water is fringed by a diverse range of habitats: reedswamp, fen, and willow-alder carr woodland.

Hornsea mere is of national ornithological importance as a refuge and feeding area for duck, including large numbers of wintering mallard, pochard, teal, tufted duck, goldeneye, wigeon, goosander, scaup, and long-tailed duck. In addition, breeding species include coot, mallard, gadwall, pochard, teal, shoveler and tufted duck, and – near the north-east limit of their British range – reed warbler.

In the past, as now, the mere and its surroundings were the focus for a diverse range of leisure activities: angling, bird watching, boating, wildfowling, winter skating, walking along the shoreline. In his long autobiographical narrative poem of c.1806 (*The Sailor; a poem*), Edward Anderson devotes a section to the pleasures of Hornsea Mere:

Many go there to fish for pleasure's sake,
But they must always pay for what they take;
When caught, they weigh it at the New Inn door,
The money it is given to the poor.
This lake is two miles long and one mile broad,
And both with fish and fowl it is well stor'd;
And in the midst of it an island lies,
Where sea-birds breed – for miles you hear their cries.
I went there in a boat one morn in spring,
The cries around me made my ears to ring;
Thousands of birds were flying round my head,

12

Plate 2. The ragged edge: the boulder clay cliffs of Holderness, embattled symbol of man's transient hold on this land. (Photographs: Stephen Harrison)

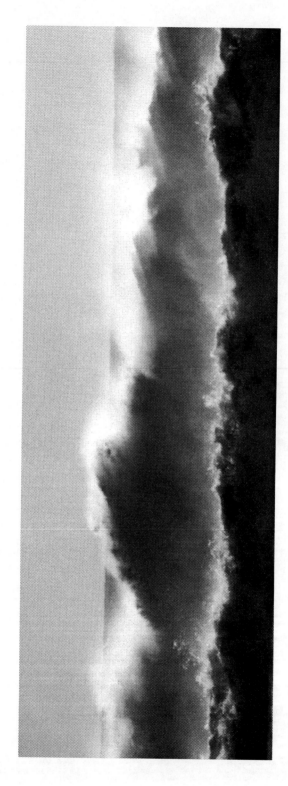

Plate 3. The vibrating and irresistible force of a winter's storm pounding the shoreline at Hornsea: a wide expanse of turbulent sea, grey-green, laced white, under a capricious sky. (Photograph: Stephen Harrison)

Plate 4. Buildings on the edge: the effects of coastal erosion at Hornsea in the early years of the twentieth century. (Photograph: Stephen Harrison collection)

Plate 5. The storm-battered remains of sea defences at Hornsea, photographed sometime between c.1900-14. These timber groynes were erected at different dates during the second half of the nineteenth century and were designed to protect residential and resort development along the cliff edge from the effects of coastal erosion. Whilst offering a degree of short-term protection to land and property immediately behind, slowing or even halting the rate of erosion, the limited lengths of such defences are ultimately ineffective. The sea simply goes around the ends and continues on its destructive path. They also restrict the supply of sediment for longshore drift and, therefore, reduce still further the width of protective beach. (Photographs: Stephen Harrison collection)

16

Plate 6. A combination of timber groynes, dumped boulders (some the size of a small car) and concrete sea wall make up the modern-day sea defences at Hornsea. (Photographs: Stephen Harrison)

17

Plate 7. Erosion caused by slippage of the cliff edge due to water percolation from the landward side. (Photograph: Stephen Harrison)

Plate 8. Approached from the west or south-west, the mere and its woodland curtain give Hornsea a picturesque aspect. Land, water, sky and the built environment meet and merge in a pleasing, almost naturalistic prospect. On a bright, sunlit day, particularly when viewed from the mereside path between Wassand and Hornsea (laid out at enclosure in the early nineteenth century), it is an enduring image of the English countryside. (Photograph: Stephen Harrison)

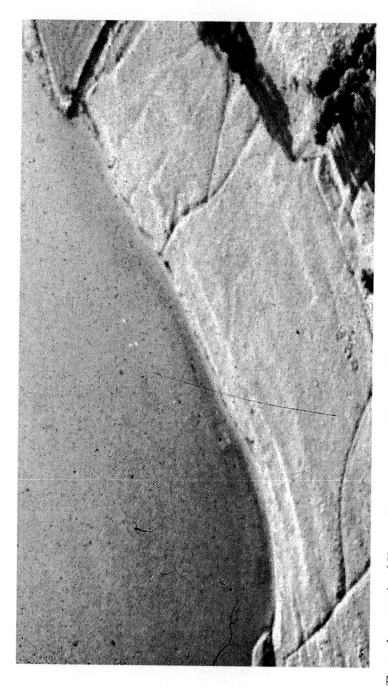

Plate 9. The southern margin of Hornsea Mere. The parallel lines just above the present-day shoreline provide evidence for once higher water levels. (Photograph: Stephen Harrison)

Plate 10. The west end and the northern side of the mere are bordered by woodland: Decoy Plantation, Springfield Wood, Low Wood, and the un-named belt alongside the Seaton road. These plantations were laid out during the nineteenth century as landscape enhancement schemes and game coverts by the Strickland-Constable owners of Wassand Hall, at the west end of the mere. (Photograph: Stephen Harrison)

Plate 11. Image of Hornsea Mere. (Photograph: Stephen Harrison)

So many nests that clear I could not tread
Without breaking their eggs, in vain to strive,
And with young birds the weeds seem'd all alive;
The old ones cry'd, Begone, they seem'd to say,
And flew close at me as I went away;
The swans so stately held their heads so high,
They too did hiss me as I pass'd them by;
They flapp'd their wings, and at me they did stare,
And seem'd to say, What business had you there?
I never saw, in countries I've gone o'er,
So many in so small a spot before.

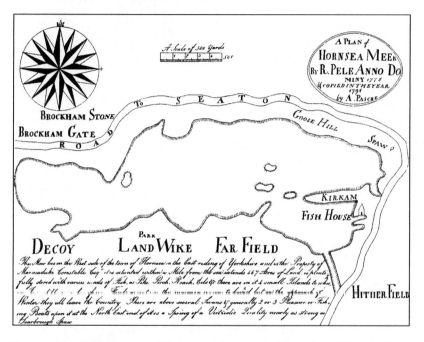

Figure 2. This 1778 plan by R. Pele is the earliest known illustration of Hornsea Mere.
The legend reads:

> This Meer lies on the West side of the town of Hornsea in the East
> riding of Yorkshire and is the Property of Marmaduke Constable
> Esq. It is situated within a Mile from the sea, extends [to] 467
> Acres of Land, is plentifully stored with various kinds of Fish as
> Pike, Perch, Roach, Eels &c. There are in it 4 small Islands to
> which an Incredible number of sea Fowls resort in the summer
> season to breed but on the approach of Winter they all leave the
> Country. There are above several Swans and generally 2 or 3
> Pleasure or Fishing Boats upon it. [A]t the North East end of it is a
> Spring of a Vitriolic Quality nearly as strong as Scarborough
> Spaw.

23

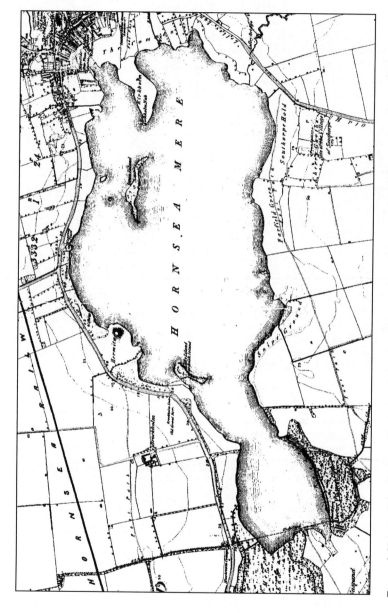

Figure 3. Hornsea Mere in the mid-nineteenth century. (Extract from 1:10,560 Ordnance Survey map (Sheet 197), surveyed 1852, published 1854)

In February 1838, during one of the severest winters of the nineteenth century, the *Hull Rockingham* carried the following report of festivities on the mere:

> The beautiful lake at Hornsea has been frozen for upwards of six weeks, during which the inhabitants of the village have amused themselves with playing at "shin-up," skating, dancing reels, and running races on the ice. A few days ago, a sum was raised by subscription sufficient to purchase a fine sheep, which was roasted on the ice over the heads of the amazed fishes, the most ancient pike in the place remembering no similar exhibition. A friend of ours has favoured us with a graphic description of the whole process, from which we make the following extract:- Having bought our sheep, we all immediately set to work in making preparations for the roasting. Some of us loaded ourselves with bricks for the erection of a fire-place, while others were engaged in constructing a capacious booth to accommodate the guests. About eleven o'clock the sheep was put upon the spit, and at three was pronounced ready for the table. It was admirably dressed and reflected much credit on the head cook, Mr W. Leeson, to whose superintendence the whole management was entrusted. Men, women, and children flocked to behold the joyous scene, some of the men being mounted. The dinner went off amidst mirth and music. Before it was ended we were called upon to leave the booth to look at a cart loaded with bricks and drawn by two horses, which was passing over the ice on the north side of the lake. Our repast being at length concluded, we divided ourselves into two parties, and forthwith commenced a game of shin-up, which was severely contested. Between eight and nine o'clock in the evening we paraded the streets, accompanied by a band of music and torch bearers; thence we returned to the ice, marched in procession round the island, and danced, sang, and shouted till the woods of Wassand echoed back our nocturnal revelry. Such was our feast, which we finished at the Old Hotel by drinking, in prime ale, health and long life to the Queen and her ministers.

In the equally severe winter of 1871, events similar to those just described were repeated on the mere: tables set up on the ice for the consumption of mutton, bread and ale, all provided free of charge, and accompanied by dancing, singing and skating. And, on Boxing Day 1890, a cricket match was played on the frozen surface of the mere.

As well as pleasures, there were dangers for the unwary, as Bedell relates:

> The mere is occasionally frozen very strongly, sometimes affording excellent skating. Without care there is danger from the open water kept in some spots, by birds, and when they are at length driven from these places, a skater may be fatally deceived by running upon them when the ice there is perhaps of only one night's production. Accidents have occurred within memory from this cause. Before inclosure, strangers descending Brockholme Hill, where the road

bends to the left, have been misled when the mere has been frozen and all covered with snow, by making direct for the lights in the town, and so getting on the ice. One winter's night, two men, with a horse and cart and some goods which they had been seizing for rent, went some distance on the ice without knowing it: the horse was drowned. Many years ago a woman of the name of Moor, who had strayed on the ice at night in a similar manner, got among the trees on the island, where she sung a psalm very loudly, to the astonishment of the town's-people, who heard it very distinctly through the still frosty night air, and presently went with lights in search of the singer.

We are not told the outcome of the rescue attempt.

The meaning of 'Hornsea'

The origin of the place-name 'Hornsea' is relatively straightforward and has a topographical meaning. The first element is derived from the Old Scandinavian *horn*, meaning a 'nook of land, projecting piece of land, headland'. The second element is from the Old English *saē* or Old Scandinavian *sáer*, both meaning the 'pool, lake'. Thus, when compounded: 'the lake in which lies a projecting piece of land'. This is entirely appropriate. At the eastern end of the mere, there is a long, narrow peninsula – Kirkholme – that, in the past, may have been longer still: some 250m offshore, the small Swan Island appears to have been a continuation of it.

CHAPTER 2

EBB AND FLOW
Introduction

People have lived continuously in and around Hornsea for the last 10,000 to 12,000 years. For the first four or five thousand of those years communities followed a sophisticated hunter-gatherer-fisher lifestyle; thereafter farming became dominant, and has remained so to the present day. This chapter will explore Hornsea's largely invisible pasts: its prehistoric, Roman, Anglo-Saxon and Viking legacies.

Although the area (along with the rest of Holderness) has only recently begun to attract the systematic attention of archaeologists, there is much within and around the town that speaks of this early occupation. The prehistory and early history of Hornsea invites endless speculation and there is a certain pleasure to be derived from the prospect of human settlement in areas where, many thousands of years later, streets would be laid out and houses constructed. The evidence ranges from the transitory campsites of mesolithic hunters, gatherers and fishers, through neolithic, bronze age, iron age and Romano-British settlements, field systems and trackways, to Anglo-Saxon burials: layers of human endeavour piled one on top of another. There are surface scatters of artefacts – more often than not individual and spatially isolated pieces, less frequently dense gatherings – brought to light by ploughing and other activities: flint or stone tools and implements, cores and waste from flint knapping, finely ground and polished stone axes, fragmentary pottery vessels, metalwork, quern stones, animal bones and other domestic debris. Disconnected and disjointed fragments from many different pasts; suggestive tokens of once much greater wholes. The evidence is of long duration, spanning almost 10,000 years and over 400 generations. Full of anomalies and contradictions and irresolutions and ambiguities as it is, these fragments from the past can also provide moments of revelation, when the town and its surroundings can be seen to harbour the secrets of the human world.

A general trend throughout these long millennia is of people gradually settling down, developing a local identity and a strong sense of, and attachment to, place. Despite the fragmentary nature of much of the surviving resource, it is possible to construct a relatively coherent narrative of how successive communities confidently responded to, exploited and organised the local landscape to meet their own particular needs and requirements, imposing their own identity on the natural world; and how, as the centuries gave way to millennia, different societies altered and restructured in their own image the world they inherited. Processes of creation, decay, adaptation and renewal have led to the superimposition of many different cultural landscapes one on top of another, generating what the nineteenth century historian F.W. Maitland called 'that complex palimpsest,' which bears comparison with an

27

overwritten document. Locally, the multiple landscapes of prehistory and the early historic periods have not entirely faded from view; if you look hard enough you can still see the ghosts.

Born to run (mesolithic: c.9,500-4,000 BC)

The story of human occupation in East Yorkshire has modest beginnings. The earliest peoples – modern humans like you and me – to inhabit the region, perhaps 10,000 or 12,000 years ago, have left only shadowy traces. Mesolithic: hunters, gatherers and fishers. From where did these hunter-gatherer-fishers originate? At this remove it is impossible to give a definitive answer. The likelihood is that the first arrivals into eastern England came from southern Scandinavia or northern Germany *via* the land bridge across what is now the North Sea; indeed, items of material culture found in East Yorkshire and elsewhere, such as the bone and antler points discussed below, have distinct parallels in this part of Europe. Alternatively, they may have penetrated the region from the south, having their ultimate origins in the Low Countries or northern France. Wherever they came from and however they arrived, it is certain that we are dealing with extremely low population levels. Although it is not possible to arrive at anything like accurate population figures, 'best guess' estimates range from as low as 6,000 to as high as around 30,000 people for the entire British Isles at any one time. Locally the density would have varied, with much higher figures for favoured locations, such as around Hornsea, with perhaps as many as between three and ten persons per square kilometre. The very small human population levels, unevenly spread across the whole landmass, contrast with likely numbers of herbivores: for example, 1,500,000 red deer, 1,350,000 wild pig, and 1,000,000 wild cattle. Given the lifestyle, minimal human population numbers were a necessary prerequisite to survival. People were probably organised in extended family units, leading a relatively solitary existence for much of the time. In these circumstances, survival depended on the absolute co-operation and integration of all members of the group. Occasionally, such groups might come together in larger – perhaps regional – aggregations for the purposes of ritual and ceremony, for the exchange of exotic items, for the selection of 'marriage' partners from a wider genetic pool, for the forging and renewal of alliances, and for the cementing of bonds. Times for gossip, feasting, and the exchange of information.

At this time, Holderness was an Amazon Basin-like landscape with an unbroken forest canopy relieved only by meandering streams and larger expanses of open water, such as Hornsea Mere. The local environmental data indicate an abundance of tree species. However, browsing and de-barking by animals may have inhibited tree growth or even preserved clearings. The degree to which the mesolithic environment contained 'wildwood' is therefore unclear and it may have consisted of a variety of woodland types, from relatively dense areas to more open 'wood pasture.' Overall, though, hemmed in by trees, their world would have been circumscribed, enclosed and dark, even though such enclosure may have been comforting. The great expanse of sky could only be glimpsed through gaps in the canopy and rarely would mesolithic hunter-gatherers have caught a glimpse of the horizon. From the perspective of the twenty-first century, a forgotten landscape.

Mesolithic people were nomadic, moving across the landscape along well-trodden pathways through the densely forested early post-glacial environment, entering into an active engagement with the surroundings; establishing temporary campsites.[1] They exploited the natural resources of wherever they happened to be. It was a lifestyle involving degrees of seasonal, annual and lifetime mobility. For the most part, not altering or manipulating their surroundings, preferring co-existence with nature, taking only what was required for immediate needs, involved in a mutualistic relationship with their environment; the forest was perceived as a benign, life-giving force. Mesolithic people were intimately knowledgeable about natural resources, confidently exploiting their environment, moving around and visiting, exchanging and feuding with other groups. Today, all that usually remains of their fleeting presence is a handful of flint cores, flakes and tools in a ploughed field.

On the dry land stretching away from the mere in all directions was woodland. Rather than continuous forest, the vegetation may have been a mosaic of small glades, coppiced trees, overgrown campsites, and cleared or regenerated plots. In between would have been a dense tangle of forest. In varying degrees, species present include: oak, beech, birch, elm, and hornbeam; alder, elder, willow, yew, wild cherry, and hazel; ash, holly, whitebeam, crab apple, pear, plum, and field maple; an understorey of bracken, gorse, hawthorn, bilberry, blackberry, cranberry, cowberry, crowberry, wild strawberry, wild raspberry, juniper, grasses, knotweed, woundwort, goosefoot, chickweed, dandelion, common nettle, vetch, dock, silverweed, and wild rose. Fungi also. This gloomy and shadowy world, full of noise and movement, was home to a diverse range of animals and birds, some migratory, others permanent. The list is long: wild cattle (aurochs),[2] wild horse,[3] red deer, roe deer, wild pig, brown hare, pine marten, badger, red fox, arctic fox, brown bear, wolf, wild cat, red squirrel, stoat, lynx, woodmouse, game birds and song birds, bees, insects, and edible grubs. A highly evocative and ideologically charged place; full of hazards too for the hunter and the unwary alike.

---

[1] However, recent excavations at Howick, on the north Northumberland coast, are perhaps beginning to alter our perceptions of mobility in the mesolithic. Here, a substantial circular timber-framed house – the only one so far known in Britain and north-west Europe – was discovered. This complex structure, with its succession of earth floors and hearths, seems, from the radiocarbon dates, to have been permanently occupied between c.7,700 and 7,600 BC. This one hundred-year occupation probably equates to about three generations of people, and implies long-term, stable settlement.

[2] In the sixteenth century, the Polish writer Gessner reported: 'The aurochses are supposed to be very like our common black bull, but larger and with a longer coat. They have two long thin horns, whitish with black tips pointing forward. The forehead with its tight curly hair has a frightening aspect. The feet are lighter in colour than those of domestic cattle. The cows are smaller and shorter than the bull. At six months it is completely black with a lighter strip on the back. The cows are seldom black. These animals are very strong, very agile and very dangerous ...' The last aurochs, a female, died in 1627. The prehistoric aurochs measured 6'6" at the shoulder and weighed up to 1,400kg.

[3] Tarpan. Mouse-grey coats, black dorsal stripe, dark manes with blonde underhairs; they were driven to extinction over a cliff-edge in Poland in 1876.

Plate 12. This modern-day children's 'den' in a woodland clearing perhaps captures much of the essence of mesolithic transience. (Photograph: Stephen Harrison)

The area around Hornsea appears to have been a favoured location, a place of transitions, where different, contrasting environments merged one with the other, offering many opportunities in keeping with a transient mesolithic lifestyle. Here, the convergence of dry land, wetland and open water provided a variety of rich pickings, not just dietary but material as well. To these first inhabitants it must have seemed a marvellous place, swarming with plants and animals and birds and fish.

A three- or four-hour walk eastwards along the banks of the meandering, sluggish outfall from the mere would have brought our hunters, gatherers and fishers to a third, contrasting environment – the coast – where an additional set of resources was plentiful: inshore fish – eels in the autumn, saithe and cod, plaice and flounder, turbot and brill, sole and skate, whiting and mackerel at other times – could be caught, along with grey and common seals; shellfish – limpets and periwinkles, cockles and mussels – could be harvested from the inter-tidal zone. The infrequent dead whale, washed ashore, would have provoked wonder or occasions for feasting or just revulsion at the smell of rotting flesh; mesolithic people – just like ourselves – would have found these giant sea mammals of considerable interest and amazement. Sea birds – guillemots and gannets, cormorants and gulls – could be netted or brought down. Much could be had from the seashore; much also could be taken from the inshore waters using nets, traps and harpoons. It is not impossible that some form of canoe or dugout was used in order to maximise the opportunities that presented themselves. At the base of the cliff line a further resource was there for the taking: nodules of randomly scattered flint, eroding out of the boulder clay, provided the raw material from which a range of specialized tools and implements were manufactured. The finding of a good nodule today brings, perhaps, the same delight as when one was found in prehistory.

Plate 13. 'The Way through the Woods' (Rudyard Kipling)
Mesolithic themes: open canopied and light in places, dense and dark in others, the uncertain wildwood and its tangled understorey provided game and edible plants, berries, nuts and fruits; well-trodden pathways, dendritic networks of trails, connected locales and patterned movement within and beyond; transient campsites in natural or people-made clearings. Major uncertainties exist about the extent to which the tree cover was a mosaic of natural and anthropogenic clearings. (Photographs: Stephen Harrison)

31

And there was the mere itself, much larger and deeper then. A graded transition from forest to open water: a semi-terrestrial environment of light, open woodland, where it was just dry enough for water-loving trees to grow; alder carr; sedge and reed beds; fringing beds of yellow and white water lilies in profusion; and then open water. The mere was bursting with life. The sky echoed with calls, many of which are unheard today. There were migrating cranes looking for a safe place to roost; spoonbills; bitterns; little egrets; herons; staggeringly large flocks of geese, greater than anything seen today; vast flocks of waders; avocets; wild swans from the arctic. Below the clear water's surface, fish in prodigious numbers wove their way playfully in and out of the luxuriant underwater gradens: roach, tench, carp, perch, pike, eels, and more besides. Except for the occasional otter or beaver, all this wildlife had only two main predators to fear: humans and, from below, the predatory pike, a fish of devastating power, for whom exhausted migratory birds always offered a welcome change from a routine diet of fish. Overhead, marsh harriers, their every twist and turn loaded with meaning, aided the human hunter. Mesolithic people would have known this domain well; it was after all part of their livelihood.

Plate 14. Hornsea Mere: a graded transition from open woodland, alder carr and reed swamp to open water. (Photograph: Stephen Harrison)

Of the mesolithic finds from Hornsea, one of the most significant, and certainly the most contested for many years after its discovery, is the bone point or harpoon that supposedly came to light during construction work for a new gasometer at the gasworks in 1905. This object, fixed to a wooden shaft, would have been used for hunting or fishing. It measures slightly less than ten inches in length, has eleven barbs cut along one side, and was manufactured from a piece of straight limb bone from a large mammal, scraped to a point at both ends. Although not radiocarbon dated, its form and character suggest that it needs to be placed very early in the local mesolithic sequence, perhaps somewhere between 10,000 and 9,000 BC. This point, the first of many subsequently discovered in the Hornsea-Brandesburton area, is now deposited in the British Museum.

32

The precise circumstances of its discovery remain obscure, clouded by the passage of time, inadequate contemporary records and, above all, by the *angst* of the turbulent and flamboyant Thomas Sheppard, curator of Hull Museums at the time, who publicly showed much scepticism as to its authenticity. Although discovered in 1905 it would be a further ten years before the object entered the public domain, beginning a controversy that would last intermittently up to the present. In 1915 the bone point came into the possession of William Morfitt (1831-1923) of Atwick.

Plate 15. Members of the Morfitt family pose with visitors outside Charlotte Cottage, Atwick. *Left to right*: Rev. R.A. Gatty, William Morfitt, Professor (later Sir) William Boyd Dawkins, Major B.B. Haworth Booth, Beaumont Morfitt, and Aaron Morfitt. (Photograph: Stephen Harrison collection)

Following his retirement as a Goole greengrocer and bread and biscuit manufacturer, Morfitt moved to Atwick with his family in 1890. He had a longstanding interest in antiquities, which was shared by his two sons, Beaumont (1856-1929) and Aaron (1863-1928), and two daughters, Margaret (1855-1905) and Charlotta (but more often referred to as Charlotte; 1866-1914). After the move to Atwick, the family would devote the next thirty years to antiquarian pursuits and the building up of a collection of archaeological and geological specimens from this part of northern Holderness, particularly from the eroding cliff line. The collection, known as the *East Coast Museum of Antiquities*, was housed in the family home, Charlotte Cottage on Church Lane, and attracted many prominent visitors from the world of archaeology. Though their excavation techniques and recording standards were lamentable (even when judged against those of the day), their industriousness and enthusiasm could not be faulted, as Canon William Greenwell, the Durham-based archaeologist and friend of the family, testified early in the twentieth century:

33

Only those who have been present at the excavations know what laborious work it is, often in the teeth of furious gales in winter on the north-east coast, to dig through very hard mud, every bit of which has to be examined with fingers numbed with cold.

Over the years an important, but at the same time poorly documented, collection of prehistoric artefacts was built up, displayed in chaotic confusion at Charlotte Cottage, but nonetheless attracting the attentions of the leading archaeologists of the time. Contemporary photographs and postcards indicate that the collection was extensive and wide-ranging. The images display a multiplicity of objects: neolithic and bronze age stone axes, worked flint artefacts, bronze axe and spear heads, bone implements, iron age and Romano-British pottery, as well as quantities of geological specimens. Crowded, cluttered and disorganised; the randomness of objects with no particular associations juxtaposed one against the other, jostling for position and space and prominence. Although lacking supporting documentary records, making the collection of little value to modern-day archaeologists, it is nevertheless true that the Morfitts rescued large numbers of artefacts that would otherwise have been lost to the sea or to agricultural operations. Much of the collection eventually found its way to the Yorkshire Museum in York, where it is still housed; other items are in the British Museum, Hull Museums and Sheffield Museum.

Plate 16. Crowded, cluttered and disorganised: the Morfitt collection on display: 'Mr Morfitt's collection ... in its way is unique, and is chiefly – if not wholly – the result of the patient, persistent, painstaking work of two or three men, who have devoted ... a large amount of time and energy to these researches; and who are doing it not for gain, but for the pure pleasure to be derived from the gratification of the antiquarian taste.' (Photograph: Stephen Harrison collection)

34

Plate 17. The past on display: a more organised grouping of artefacts in the Morfitt collection. This probably represents a coherent assemblage of, in the main, iron age objects excavated from the eroding cliffline at Atwick. (Photograph: Stephen Harrison collection)

But, to return to the Hornsea bone point: Beaumont Morfitt allegedly purchased this object on 24 January 1915, paying 5s to the un-named finder or his family. When the point was bequeathed to the British Museum in 1928, its provenance was stated as 'the site of the Hornsea Gasworks under 12 feet of peat and 200 yards from the mere'. This was where the confusion and the controversy began. The 'Great Holderness Harpoon Controversy' was set to unfold. Subsequent observations and limited fieldwork on and around the site of the former gasworks failed to establish the presence of peat deposits in this area. Later, this was compounded by the denials of gasworks employees that neither the bone point nor any peat deposit was ever found on the site, though, it has to be said, these statements were not made until 1922, some *seventeen* years after the initial discovery; for whatever reason, deliberately or otherwise, memories became clouded or faded with the passage of time. Intriguingly, however, when members of the Hull Scientific and Field Naturalists' Club visited Hornsea Mere in August 1902, they examined a deep section exposed during the construction of the new gasometer, which comprised beds of gravel, shell marl and *peat*. On balance, the stated geographical location of the find-spot appears to be reasonably secure.

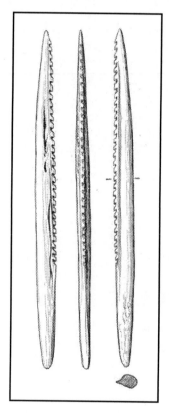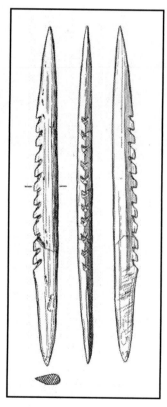

Figure 4. The Hornsea barbed points: *left*: the original 1905 Morfitt find; *right*: the 1932 J.A. Stocks discovery. (Illustrations: *Proceedings of thePrehistoric Society 22* (1956). Reproduced by permission of the Prehistoric Society)

Meanwhile, A. Leslie Armstrong, an amateur archaeologist from Sheffield and friend of William Morfitt, entered the scene. He was responsible for bringing the find to wider attention, delivering a paper before the 1922 Hull meeting of the British Association. This was followed up by a note in the September 1922 issue of the anthropological journal *Man*, which also discussed a second bone point from nearby Skipsea (this, too, a Morfitt discovery). In the article Armstrong compared the Hornsea and Skipsea bone points with similar examples from Maglemose in Denmark and concluded that the local finds were also of Maglemosian or Mesolithic date, making them around 10,000 years old. At this time, these were the only known examples of such objects from the British Isles. He went on to argue that they represented some of the first evidence for Maglemosian/Mesolithic hunter-gatherers not only in East Yorkshire but the country as a whole. If his identification and interpretation were accepted, Armstrong would have achieved a considerable coup, greatly enhancing his reputation in archaeological circles. Instead, all he succeeded in doing was bringing down the wrath of Sheppard.

Thomas Sheppard immediately took issue with Armstrong's statements, questioning the authenticity of the find, arguing that it (along with the Skipsea example) was a forgery, claiming that it was no older than Armstrong himself. In particular, he doubted their authenticity because of their sharp, smooth condition, which, he claimed, was inconsistent with their supposed great antiquity. Sheppard's argument that they were forgeries, based upon nothing more than the rarity of such objects in the 1920s, carried much weight at the time.

On 14 September 1922 the following anonymous poem appeared in the *Eastern Morning News*:

> Long years ago – so long – no-one knows,
> There came a man from Maglemose.
> How he got here without clothes,
> From Maglemose to Holdernose,
> Without the frost-bite in his toes,
> Is more than we can *dare* suppose.
>
> This man a long bone harpoon throws
> (Just like those found at Maglemose);
> He aimed at an elk (or deer),
> The harpoon pierced it like a spear;
> It no doubt killed that elk (or deer),
> In what was once called Skipsea Mere.
>
> From long ago, in silt (or clay)
> The harpoon and elk did stay,
> 'Til Mr Morfitt passed one day.
> The fourteen feet it penetrated
> And then it stopped; or so 'twas stated.
>
> The rod touched something firm and bony
> (so different from an object stoney);

Then Mr Morfitt dug deep down
The fourteen feet, and got renown
By finding something quite unknown,
(Except for one in Hornsea town).

How he dug, well no-one knows;
But he found trace of Maglemose!
He put it in his small museum,
Where with the other all could see'em.
They rested there for years and years
Until the British Ass[ociation] appears.

Then an Armstrong long and weary,
Gave a most enthralling theory;
How the man from Maglemose
In the Baltic, *that* one knows,
Came to Atwick (or quite close),
While in search of food and clothes.

Then a Sheppard roared like thunder,
'There has been a fearful blunder,
The harpoon from Maglemose,
Is not as old as you'd suppose';
And in a manner most indecent,
Said the harpoon was quite recent!

Ever the self-publicist, it is likely that Sheppard himself penned this piece of doggerel, which neatly summed up his scepticism about both objects.

The allegations, expressed in Sheppard's usual forthright and assertive manner, caused a storm. As happens in such cases, people took sides. A long and bitter debate followed, conducted in the letter columns of newspapers and the pages of learned journals, and from the floor of society meetings.

Two committees of enquiry were subsequently convened to look into the finds. The first, purporting to represent the British Association but in reality an *ad hoc* affair, reported that 'in type, general facies, colour, and in the partially mineralised condition of the bone ... both the Holderness harpoons are genuine antiquities.' Slightly later, in 1923, a committee under the auspices of the Royal Anthropological Institute was formed. It ambiguously concluded that 'In general we see no evidence in the objects themselves that is conclusively against their genuineness.' This report added: 'A curious feature is that the workmanship of the barbs in the two harpoons is so similar to point to their being the work of the same individual, though found 4 miles apart.' Sheppard seized on this as another indication of their forged nature. However, modern examination has conclusively shown that the techniques of manufacture are different in both examples.

There, after a further flurry of letters and articles, the matter seemed to rest. That is, until 1929, when Sheppard resurrected the whole issue again. In that year, following the death of Beaumont, the last surviving member of the Atwick branch of the Morfitt family, he released evidence which he claimed to have previously held back out of deference for William Morfitt's feelings. Allegedly, before her death in 1914 Charlotte Morfitt told Sheppard 'that her brother Beaumont made these harpoons from the leg bone of a Red Deer.' Claim and counterclaim ensued once more. Captain William Middlebrook, a friend of the Morfitt family and an executor of Beaumont's will, published a series of articles in the *Hull Daily Mail* defending the family. The question was asked of Sheppard: 'Why wait until now to bring this further revelation forward?' To which he had no satisfactory answer. After all, William Morfitt, whose feelings he was supposedly saving, had died in 1923 – six years previously. At the time, very little credence was attached to Sheppard's latest charge.

From the 1930s perceptions began to change. Gradually, both the Hornsea and Skipsea bone points came to be regarded as genuine. Similar artefacts, some exhibiting the same techniques of manufacture, began to turn up with increasing frequency across the British Isles, in contexts which were unequivocally early prehistoric. In particular, around thirteen bone points have been discovered locally since the Second World War, as a result of commercial gravel extraction in the Hornsea – Brandesburton – Leven area. If the Morfitt artefacts were forgeries, they were fortunate indeed in having chosen a locality where a considerable number of genuine bone points would be discovered in later years. In essence, there is nothing to suggest that they are modern forgeries.

With Sheppard's death in 1945, the controversy also came to an end. What motivated him? The outpouring of angst ultimately had its origins in the early years of the twentieth century, in or around 1903, when Sheppard fell out with the Morfitts. The reason for this breakdown in relationships is not known, but in all likelihood was probably caused by their rivalry as collectors. Thereafter, Sheppard took every opportunity to 'rubbish' the Morfitts and their antiquarian endeavours. It is also likely that he felt frustrated at being unable to add the bone points to his, that is, Hull's, collections. If he could not have them, then nobody would. Sheppard's objections to the genuineness of the artefacts had little validity, depending on subjective interpretations and superficial discrepancies in the information. The stance he took was, it has to be said, fuelled by the failure of the Morfitts to keep adequate records of their discoveries.

No attempt has been made to date the Hornsea and Skipsea bone points. The Morfitts soaked them in 'a fairly strong solution of glue' to aid their preservation. This would have contaminated them, rendering radiocarbon dating non-effective. However, stylistically similar bone points have been dated: one, dredged up from the Leman and Ower Banks in the North Sea, provided a date of around 11,749 years before the present; another, found in a gravel pit at Sproughton, near Ipswich, gave a date of 10,910 years before the present; and, a more local example, found at Gransmoor in Holderness in the early 1990s, has been dated to between 11,500-11,000 years before the present. It is likely that both the Hornsea and Skipsea specimens are of a similar age.

A second bone point was discovered on the foreshore at Hornsea in 1932 in somewhat unusual circumstances. A Mr J.A. Stocks was:

walking out with his dog just after high tide and just below high tide mark about ½ mile south of Hornsea, ½ mile from the then end of the parade and round the other side of a little cape. He was looking for something to throw for his dog and saw what seemed to be a "stick" protruding from a lump of seaweed. He picked it up and feeling with his fingers that it was notched did not throw it to his dog but took it home instead … There was no peat or anything adhering to it. It was just tangled up in the seaweed, and might well have been flung up by the waves with the seaweed.

The find was not brought to attention until after the Second World War, no doubt a reflection of the controversies surrounding the earlier discovery. Immediately accepted as genuine, this example, fashioned from stag antler, is also slightly under ten inches in length, is tapered at both ends, and has thirty close-set barbs along one edge.

The most commonly found artefact of the mesolithic is the microlith. These consisted of small flint or other stone blades worked along one or more edges to form barb-like tools, which were then used in combination to form composite artefacts such as arrowheads or craft tools. Early mesolithic microliths are generally broad (that is, the width is normally greater than 8mm) and with a limited variety of shapes. Later mesolithic microliths decrease in size (that is, the width is generally less than 8mm) and become geometric with more varied shapes.

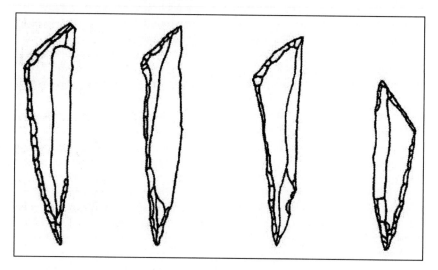

Figure 5. Examples of later mesolithic microliths from Hornsea.

Over the last one hundred years microliths, dating to both the earlier and later parts of the period, have been found at a number of locations within Hornsea parish. In general terms, mesolithic activity is distributed more or less continuously across the parish, but varies in intensity from one location to another. Usually they have been found as single isolated items, opportunely picked out of the plough-soil by sharp-eyed observers; on other occasions,

40

larger surface scatters have been found, concentrated in small areas, where tool-making and food processing activities were taking place, perhaps positioned on paths of movement through the landscape. These are perhaps best defined as activity areas: putative temporary campsites, with multiple episodes of short-lived occupation; people stopping at places used in the past in order to replicate and reaffirm the significance of those places in their mobility cycle, implying that such places had become important and remembered. The *longue durée* of repeated visits to the same places suggests some concern with time depth and previous histories of occupation. The single finds are perhaps best accounted for as accidental losses during the course of hunting expeditions. When plotted, two trends are seen in the distribution of these artefacts: the isolated finds are widely scattered across the parish; the concentrations, however, show clear patterning. They are located on the higher ground overlooking the northern and, to a lesser extent, southern margins of the mere; and, for the most part, preferentially located on gentle south-facing slopes. Those findspots to the north of the Mere are of particular interest. When plotted, scatters of lithic material can be seen to occur in a broadly east-west line across the parish, which may reflect an important emerging axis of movement. In general they are sited on or near hillocky deposits of Devensian sand and gravel that extends westwards through Seaton and Catwick into Brandesburton and Leven parishes and the river Hull valley. Over the years significant numbers of portable mesolithic artefacts have been recovered from this area, especially so from around Brandesburton, which is notable for its series of barbed points, similar to those from Hornsea, discovered during large-scale sand and gravel extraction. Although no definite mesolithic settlements have been identified, all this evidence points to frequent repeated visits.

The sand and gravel outcrops were perhaps meaningful to mesolithic people in many ways: the light, freely-drained sands and gravels offered an effective physical routeway through what was otherwise a predominantly waterlogged, marshy environment at this time. Certainly, many of the findspots overlook what would have been open water, offering plentiful opportunities for hunting and fishing and the procurement of a diverse range of other resources. Importantly, these findspots are located in a zone which reinforces the perceived significance of physical boundaries in the landscape. The contrasts between the blue of the open water, the light coloured soils of the ridge and the heavier, darker soils of the surrounding areas, together with the seasonality of the vegetational cycle and the different densities of tree cover, may have, on the basis of ethnographic parallels, held symbolic significance for mesolithic communities operating in this part of East Yorkshire. The convergence of water, clay and sands and gravels, together with their contrasting environmental complexions, and the different sounds, smells and colours associated with each, would have been important in formulating the mesolithic experience of this particular landscape. Altogether, it can be argued that this locale was both visited in the mesolithic and assigned meaning, perhaps as part of a mythological understanding of the world: hunter-gatherers would have derived ideas and sentiments of cosmological significance from their 'construction' of the landscape they inhabited. The named pathways and places that they visited in their seasonal cycle of movement would probably have had great significance to the histories of individual groups in their claims to territorial rights over specific resources.

In sum then, the mesolithic was a world of scattered concentrations of population, relative isolation, and repeated movements. In an inhabited landscape already filled with symbolic meaning and important places, repeated visits to the same locales indicate that there was already a commitment to place.

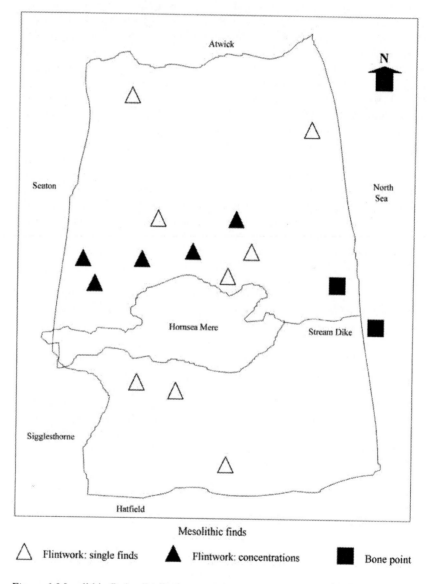

Figure 6. Mesolithic finds: distribution map.

Ways of Working, Ways of Life (Neolithic: c.4,000-2,200 BC)

The end of the mesolithic is poorly defined in the British archaeological record, but the beginnings of cultural change can be detected from around 4,500BC. A new age was slowly emerging: the neolithic, a new way of being, a new way of engaging with the world This was part of a broader pattern of economic, social and cultural transformation that was sweeping across the temperate forestlands of north-west Europe during the fifth and fourth millennia BC.

The neolithic material culture which gradually replaced that of the mesolithic was very different in character. In place of microliths, a transient lifestyle and little trace on the landscape came tombs, enclosures, domestic plants and animals, pottery, polished stone axes and other new lithic styles. The manner in which this transition took place is the subject of continuing debate. At the core of this debate is the extent to which the local mesolithic populations of the British Isles were involved in the process of cultural transformation – that is, whether they took up continental material culture themselves, or whether these new monument and artefact styles arrived in the British Isles with migrant communities. At the moment it appears that different elements of the neolithic cultural repertoire arrived at different times over a protracted period. Within such a scenario there is ample room for both indigenous and continental communities to have played a part. Nor is it at all obvious why neolithic culture was adopted in the British Isles. What is clear, however, is the wide geographical area of mainland Europe, from Denmark to Brittany, from which this new culture was 'imported.' As a result the British neolithic has a distinct identity and does not merely reproduce the material culture of any one area of continental Europe.

Plate 18. The neolithic was a time of new concerns and attitudes: new ways of living, new ways of being. The opening up of the forest canopy or the consolidation of older clearings during this time was a precursor to residential semi-permanence or permanence, the clearing of the ground being one of the ways in which people can make a commitment to place. Freed from cover by wind, fire and human agency, cleared ground also created the space in which to experiment with the growing of cereal crops, as well as the grazing and management of domesticated animals. (Photograph: Stephen Harrison)

43

Plate 19. The dull, ringing strike of the axe deep in the forest still resounds within mind. Stone and flint. The axeheads flashing in the sunlight had begun to eat away at the edges of what was obscure and threatening. With this the end of passivity had gone; now we would seek to impose our will on things and to shape nature to our needs. So the dark forest, and all its spirit awe, dwindled; and out in the newly created open spaces the building began. (Photograph: Stephen Harrison)

Just how soon the mesolithic forest disappeared is far from clear. Given the almost ubiquitous forest environment of the earliest neolithic it follows that the occupants of this area were predominantly forest dwellers who obtained a living from the woodland and its resources rather than as farmers or herdsmen.[4] A lifestyle, initially at least, very similar to that of the mesolithic. In essence: part-time hunters, gatherers, fishers, herders and horticulturalists. People living the pioneer life. That the old traditions of hunting and gathering persisted can be seen as a necessary component of the new economic regime, guarding against the failure of other, agriculturally derived resources. Even so, to agriculturalists, by virtue of their activities, the forestlands must have been intimidating, threatening and dangerous places.

Later, as the period unfolded, inroads were made to the forest: clearings were created by felling or by controlled fire setting for arable and pastoral activities. Repeating a picture common across much of lowland Britain at this time, the Hornsea landscape was a mosaic of woodland and localised clearings. A landscape of woodland, paths and places, some fixed, others transitory. In time, clearings coalesced to form larger treeless areas. The appearance of the landscape was changing. This was a gradual process. Through long generations, people creating openings in the forest: a direct struggle with nature, clearing wild land, breaking in new ground, establishing settlements, building monuments. Not until the succeeding bronze age was the local landscape largely devoid of tree cover.

Neolithic settlement in this area is difficult to prove, giving the impression of a country without people. No monuments, either upstanding or visible as cropmarks or soil stains on aerial photographs, have yet been recognized as dating to this period. On the surface this would seem to indicate that the major node of activity during this period was some distance to the west, on the chalklands of the Yorkshire Wolds, where evidence is plentiful.

However, over the last century or so, several locations within the parish have yielded surface finds of axeheads and flint implements: although not structural in the sense of postholes, ditches or pits, these are significant indicators for a neolithic presence in the area. If the relative frequency of material found at a comparatively small number of findspots is typical for the parish as a whole, as evidence from elsewhere in the country would suggest, it becomes clear that the area was well populated and extensively exploited during the period.

Finely ground and polished greenstone axeheads, representing the ultimate in neolithic technology, have been found in the parish. Four complete or fragmentary examples are currently known. It is likely that this type of axe was of long duration, from the beginning of the neolithic until the early

---

[4] Support for this view can be had from excavations in 1992-93 in advance of the construction of the Leven-Brandesburton bypass, some half-a-dozen miles to the west of Hornsea. Here, two pits, possibly related to an undiscovered settlement, were excavated. In addition to numerous fragments of pottery and charred wood, both pits contained caches of hazelnut shells. The contents of the pits were dated to the first half of the fourth millennium BC, that is, to the earlier neolithic. The hazelnut shells offer a pointer to the ongoing importance of foraging as an economic activity.

Plate 20. Neolithic and bronze age material culture from Hornsea parish. *Top*: finely ground and polished greenstone axehead, a quintessentially neolithic artefact; *Bottom left*: barbed and tanged arrowhead of early bronze age date; *Bottom centre*: leaf-shaped arrowhead of neolithic date; *Bottom right*: neolithic pebble mace-head with hourglass perforation. These surface finds came from an area to the north-west of the town. (Photograph and finds: Stephen Harrison collection)

bronze age, when metal became plentiful and widely available. An examination of these greenstone axes suggests that they could have come from the well-known Langdale Pike axe factories in the Lake District, although a regional study has speculated that they were perhaps manufactured locally using Langdale-type stone found as glacial erratics in the boulder clays of Holderness (but this latter view, it has to be said, has not found general acceptance amongst archaeologists). If the greenstone axes originated in the Lake District – either as rough-outs or finished items – then it is to be assumed that they were traded 'down-the-line,' along well-used routeways through the Pennine valleys before reaching their final destinations. Alternatively, direct procurement from these distant sources in north-west England cannot be entirely ruled out.

In addition, two complete and three partial flint axeheads have been found, again as chance surface finds, manufactured from locally derived raw materials. Good quality flint outcrops are to be found around Flamborough Head, fifteen miles to the north, or nodules of the material can be readily picked out of the boulder clays of Holderness, where it occurs as glacial erratics.

The main users of the greenstone and flint axes were neolithic farmers, clearing woodland in order to create the arable and pasture lands needed for their mixed farming regimes. Although no settlements have been found, the

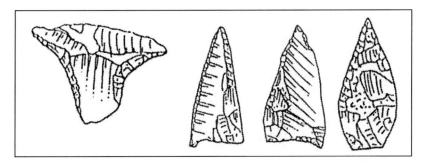

Figure 7. Neolithic flintwork from Hornsea: arrowheads. *From left to right*: chisel-shaped arrowhead; oblique arrowhead; oblique arrowhead; and leaf-shaped arrowhead. (Stephen Harrison Collection)

spatial distribution of axeheads strongly suggests that all parts of the parish were utilised by neolithic communities.

Small scatters of flintwork have come from locations in the eastern and northern parts of the parish. For the earlier neolithic the most conspicuous and diagnostic of these finds have been leaf-shaped arrowheads, which replaced the composite microlith projectile points of the mesolithic. Also of this period, but much more difficult to distinguish from similar tools of the mesolithic, are serrated blades, scrapers, and knives. A number of these latter finds have come from areas overlooking the mere, suggesting that neolithic people, like their predecessors, were actively exploiting the resources offered by this watery expanse. By the later neolithic these forms were replaced by a much more distinctive tool-kit: chisel-ended and oblique arrowheads, highly finished knives, and side-, end- and horseshoe scrapers. Again, examples of these artefacts have been recovered from widely scattered areas across the parish.

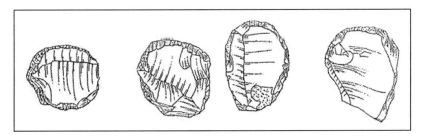

Figure 8. Neolithic flintwork from Hornsea: scrapers. (Stephen Harrison Collection)

Few neolithic places around Hornsea are located in continuity with hunter-gatherer sites. In many cases it appears that farmers are celebrating new places through a repertoire of material culture that includes many new forms and expresses their relationships with distant places.

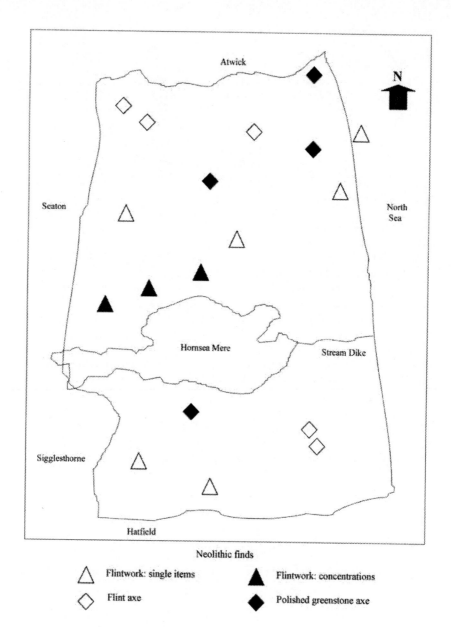

Figure 9. Neolithic finds: distribution map.

New Traditions (bronze age: c.2,200-700 BC)

Around 2,200 BC the neolithic began to give way to the bronze age: as with all period transitions beginnings and ends are not precise historical events but gradual processes of change that occurred in different places at different times and with different durations. The bronze age is associated with the movement of settlers from Europe, bringing with them the ability to manufacture implements from copper, and subsequently from bronze. Bronze, an alloy of copper and tin, forms harder cutting edges and is easier to cast than copper, and was suitable for a wide variety of tools and weapons. This amazingly versatile material represented the pinnacle of technological achievement in the ancient world, a revolutionary development; it was to bronze age societies what the microchip is to us. Throughout the period, bronze was used side-by-side with implements manufactured from flint and other stone. Other features associated with the bronze age include the introduction of new forms of pottery vessels – elaborately decorated beakers, and food vessels and collared urns – and flint tools, altogether different from the preceding neolithic; and the widespread disposal of the dead under round earthen mounds.

What of the evidence from Hornsea? As with the neolithic, so too with the bronze age. Currently, this period in and around the town is little understood, known only from a handful of flint tools picked up as surface finds from ploughed fields or found eroding out of the cliff edge. The absence of identified settlements and burial monuments is probably more apparent than real, reflecting the lack of archaeological fieldwork in the area. Since the days of William Morfitt and family there has been little active work by archaeologists in the parish. Almost certainly, as is becoming increasingly clear from elsewhere in Holderness, the evidence is there, waiting to be discovered.

Flint tools of bronze age date – barbed-and-tanged arrowheads, and scrapers – have been found at various locations across the parish. Although few in number, they do indicate a bronze age presence in the local landscape, but the character of any permanent settlement is not at present known. The distribution of finds broadly parallels the pattern already identified for the mesolithic and neolithic, clustering on the higher ground to the north of the mere, on the natural gravel ridge which crosses the parish from west to east. With one exception, all the finds of this date have been single items. In 1994, to the north-west of the mere, a small concentration of flint tools and flint waste, thirty-seven pieces in all, was recovered from the surface of a newly cultivated field. These items, collected from an area measuring approximately 3m by 3m, may represent evidence for an as yet undiscovered settlement – or perhaps it was just somewhere where somebody sat down and produced a small number of tools to replace those lost whilst out hunting. In any event, these are the ephemeral remains, the signature, of a routine task completed at this spot three thousand and more years ago.

In 1995 palaeoenvironmental work by Hull University's Centre for Wetland Archaeology (Humber Wetlands Project) took place at Seaton, to the west of the town, in the former wetland valley connecting Hornsea Mere to the Hull valley. Evidence for active and deliberate woodland management – alder and hazel coppicing and the working of oak – and clearance was found. Analysis of the chopping facets on felled timber clearly showed that both stone axes and metal blades had been used; in addition, and associated with this timber, a small collection of flint flakes and a flint blade-like object were discovered. All this points to a later prehistoric date, that is, somewhere in the bronze age or iron age. Woodland clearance is best seen in the context of agricultural intensification. At Seaton the environmental impact of clearance was also seen: once cleared of its vegetation and brought into arable

49

cultivation the soils became susceptible to erosion, with surface run-off of sediment being transported down-slope and deposited in the valley.

It is likely that by the later part of the bronze age there was an open, cleared landscape in the Hornsea area. Of course, pockets of woodland would have remained, especially in and around marshy hollows and along the fringes of watery places. Life would have been more settled, less nomadic, and perhaps, because of the heavy and intractable boulder clay soils, based largely on pastoralism. By analogy with evidence from elsewhere, it is assumed that local societies were dwelling in small farmsteads scattered across the landscape. These are likely to have been concentrated on the lighter, gravely soils. Areas closest to the farms would have been given over to the cultivation of cereals in small fields, while extensive pastures, providing grazing for sheep and cattle, would have dominated the landscape beyond. With an absence of fertilisers, the arable areas would have quickly become exhausted, and it is possible to envisage a patchwork landscape with settlements and their surrounding fields frequently shifting to new, adjacent locations.

Organisation in the landscape (iron age: c.800 BC-AD 71)

From about 900BC iron gradually displaced bronze as the principal metal for the manufacture of tools and weapons, marking the transition to the iron age. The iron age in East Yorkshire saw the emergence of a distinctive local tradition known as the Arras Culture, named after the type-site at Arras, near Market Weighton, and partially excavated in the early decades of the nineteenth century. This culture, confined as it is to eastern Yorkshire, might represent the geographical distribution of an immigrant tribe, known from Roman literary sources as the Parisi, who possibly originated from northern France. Just why such a movement took place is not known. Alternatively, this culture may have developed as a result of long-distance contact between communities living in East Yorkshire and northern France – that is, the exchange of knowledge rather than people. Somewhat atypically the Arras culture is defined almost exclusively from the burial record, the main characteristics of which may be summarised as: the development of large cemeteries, often containing upwards of 500 graves each; the definition of individual graves by a covering mound set within a square- or circular-ditched enclosure; and an elite burial tradition involving the placing of a dismantled two-wheeled vehicle (often referred to as a chariot or cart) with the corpse. Set within a wider context, this funerary tradition is of great importance for British iron age studies: in most of the rest of Britain iron age societies did not bury their dead with any readily recognisable and archaeologically recoverable burial rite.

But there is more to the local iron age than a concern with the dead and their proper and fitting disposal. The eight hundred or so years of this period probably saw major structural changes in the way in which the local landscape was inhabited, including the expansion of settlement and the intensification of agricultural pursuits. Both are predicated on population increase. It is also clear that the later part of the period in particular saw radical changes in the use of the landscape, from stock rearing to cereal cultivation; and there is increasing evidence for human occupation in areas previously considered to be marginal.

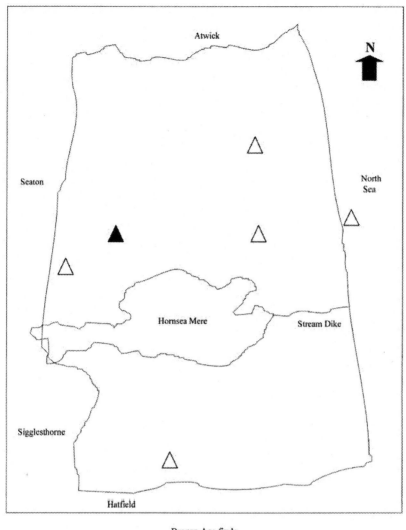

Atwick

N

Seaton

North
Sea

Hornsea Mere

Stream Dike

Sigglesthorne

Hatfield

Bronze Age finds

△ Flintwork: single finds   ▲ Flintwork: concentrations

Figure 10. Bronze Age finds: distribution map.

The iron age in Hornsea is known only from chance finds. And yet, of all the prehistoric periods, evidence for this one is the most plentiful. In particular, large quantities of pottery have been discovered at various locations across the parish over the last one hundred or so years. The Morfitt family recovered much of this material in the early years of the twentieth century, either from the eroding cliff edge or from fields adjacent to the coast. From the cursory notes compiled at the time of finding, it appears that concentrations of pottery fragments – representing jars, cooking pots and storage vessels – and other artefacts – animal bone, burnt stones and small

51

amounts of metalwork – were discovered at a number of now unidentifiable locations near to the coast, both to the north and south of the present town. More recently, fieldwalking in western parts of the parish has produced a similar range of material. Using the recovered ceramics as a chronological indicator it can be seen that the evidence spans the entire iron age, but with a noticeable increase in frequency for the later part of the period, that is, from about the third century BC down to the beginning of the Roman occupation towards the end of the first century AD. What conclusions? These dense scatters of domestic material can, in all probability, be interpreted as the sites of small farmsteads, similar to the large number of better documented examples that are known from, in particular, the Yorkshire Wolds. Across the parish these scatters seem to have an average spacing of around 2km. The fact that such scatters are more or less evenly spaced can be explained in terms of spatial competition for the available resources. In other words, the territory surrounding these sites can be viewed as the minimum size capable of sustaining settlements with an iron age economy.

As with the better-known examples elsewhere, these Hornsea farmsteads would have consisted of small enclosures containing one or more roundhouses – constructed from timber uprights, wattle and daub walls, and thatched conical roofs – and perhaps granaries and other agriculturally related buildings. Small square-shaped fields would have surrounded the farms and a network of tracks would have connected the farmsteads to each other and the wider world; indeed, cropmarks on aerial photographs of the parish indicate the probable remains of some of these features. If the same pattern existed to that known from other parts of East Yorkshire, a mixed arable-livestock farming regime was followed, with the emphasis on each component varying at different times. At Hornsea, this would, presumably, have been supplemented by harvesting the available resources from within and around the meres, as well as those that could be obtained from the nearby seashore and coastal waters. Notwithstanding these additional resources, it is possible to envisage the local landscape during the iron age as open, well settled and intensively exploited.

A perfunctory note in the archives of the Yorkshire Museum in William Morfitt's hand relates the discovery of a probable iron age cart (or chariot) burial at Hornsea, somewhere in the block bounded by Hartley Street, Cliff Terrace, Cliff Road and the Esplanade:

> 1904. The Old Gashouse North End Promenard. While digging at Hornsea in the Gravil bed (a hill) near the old Gas house on Jany 4th 1904 I unearthed spearheads of Iron and one spearhead with Iron haft and blade of bronze, also what appeared to be thin wheel tyres of some light vehicle and bits of horse trappings very much corroded. Evident of Saxon period.

Given that the finds are now lost, the written description is rather problematic, ambiguous, leaving much to be desired. Despite the reference to 'Saxon' and earlier doubts as to the nature of what was being described, it is fairly clear that we are dealing with an iron age cart or chariot burial. In particular, the mention of 'thin wheel tyres' is suggestive of the iron age rather than of the

Anglian period. Also, iron spearheads (and other weapons) are known from other cart burials in the region, at Wetwang Slack and Kirkburn. If this interpretation is correct, it is the only known discovery of an iron age cart burial in Holderness, extending the distribution of this small group of highly distinctive finds off the Yorkshire Wolds and into the surrounding lowlands.

Unfortunately, beyond noting its discovery and potential significance little can be added.

A further iron age discovery needs to be mentioned. Some time in or slightly before 1905 a rare gold coin was 'found on the sands near Hornsea … undoubtedly washed from the cliffs' by a Mr W. Bearman. Unfortunately, the precise findspot is not known. The coin was presented to Hull Municipal Museum by the finder, but is presumed lost following the destruction of the museum by German bombing in June 1943. From a brief written description and accompanying illustration by Thomas Sheppard, the coin is identified as a Coritanian [5] gold stater, showing a debased headband of Apollo on the obverse side and a horse facing left on the reverse, dating to the late first century BC or early first century AD. A similar coin, now in the British Museum, was found at Atwick by William Morfitt in 1903 or 1904.

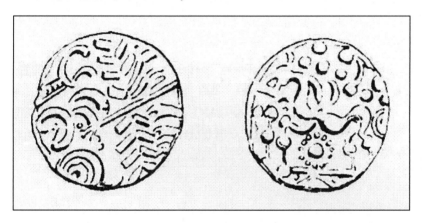

Figure 11. The Coritanian gold stater from Hornsea. (Illustration: *Quarterly Record of Additions, No. XII*, Hull Museum Publications (March 1905): 11-12)

Broadening the horizons (Romano-British: AD 71-410)

In the summer of AD 43, in the third year of his reign, the Emperor Claudius ordered the invasion of Britain. Under the command of Aulus Plautius, four legions of the Roman Imperial Army plus auxiliary units (perhaps 40,000 troops in all) landed on the south coast, in modern-day Kent: a forceful and bloody attack by the greatest superpower of the ancient world brought the foggy wilds of Britain within the orbit of the Roman Empire. Annexation. Occupation. *Pax Romana*, the introduction of a major road network, new and expanded focuses of economic demand (towns, the military market, and taxation), a highly developed coinage system, and a limited, but

---

[5] The Coritani were an iron age tribe in Lincolnshire, in the area between the rivers Trent and Nene.

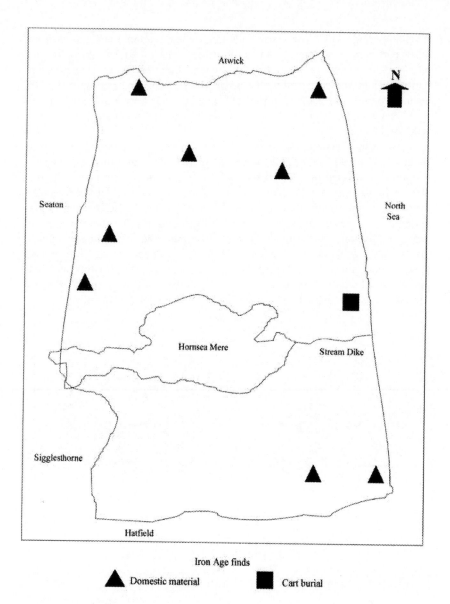

Figure 12. Iron Age finds: distribution map.

important, inflow of people (soldiers, administrators, traders, entrepreneurs, and settlers) from widely different cultures throughout the Empire were just some of the new forces that helped to foster fundamental changes in the movement of people, goods, ideas, social relations, economic strategies and settlement types and locations over the next 350 years.

By AD 48 Roman legions had advanced to take into the Empire that part of Britain which lay to the south and east of a line from the Bristol Channel, by way of the lower reaches of the Severn, the Warwickshire Avon and the Trent, to the Humber headlands. The speed with which the conquest was accomplished suggests that, after some initial and piecemeal conflict in

54

southern Britain, no great resistance was offered by the native populations in the subjugated areas. After the initial pacification, and although the intended strategy was for total conquest, the Romans seem to have been content with a new imperial province in south-east Britain, separated from the barbarian north and west by a frontier zone roughly along the course already described earlier in this paragraph.

However, all this was to change within a couple of decades. In 71 the *Legio IX Hispana*, under the command of the provincial governor Q. Petillius Cerialis, crossed the Humber and began the protracted incorporation of northern Britain into the Empire. This move was prompted by a rebellion of the Brigantes, a tribe whose territory lay immediately north and west of East Yorkshire. After crossing the Humber a military base was established at Brough, from where a road network, cutting across the grain of the land, was constructed northwards. From Brough a major route ran north, through present-day South Cave and Sancton, to a point just south of Market Weighton, where it divided: one branch extended north-west, via Shiptonthorpe and Hayton, to York, where a legionary fortress, civil settlement (*canabae*) and, later, a town for retired military veterans and their families (*colonia*) was established (in 71, c.71 and the early second century respectively); the other route continued more or less northwards across the Wolds to Malton, where a fort and, subsequently, a small town (*vicus*) was also inscribed on the landscape (in c.71 and the last quarter of the first century respectively). Over time, many other minor routes were also established, some using pre-existing routeways such as the Woldgate, extending westwards from Bridlington to York.

It is abundantly clear that the Roman incorporation of East Yorkshire into the greater empire was not a particularly significant event for the people farming in the region. There would, of course, have been new taxes to pay, a new range of consumer durables available in the distant market towns, and a new network of roads making travel easier for those with time and inclination. But for the most part life was little changed. Farms continued to be owned and worked by families whose ancestors may have broken the land many centuries earlier, perhaps even before iron had come into general use. Certainly, all the evidence would seem to suggest that the Parisi were not perceived as a threat; the annexation of East Yorkshire was seemingly achieved by peaceful means. Over the years many natives bought into the Roman way of life, adopting the distinctive traits of Roman material culture and, to some degree, became Romanised – or Romano-British. For instance, excavations at a number of local Roman villa sites, such as that at Rudston, have demonstrated that they were expanded and developed in the second and third centuries AD out of existing iron age farmsteads – in effect, as fortunes grew, their native owners threw away their roundhouses and built new, linear houses in the Roman manner. By doing so, they were perhaps seeking to display their wealth and status by conspicuously emulating aspects of the new culture, thereby outwardly (at least) affiliating themselves with the Roman state.

The Roman conquest had a significant impact on the economy of East Yorkshire. The agricultural base witnessed a shift from pastoral farming to cereal production – presumably, to supply the local military garrisons and newly founded urban centres, and as a medium by which taxes could be paid.

New industries were established, particularly those concerned with ironworking and pottery production, as at Crambeck, near Malton, and in the Holme-on-Spalding Moor area. Pottery from these centres, a hard, blue-grey wheel-turned fabric, is ubiquitous across the parish. 'Exotic' goods, from the length and breadth of the Empire, were imported and widely available, emphasising the fact that the region became locked into a sophisticated empire-wide market, resulting in the redistribution of agricultural produce, natural resources, and consumer goods and services across the Roman world. Locally this is seen by the finding of amphora, large pottery vessels for the shipment of wine, olive oil and other liquid-based products, which originated as far away as Spain, Italy and North Africa. Also, fine pottery produced in Oxfordshire and Northamptonshire has been picked up from various locations within the parish.

It is now clear that by the iron age the landscape was fully occupied: there were settlements everywhere and very few areas of unexploited land. This state of affairs continued in the Roman period, when relative peace and prosperity, allied to improving climatic conditions, encouraged population growth and even more intensive land use and settlement. It is not surprising therefore to find evidence of occupation in Hornsea parish during the 350 years of Roman rule.

Although no Roman period excavations have taken place in the parish, cropmarks on aerial photographs and surface finds of material culture do indicate that the area was intensively occupied at this time, particularly, judging from the dating of diagnostic artefacts, during the third and fourth centuries AD. The distribution of portable artefacts – collected by the Morfitts and others – is broadly consistent with the cropmark evidence for sites, which on morphological criteria, can be dated to this period.

In the late nineteenth and early years of the twentieth century members of the Morfitt family regularly picked up items of Roman date during their frequent fieldwork outings. Exact provenancing is a problem, but it seems that their finds came from one of two areas: material eroding out of the cliff face or from scouring the fields between the Atwick parish boundary and the northern outskirts of Hornsea. These activities resulted in the accumulation of large quantities of artefacts – mainly pottery and animal bone, but also the occasional piece of metalwork (usually the remains of copper alloy – bronze – brooches).

In recent years, this author has found quantities of Roman-period pottery, much of it dating to the third and fourth centuries AD, scattered widely across the parish. Much of this is likely to derive from the same findspots as the material collected by the Morfitt family; unfortunately, in the absence of written records, this cannot be verified. Pottery of the same date has been collected from gardens and other open spaces within the present built-up area of the town. Here, concentrations of material in two particular areas are of potential significance. The first, around Mount Pleasant, on the gravel ridge extending westwards towards Brandesburton and Leven, has produced, in the early years of the twentieth century as well as more recently, quantities of pottery and a limited range of other items (bone, burnt stone and

Figure 13. Early twentieth century illustration of reconstructed Roman pottery in the Morfitt collection. No longer identifiable within the surviving collection, they appear to be typical greyware products of third-fourth century date from the Holme-upon-Spalding Moor kilns. (Illustration: Stephen Harrison collection)

fragments of brooches). This may indicate the presence of some form of settlement, probably a farmstead, under this part of the modern town. To the east, along the coast in the area of Cliff Road, Esplanade, Hartley Street and Promenade Villas, similar second/third/fourth century pottery has been discovered over the years in sufficient quantities to indicate that a settlement may exist here also. In this area, significant detail was added to the scatter of surface finds in 1995, when the then Humberside Archaeology Unit carried out a watching brief on the site of the Granville Court Hotel, which was being developed as a nursing home and day care centre. Here, monitoring of the development revealed a north-east/south-west aligned linear ditch, containing a few scraps of pottery and a copper alloy head-stud brooch of second century AD date. This u-shaped ditch was between 0.85m and 1.10m in width, and had a maximum surviving depth of 0.50m. Earlier, in 1982, during the excavation of the Anglo-Saxon cemetery on the same site (see below), a similar north-east/south-west aligned ditch was noted, running parallel to the 1995 discovery. Together, these ditches are interpreted as either field boundaries or the flanking ditches for a track or droveway. Other, slighter ditches or gullies were recorded in 1995. These were of unknown date and function, but probably associated with the two main ditches. Taken together, all the evidence reinforces the impression that a farmstead or settlement exists in this vicinity. This material has come from the same general area as the iron age cart burial and Anglo-Saxon cemetery, and is likewise situated on the same gravel ridge as Mount Pleasant. From elsewhere across the town, a light background scatter of pottery suggests the presence of other settlements or the spreading of domestic refuse, incorporating broken vessels and other discarded objects, on arable fields to aid soil fertility.

Broadly speaking, there is continuity of settlement on many sites from the iron age into the Roman period. This is evidenced by the finding of both iron age and Roman artefacts together at the same location, suggesting the longevity of occupation at such places. In other areas, only Roman material has been found, mostly dating to the second and, more particularly, to the third and fourth centuries. Here, the evidence points to newly established settlements at this time. Of course, it is not possible to say how many of the occupation zones were in use at the same time, but the overall impression is of a countryside filling up with both people and settlements. A busy landscape. It is also important to remember that these observations are based on the collection of surface finds; excavation may eventually tell a different story.

The later third, fourth and early fifth centuries were a time of crisis across northern and western Europe, characterised by economic decline and political and military instability. These events marked the beginning of the end of the Roman Empire in the west. As far as we are concerned, the prosperous infrastructure of Roman Britain came under increasing attack from overseas raiders. The attackers, 'barbarians' from north Germany, Schleswig-Holstein and the Low Countries, sailed across the North Sea and then up the principal rivers, penetrating far into the interior of Britain, wreaking havoc to the economy and social fabric of both town and country. The Humber estuary, facing eastwards towards the homelands of these raiders, must have been particularly inviting, providing access to all the main rivers draining Yorkshire, Lincolnshire and much of northern Britain. The Roman authorities responded to these frequent and persistent threats by defending the main centres of population and by the gradual construction of a network of coastal defences – forts and signal stations (watchtowers) – along the province's southern and eastern coastline – the so-called Saxon Shore Forts. During these years, too, the legionary fortress at York became the headquarters of the duke of the Britains (*dux Britanniarum*), who was almost certainly responsible for the defence of the country. However, during the later fourth and very early fifth centuries matters came to a head. Hostile raiding increased apace, becoming endemic. Rome could no longer sustain its interest in Britain and around 410 the imperial authorities decided to withdraw completely. It was an ordered departure. Troops departed to defend other frontiers; and the people of Britain were left to defend themselves. The market economy collapsed. Coinage disappeared, to be replaced by bartering. Centralised state power disintegrated. A unified state breaking down into discordant parts. Within the span of a single lifetime the economic and social structure of those parts of Britain which had been under the control of the Roman Empire for nearly four hundred years changed beyond recognition. Roman Britain passing into history.

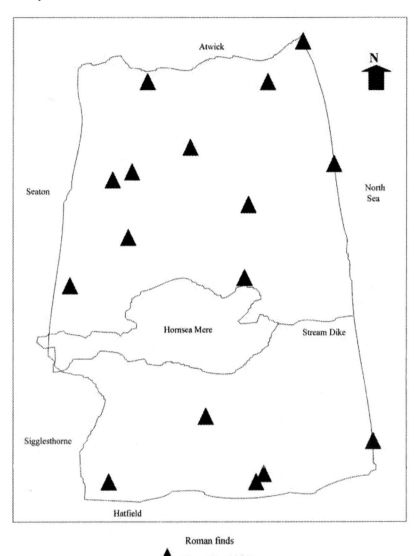

Figure 14. Roman finds: distribution map.

Seeing in the dark (Anglo-Saxon: c.AD 410-875)

Changing times. Just beyond Britain's eastern shores others were lurking to fill the void left by the Romans: Angles, Saxons and Jutes. The English. As Bede was to write a little over three centuries later, the English:

came from three very powerful Germanic tribes, the Saxons, *Angli*, and Jutes. The people of Kent and the inhabitants of the Isle of Wight are of Jutish origin and also that people opposite the Isle of Wight, that part of the kingdom of Wessex which is still today called the nation of the Jutes. From the Saxon country, that is the district now known as Old Saxony, came the East Saxons, the South Saxons, and the West Saxons. Besides this, from the country of the *Angli*, that is, the land between the kingdoms of the Jutes and the Saxons, which is called *Angulus*, came the East *Angli*, the Middle *Angli*, the Mercians, and all the Northumbrian race – that is those people who dwell north of the river Humber – as well as the other peoples of the *Angli* (*A History of the English Church and People*).

The fifth century was a time of considerable confusion (as, archaeologically and historically, it still is), giving rise to the term 'Dark Ages.' Apart from residual items of material culture there is no evidence of continuity between late Roman Britain and what came after. Complete collapse followed, for the best part of one hundred years, by chaos and then, from the late fifth and early sixth centuries, by the beginnings of a return to a complex, but very different, society. A period of profound, even revolutionary change, at the end of which grandparents were wearing totally different clothing and jewellery from their grandchildren, speaking a different language and embracing a different religion. The documentary sources are few, ambiguous and often written decades, if not – as in the case of Bede – centuries later. The Byzantine historian Zosimus implies that Roman rule in Britain ceased in 410. The earliest presence of 'Saxons' in Britain was, according to Constantius' *Life of St Germanus*, in 429. A Saxon take-over of Britain – the *Adventus Saxonum in Britanniam* – is assigned to 441 by the *Gallic Chronicle* and to 449 by Bede in his *History of the English Church and People*. Exiguous and fragmentary as they are, these sources do suggest a time-lapse between the end of Roman rule and the arrival of Germanic incomers. The archaeological evidence supports the picture that these near contemporaries paint – at least in East Yorkshire and the north of England. No Roman coins found on sites in the region can be dated to later than about 408, and those of the later fourth century occur infrequently. A similar end date for Roman mass-produced pottery is evident. This corroborates the written sources and suggests that Roman rule in northern Britain was fatally disrupted by around 410. The minting of coins and the mass-manufacture of pottery in the region had been made possible by the presence of troops, as a captive market, and their payment in coin which could then be used to purchase manufactured goods. In any event, the earliest detectable presence of 'barbarians' in East Yorkshire comes from the cremation cemetery at Sancton, just to the north of the Humber and adjacent to the old Roman road from Brough to Market Weighton, Shiptonthorpe, Hayton and York, which dates to the later fifth or early sixth century.

What happened between the end of Roman Britain and the arrival of the Germanic immigrants? What became of the native British population once the Anglo-Saxons began to colonise the country? More specifically, was the colonisation accompanied by extensive settlement, displacing or reinforcing the indigenous population, or was there rather a take-over of the lands of the British by an incoming elite? These questions have vexed historians and archaeologists since the nineteenth century and are really no nearer resolution now than they were one hundred and fifty years ago.

What is certain, however, is that the traditional view of the end of Roman Britain in an orgy of conflagration and slaughter, followed by the movement of Anglo-Saxon settlers into a desolate wasteland, avoiding or ruthlessly obliterating all cultural traces of their predecessors and imposing their own Germanic culture and patterns of nucleated villages and open fields, is no longer tenable.

In the twilight years of the Empire the Roman authorities invited Germanic mercenaries to help shore up Britannia's collapsing defences. After 410 these groups stayed, serving opportunistic native aristocratic masters who were vying with each other to fill the power vacuum left by the departing Romans. If any reliable impression can be gained from the legend of Vortigern, Hengist and Horsa it is that Saxon mercenaries serving British rulers could have provided the bridgehead for a subsequent larger-scale colonisation by economic migrants, who were escaping the worsening economic conditions caused by rising sea-levels and climatic deterioration in their north German homelands. It is important to emphasise the relatively small-scale and peaceful nature of these migrations. The traditional view is of massive, unrelenting waves of immigrants swamping the native population, a cataclysmic event that overwhelmed late Roman civilisation to such an extent that little trace of it was left in Anglo-Saxon England. War and pandemonium. Modern research tends not to support such a vision of catastrophic change. Instead it is now suggested that only thousands rather than tens of thousands of people were involved. An alternative hypothesis sees the colonisation as the resettling of a numerically small warrior elite on an indigenous peasantry. Whatever the mechanisms (and this is no place to go into the complexities of the evidence or arguments), what is certain is that substantial (unquantifiable) numbers of immigrants settled in the lowlands of eastern England, particularly in East Anglia, Lincolnshire and Yorkshire. Gradually the settlers became dominant and the native Britons were assimilated into a new, alien culture. Amongst the indigenous population a process of de-Romanisation took place, that is, the gradual disappearance of the physical trappings of Romano-British culture in the face of a new cultural formation. The old Roman ways became little more than a memory, replaced by a Germanic language, laws, institutions, customs and religion within a new, but not particularly united, country – England. Reorganisation among the ruins. Eventually the incomers went on to develop one of the most sophisticated and organised societies in early medieval Europe, the first nation state.

East Yorkshire has provided much archaeological evidence for the settlement of the *Angles*. Eventually, probably in the early sixth century, the Anglians went on to found the kingdom of Deira, which stretched from the Humber to the Tees and inland as far as the Vale of York and the Pennine foothills; within this broad geographical and political entity, East Yorkshire, more particularly the chalklands around Driffield, formed one of the state's core areas. Much of the available evidence comes from cemetery excavations, often from poorly documented eighteenth and nineteenth century investigations. Around seventy-seven definite or probable Anglo-Saxon inhumation cemeteries are currently known in East Yorkshire: forty-five flat cemeteries (including the one at Hornsea; see below), twenty-three inserted into bronze age round barrows, seven placed into later prehistoric linear earthworks, and two inserted into iron age square-ditched barrows. In addition there is one large cremation cemetery at Sancton, evidence for cremation burials at Garton-on-the-Wolds and Swine, several cremations with inhumations at Driffield, and circumstantial evidence for cremations at Nafferton and Kilham. Parts of only four of these sites – Garton Station, Sancton, Sewerby and West Heslerton – have been excavated to modern standards.

There are certain or possible Anglo-Saxon settlement structures at half a dozen locations across the county, most notably at Cottam, Newbald, Elmswell, Rudston and West Heslerton. Concentrations of sites, mostly indicated by surface finds of pottery and metalwork, are to be found in the Driffield area, in the Great Wold Valley to the east of Rudston, on the western escarpment of the Wolds around Acklam, and on the coast from Sewerby northwards. Scattered sites are also to be found in the Vale of Pickering. There are few in Holderness and none so far identified in the Vale of York. Elsewhere stray finds suggest possible further occupation areas.

What does all this fragmentary and often ambiguous evidence tell us about the actual process of settlement? Excavations at the Sancton pagan cremation cemetery, near Market Weighton, suggest that areas adjacent to the Humber were colonised first, probably in the mid-fifth century, and that this settlement had close affinities with that in north Lincolnshire. In a detailed study of grave goods accompanying burials, the historian John Hines has suggested that the rest of East Yorkshire was a zone of secondary settlement, peopled by immigrants from southern Scandinavia in the later fifth or early sixth centuries. This phase was characterised by a tradition of inhumation, as opposed to cremation, burial. This was a time of consolidation and expansion, with communities growing in size, settling peripheral areas, and probably appropriating large tracts of land hitherto in the hands of native Britons. It is most likely that the political kingdom of Deira was established during this time. This was one of a dozen or so kingdoms founded along the North Sea coast during this period.

Hornsea along with the rest of Holderness has provided very little physical evidence for Anglo-Saxon colonisation. Place-name evidence is the most abundant. In the vicinity of Hornsea, the following place-names are indicative of an Anglo-Saxon presence:

- Mappleton – the 'farm by a maple-tree'
- Hornsea Burton – the 'fortified farmstead'
- Seaton – the 'farmstead near the lake' (that is, Hornsea Mere)
- Catwick – the 'dairy farm of Catta or of Catta and his people'
- Beeford – the settlement 'near the ford'
- Bewholme – 'at the bends in the stream(s)'
- Nunkeeling – the settlement of Cylla and his people.' The 'Nun' element was added in the twelfth century, from the Benedictine Nunnery founded here in about 1150

- Skirlington – 'Scirela's farm'
- Dunnington – Dudda's farmstead'
- Bonwick – 'Būna's dairy farm' or the 'dairy farm near the reeds'
- Ulrome – 'Wulfhere's homestead'
- Lissett – the 'dwelling near the pastureland'
- Barmston – 'Beorn's farmstead'

One point needs making. It does not necessarily follow that place-names reflect the ethnic composition of the settlements that bore them. The English names could very well have been coined by a not very numerous English ruling elite without any reference to the language spoken by the inhabitants of the settlements to which they were given. It is hard to avoid the conclusion, though, that the population in this area came to regard itself as predominantly English and was principally English speaking.

The only direct evidence for an Anglo-Saxon presence at Hornsea itself is the inhumation cemetery, first recorded in the early twentieth century. In the summer of 1913 workmen levelling a natural gravel ridge for the construction of a bowling green in the grounds of the new Hydro Hotel at the north end of the promenade, came across human bones and artefacts. A press report of the discoveries, initially thought to be Roman, caught the attention of Thomas Sheppard of Hull Museums. Ever alert to the possibilities of increasing the museum collections, Sheppard, after an initial refusal, was eventually given permission to 'superintend the remainder of the work:'

> Together with my assistant I visited Hornsea and found that a number of human bones had been excavated and that various small beads, and one or two brooches had been found, and had been divided among the workmen and others interested. With one or two important exceptions it was possible to secure the various specimens [for Hull Municipal Museum].

He was able to record twelve inhumation burials of Anglo-Saxon date. Here is his description:

> So far as could be judged from the bones remaining, they mostly occurred in a row extending east to west. Skeletons Nos.1 to 8 were roughly parallel with each other, and with one exception (No.2), had the heads pointing to the south. In that exception the head was to the north. Skeleton No.9 had the head to the south-west, whereas at the end of the same row skeleton No.10 had the head to the west. Facing No.10, at a distance of three yards, was skeleton No.11, also with the head to the west. Skeleton No.12 (near No.1) had the head to the north-west. Between 11 and 12 there may have been other skeletons forming a second row, but, if so, they had been removed some time previously without any record being kept. In most cases the skeletons are stretched out at full length, but in Nos. 2, 10, and 11 they are buried in a crouched position, which seems to be a not unusual feature in Anglo-Saxon burials in East Yorkshire. One of the skeletons (No.11) was that of a child.

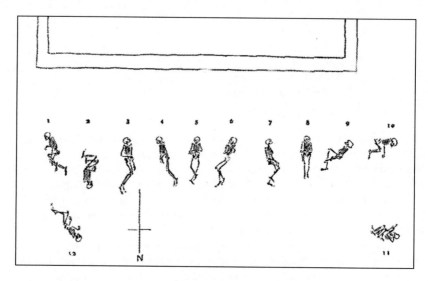

Figure 15. The Anglo-Saxon cemetery at Hornsea as recorded by Thomas Sheppard. (Illustration: *Transactions of the Hull Scientific and Field Naturalists' Club* 4 (1913))

He then went on to describe the various items of grave goods that accompanied the burials:

> With skeleton No.1 was found the square-headed brooch, a food vase, key, and the annular brooch. Near the hip-bones of skeleton No.2 was a small iron saxe or knife, and a silver disc. With skeleton No.3 occurred the most important set of objects met with during the excavations. Near the right shoulder was the elaborately-ornamented fibula; near the left wrist was the annular brooch, with the iron pin still in position; at the feet, to the left of the skeleton, was the food vase. With skeleton No.9 was found the long square-headed brooch. With No.10 a similar brooch was obtained, together with an annular brooch and a necklace, and at the feet of the skeleton was a vase. With skeleton No.12 were found an irregular mass of jet, a fine spindle-whorl of jet, a ring brooch, bronze clasps, and two small fragments of bronze, sharper on one side than the other, after the manner of a knife-blade. These probably belonged to a belt. Other brooches, etc, were obtained, but as they had been found before we arrived, it is difficult to allocate them to any particular skeleton.

In 1981 a planning application to build eleven houses in the grounds of the Hydro, by now renamed the Granville Court Hotel, was approved. As a consequence of the 1913 discoveries on the site, a condition was attached to the planning consent which allowed for a small excavation to be undertaken prior to any development. This investigation, carried out by the then Humberside Archaeology Unit, took place early in the following year. This work uncovered a further six inhumation burials, to the north of Sheppard's explorations. Unlike the earlier burials, these were not regularly laid out in

64

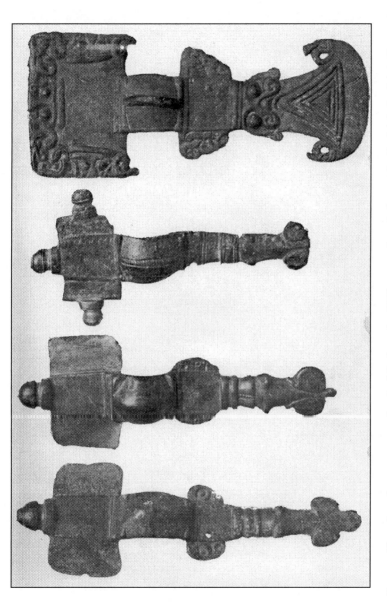

Plate 21. Copper alloy cruciform brooches, accompanying burials from the 1913 excavation. *Left to right:* Burial 9, Burial 1, Unassociated, and Burial 3. (Photograph: *Transactions of the Hull Scientific and Field Naturalists' Club* 4 (1913))

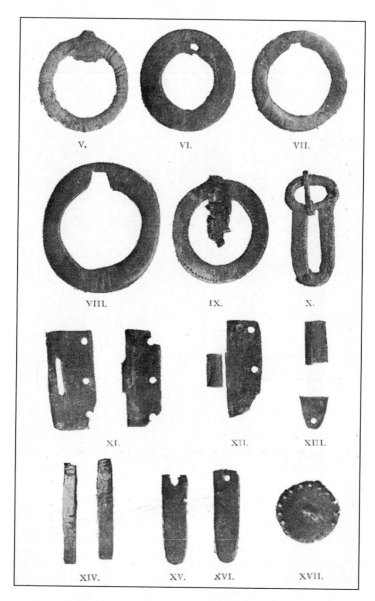

Plate 22. Metal artefacts from the 1913 excavation.

Top row, *left to right*: Copper alloy annular brooches from Burial 3, 1, and 10

Second row, *left*: copper alloy annular brooch from Burial 10; *centre*: unassociated copper alloy annular brooch; and *right* unassociated copper alloy buckle.

Third row, *left to right*: copper alloy sleeve clasps and strap ends from Burial 12.

Fourth row, *left to right*: copper alloy strap ends from Burial 12 and silver disc from Burial 2.

(Photograph: *Transactions of the Hull Scientific and Field Naturalists' Club* 4 (1913))

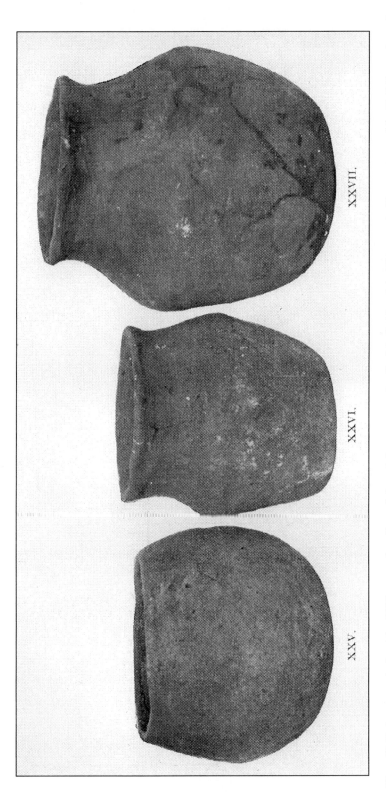

Plate 23. Pottery vessels from the 1913 excavation. From *left to right* accompanying Burials 3, 10 and 1. (Photograph: *Transactions of the Hull Scientific and Field Naturalists' Club* 4 (1913))

rows, but seemingly haphazardly placed. The 1982 burials were fragmentary, making any determination of gender and age difficult. Quoting from the excavation report:

> Burial 1 was thought to be that of an adolescent, possibly male, and perhaps aged between twelve and sixteen years. Burial 2 was the most complete skeleton and thought to be that of a female, aged between twenty-five and thirty years. Burial 3 was very fragmented: the robust bones may suggest a male under the age of forty years. Burial 4 was also found in a fragmentary state, but was possibly a female adult. Burial 5 contained a nearly complete female skeleton, possibly between the age of twenty-five and thirty-five years. Lastly, Burial 6 was possibly that of a female adolescent.

Taking the 1913 and 1982 burials together, the majority were placed on their right-hand side, and most were semi-flexed, that is, with legs slightly drawn up. Arms were either folded on the chest or in irregular positions. In nearly all cases the head was looking straight forward, with the orientation to north, south, west, south-west, north-west or south-east.

The 1982 excavations produced grave goods similar to that of 1913: bronze cylinders, bronze fragments; iron and copper alloy annular brooches, copper alloy strap ends, copper alloy pins, iron knives, amber and glass beads, and pottery. These are typical for the period. But, with an average number of goods per grave at 1.5 it is a relatively poor cemetery, representing a low social status and relatively impoverished community; at Sewerby Anglo-Saxon cemetery, to the north of Bridlington, for example, the average number of items accompanying each burial was 2.2. Or, conceivably, other, 'richer' graves have yet to be discovered.

What of date? Using the accompanying diagnostic artefacts, the brooches in particular, it is possible to say that this cemetery was of long duration, in use between the late fifth and seventh centuries, with the majority of burials dating from the mid- to late sixth century. In other words, the cemetery contains both Pagan and Christian burials, spanning the conversion period as it does.

Altogether, the layout of the Hornsea cemetery is unusual. The two areas are different, organisationally and spatially: regular rows from the 1913 excavation, haphazard placement from the 1982 work. The overall distribution of burials is irregular: in the southern part, that excavated by Sheppard, they were all placed in close proximity, in graves that must have had above-ground markers to prevent disturbance by later interments; in the northern area, the burials were widely spread, without apparent order. This can be taken to indicate either (1) no competition for space within the cemetery or (2) the subsequent, unrecorded disturbance and destruction of burials (Before the Hydro was built in 1913, this area was under intensive cultivation; over the centuries, ploughing many have destroyed many burials). If we take the evidence at face value, the arrangement is puzzling, anomalous. No other excavated East Yorkshire Anglo-Saxon cemetery exhibits this patterning. There is no evidence to suggest one area being earlier or later than the other. Nor is there any evidence for segregation by sex or age. Why the cemetery

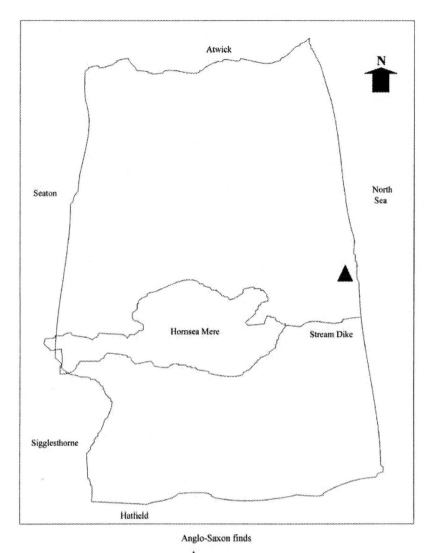

Anglo-Saxon finds

▲ Cemetery

Figure 16. Anglo-Saxon finds: distribution map.

should be organised in this way is not known. As both excavations are likely to have touched only a portion of the whole cemetery, future work may provide an answer to this question.

The finding of part of an Anglo-Saxon comb on the adjacent cliff in 1970, strongly indicates that part of the cemetery has been lost to coastal erosion. This object, now in Hull Museum, has incised latticework decoration on the plates, which hold two rows of teeth in place, and most probably was an item of grave goods accompanying a burial.

It is likely that the gravel ridge on which the cemetery was established would have been a prominent location, an island surrounded by lower boulder clay plains. A raised area of drier land with wide vistas: a landmark to be seen in an otherwise flattish countryside. This may have been one of the attractions for iron age, Roman and Anglo-Saxon activity here.

The location of any settlement that possibly served the cemetery is not known. Presently, the cemetery represents the only Anglo-Saxon evidence from Hornsea.

Sharing out the land (Viking: c.AD 875-1066)

In the ninth century Scandinavian invaders threatened to overwhelm Anglo-Saxon England. After a series of bloody campaigns they managed to establish a permanent presence in eastern England, occupying territory that became known as the Danelaw. Part of this conquest involved East Yorkshire, where Viking settlement began in the mid-870s, following Hálfdan's seizure of York and the kingdom of Northumbria. In 876, according to the *Anglo-Saxon Chronicle*, 'Hálfdan shared out the lands of the Northumbrians, and they [the Scandinavians] proceeded to plough and to support themselves.' This is corroborated by the anonymous tenth or eleventh century text *A History of St Cuthbert*, which states that the Vikings 'rebuilt the city of York, cultivated the land around it, and remained there.' The implication of both texts is that the Scandinavians took possession of the land of Northumbria and settled on it. We have no way of knowing how many Vikings settled in East Yorkshire, or whether it involved men of peasant class, perhaps accompanied by their womenfolk and children, or an elite force composed of aristocratic adventurers. Recent research would tend to indicate that the Viking settlement of East Yorkshire did not radically disrupt the existing pattern of occupation, and that over time a distinctive Anglo-Scandinavian culture flourished.

Place-names derived from the Viking language are widespread in Holderness, as they are across the rest of Yorkshire. They cannot, however, be used to assess the level of Viking settlement in a simple way; in the light of recent research, it is no longer possible to regard a village with an Old Norse name as one necessarily settled by Vikings. The new settlers could simply have renamed many existing settlements.

Other than place-names there is no physical evidence for a Viking presence in the immediate vicinity of Hornsea. As discussed in chapter 1 the name Hornsea may be wholly Scandinavian or it could be an Anglo-Saxon/Viking hybrid. Scandinavian place-names in the immediate area include:

- Northorpe – the 'north hamlet (see below, chapter 3)
- Southorpe – the 'south hamlet' (see below, chapter 3)
- Wassand – the 'sand bank or sandy shore near the ford'
- Sigglesthorne – 'Sigel's thorntree'
- Withernwick – the 'dairy farm belonging to the lost settlement of Withthorn'
- Atwick – 'Atta's dairy farm'

Summary

Taking the long view, although the evidence for pre-medieval settlement within the modern built-up area is meagre and equivocal, we should not take this to mean that the place was of no interest or significance to people in prehistory or early historic times. We can point to circumstantial and topographical evidence, as well as finds, to show that the area had been a focus of activity since the mesolithic period. But we can hardly pretend that the evidence is thick on the ground. Any meaningful understanding of the archaeological remains of the prehistoric, Romano-British, Anglo-Saxon and Viking periods within the town's boundaries is dependent on the patterning of discoveries made within the surrounding areas. When viewed as a whole – that is, Hornsea in the context of this part of northern Holderness – the evidence indicates a landscape becoming progressively more manipulated by human intervention through time, more settled.

CHAPTER 3

ORIGINS OF PLACE

Introduction

1066. A tangled web of momentous events. A year of crises. A year of two
invasions, three battles and two coronations. A year when a French-speaking
Norman triumphed over an Anglo-Saxon and a Scandinavian. A convulsive
and fateful year for England. A year that brought together the three greatest
European military leaders of their day: Harold II of England, scion of one of
the most ambitious family dynasties in Anglo-Saxon England; Duke William
of Normandy, William the Bastard as his contemporaries called him, William
the Conqueror as he proved to be; and the Norwegian King Harald Sigurdson
– Harald Hardrada, Harald the Ruthless – the most feared warrior in northern
Europe. Three powerful and ambitious men who had fought their way to
authority in their respective countries and who now, in three short weeks of
bloodshed in the autumn of 1066, were to fight to the death for the greatest
prize of all: the English throne.

These tumultuous events, played out on a large canvas, provided the
scene and setting for a multiplicity of subsequent local narratives.
Repercussions, reverberations. National events shaping the destinies of people
and place: like ripples on a pond, reaching out, spreading, the effects were
everywhere felt. New identities, new axes of power and authority. Ultimately,
the direct origins of modern-day Hornsea can be traced back to those years
and to the succeeding three or four centuries.

Beginnings: towards a geography of place

The first documentary reference to Hornsea occurs in the *Domesday
Book* of 1086, a national survey compiled for taxation purposes, but also
containing a broad social and economic description of the country. The entry
for Hornsea reads:

> In Hornsea Morcar had 27 carucates of land taxable, the same
> number of ploughs are possible there. Now Drogo has there 1 plough
> and Wizo, his man, [has] 1 plough; and 9 villagers and 3
> smallholders with 1½ ploughs. There is a church and a priest.
> Meadow, 60 acres.
>
> To this manor belongs this jurisdiction: [Hornsea] Burton, 2
> carucates; [Sou]thorpe, 1½ carucates; [Long] Riston, 2 carucates and
> 6 bovates; [North] Skirlaugh, 6 oxgangs; [High] Skirlington, 5
> carucates. Together 11½ carucates of land taxable, where 12 ploughs

are possible. Now Drogo has there 2 freemen and 3 villagers with 2 ploughs.

Value before 1066 £56; now £6.

The interest lies in the detail.

Of particular note is the information concerning landownership in 1066. At the time of the Norman Conquest, the Anglo-Scandinavian Earl Morcar held Hornsea as one manor of twenty-seven carucates. Originally the amount of land a team of eight oxen could plough in a year, the carucate was used as a unit of tax assessment – geld – in *Domesday Book*, and cannot, in any meaningful sense, be converted into acres or hectares. Morcar was the most powerful individual in the north in 1066, having what almost certainly amounted to a vice-regal role in the region. The younger brother of Earl Edwin of Mercia, Morcar had been created Earl of Northumbria in 1065, following a successful rebellion prompted by the harsh rule of the then earl, Tostig, the younger brother of Harold Godwinson and heir-apparent to the English throne. Ousted from his earldom, Tostig fled to the court of Baldwin V in Flanders, subsequently forging an alliance with King Harald Hardrada of Norway for an invasion of the north of England. In mid-September 1066, in a campaign that was brief, bloody and, for them (as for many of their followers), terminal, Hardrada and Tostig invaded East Yorkshire *via* the river Humber. On the 20th of that month, they defeated an English army commanded by Earls Edwin and Morcar at Fulford, just outside York. Five days later, after a forced march from London, Harold Godwinson, King of England since January 1066, defeated and killed both Hardrada and Tostig at the battle of Stamford Bridge. In the event the outcome was an empty victory, only serving to guarantee the result of the next – and final – engagement of the year. The victory celebrations at York were short-lived, interrupted by the news that William of Normandy had landed on the south coast and was making a bid for the English crown. Harold had no alternative but to meet the challenge. He marched the remnants of his weary army southwards, only to be defeated and killed at the battle of Hastings on 14 October. Just as the battle of Stamford Bridge finally settled the Scandinavian threat, the battle of Hastings decided the fate and future destiny of Great Britain.

A new king. William's authority was legitimated by military conquest and his power maintained through force of arms and terror campaigns against the indigenous population.

In order to maintain some semblance of continuity in the north, King William allowed Morcar, who had not fought at Hastings, to remain Earl of Northumbria. It is feasible that William regarded the native Anglo-Scandinavian aristocracy – men like Morcar – as his best buffer against the threat of new Danish invasions of the north of England, in 1085 by Knútr the Good, son of the Danish King Sveinn Estriðson, and later, in 1098, by King Magnús 'Barelegs'. Initially, Morcar pledged his loyalty to William, but, like all the northern earls, did not willingly accept Norman rule. The scene was set for conflict. In 1068 Morcar led an unsuccessful northern insurrection against William, for which he was pardoned. Three years later, in 1071, he joined Hereward the Wake on the Isle of Ely and took part in another short-lived

73

uprising. Following a land and water-borne assault, Hereward's revolt quickly collapsed. Morcar was captured and, for his part in the rebellion, all his estates were forfeited to the crown. Morcar never regained his land and remained a prisoner until 1087, when William, now on his deathbed, had him freed. Freedom was fleeting. Morcar was subsequently imprisoned by William's successor, William II, and died in captivity.

Reference has already been made to the word 'manor.' How should we define this word? Over the years there has been much argument as to what constituted a manor. In the context of the *Domesday Book* it is best envisaged as a landed estate, of greater or lesser size, owned by one man, who was responsible for the payment of geld – taxes – due from himself and his unfree tenants. It was a landholding organised and managed from a central place, known as a *caput*, but which often had interests in outlying places called *vills*.

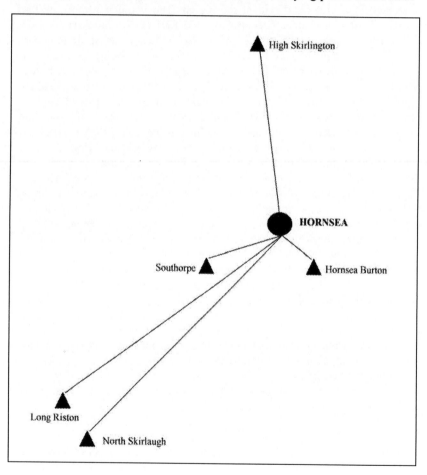

Figure 17. The Domesday geography of Hornsea.

In addition Hornsea had jurisdiction (soke) over, but not ownership of, five other townships: Southorpe and Hornsea Burton in Hornsea, High Skirlington in Atwick, and Long Riston and North Skirlaugh in Swine.

74

'Soke' (or *soc*) is understood as a relatively loose bond between a lord and man, a form of lordship that was exercised over freemen and their land. The word itself is derived from 'seek' and refers, under the laws of the later Anglo-Saxon kings, to the duty incumbent upon a freeman to 'seek a lord' who would support him in the courts and generally stand surety for him. In return for this protection, the sokeman would perform services for, and pay customary and other dues to, the lord, who would also receive monetary payments for any minor breaches of the law on the part of the sokeman. The sokeman was responsible for the payment of geld on his holding and this would be rendered at the lord's *caput*.

Turning to the agricultural exploitation of Hornsea, the *Domesday* entry states that twenty-seven ploughs were 'possible' there. If it is reckoned that each plough was capable of coping with 100 acres/40 hectares each year, then this gives an indication of the primary importance of grain production on the estate in 1066 and the immediate pre-Conquest years. However, in 1086 only three-and-a-half ploughs were recorded. This implies a massive scaling down in arable activity between the two dates. Such decline needs to be seen within the context of a concomitant reduction in the size of the resident population.

The *Domesday* survey was not intended as a population census and numbers are not always given for individual places. For Hornsea, though, we are fortunate in having some demographic detail. The entry lists fourteen people, all of whom we can assume were resident: Wizo, who was described as 'Drogo's man,' a priest, nine villagers and three smallholders. This seems a very low population even when, as we know, *Domesday Book* tended to omit certain categories of people, such as millers and other specialists. The recorded figure must represent a minimum. If we assume that each person listed was the head of a household containing at least 4.5 members, then we arrive at an estimated total of sixty-three people, sixty-four when we include the unmarried priest. Taking the 1852 parish area of 3,332 acres/1,348.5 hectares, we can calculate a rough-and-ready *Domesday* population density of 12.30 persons per square mile/4.75 persons per square kilometre. The *Domesday* population of Hornsea was very low, certainly nowhere near enough to ensure the viable exploitation of the entire estate.

Cause and effect: a much-reduced population leading to low levels of economic exploitation. What brought about a systemic failure of such catastrophic proportions? The documents are silent. A probable cause is to be found in the terrible events of the winter of 1069-70. In the years immediately following the conquest of 1066 the north of England was in a state of constant open rebellion against William. The broad outline of what happened in the North during the 1060s is clear enough from contemporary or near-contemporary sources. The Northumbrians, motivated by memories of former independence and by the presence of many Scandinavian settlers, were hostile to any close control by a southern-based monarch, who was seen by most, and this despite his own Viking roots, as an unwelcome outsider. Between 1067 and 1069 there were at least four major rebellions in the area between the Humber and Durham. The last of these, in September 1069, was the most serious, and the one that William had most difficulty in suppressing. On this occasion, the Northumbrians were assisted by a large polyglot gathering of happy-go-lucky adventurers from Scandinavia, Poland, Saxony and Friesia, led by Osbeorn, brother to King Swein of Denmark. During the course of this rising, and adding insult to injury, William's two new castles at York were captured and their garrisons massacred. Determined once and for all to bring the area beyond the Humber to heel, the King swore revenge and, with devastating effect, unleashed his army on the communities of the northern counties – the so-called 'Harrying of the North,' described by the historian Edward Freeman in 1871 as 'that fearful deed, half of policy, half of vengeance, which has stamped the name of William with infamy.' Shock and awe, in the language of the present. With more than a little hint of partisan exaggeration, the contemporary *Anglo-Saxon Chronicle* records that William 'utterly ravaged and laid waste the entire shire' of Yorkshire. More than fifty-five years later, in 1125, Orderic Vitalis, in compiling his eponymous *Ecclesiastical History of Orderic Vitalis*, wrote that William adopted a scorched earth policy 'north of the Humber,' burning all food supplies, driving away livestock, and slaughtering countless people. He went on, 'in consequence ... so terrible a famine fell upon the humble and defenceless populace, that more than 100,000 Christian folk of both sexes, young and old alike, perished of hunger.' The medieval mind was prone to exaggerate, especially where figures were concerned. It delighted in good round numbers, and was accustomed to make confident statements entirely without adequate data. So 100,000 deaths can be confidently dismissed; it should more realistically be read as meaning 'many.' Hugh the Chantor, writing at about the same time as Orderic, described how the Normans destroyed York and the 'whole district around it ... with the sword, famine and flames' (although, admittedly, there is no current archaeological evidence to substantiate this claim). Whatever the precise truth of these and similar statements by Anglo-Saxon annalists and later chroniclers, and they are deeply flawed as historical source material, it is abundantly clear that the hapless northerners suffered grievously from William's wrath during the winter of 1069-70. The effects of the harrying were, perhaps, further compounded by the activities of the rebels themselves, as well as by a Scottish invasion of the northern shires in the same year. Overall, large swathes of Yorkshire and adjoining counties must have resembled a wasteland; and the consequences of that destruction were still very much apparent in 1086 when *Domesday Book* was in process of compilation.

Lords of the manor

Following the forfeiture of Morcar's estates, William I granted Hornsea, along with the rest of Holderness, to Drew de Bevrère. Drew, also known as Drogo, is a shadowy figure. Little is known about him: he was a Flemish adventurer who fought alongside William at Hastings; and he was married to a kinswoman of William. For his services at Hastings and presumably also because of familial ties, William entrusted Drew with the lordship of Holderness. He made his residence at Skipsea, half-a-dozen miles north of Hornsea, where he had a motte and bailey castle constructed. According to the *Meaux Chronicle*, written some two hundred years after the event, Drew supposedly killed his wife in a fit of temper sometime before

September 1087, secretly burying her body within the confines of his castle. Before news of this leaked out, he went to William and asked for money so he and his wife might return to Flanders. With this Drew fled and sought refuge at the court of Baldwin V, renowned as a safe haven for all manner of renegades and misfits. Beyond confiscating his English lands, William appears not to have sought revenge, and Drew seemingly spent the rest of his life in exile in Flanders.

After Drew's flight, his lands in Holderness had been transferred to Odo of Champagne, Count of Aumale, by September 1087. In 1088 or shortly thereafter, Odo granted the manor of Hornsea and the tithe of fish (from the mere) to the abbot and abbey of St Mary, York. Sometime after 1090, his son and successor, Stephen, gave the church at Hornsea to St Mary's.

The Benedictine abbey of St Mary's was founded in 1086, following a move from Lastingham on the southern fringes of the North Yorkshire Moors. Odo's initial gift of Hornsea was just one of a large number of similar endowments made to the monastery by influential landholders from across Yorkshire and elsewhere in the years immediately following its foundation. Over the coming decades and centuries many other estates were likewise granted to the abbey. These, together with the many privileges granted by successive kings of England, eventually resulted in St Mary's becoming the wealthiest and most powerful monastery in the north of England.

When an abbot accepted such a grant as Hornsea he became the lord of the manor, was entitled to the profits of the demesne land, and had rights over customary tenants, rents and labour services, and the perquisites of lordship, including profits from the manorial court. In practical terms there was little difference between manors under lay control and those under monastic control.

Hornsea was to remain a property of St Mary's until the dissolution of the monasteries in the sixteenth century.

Medieval topography

The shape of Hornsea (that is, the historic core around the church and market place) can be regarded as the product of the interaction of several different influences and processes working within a framework of physical and historical constraints – such as the physical constraints of the site, inherited patterns of land parcels and boundaries, seigneurial controls, and pressures generated from within the community itself. The effectiveness of the various influences and the extent of their impact upon the village plan are likely to be subject to temporal fluctuation. While the study of the present arrangement of village streets and open spaces, property boundaries and public and private buildings is entirely justified in its own right, it is also apparent that these aspects of village topography cannot be understood without reference to their past development. The greatest problem in projecting morphological studies back into the historical dimension is to gauge how far back in time one can safely project the various individual surviving elements; and the greatest pitfall lies in the over-ready assumption that settlement forms or the disposition of any elements within them were

Plate 24. Medieval pottery from Hornsea. Pottery manufactured in Beverley, Scarborough, Holme-upon-Spalding Moor, York, and Brandsby (North Yorkshire) has been found at Hornsea, covering the period from the eleventh to the fifteenth centuries. Vessel types range from coarse cooking and storage pots to finely glazed and decorated tableware, cisterns, lamps, dripping dishes, and urinals. Although varying greatly in size and shape there were three basic vessel forms throughout the middle ages: jugs and jars and bowls. From the fourteenth century the range of shapes and forms shows greater variety as pottery begins to replace treen or wooden objects, such as wooden drinking bowls. In addition, smaller quantities of pottery from further afield has turned up: Rhenish wares of the twelfth century; northern French wares of the early thirteenth century; and south-west French and Low Countries wares of the later thirteenth and fourteenth centuries. The European fabrics would have been imported through, and then distributed from, Hull and Beverley. Most pottery had a limited distribution around the area in which it was produced: it was bulky and heavy to move over long distances, particularly at a time when transport was limited; and it could easily be broken. Generally, it was only fine, high quality wares and specialized vessels that were traded over wider areas. Hornsea's role as a market centre for much of northern Holderness probably accounts for the wide and diverse range of pottery found in the town. (Photograph and finds: Stephen Harrison)

necessarily static over any period longer than that for which stability can be proven.

What we cannot assume is that the form of the town today – or what can be shown on the earliest available cartographic source – necessarily reflects the broad outlines of the village in medieval times; even less can we assume that it represents the essential shape of the *Domesday* vill or of the first Anglo-Saxon settlement.

The justification of the morphological approach is the belief that the village plan contains evidence of its own historical development. From a study of Hornsea's archaeology, layout, place-names and the few surviving documentary sources, it is possible to identify a series of distinctive stages (or phases) through which the settlement has evolved over the last one thousand or so years. But first we need to place developments during the medieval period into their immediate context.

At various times in the later nineteenth and earlier twentieth centuries sporadic scatters of (now lost) Roman pottery and other artefacts were recovered from the vicinity of Mill Lane and Mt Pleasant during building work. Such evidence is perhaps suggestive of an as yet unidentified Roman settlement on the glacial ridge overlooking the present market place. This is not, however, to imply any continuity between a putative Roman period settlement and the later, medieval village. The precision of the juxtaposition of these settlements makes the inference of some direct relationship between them very tempting; however, it should not be forgotten that a gap of at least eight centuries separates the two settlements. At present this chronological gulf cannot be bridged. The density of Roman settlement sites in the parish (see above, chapter 2) is such that an occasional fortuitous coincidence with the medieval village is inevitable. On present knowledge, therefore, the juxtaposition is not meaningful in terms of any form of continuity.

Moving forward in time to the Anglo-Saxon centuries, it will be remembered that a cemetery of this period was discovered during the building of the Hydro Hotel in the early years of the twentieth century (see above, chapter 2). This burial ground lies c.1km north-east of the parish church and the historic core of medieval Hornsea. Evidence for contemporary settlement has yet to be discovered.

Domesday Book contains little information about actual settlements because the compilers were primarily concerned with recording details of landownership and land values for taxation purposes. There is no information about the physical character of Hornsea at the time of the *Domesday* survey. The record of nine villagers and three smallholders does not necessarily imply that they were living in a single nucleated community on the estate or that their dwellings lie buried beneath modern-day Hornsea in the vicinity of the church. Two possibilities may be put forward. If we assume that the present church occupies the same position as that recorded in 1086, then it may have provided a focus for a loose, uncoordinated collection of houses and other buildings. Despite sporadic archaeological investigations in the area of the present market place, no evidence for an early settlement has come to light. Absence of evidence, however, is not evidence of absence. Alternatively, a dispersed settlement pattern – as is known from elsewhere in the country – could have existed, with individual farmsteads scattered across the estate, with the name Hornsea referring to the territory rather than a single concentration of dwellings.

Let us now turn our gaze upon the post-1066 period. The direct origins of modern Hornsea can be sought in the early years of Norman rule. This Phase I settlement appears to have been constructed *de novo*. It seems highly likely that the population of Hornsea had moved (or more probably been moved) into a nucleated settlement by the late eleventh century. This was a regularly planned linear layout of rectangular tofts and crofts arranged in orderly lines on both sides of, and at right angles to, a main street extending westwards from the church (the present Westgate), with a parallel back lane to the south (the present Back Westgate). Both streets were on a slightly arced east-west alignment following the lower, south-facing slope of the glacially derived ridge of sand immediately to the north. This topographical feature, together with the mere immediately to the south, encouraged linearity in the settlement plan. (Essentially this was a street village, typical of many that can still be seen across the Holderness landscape today; similar broad arrangements can be seen locally at, for example, North Frodingham and Burstwick) The new village, as proposed here, was a rectangle of properties some 250m east to west by 75m north to south. The main features of this village were present when Hornsea first appears on maps from the late eighteenth century, which suggests that the geometric characteristics are nothing other than historic in origin.

Although no surviving documentary sources refer to these events, ecclesiastical agency is suspected. The acquisition of Hornsea by St Mary's Abbey, York, in about 1088 provides a suitable context for this reorganisation. A colonising venture, a settlement laid out at one moment in time: a conscious monastic creation.

This hypothesis is tentatively supported by the pottery sequence. Significantly – and as a crude indicator of the beginnings of domestic occupation in the Westgate area – pottery fragments collected from gardens and foundation and service trenches starts no earlier than the late eleventh or early twelfth centuries: thereafter there is an almost uninterrupted sequence down to the present time. Of the earliest pottery, two types are present: (northern) gritty (or pimply) ware and splashed glaze ware. Gritty ware is a white, pink, reddish-yellow or light red (and occasionally grey) fabric and is distinctive on account of its many protruding angular or sub-angular quartz sand inclusions. Vessel types consist of cooking and kitchen wares, with some bowls. The source of manufacture is not known, but gritty ware has a wide, almost ubiquitous, distribution across the East Riding. Splashed glaze ware comes in similar fabrics to gritty ware, but has sparse and pitted brown or yellow or olive green glaze applied to its external surfaces, and consists mainly of jugs and pitchers. The location of the kilns producing this pottery is also not known. It has a similar distribution to gritty ware.

The sources do not allow a detailed reconstruction of the first medieval village. A document of c.1200 describes a house lying 'at the end of the vill of Hornsea towards Seaton,' which must imply that the village consisted of houses grouped together. Another of 1225 refers to 'a messuage, croft and garden lying along the road to Seaton,' also presumably on what was to become Westgate. But individual descriptions such as this add up to an impression rather than to a precise picture of the settlement.

Manors were economic units, to be exploited and from which profits were to be derived. It is self-evident from the *Domesday* entry that Hornsea was very much under-exploited in 1086. It was inevitable therefore that following the transfer to St Mary's the new monastic proprietor would take steps to bring the estate to maximum productivity in as short a time as possible. Amongst other measures this presumably involved the laying out of a new, nucleated village and repopulating it. Having the population concentrated in one location also meant that a greater degree of control could be exercised over the community and, furthermore, that the territory of the estate could be more efficiently exploited. How was the village repopulated?

Given that the population level recorded in *Domesday Book* was so low, this was presumably achieved through the compulsory relocation of tenants from other estates belonging to the abbey. In an age when surnames indicated occupational affiliation or place of origin, these give some clues. Surnames giving a place of origin other than the recorded place of residence (called 'binominal locatives') are useful in this respect. Surviving documents of the late eleventh and early twelfth centuries mention a handful of people, then residing in Hornsea, who might originally have hailed from other parts of the East Riding: John of Acklam, Peter of Escrick, William of Skirlington, William of Cottingwith, John of Elmswell, Walter of Howden. In each of these places St Mary's had an estate. This is not a complete listing, but does give some indication of the areas from which St Mary's drew to repopulate Hornsea (assuming, of course, that the person came from the place; we should bear in mind that the place-name might have become a surname which was passed down the generations).

Nucleation of settlement may also have been accompanied by a reorganisation of the estate's agricultural system: in particular, the laying out of the two great arable fields which were worked throughout the medieval period and later. Again no documentary sources exist to give a date for the creation of the open fields but their morphology and early manner of operation suggests that they too, like the village, were deliberately laid out at one moment in time. The repopulation of Hornsea would be a suitable context for this event. Two strands of evidence are important in this respect: one, what is immediately striking about the medieval open field system at Hornsea (and which is also, incidentally, common to the rest of Holderness) is its simplicity and uniformity of layout. Where they can be reconstructed, the individual strips are found to lie parallel to one another (generally aligned north-south or east-west) over the greater part of the arable area, and were of considerable length; two, the organisation of individual holdings mirrored this structural simplicity. It is clear from later twelfth and (mainly) thirteenth century documents that the strips belonging to an individual farm were grouped together, not inter-mixed and scattered haphazardly across the entire arable zone. These two features suggest a planned origin undertaken as a single event; they are incompatible with the irregularity and complexity that is usually associated with slow organic growth.

In Hornsea's case reorganisation and rationalisation obviously paid off. Within twenty-odd years, by 1203, the place was one of the four wealthiest manors in Holderness (along with Humbleton, Swine and Patrington; all, incidentally, ecclesiastical properties). Seeking to realise the value of the property, aggressive exploitation by the monastic proprietor, mirroring the preoccupations of the laity with wealth and power, was the key to success. This was founded on improved and centralised organisation and increased technical efficiency. Essentially, St Mary's demand for rent stimulated peasant production at Hornsea.

Phase II in the settlement's evolution can be dated to the mid-thirteenth century and relates to an episode of reorganisation, which resulted in a large-scale alteration to the village plan. This involved: (a) the laying out of a market place between the church and the mere, (b) the laying out of new property plots around parts of the market place, and (c) the incorporation of the Westgate area into the new arrangement. Together, they fundamentally changed the physical character of the place. This was a process of internal movement and adjustment associated with the granting, by Henry III in 1257-58, of a royal charter allowing St Mary's abbey to hold a weekly Monday market at Hornsea. It is perhaps worth noting that the granting of this charter more or less coincided with the beginnings of the abbacy of Simon de Warwick (1258-96), who was instituting plans for the rebuilding of St Mary's Norman church. This programme of work needed financing. The abbey needed to increase its income. The rationale behind the establishment of a market at Hornsea (as happened elsewhere on the abbey's estates at this time) should be seen within this context, a requirement to increase income levels in order to pay for the new building project. At Hornsea this was to lead to future troubles.

A document of the same year refers in passing to the 'new market place near the church' and the destruction of an unknown number of properties on what must then have been the south side of Westgate to accommodate it. This presumably is the origin of the present-day market place. A further document, this time of 1260, mentions an 'east' end and a 'west' end, referring to areas near the church (east) and Westgate (west), separated by the newly acquired market place. This topographical distinction has not survived through to the present time.

Today's Market Place is fossilised as a closely built-up and constricted east-west triangular area. Its apex, by the church, converges on the junction of Southgate and Newbegin; the broad base of the triangle is formed by the junctions with Westgate (in the south) and Mill Lane (in the north). The present size and shape is a product of progressive infilling since at least the later seventeenth century. Topographical analysis and the negative evidence from recent archaeological investigations combine to suggest that Market Place is the remnant of a once much larger public and communal, and social and economic, space.

From recent archaeological work in the vicinity of Mill Lane (that is, on the western side) it seems that the thirteenth century laying out of the market area involved the cutting back and levelling of part of the ridge of glacial sand to provide a flat, open space below the church. It is also apparent that this side of the market place was left open, not built upon, from the thirteenth to sixteenth centuries. Furthermore, this work also indicates that infilling and a consequent reduction in size has taken place on the north side. Here it is suggested that the area now occupied by Old Hall and the shops now fronting Market Place extended perhaps as far back as the moated Rectory House site (now on the western edge of Hall Garth Park). In this arrangement the eastern apex would still have been formed by the church, which, on its slight rise and with a large open space in front of it, would have commanded and framed the view of the market area. If this 'reading' is correct the market place would still have had a broadly triangular form (with perhaps a less formal boundary along its northern edge), but covering an area four or five times larger than the present space. Given its present size it is difficult to see how Hornsea could have functioned as the premier market centre in northern Holderness during the middle ages.

The establishment of a weekly market at Hornsea was part of a general upsurge in the foundation of markets at this time, manifesting the optimism of an age of economic expansion, great inflation, when the price of corn and livestock doubled, even tripled, and dramatic population growth. An age when swords were converted into ploughshares, spears into scythes. The market at Hornsea served a wide area, a hinterland taking in much of northern Holderness; it provided an outlet for the surplus produce of the local countryside – the grain, malt, livestock, fish, bread and ale – as well as the cheap fabrics and leather goods made in the district. Markets benefited almost everyone. For the lord of the manor – the abbey of St Mary's – the market provided direct income, as well as an occasional outlet for the produce of the demesne. The abbey collected tolls on goods sold, rents for stalls, levies such as picage (when poles or pegs were driven into the ground to anchor the booths more securely), and the assize of bread and ale. As well as self-interest, the founding of the market by the Abbot of St Mary's was also a show of charity, catering for the localised needs of the tenantry on the estate: smallholders, tradesmen and craftsmen. It was primarily the local population that the market benefited. It helped them to sell their surplus grain, their old livestock, their hens and eggs, their cheese, and their wool, and to buy from the outside world such essentials as salt. The smallholder and the landless labourer could buy the food they themselves could not produce, and perhaps arrange for casual employment at hay-making or harvest. The village craftsmen might find their iron for the smithy, timber for the carpenter, yarn for the weaver. For the villagers' families the market offered social contact with neighbours, and opportunities for family members, particularly unmarried women, to make precarious livings as stallholders or hucksters. Essentially, the market at Hornsea served as a regional entrepôt for distributing the produce from, and requirements of, the countryside. At the same time it is important not to lose sight of the fact that the bulk of commodities sold were produced by the peasants in search of money to pay rents, taxes, judicial fines, and to purchase industrial products. Nor should another function be forgotten: the market place was not only an economic nexus but, just as importantly, a social nexus too – a gathering-centre for news, gossip, rumour.

We have no direct way of knowing what was sold in the market at Hornsea during the medieval period; or of the quantities of goods passing across the stalls and booths. The documents simply do not survive. However, the general character of produce changing hands can be gained from a document of 1274, a complaint by the villagers that Simon de Warwick, the abbot of St Mary's, was levying excessive tolls at the market. The abbot was alleged to have exceeded:

> The liberty in taking toll, as he takes ½d for a measure of rye-corn and barley and for the measure by which it is measured ½d, ½d for the hide of ox or horse, ½d for sheepskin, ½d for the horse load of whatever it might be; and he takes chiminage [that is, a toll for passage through woods and forests].

This complaint appears in the Yorkshire Hundred Rolls – the records of a judicial commission established by Edward I to investigate improper alienations and encroachments on royal lands and privileges and to inquire into the misconduct of local government officers which was believed to have multiplied during the troubles of the previous reign.

The same document also draws attention to the excessively high rents imposed by the abbey on its tenants at Hornsea:

> The abbot's villains distrain within the bounds of Hornsea for their debts as if they were the king's burgesses, and this has been done for the past three years.

The 'gallows, a tumbril and pillory and prison' at Hornsea were said to have been used coercively, as deterrents, sanctions to be imposed against non-payment.

Mild social unrest threatened to disturb the feudal status quo at Hornsea in the early and mid-1270s. An escalation was avoided when the Hundred jury issued a writ against the abbot, forcing a reduction in both tolls and rents.

This episode needs to be seen as an attempt to protect the abbey's income at a time of generally rising prices and, more importantly, in the context of Simon de Warwick's ongoing building programme on the abbey church and precinct. As already mentioned, the financing of this construction work largely depended on raising the abbey's income levels. Resorting to the imposition of higher market tolls and increased rents were obvious expedients, designed to swell the abbey's exchequer. But, as is clear from the events in Hornsea, it was risky. The abbey existed and fuelled its expansion by taking the product of its tenants' labour or the labour itself (through the performance of labour services). The directness of this appropriation meant that any attempt by the abbey to increase its income was felt immediately, generating antagonism between the small-scale agricultural producers and their landlord. Aggressive economic exploitation was all well and good, but could, as happened in this case, be counter-productive if the tenantry collectively asserted their opposition. A victory for the village community over its lord, solidarity brought about by external pressure. In its own small way, this defensive episode of peasant self-interest was part of a more general movement, which ultimately led to the development of peasant self-consciousness.

A further addition to the village plan (Phase III) came about in 1275, when Edward I granted a charter for the holding of an annual fair on or about 6 December, the Patronal Feast Day of St Nicholas, the patron saint of the parish church – a religious holiday when no work was done. This fair was held to the south of the main market area, on Mereside, in an area still known as 'Fair Place.' This was a large grassed space fringing, as its name indicates, the mere's edge. Like the market, the fair allowed the abbey to increase its manorial profits from tolls, rents and the like. The holding of a December fair – for the obvious reasons of weather – is somewhat unusual: most fairs took place between May and September. Too late in the annual agricultural cycle for the sale of harvested grain and autumnal-culled livestock, it concentrated on the sale of luxury items and, to a lesser extent, on livestock-on-the-hoof.

Conspicuous consumption. The medieval equivalent of our own Christmas shopping. Agrarian producers made money at markets and spent it at fairs. It was also an occasion for festivities, to celebrate the feast day of St Nicholas.

A further charter was granted, this time by Edward III in 1358, for the holding of a second annual fair, also on Fair Place. This event took place over three successive days, between 31 July and 2 August. Again too early for the sale of the current grain crop (the medieval harvest, unlike or own, usually took place in September), the emphasis of this event was on the sale of livestock-on-the-hoof, a tradition that continued into the later nineteenth century, and hides. Locally, during the thirteenth and, more particularly, in the fourteenth century, a thriving leatherworking industry developed and, to a great extent, this particular fair specialised in the sale of its products. Sporadic references to tanning and the manufacture of shoes, belts and other items occur. We must be aware of the danger of constructing a local industry from accidental documentary survivals, but it does, however, fit in with later medieval and early modern evidence about the existence of a leatherworking industry in the district. There was, for example, a leatherworking industry of some importance at nearby Seaton from at least the 1340s. This may have developed because of the proximity of the market at Hornsea: the short distance and, therefore, low transportation costs, leading to greater profitability for the producers, may have triggered this industrial development.

Fairs provided a break from the routine of rural life and an opportunity to buy the wares of travelling pedlars. They provided entertainment and diversion: entertainments by jugglers and girls of doubtful virtue; the exchange of gossip from a wider area – news of the plague or some other epidemic sweeping the land, or the French wars, or rumours of taxation and unrest. To the villagers the fair brought a touch of the exotic and the hint of a world over the horizon. They were as much social as economic events.

The main access to the Hornsea fairs was along what is now known as Scalby Place, whose plan still betrays something of its medieval origins. Where it joins the market place at its junction with Westgate it is wide. From there it gently tapers until it opens out on to Mereside. This arrangement gives a tunnel-shaped plan, allowing for the greater control (and perhaps separation) of livestock as it entered the fairground. It is uncertain whether Scalby Place (by whatever name it was then known) existed prior to the founding of the fairs, or whether properties were demolished to create the desired access to Mereside. Similarly, it is not known whether the road dates to 1275 or 1358 or to some intermediate period.

Finally, in 1466, the right to hold a second weekly market, on Thursdays, was granted to the abbey by Edward IV. This market was focused on the eastern end of the existing market place, around the junction of Newbegin with Southgate, and involved no alteration to the existing plan of the village. This development may account for the greater than usual width of Newbegin at this point, in front of the church. A market cross was erected more or less on the junction of the two streets, somewhere in the vicinity of the present-day traffic lights.

A fourth phase in the physical development of Hornsea can be identified. This dates to the later fourteenth and fifteenth centuries and consisted of residential extensions along the main southern and eastern approaches – that is, Southgate and Newbegin respectively. Properties also extended for some little distance from the market place along Eastgate, but just how far is uncertain. These are the few known facts. Concentrations of fourteenth and fifteenth century pottery have been recovered from gardens and the like clustering, around and extending away from the market place. These are centred on the approach roads of Eastgate, Newbegin and Southgate; and the pottery spreads, as currently defined, extend for between one and two hundred yards along these routes. The impression gained is of fairly densely built-up areas around the junctions with the market place, becoming less so as one moves further away. Very few fragments of pre-fourteenth century pottery have been found in these areas, strongly suggesting that new development was taking place on hitherto unoccupied land – unoccupied, that is, by residential buildings.

Just how much of this central area – Market Place and the junction of Southgate and Newbegin, and Westgate – was built-up in the middle ages is uncertain. In the village's heyday, between the twelfth and fourteenth centuries, the market place frontages may have been fully occupied. It is likely, though, with later decline some of these would have become abandoned. Like many other places, Hornsea suffered decline in the later medieval and early post-medieval periods. In the seventeenth and eighteenth centuries landowners were able to buy up vacant plots in the centre of Hornsea and amalgamate them into large gardens. Finally, in the nineteenth century, the place expanded in all directions, but more particularly to the east and south.

Although the general sequence can be identified, precise dating of the early phases of morphological development is not yet possible. Specific streets are mentioned in the middle ages: Market Place; Westgate (the road leading to Seaton and Sigglesthorne and beyond); the road northwards to Atwick; Southgate (the road to Rolston); and Newbegin. The last is particularly significant. Newbegin ('new building(s)') was first mentioned in the 1270s. It can best be regarded as an extension to the built-up area in response to population growth. Just how far along Newbegin any such development extended is not known at present.

In this tour of medieval Hornsea one further structure needs to be mentioned. To the north of the church, in the western part of what is now Hall Garth Park, are to be found the earthwork remains of Rectory House. As its name implies, this was the site of the medieval rectory. Today, we are confronted by the truncated remains of a broadly rectangular enclosure surrounded by a moat (still a prominent feature in the landscape after 500 years of disuse), with a well-defined entrance on the east-facing side. Within this compound – the moat more symbolic, implying status, than defensive – on the level platform which occupies the interior, a substantial medieval house and other buildings once existed. Nothing is known of the character of these buildings or their date of construction. Only one reference has been found: in 1397 the incumbent had a licence to celebrate divine service in the rectory house. Was this because the church was undergoing one of its periodic building programmes? Probably we will never know.

In 1423 the status of the parish changed: it ceased to be a rectory (that is, where the incumbent – a rector – retained all the tithes) and became a

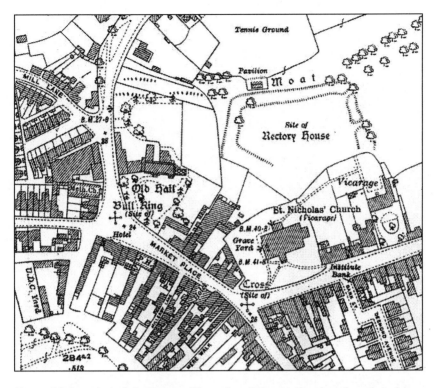

Figure 18. Location of the Rectory House in relation to church and market place. (Ordnance Survey 1:2500 map extract, Sheet 197.3, published 1927. Reproduced by courtesy of the Ordnance Survey)

vicarage (that is, where all tithes passed to a chapter or religious house or layman; in this particular instance to St Mary's Abbey). As well as an annual stipend of forty marks (£26 13s 4d), the following reverted to the newly instituted vicar:

> All the tithes of wool, lamb, lime, hemp, pigs, brood geese, foals, eggs, hens, ducks, pigeons, onions, leeks, and fruits of gardens through the whole parish; also two oxgangs of land of the said church, or else of the demesne land of the abbot and convent. Moreover, the vicar shall have all the tithes of garbs (what sort soever), and of hay, lamb, and wool (whether they consist in wool or lamb, or money paid), and of all calves, foals (whether by head or kind titheable), also all mortuaries, as well quick as dead, with arms of knights, esquires, or others, and all oblations, obventions, and minute tithes, and all other singular emoluments to the chapel at Riston (depending on the church of Hornsea) and to the village of Arnold, any way belonging.

87

Plate 25. The east-facing moat with causewayed entrance that surrounded Rectory House. The platform on which buildings were situated is on the right (Photograph: Stephen Harrison)

In addition,

> The vicar shall have one mansion at Riston, built at the first by the abbot and convent, and two oxgangs of land, to the chapel thereof appertaining, for which he shall bear all burdens; and one chaplain to serve the said chapel, and bear all other burdens incumbent upon the same. But as to burdens ordinary, and extraordinary, incumbent upon the church of Hornsea, such as archdeacon's procurations, synodals, payment and collection of Peter's Pence (excepting all burdens pertaining to the chapel of Riston, which the vicar shall in future bear) the said abbot and convent shall, at their own cost, bear or pay for ever.

The income from this new arrangement clearly proved insufficient. In 1493 Master William Otwey, the pluralist vicar, argued a case before the York Consistory Court against St Mary's for an increase in his income. From the accounts produced in evidence, covering the period 1481 to 1493, now amongst the Cause Papers at the Borthwick Institute of Historical Research in York, it seems that the tithes and land in Hornsea did not produce the expected revenue. Although it was calculated that St Mary's income from tithes was £60 per annum, the vicar's income was never more than £4 or £5 per year. Interestingly, the annual income at Riston, with less than half the population of Hornsea, ranged between £10 and £15. No reasons for this shortfall are given. Was the original figure of 40 marks unduly optimistic? Or may it have resulted from endemic disease within the parish's livestock population. Previously, in 1481, it was stated, rather ambiguously, that no tithes on sheep had been collected 'because of accident'; and one of Otwey's witnesses said that he remembered a time when four men of Hornsea owned more cattle and sheep than all the parishioners put together in 1493. Or, alternatively, might this have been caused by a conversion of pasture to arable? We have no way of knowing. Despite the presentation of detailed accounts, the augmentation case was lost. In a neat piece of legal contradiction, the abbey admitted that whilst the income of the vicarage fell below the stipulated 40 marks, it was still perfectly adequate. Whilst this was undoubtedly true in normal circumstances, the abbey's defence studiously and pointedly ignored the heavy expense incurred by Otwey, as evidenced in the accounts, on necessary repairs to the vicarage house between 1487 and 1490 (see below). For reasons best known to himself Otwey failed to capitalise on this point, the strongest part of his claim. Whatever, the abbey's argument persuaded the court in its favour. Frustrated and outraged by the judgement, Otwey took his revenge on St Mary's. On the afternoon of Easter Sunday 1494, in a highly public show of defiance against ecclesiastical authority, he unlawfully commandeered the abbey's boat and nets and went fishing for bream and pike on the mere. Not surprisingly, this blatant act, infringing as it did St Mary's much guarded monopoly on the produce and benefits of the mere, brought down the abbot's wrath on the troublesome vicar. For so deliberately and wilfully violating the liberties and franchise of the abbey, the ultimate penalty was imposed: excommunication, exclusion from participation in the sacraments, from formal communion with the Church, a final sanction imposed when all other avenues have failed. To us, living in a highly secular world, this seems extraordinarily drastic, since excommunication meant eternal damnation. In effect, an excommunicated person became an outcast, a religious leper. Evidently, though, this state was short-lived; after due penance, Otwey was restored to his living and died in office in 1499.

The 1423 change in status also resulted in St Mary's building a 'manse adjacent to the cemetery, with a hall, chamber, kitchen, garden and sufficient close [much of which is now Hall Garth Park] to accommodate the vicar.' Clearly it was a substantial range of buildings. This new complex, immediately east of the church, was constructed more or less on the site of the present vicarage on Newbegin, if anything, though, closer to the street frontage than the present house. It is not known what happened to the Rectory House after 1423; possibly it became the home of, and administrative centre for, St Mary's bailiff in Hornsea. After the dissolution the property passed to the crown, with recorded occupation until the late seventeenth century. In 1611, Michael Warton sold the Rectory House to Robert Moore. Moore then conveyed the property to Peter Acklam in 1651, and it may have been this house in which Acklam had six hearths in 1672. Shortly afterwards Acklam demolished the house, replacing it with what is now the Old Hall in Market Place, on a more spacious plot immediately adjacent to the old site. When another Peter Acklam sold Old Hall to the Rev. Charles Constable in 1821 it was described as the mansion house of the rectory, implying that it was the successor of the earlier dwelling.

Unfortunately we have no details regarding the character or layout of the 1423 buildings. In general terms medieval parsonages or vicarages tended to be large and substantial; they had to accommodate not only the incumbent but also his live-in chaplain(s) and servants, and guests. Many such buildings had two storeys and included a hall, parlour, kitchen, priest's chamber and rooms above – broadly in line with the quoted description of the Hornsea vicarage in the above paragraph. What we do have, however, is a set of parish accounts covering the period 1481-1493. These accounts, preserved in the Borthwick Institute of Historical Research at York, provide an insight into the rectory complex, particularly as regards ongoing maintenance and repairs in the later fifteenth century. The following is a selection of the relevant entries:

In 1485-1486   Expenses for the vicarage of Hornsea

Item payd for tymber to Thomas Wheitley	5s
Item payd to Antony Thomson for makyng	5s 4d
Item payd to William Ibowcher for thakk	2s
Item payd for the caryage of the same	4d
Item payd for nalez	2d
Item payd for drawyng of thakk	6d
Item payd for taking the kechyng end	4d
Item payd to Robert Marchall for wallyng 7 days	2s 7d
Item payd to Robert Hyk for wallyng 3 days	13d
Item payd to John Gymlyng for thekyng 6 days	2s 3d
Item payd for serving of the same John	9d
Item payd for a cartfull of stray at Mapilton	18d
Item payd for lyme 1 schowld & ahalff	6s
Item payd to the tellers for vii days and 1 halff	6s 3d

Two points can be made in relation to the above list. First, that significant repairs were undertaken at this time, particularly the replacement of the thatched roof. These repairs can be interpreted as the renewal of dilapidated materials, possibly for the first time since the construction of the building in 1423. Second, that at least some of the walls were constructed from a daub mixture. Clay was mixed with chopped straw and hay and lime to make a daub, which was then spread over a wattle framework. This was a common construction method in Holderness at the time.

In 1487 and again in 1488 further building work was undertaken, when a total of £4 9s 7d was spent. Here are some of the items listed:

1487	For spars bought from Hull brig	22d
	Item Richard Hewitson and John Waltam carpenters	12s
	Item for Robert Marshall for the earth work	3s
	Item for Antony Thomson for tiles	16s
	Item for carriage [of tiles]	2s
	Item from Richard Clarke of Beverley iiii quarters of lyme	4s
1488	For two couppyll of spars bought from Hull brig	10d
	Item for carriage [of spars]	6d
	Item for Antony Thomson for the sawn waynskot for the window	10d
	Item for Richard Hewitson for mending ii windows in the hall	11d

Suitable timber was apparently scarce around Hornsea. That needed for repairs to the vicarage was brought from Hull to Hornsea Beck by sea, as the above makes clear: These 'spars' are basic constructional elements and indicate that the buildings had a cruck framework. What is not clear is this: do they represent replacements for existing timbers, are they for extending the house, or are they for additional buildings on the site? No answer is, unfortunately, forthcoming from the extant sources.

Both the markets and fairs were responsible for bringing prosperity to Hornsea and to increasing the size of its resident population, especially during the thirteenth and early fourteenth centuries and again in the fifteenth century, after the ravages of the Black Death and other associated epidemics. Hornsea was an important locale in northern Holderness.

Some measure of Hornsea's wealth and locally pre-eminent position can be gained from the 1334 lay subsidy returns, in which the village was assessed at £3 6s 8d for taxation purposes. This is greatly in excess of the surrounding villages, whose assessments are listed below in descending order of value:

Catwick and Catfoss	£1 17s 10d
Mappleton	£1 13s 4d
Hatfield	£1 10s 0d
Hornsea Burton	£1 8s 0d
Atwick	£1 8s 0d
Southorpe	£1 6s 8d
Rolston	£1 6s 8d
Bewholme and Arram	18s 0d
Goxhill	18s 0d
Northorpe	13s 4d

Seaton and Sigglesthorne are not listed in the returns.

Of the seventy-seven vills in Holderness, Hornsea ranked equal eleventh (with Brandesburton) in value, and its £3 6s 8d assessment was well above the average for all vills in the sub-region, which was £2 4s 6d.

Earlier in this chapter an attempt was made to reconstruct the *Domesday* population of Hornsea. What were the effects of population growth in the three centuries after 1086? The next source after *Domesday Book* is the Poll Tax of 1377. This record allows us to count the number of taxpayers, as the tax was levied at a standard rate of 4d from every person over the age of fourteen years. Because relatively small numbers of people were exempt, it provides a reasonably reliable indication of the size of the rural population at this date, though the amount of evasion is inevitably uncertain. In 1377 there were 271 tax-payers in Hornsea, 264 in Hornsea Beck, 96 in Hornsea Burton, 28 in Southorpe, and 7 in Northorpe: 666 tax-payers in total. The tax reveals a density of 128.08 tax-payers per square mile/49.41 per square kilometre across the parish, an extrapolated actual population density of around 253 per square mile/97 per square kilometre; this is over twenty times the figure for 1086.

(We do not know how the 1377 parish population compares with that of a generation or so earlier, that is, in the years immediately before and after the Black Death of 1348-49. The documents are simply not there. The Black Death and subsequent epidemics were lethal beyond imagining, affecting this part of Holderness in much the same way as other regions, leading to a loss in the long-term of about half the rural population. These epidemics and the consequential population decline, together with a climatic downturn, had major adverse effects on the countryside: land fell vacant, thereafter to lie waste, or be converted into pasture, or amalgamated into peasant holdings that became much larger than those of the later thirteenth century. The discipline exerted by lords slipped as the scarcity of tenants strengthened the position of those who remained. Peasants were able to secure rent reductions. Many others migrated. There was little profit to be made from large-scale arable farming and much land was converted to pasture. Feudalism began to break down, paving the way for new social and economic forms and relationships).

The next series of useful statistics is dated 1490, towards the end of the middle ages. In that year Master William Otwey, vicar of Hornsea, in connection with a tithe dispute he was bringing before the York Consistory Court (see below), recorded the population of his parish: 340 'and more' souls in Hornsea, 240 in Hornsea Beck, 50 in Hornsea Burton, 30 in Southorpe, and 14 in Northorpe. An absolute total of 674 people, slightly (and unquantifiably) higher when the 'and more' is taken into account. These figures give a density of 129.61 persons per square mile/50 persons per square kilometre.

If an estimated total population of around 1,320 in 1377 is accepted and if Otwey's absolute figure of 674 (or thereabouts) is correct, then there is a deficit of around 620 people between the two dates, indicating a sustained demographic trough. When averaged out over the 113 years, this represents a loss of 5.73 persons per year. Not many. Cumulatively, however, 49% of the entire population seems to have disappeared. Can we reconcile the difference? Unfortunately not. The surviving documents do not even begin to provide an answer. Possible reasons may, however, be suggested: recurrent outbreaks of

Place	1377 Estimated population	1490 Actual population	Change
Hornsea	540	340	- 200
Hornsea Beck	520	240	- 280
Hornsea Burton	192	50	- 142
Southorpe	56	30	- 26
Northorpe	14	14	no change
Total	**1322**	**674**	**- 648 (49%)**

Table 2. The changing population of Hornsea parish: 1377 and 1490

disease, with continued high mortality rates; low birth rates; with disintegrating feudal relations, high levels of outward migration; deliberate depopulation brought about by the conversion of arable lands to pasture, reflecting a shift from labour-intensive cultivation to less labour-intensive stock rearing; the loss of acres through coastal erosion, particularly as it affected Hornsea Beck and Hornsea Burton, forcing people to leave the area. Any of these, singly or in combination, could have been responsible for population decline.

Incidentally, this decline was not confined to the fourteenth and fifteenth centuries. The long-term downward trend continued, not so dramatically, for the next 300 years. In the 1670s there were an estimated 590 people living in the parish; and in 1801, in the first national census (the first accurate record of population data), 533 people were enumerated. In broad terms then, the 319 years between 1490 and 1801 saw a further reduction of somewhere in the region of 140 people (21%). It was not until after 1861 that the resident population began to approach the postulated 1377 figure again.

The parish church

The parish church dedicated, appropriately enough for a coastal parish, to St Nicholas, the patron saint of sailors, is located in a slightly elevated position on the eastern edge of the triangular market place, where the southern apex meets with Newbegin and Southgate. The presumption is that it was built on the site of the church mentioned in *Domesday Book*. The character of this earlier church is not known; certainly no structural evidence survives in the present building.

Surrounded by the artefacts and clutter of the modern age, and, in consequence, difficult for our eyes to appreciate, the church, during the middle ages (and indeed up to the nineteenth and early twentieth centuries), dominated the local scene, the focal point, an unambiguous landmark, for people approaching the settlement from all directions. A clear and unobstructed sight.

The gutting and restoration of Hornsea church by Sir G.G. Scott in 1866-67, following more than a century of neglect and dilapidation, scraped away much of its history along with its seventeenth century plaster and eighteenth century woodwork, but the fabric still contains sufficient clues to speak of its origins and evolution. Looking behind Scott's makeover, the cobble and ashlar building is, essentially, of thirteenth century date, with additions and alterations of the fourteenth and fifteenth centuries. It consists of a four-bay chancel with a clerestory, north and south aisled chapels and an eastern crypt, a four-bay aisled nave with a south porch, and a three-stage crenellated west tower with eight crocketed pinnacles, which is embraced by a western extension of the nave aisles.

On entering the church today one is confronted by a stark and simple perspective. For the medieval parishioner the scene was very different. The interior was redolent with the trappings of piety. It was densely peopled with saints, whose images filled the building. In the chancel – that sanctified stage on which the mass was said – to either side of the high altar, as decreed by canon law, were the principal statues of the Virgin and the patronal image of St Nicholas, each in decorated niches ('tabernacles') hung with curtains. Over the church's side altar, where weekday masses were celebrated, was the image of Jesus. This was possibly an image of the infant Jesus, but more likely to be a standing figure of Christ holding a globe – the 'Salvator Mundi.' The cult of the Holy Name of Jesus, reflected in the spread of Jesus altars and celebrations of the Jesus Mass in parish churches across the whole of England and nourished by devotional texts and practices emphasising the tenderness and accessibility of the human Christ, was one of the main growth areas of late medieval lay piety. Other niched figures were to be found against pillars and walls round the church. We have fleeting references for: the Sunday Christ, a 'Man of Sorrows' representation of Jesus pierced by the tools and implements of work; St Anthony, healer of men and farm animals; St Anne, often depicted teaching the young Virgin Mary to read, or with the adult Mary and her child Jesus. St Anne was a barren woman made miraculously fecund; for obvious reasons she was a devotional favourite with married people, anxious in one way or another about childbirth and posterity.

Contrasting with the obligatory statues of the Virgin and St Nicholas, all these other images represented devotional choices made by the parishioners of Hornsea. They were located in the body of the church, close to the congregation who maintained lights before them, and to whose anxieties and hopes they held up a devotional mirror. Included among them was another representation of the Virgin, Our Lady of Pity, the stricken figure of Mary at Calvary, weeping over the body of her dead son laid in her lap. This was a powerful image that appealed to medieval people, both as a model of the appropriate devotional response to the sufferings of Christ, the tears of Mary a symbol of the penitent heart, and also as a reminder for their own predicament in the universal experience of death and bereavement.

These images and the cults they represent all have an immediate and obvious resonance in the lives of the people of a farming community like Hornsea. Though the figures of Jesus and Mary are essentially devotional, emblematic of the central affirmations of the Christian faith, all the rest are holy helpers, embodiments of religion harnessed as much to the everyday material needs as to the spiritual longings of labouring and suffering men and women. Piety for practical people. All this and more was to be swept away by the Tudor Reformation.

Plate 26. The parish church of St Nicholas. (Photographs: Stephen Harrison)

During the middle ages the parish church also held altars belonging to four religious guilds: Corpus Christi, Holy Trinity, St Catherine, and St Mary. Documentary references to these guilds are few and far between. The origins of these institutions – providing protection and mutual aid for their members, as well as organising religious processions – is not known; they were certainly in existence by 1422, when the rector of Hornsea, Anthony St Quintin, died. By the terms of his will he left 10s each to the guilds in Hornsea church. Sometime after this date, the guilds acquired property in the village, either by purchase or construction. Guildhouses belonging to Corpus Christi, St

Catherine, and St Mary are recorded in Newbegin, Southgate and Westgate respectively; it is possible that the guildhouse of Holy Trinity – associated with mariners and alternatively known as the Shipman's Guild – was at Hornsea Beck. In 1528 Robert Metham, bailiff for St Mary's Abbey, by his will, left a quarter of barley to the guilds. As religious institutions all guilds were suppressed in 1549; however, as social and craft organisations, promoting trade and commerce, they persisted after the Reformation. Outside the urban centres of Beverley and Hull, Hornsea, along with Patrington in southern Holderness, had the largest concentration of guilds in late medieval East Yorkshire. That these were all active at the same time in Hornsea is an indication of the high level of commercial activity in the place, reinforced by its central position in northern Holderness and its market function.

Later documents allow us to locate the sites of the guildhouses with some degree of accuracy. The manor court rolls of 1671 refer to 'one house, called the Guilds house and garth in Newbegin.' This refers to the property of the Guild of Corpus Christi. Subsequent sporadic references (in the manor court rolls up to 1814) enable the site to be located with precision. In 1746 the guildhouse passed into the possession of Peace Bedell and later to John Bedell, the father of the Hornsea historian E.W. Bedell. At the beginning of the nineteenth century, in 1805, a 'cottage in Newbegin called Guild House together with three cottages lately built there on' was sold; and two years later the following entry occurs in the manor court rolls:

> The dwelling house lately erected upon a parcel of a cottage in Newbegin called by the name of Guild House and the Garth thereto together with the Yard and Garden and all that garth containing by estimation two roods lying on the South side or back side of the said three several tenements.

The site, on the south side of Newbegin, almost opposite the Hornsea Museum and to the west of Willows Drive, was that occupied by Tower House (a 1811 remodelling of the three cottages, together with extensions and envelopment behind a Georgian façade by Hull merchant George Adler; in 1842 it was bought by William Bettison, a Hull merchant and part proprietor of the *Hull Advertiser*, who, in 1844, constructed The Tower – a folly – in the grounds. This brick-built circular structure, a fairy tale tower complete with crenellations, was known disparagingly at the time as 'Bettison's Folly). Interestingly in view of its past associations, when the house was demolished in 1966 it was replaced by an old people's home. Today, only the Tower remains. There are no known descriptions or illustrations of the guildhouse.

The guildhouse of St Catherine in Southgate receives a first mention in the manor court roll of 1651, when a 'cottage near Gildhous hill' was sold. This reference is indirect, as are most later ones. The name is topographical. *Guildhouse Hill* – the hill on which the guildhouse stands. Nevertheless, the site can be pinpointed with some certainty. In 1688 a George Barnes bought '… a cottage in Southgate called Gildhall House.' This was the last specific reference to a guildhouse here; the presumption is that it was demolished sometime later. However, the site was frequently referred to as Gildas Hill until at least 1756: for example, in 1734 Mary Foster surrendered '… a cottage in Southgate near Gildas Hill commonly called White House with the yard and outhouses belonging to the beck thereof' is recorded; and in 1756 John Brough of Rolston acquired '… a cottage near Gildass hill called White House.' The un-named beck referred to in the 1734 entry is the Stream Dyke. It would appear, therefore, that the White House was situated alongside the stream. In 1719 Francis Coulson surrendered half of the White House along '… with 7½ yards of the Garth from the North west corner of the orchard wall fronting the street to the South west corner of ye said White House.' From this description it can be seen that the property lay on the north side of Southgate; and a 1722 entry in the manor court rolls refers to '… a cottage in Southgate near Gildas Hill commonly called White House and two cottages adjoining upon football greene' This latter reference places the property on what is now the cemetery. The Local Board of Health bought the White House, together with two acres of adjoining land, in March 1884 for the provision of a town cemetery; in July of that year, the White House, along with its associated farm buildings, was demolished. Locally, the highest ground is a little to the north of the cemetery; presumably this was the site of the guildhouse. There are no known descriptions or illustrations of the building.

Rather less is known about the guildhouse of St Mary in Westgate. There are no specific references in the manor court rolls (or indeed elsewhere) to the property in Westgate. There are, however, repeated mentions of a cottage near 'Gildhill.' Topographical analysis and study of the rolls identifies the area around Westgate House (built c.1866, possibly for Elizabeth Bainton of Hornsea, to designs by the Beverley and Driffield architect William Hawe), on the high ground on north side of Westgate, as the most likely candidate for the location of the guildhouse. Coincidentally Westgate House has a similar later history to Tower House; in 1955 it was purchased by Hull Corporation and converted into an old people's home.

Except for its physical presence, nothing at all is known about the Holy Trinity guildhouse at Hornsea Beck. Presumably it was lost to coastal erosion at some early date and not replaced.

This discussion so far has concentrated on the physical growth of Hornsea. But, throughout the middle ages, the parish also contained four other settlements, all of which were to be abandoned by the seventeenth century: the hamlets of Southorpe and Hornsea Burton (both mentioned in the *Domesday Book*), and Northorpe and Hornsea Beck.

Southorpe This township and hamlet lay to the south-east of Hornsea, to the south of the mere, and covered around 560 acres/227 hectares. The township boundaries were: Foss Dike in the east, Hornsea Mere to the south, the parish boundaries with Mappleton and Hatfield in the south, and the boundary with Sigglesthorne parish in the west. The name 'Southorpe,' derived from Old Scandinavian for the 'southern or outlying farm,' implies a secondary foundation, and may represent a daughter hamlet of Hornsea: fission, for whatever reason, from the older settlement. Although referred to in *Domesday Book* as a soke of Hornsea there are scant references to the place throughout the medieval period; altogether it is more out of focus than sharply defined, warranting little more than a passing mention every once in a while. The 1334 lay subsidy assessed Southorpe at £1 6s 8d; this was well below the £2 4s 6d average for all Holderness vills, and is indicative of a relatively poor community. In 1377 there were only twenty-eight poll-tax payers, suggesting a total population of around sixty. By 1490 the number of inhabitants had fallen to just thirty. During the early part of the seventeenth century there were only three or four inhabited cottages at Southorpe. The slide to complete abandonment continued: an empty, ruinous house was all that remained in 1650.

Whilst the abandonment of Hornsea Beck, Hornsea Burton and, possibly, Northorpe came about as a result of coastal erosion, the same cause cannot be applied to inland Southorpe. Some other reason(s) must be sought. The documents offer no clues. Instead, we must rely on informed speculation. Proximity to Hornsea, with its parochial and manorial administrative functions and market, may have made Southorpe, as a subsidiary place, vulnerable to decline and eventual desertion. In other words, Hornsea's high status within the local settlement hierarchy may have protected it from decline, to the disadvantage of Southorpe. Taking an England-wide perspective, and judging from fourteenth century tax assessments, it was the smaller and poorer settlements that were, on the whole, more likely to become deserted. Such places were more sensitive to the economic and social crises of the later middle ages: population decline following the plague epidemics of 1348-49 and subsequent outbreaks; harvest failures; livestock disease; agrarian crises caused by a switch from cereal growing to pasture; internal strains in communities short of labour and threatened by the ambitions of a few better-off farmers. Geology may also have played a part. Southorpe lies exclusively on boulder clay and this, with the heavy, unmanageable soils which it tends to produce, may have been a contributory factor in the eventual desertion of the settlement. This last point may not, however, be of particular significance, since much of Hornsea itself is situated on these soils.

At the south-east corner of the mere, on a gentle north-facing slope just above the shoreline, the substantial earthworks of the village are preserved in pasture: clear remains of deep holloways formed by the passage of many people, carts and animals, toft boundaries and house sites. As Southorpe is now completely deserted the complexities of its medieval layout can be seen free of later development. The earthworks extend over an area approximately 200m by 150m. In plan they are complex, confusing even: the digging of later drainage ditches has not helped matters. Running east to west, parallel with the mere, a number of tofts, extending up the slope, are arranged in a regular row along a broad holloway. A small, compact settlement.

Hornsea Burton This township and hamlet lay to the south of Hornsea, and comprised around 410 acres/166 hectares. The township boundaries were: Stream Dike in the north, Foss Dike in the west, the boundary with Mappleton parish in the south, and the coast line in the east. The derivation of the name 'Hornsea' has been referred to elsewhere in this book; the 'Burton' element is Anglo-Saxon and means a 'fortified farmstead.' Until the early thirteenth century the place was simply known as 'Burton;' probably, the prefix came into common usage in order to distinguish this Burton from the many other Burtons that existed across the face of the East Riding. Like Southorpe, Hornsea Burton is recorded as a soke of Hornsea in *Domesday Book*. In 1334 the lay subsidy assessment was £1 8s, well below the Holderness average of £2 4s 6d. The implied poverty of the settlement is probably a reflection of the difficulty in deriving a livelihood from the intractable, often waterlogged boulder clay soils on which the township was located, making it especially sensitive to both climatic changes and economic and agrarian recession. There were ninety-six poll-tax payers in 1377, but only fifty inhabitants in 1490. This suggests a population reduction of around 70% between the two dates. In 1663 there were eight houses; in the only known extant reference to the morphological character of the place, these properties were located close to a small common or green, fringing its southern and eastern sides. Thirty-four years later the hamlet was nothing more than a memory, the built-up area uncompromisingly described in 1697 as having been wasted, that is, destroyed, by the sea. The place did not disappear in one cataclysmic event, at one precise moment in time, but, rather, in piecemeal fashion, with properties progressively falling victim to coastal erosion, their inhabitants, according to the few surviving references, withdrawing as and when necessary to the inland safety of nearby Hornsea proper.

Hornsea Burton had its own open fields and common meadows and pastures throughout the middle ages. The layout of the fields is unknown, but small pockets of plough-reduced ridge and furrow still survive in various locations, most prominently by the side of Hornsea Burton Road. The lands of Hornsea Burton were enclosed by private agreement in about 1663. Under this enclosure, Marmaduke Constable received 103 acres, William Audas 92 acres, four others received between 40-70 acres each, and two others between 15-20 acres. The 8-acre common was left unenclosed. Four of the landowners had equal shares in the common, while the cattle of two others were allowed access to the pond on its northern edge. Enclosure resulted in the parcelling up of the former open fields and pastures into small, compact and irregularly shaped fields, bounded by quickthorn hedges. Until the town expanded over this area in the twentieth century, these fields still formed a feature in the landscape, contrasting with the larger, more regular ones that were laid out across the rest of the parish following parliamentary enclosure in the few years after 1801.

Northorpe The township and hamlet of Northorpe lay immediately to the north of Hornsea, and contained approximately 440 acres/178 hectares. The township boundaries were: the present-day Atwick Road in the west, the Atwick parish boundary in the north, the township boundary with Hornsea in the south (somewhere a little to the north of Eastgate), and the cliff line in the east. As with Southorpe, the name 'Northorpe' is derived from Old Scandinavian and, in this case, means 'northern outlying farmstead,' again implying a secondary foundation from, probably, Hornsea. Despite its seemingly pre-Conquest linguistic origins, the place is not mentioned in *Domesday Book*. The earliest documentary mention of Northorpe appears to be 1198; thereafter references are few and far between, or have yet to come to light. It seems always to have been a small and poor settlement, its viability uncertain at the best of times: on the edge, a marginal existence. In the lay subsidy of 1334 it was assessed at just 13s 4d, making it one of the poorest East Riding settlements at that date, a good indication of its relative poverty. There were just seven poll-tax payers recorded in 1377, giving at total population of somewhere between fifteen and twenty; the demographic consequences of the Black Death of 1348-49 and the subsequent plagues of

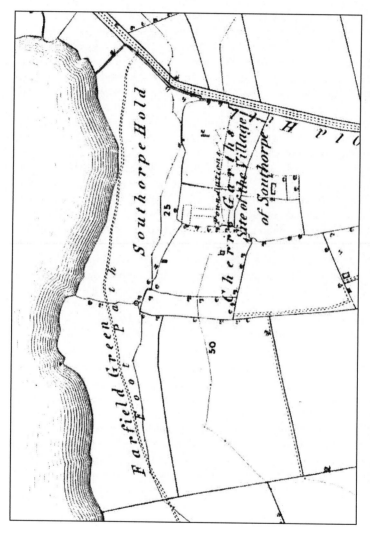

Figure 19. The site of Southorpe deserted village. (Ordnance Survey 1:10560 extract, Sheet 197: surveyed 1852, published 1854. Reproduced by courtesy of the Ordnance Survey)

the 1360s is unknown. If Northorpe did suffer a population downturn at this time, it evidently did not recover: over one hundred and ten years later, in 1490, when he came to compile his parish-wide census enumeration, William Otwey, vicar of Hornsea, recorded only fourteen souls at Northorpe – perhaps two families, three at most. We can imagine a slow decline into obscurity and eventual abandonment. Certainly, by the late sixteenth century the place had altogether disappeared as a separately functioning entity.

Why did Northorpe come into existence as a separate hamlet? Unfortunately, the documents are silent. However, given its apparent late twelfth century foundation, a probable reason can be put forward. The answer is most likely to be found in the out-migration of part of the existing population of Hornsea, brought about by demographic expansion, which in turn led to a reallocation of productive resources across the parish. During the twelfth century and the thirteenth England, along with the rest of Europe, experienced a period of massive population growth; in England, it is thought that the population doubled from somewhere between three or four million in 1086 to around eight million on the eve of the Black Death. The founding of Northorpe may reflect this growth at the local level.

The settlement no longer survives; a reminder of it is preserved in the name of the present-day Northorpe Farm, alongside Atwick Road, about one kilometre to the north of Hornsea. It is not known, however, if Northorpe Farm represents the actual site of the hamlet; no earthworks remain to be seen here – or, in fact, anywhere within the former township boundaries. However, Poulson (1840) notes that 'some aged people of Hornsea still recollect to have [*sic*] seen stones, &c. dug up, which seemed to have formed parts of buildings. North field farm and North field, are all, in the vicinity of the presumed site, which now remain.' The possibility remains that the settlement was lost to coastal erosion. It is not possible, therefore, to comment on the morphology of medieval Northorpe.

We do not know precisely when Northorpe became deserted. The last reference to properties occurs in the manor court rolls for 1691, when Peter Acklam senior died seized of 'one cottage in Northorpe and one cottage called Hopergreen in Northorpe.' Like many such settlements, abandonment was probably a long-drawn out affair, with gradual depopulation over many years. It is probably safe to assume that the Northorpe was no more by around 1700.

Hornsea Beck Now lost to the sea, this hamlet, within the parent township, was located around the mouth of Stream Dike, a couple of kilometres to the east of Hornsea, and is best regarded as a satellite of Hornsea village itself, a fishing and trading community developing on the shore of a rural manor. Standing back-to-back, the contrast between the two could not have been greater: the one looking inward with its horizons firmly focused on the land and all it had to offer, the other looking outward to the far horizon over a glistening sea. The 'Beck' element of its name was presumably taken from the Stream Dike. One point needs emphasising: until it was straightened and given a direct easterly route to the sea in 1846 the Stream Dike occupied a more north-easterly course, with its outfall some way to the east of the Marine Hotel. Here, according to sixteenth and seventeenth century cartographic sources, a narrow spit of land projected seaward, giving a sheltered anchorage on an otherwise bleak, windswept and storm-battered coastline. It was around this promontory, immediately south of Stream Dike, that Hornsea Beck apparently clustered, the topographical feature providing the rationale for the development of a small community that was focused on fishing and sea-borne commerce.

Little is known of Hornsea Beck's origins or development. Speculating for a moment, the place probably originated on waste, perhaps reflecting an expansion in the manor's stock of landless cottagers in the late twelfth century or early thirteenth. Certainly, it was in existence and functioning as a port by 1228 when merchant Walter de Spinney, under the terms of his will, left Meaux Abbey, which had existing landholdings in the place, his 'whole profit of merchandise and of every ship applying at the port of Hornsea.' This granting of tolls was disputed, manorial and seigniorial interests making themselves felt, and the abbey never did receive the benefit. As the *Meaux Chronicle* relates:

> But Walter did himself give unto us two locks in that same place, and all his toll and boardtoll at the sea, nothing being with-held, which pertained to him and his ancestors at the sea of Hornsea-beck, on the clear understanding that all the aforesaid toll and boardtoll should be towards our hospitium, our own ship excepted, the toll from which he assigned to the needs of our convent. The toll even is on all goods and the boardtoll is on every ship mooring to the shore *four pence*. But, however, revenues of this kind in that place we never had, especially seeing that all revenues of this nature on the northern side of the stream, called the Beck, are known to belong to the lordship and liberty of the vil of Hornsea, and on the southern part of the said stream, on the shore of Burton, to the lordship of Holderness.

It was Meaux's misfortune that the place straddled the jurisdictional boundaries of the manor of Hornsea and the lordship of Holderness. However, one important consequence of the dispute was that St Mary's Abbey, as lord of the manor, agreed to maintain the pier and harbour at Hornsea Beck – monastic investment with an eye to future profit – and was the only such facility between Bridlington in the north and Ravenserod at the mouth of the Humber. The character of this quay is not known. Presumably it was a stone and/or timber construction, an extension of the promontory already referred to above; a wall thrown out into the open sea, possibly with a gentle curve, which gave deep water for ships loading and unloading and which also acted as a breakwater, protecting craft lying in the lee.

In 1390 Robert Tilcot, a wealthy fisherman of Hornsea Beck, willed to his wife Johan 'a ship called *Fartoft*, with the cocks and small boat, in order that she may provide a chaplain to celebrate for a year in the church of Hornsea, for his own soul, and the souls of his father and mother.' He also left a small vessel, the *Maudlin*, to his brother William, and another, the *Garland*, to John Skelton for the same purpose. To his nephew Robert, the son of William Tilcot, he left 'four nets, called sparves, two of an ordinary, and two of a better kind.' These were probably seine nets.

Something of the character of this shoreline place can be gleaned from the scant medieval documentary record. From 1263 there is a mention of newly built cottages 'at the sea wall,' next to existing properties, perhaps resulting in a terrace; such an arrangement is often found in fishing villages where space was at a premium. Reference in 1267 to a cottage at the end of the street leading to the quay may add weight to this supposition. Hornsea Beck was a landless community, the inhabitants having no agricultural resources from which to derive a livelihood: no arable open fields, no common pasture or meadow. No farm work? Not quite. Some residents, a minority judging from the sources, had rights in the land of Hornsea proper. For instance, in the will of Robert Tilcot already referred to, as well as the boats he left his '… horses, cattle, and husbandry utensils, and all his corn in the town and the fields' to his wife Johan. The lack of land even extended to the properties themselves. A document of 1306 speaks of five cottages without gardens or any kind of land attached; and a another of fifty years later lists fourteen cottages without gardens or land, and only three with gardens. Interestingly, two of these plots were described as 'gardens for hemp.' It is worth speculating that the processed fibres from this plant were used in the manufacture of fishing nets. Other documents record the presence of fishermen (fishing more or less on a full-time basis; and, of course, their anonymous womenfolk, hidden deeply, but mending nets, tending hemp gardens, gutting and curing), a sprinkling of merchants, traders, innkeepers, bakers, millers, and craftsmen – the latter category including smiths and carpenters, presumably occupied on the repair and building of boats. All this must have given the settlement a special and distinct character and quality of life in the middle ages.

Throughout the medieval period Hornsea Beck was clearly a thriving coastal community. The settlement was not valued separately for the 1334 lay subsidy payment, but subsumed within the £3 6s 8d assessment that Hornsea paid. Even so, it must have been a relatively wealthy place. There were 264 poll-tax payers in 1377, perhaps indicating a total population of around five hundred people, quite a sizeable nucleation by the East Riding standards of the time. In 1490 the total population was put at 240 by the vicar of Hornsea; still large, but a substantial decrease on the 1377 figure. Depopulation is best accounted for through the effects of coastal erosion. As the sea advanced the inhabitants retreated little by little to the parent village.

The threat from coastal erosion was all too real, affecting the long-term viability of the settlement. For example, in 1334 Meaux Abbey held twenty-six acres of cliff top land at Hornsea Burton, let at an annual rental of 2s per acre; by January 1400 the sea had swallowed all. Throughout the sixteenth, seventeenth and eighteenth centuries we catch glimpses of the unequal struggle with the sea and the inevitable long-term, piecemeal disappearance of the hamlet from the historical record. It was a losing and ultimately futile battle. Many documents record successive episodes of storm damage to the pier and ongoing disputes over its repair. By the early years of the sixteenth century it was in a poor condition. In 1555, according to evidence given to a tithe dispute case, 'The said Key of Hornesey about thirty or forty years ago was once and again in great ruin and the Abbot and Convent put off the repair of the same for a long time on account of the great expense necessary.' In response to the abbey's inaction, the fishermen of Hornsea offered to give additional 'dolles or cadolles' of fish, amounting to the equivalent of 'a mans right of fyshe of every shypp of the parish belonging to the sayd Key for every tyme that the sayd shypp goeth furthe a fysshyng.' The abbey remained unmoved, repairs were not carried out and, in any case, all hopes of a successful resolution were dashed when the monasteries were dissolved.

After the dissolution, the manor of Hornsea passed to the Crown. Appeals for assistance in rebuilding the pier were made to the Privy Council in 1549:

> A platt sent by Richard Mansell of Hornsey Beck, declaring the pere [pier] to be ruined whereby the King lost certain yearly rentes, his Lordship must send thither summe man of skill to consider what stuff is there towards the reparacion of the pere and what more shall be nedefull and what may be the charges thereof.

The appeal succeeded and at long last repairs were put in hand. As it turned out, though, both funding and materials proved inadequate. So, in 1553, a second exchequer payment was authorised:

> Mr Chaucellour to direct out of his warrant for the diffrayment of £1,000 more than the other thousand poundes that hath byn by the ordre of the Kings Majestie all ready bestowed about the peere of Hornsey so as the woorkes may be fynisshed out of hande.

Even so, the rebuilt pier was unable to withstand further storm damage and the effects of coastal erosion. Evidence to a 1609 commission of enquiry stated:

> We find decayed by the flowing of the sea, in Hornsea Beck, since 1546, 39 houses, and as many closes adjoining. Also we find, since the same time, decayed in ground the breadth of 12 score yards throughout the field of Hornsey, being a mile long, and parcel of the aforesaid manor. We further find that there will be great hurt and damage to the king's demesnes and pasture grounds near adjoining the said Hornsey Beck, within the manor of Hornsey, to the great hurt and impoverishing of the inhabitants of Hornsey, if that a present remedy be not made, either by re-edification of a peare [pier] or some other good defence for the same, for the safeguard of the said lands and country adjoining. And further, for the charge of the same, we find that the last peare built at Hornsey cost £3000 or thereabouts, and it will cost much more than it did then ... John Galloway, of Hornsea, pannierman, of the age of 80 years, says he had known 39 houses and 39 closes wasted away, of the yearly rent to the king of 58sh 6½d, and that there doth usually every year waste the breadth of 40 feet, which is more than heretofore; and that there are divers meadows and pasture grounds, called the King's Demesnes, of the yearly value of £11 18s, ancient rent, which will in a short time be wasted and consumed, with a great part of the town of Hornsey, without a peare, which he thinketh will amount to 2500 trees. Edward Harrison, of Seaton, husbandman, aged eighty years, says that he has known 300 yards washed away, and that there was a

peere at Hornsey Beck, during the continuance whereof the decay was very little.

The westward march of the sea continued unabated. The manor court rolls show that there were still inhabited cottages at Hornsea Beck in the later seventeenth century. The last mention of such properties is in 1744. Quoting from Thomas Sheppard's *The Lost Towns of the Yorkshire* Coast (1912), on 1 November 1757 Joseph Harrison measured

> [T]he distance from the north-east corner of Robin Maudley's house, at the seaside [that is, at Hornsea Beck; is this the house referred to in the court roll entry of 1744?], to the edge of the cliff, along the balk, next the ditch, it was 61 yards 4 inches. April 2nd 1759 … the distance was then 50 yards, so that in one year and five months the sea had gained 11 yards and 4 inches; at the same time the distance from the beacon to the edge of the cliff was just 19 yards. The foundations of the house alluded to were washed away in 1785, and the beacon was removed about 14 years before that. In the year 1786 the distance from the church to the seaside was measured by Mr John Tuke, surveyor, of York, when it was found to be due east 1113 yards. Mr Harrison took the distance from the cliff in 1759. The distance from the church (east end), in December 1876, was only 1000 yards, making a deficit of 133 yards from the period of its ad-measurement by Mr Tuke.

In a letter of 19 September 1787 to the Rev. William Dade, William Wytehead, the rector of Atwick and curate of Hornsea wrote:

> [T]he place where the stream dyke empties itself into the sea for about eight months in the year is … called the Beck; near this beck the town was situated. Two or three years ago the Beck took another current to the sea 140 yards southwards from the place where Robt. Maudley's house stood by the sea, overflowing its banks, and filling up with sand its ancient course, so that Mr Bethell's manor is increasing in the same proportion as Mr Constable's is decreasing … Hornsea Beck has now altogether disappeared.

Wytehead's comment that 'Hornsea Beck has now altogether disappeared' is supported by cartographic evidence. On John Tuke's 1786 map of Holderness, the legend 'Site of the Town of Hornsea Beck' is placed to the east of the cliff line, on what was by then the foreshore. So, after a protracted fight with the sea, and the piecemeal abandonment of properties from at least the late sixteenth or early seventeenth centuries onwards, the hamlet had finally succumbed to its inevitable fate by 1785.

Agriculture

In medieval society, as in all pre-capitalist economies, agriculture predominated over industrial production. The peasants, who were overwhelmingly the principal producers, certainly put some of their produce on to the market in order to acquire cash to buy industrial goods and products like salt, and especially to be able to pay rent and taxes. But most of their production was for self-subsistence and economic reproduction. Most peasants lived in traditional communities, which probably pre-dated feudal lordship. High proportions of peasants were legally servile or, if of free status, were nonetheless dependent on the power of the landlord. By their labour peasants provided not only their subsistence requirements but also the income of the landlord. Extraction of rent, whether through labour services, in kind, or as a cash payment, could be seen by the peasant producer as an appropriation of his product.

In Hornsea there were two large open arable fields (that is, land without fences or other physical divisions between properties), East Field and West Field, which, together with blocks of meadow, pasture and wasteland, spread out in a wheel with the village at its hub. The arable lay in almost continuous tracts over much of the parish, with other resources such as meadow, permanent pasture and small pockets of woodland being located on its fringes. Both fields were on the higher ground to the north of the village, between the present-day Atwick road and the parish boundary with Seaton. The course of Bewholme lane (laid out as a formal routeway at enclosure in the early nineteenth century) is the likely boundary between the two fields. Although precise acreages are difficult to come by, and were apparently subject to slight variation at different times, the total amount of land contained in the fields was around 800 acres, more or less equally divided between the two. This accords well with early sixteenth century statements that the fields of Hornsea and the hamlet of Southorpe collectively contained ninety-five bovates, where the notional value of a bovate is taken to be ten or twelve acres (there being about 350 acres in the single open field belonging to Southorpe).

Each year approximately one-half of the land was left fallow, the remainder being cultivated; both winter- and spring-sown crops were grown in one field while the other was fallow. The vast fields adjoined similar expanses in nearby villages, Atwick, Seaton, Sigglesthorne, and Hatfield; and within the parish itself, the fields of Hornsea would have merged with those of Northorpe, Southorpe and Hornsea Burton, only differentiated one from the other by boundary markers, grassed balks or drainage channels. The countryside was in a most literal sense open. Such an open landscape was of course different from the planned, enclosed landscape that came in to being following the enclosure of the parish in the early nineteenth century, with its varied network of hedgerows and drainage ditches. Yet in its openness and ecological poverty it was probably not so very different from the 'arable prairies' that have resulted from the removal of those hedges in the decades since the Second World War.

The open field system was to be found across the whole of lowland England during the middle ages. The smallest and most fundamental unit within the arable open fields was the 'land' or 'rigg', a long narrow plot separated from its neighbours by a drainage furrow; in terms of tenure it was held by either a single individual or occasionally by two or more joint farmers. A group of parallel lands formed a furlong, also known as a 'flatt', and there were balks or green access lanes between furlongs. The length of a

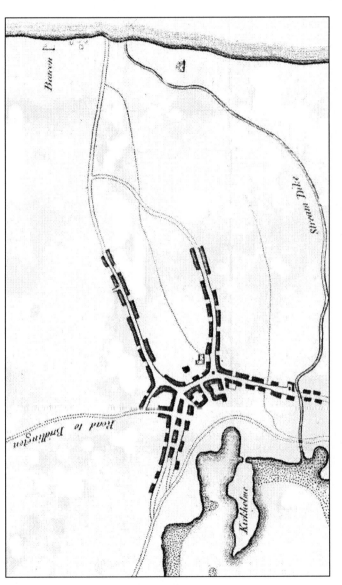

Figure 20. Extract from a c.1784 map showing Hornsea and Hornsea Beck (Hornsea Beck is the small cluster of open rectangles just below the legend 'Beacon,' top right). The open rectangles of Hornsea Beck are used to indicate abandoned house sites or foundations; Hornsea Beacon was moved inland to the position depicted about 1771; and the Stream Dike is shown on the new course alluded to in William Wytehead's 1787 letter to William Dade.

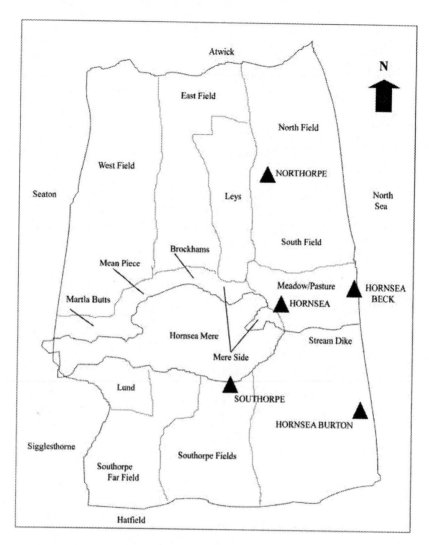

Figure 21. Medieval Hornsea was a rectangular block of territory running north-south for about 3km and was just over 4.5km east-west at its widest. North of the village, on high ground between 20m and 27m above sea level, the land was divided into two large arable fields; then, to the south, around the mere, in the 'bottomlands,' pasture and meadow were located in a narrow east-west strip; further pastures were situated to the east of the village, running towards the coast. The rest of the parish was divided between the hamlets of Southorpe, Northorpe and Hornsea Burton, each with its own agricultural system, and Hornsea Beck, which is best regarded as a port facility for the parent settlement.

land depended on the length of the furlong in which it was located. Lands were ploughed along their length, the plough being turned on a headland. The normal practice was to plough each land into a ridge; in time this traditional method of ploughing gave a reverse-'s' shape to the ridge when seen in plan. The furrows between lands had two functions: they invariably ran down the slope and therefore acted as drainage channels; in the absence of hedges or other fencing, they could also mark property boundaries. The alternation of ridges and furrows gave the fields a corrugated appearance. Farmers had their land distributed across the open field system. As well as each individual getting a share of good, medium and poorer quality land, this also helped ensure that all members of the community had an equal commitment to, and a sense of shared responsibility for, the fields.

In medieval Hornsea there was an intimate relationship between society and environment. The open field system fostered a sense of community: you could talk to the man working the next strip; you could see the shared ditches; you could tell the time of day by the movement of the common flock or herd from the village watering hole to the pastures and back. Once a year everyone would gather to 'beat the bounds' – that is, to walk around the perimeter of the parish as a way of marking its boundaries, walking the edge in order to confirm the land within (a tradition that, incidentally, continued up to the beginning of the nineteenth century). This was an important annual event: individuals, through a collective perambulation of the parish boundary, symbolically reaffirmed their presence in the landscape, thereby creating a sense of place and spatial order through dwelling, social activity and existence, in turn generating social identity.

At Hornsea – as across much of England as a whole – most of the ridge and furrow has disappeared, levelled by intensive ploughing over the last couple of hundred years or so. Small pockets do, however, survive, fossilised in present-day permanent pasture. These relict features, together with patchy soil stains and cropmarks on aerial photographs (showing the ploughed-out traces of former ridge and furrow), allow some observations to be made on the character of Hornsea's medieval ridge and furrow. Generally, the ridge and furrow ran in a north-south direction, with the strips being up to 1000m in length, around 7.5m wide (a width common across Holderness during the middle ages), and, where the physical evidence survives, about 1m in height. The furrows, separating the ridges, have an average width of about 3.5m.

Hornsea's agricultural system was based on mixed farming, with subsidiary interests in fishing and wildfowling. The farming unit in the north of England during the middle ages was the bovate or oxgang, a holding which varied in size between townships, and included areas of arable, pasture and meadow. At Hornsea during the thirteenth and early fourteenth centuries, each bovate contained around twelve acres of arable, with sufficient amounts of pasture and meadow for two draught oxen, one horse, ten cows and calves, thirty sheep and six pigs. Oxen were used for ploughing the arable. As they are nearly always mentioned in pairs, this would suggest that they, rather than horses, were the usual draught animals; certainly, on the heavy soils of Holderness they would be more capable than horses. The average size of arable holdings at this time was between 40 and 50 acres. In the later fourteenth century, when population levels were much reduced in the aftermath of the Black Death, the size of individual arable holdings increased to between 70 and 100 acres, with unknown increases in the amount of attached pasture and meadow. At the same time, the amount of land under arable cultivation decreased, reflecting low population levels. In 1374 and again in 1390, for example, there are references to pasture newly taken in from the ploughlands. Unfortunately the total amount of conversion is not known.

The late fourteenth century increase in pasture is associated with a greater emphasis being placed on livestock farming. Once again, this is a reflection of reduced population levels. In demographic recessions when labour grew scarce arable yields would inevitably diminish. Thus, the land/labour ratio may explain the change from arable to pastoral farming in the late middle ages. As animal husbandry is less labour intensive than arable farming, a change may have been the natural response to labour shortage in a period of low population.

There are few references to the types of crops grown at Hornsea during the medieval period. What sources there are mention wheat, barley, clean rye, maslin or massledine (that is, a mixture of wheat and rye), and oats, along with beans, peas, flax and saffron. No information has survived on yields, but cereal crops would have produced something under one ton per acre.

The arable accounted for around three-quarters of the total acreage, the remainder consisting of pasture, meadow and waste. The largest single pasture was The Leys, a broad rectangular swathe of grassland situated to the north of the village, between the open fields of Hornsea and Northorpe, containing in excess of 100 acres. The name is still preserved in the modern landscape, in Leys Hill and The Leys on the outskirts of the town, across which the present B1242 runs on its way to Atwick. Another block of pasture lay to the east of the village, divided into separate areas known from at least the sixteenth century as Chrystals, How Carr, and Holmes, perhaps totalling another 100 acres or so. Today, this area is covered by housing: Cliff Road, Chrystals Road, Constable Road, Marine Drive, New Road, Park Row, Railway Street, Sands Lane, Wilton Terrace, Eastbourne Road, and Burton Road. A narrow sweep of pasture lay between the mere and the present-day Hornsea to Seaton road, its separate parts known as Martla Butts, Mean Piece, and Brockhams. To the east of this, a further area lay between the village and mere, known appropriately enough as Mere Side. And yet other areas of pasture lay intermingled with the arable. It was in the pasture areas, on the short, tussocky, unimproved grassland that the villagers had the right to communally graze their livestock.

If any of the medieval abbots of St Mary's were able to visit Hornsea today, he would find much that was familiar in the mosaic of arable areas, grasslands, and copses of mixed deciduous woodland. The landscape of his mind, and the thought processes with which he and his contemporaries viewed the world around them, would, however, have been very different indeed. It is not merely that the whole structure of society was different: beliefs about what was important and what was insignificant differed; and the basic assumptions behind everyday life, including such concepts as cause and effect, and the role and position of humanity in relation to the universe, were fundamentally dissimilar. Unlike today, people were in close contact with their environment – the plants, the animals, and the soils that supported them. Activities in field, meadow and coppice were tightly constrained by the weather. Of necessity, communities acquired – through experience, and trial and error – a compendium of practical knowledge: about plants used as sources of food or for medication, or indeed decoration, fish taken from the

110

streams and rivers, lakes and the sea, and animals and birds that were hunted; as well as on such matters as soils, weather patterns, and the management of woodland.

Although of the later seventeenth century, a letter from a W. Lambert to Abraham de la Pryme provides the following lively and enthusiastic description of Hornsea Mere and its environment:

> The marr is a mile and a half in length, and in one place near a mile in breadth; it is fed by waters that run into it off the adjoyning higher grounds from the north, south and west; eastwards it runs into the sea, in a ditch called the stream dike, when the clow is opened; there are many springs in it also; the soyl is, in some places gravely, in others a perfect weedy morass. The water is always fresh. It is well replenished with the best pykes, peirches, eles, and other fish; the three named the best and largest that ever I saw or tasted. I have taken pykes a yard long, and peirches sixteen inches … I had almost forgot to add that there are three hills (islands we call them) in the marr, two of them, at the season of the year, are so full of tern-eggs and birds as can be imagined. A man must be very careful not to tread on them.

The account chimes well with later descriptions. The fish species are still to be caught and the terns still congregate. There is, however, little detail in the description of species, nothing on behaviour or what we would today call ecology. The species mentioned are apparently valued as food. In a sense the letter is an economic document. Even so, such practical details are rare.

The wider economy

Brief mention has already been made of the development of a leatherworking industry at nearby Seaton in the early decades of the fourteenth century. At Hornsea itself the beginnings of commercial-scale leatherworking, that is, supplying mass-produced commodities for sale on the open market rather than one-off items produced for consumption by the individual manufacturer and his household, can be detected at around the same time, becoming entrenched in the fifteenth, going on to peak in the sixteenth and early seventeenth, before declining and disappearing altogether in the later seventeenth and early eighteenth centuries. References throughout the fourteenth century to tanning and the manufacture of leather items indicate an active cottage industry in and around Hornsea, carried on in workshops attached to dwellings, in back gardens and in properties adjoining the Stream Dike. In 1347, for example, a cut was made from the Stream Dike to supply water to tanning pits in the garden of William de Hornsey; in 1354 hides were being stored in an outbuilding belonging to John de Rolston, who is described in one document as a 'worker in leather' and in others as a cobbler.

Owing to the paucity of early references, really no more than fleeting mentions when they occur at all, it is not possible to assess the scale of leatherworking within the community or the numbers involved, except to say that it was small-scale and, initially at least, *ad hoc* in character. It is clear,

111

Plate 27. During the middle ages – as in earlier and later times – woodland management created valuable resources. Coppicing fostered the growth of underwood for tool hafts or the flexible rods to weave into the fabric of buildings, baskets and hurdles, and generated browsing for animals. (Photographs: Stephen Harrison)

however, that for many, this was a part-time activity carried out in slack times during the agricultural round, the sale of products providing a welcome financial boost to cash-poor household economies. But for a small group of others it increasingly became a full-time occupation: craftsmen, divorced from direct production on the land, earning a living from the sale of commodities in the market place.

These activities, here and elsewhere in rural East Yorkshire, brought vociferous complaints from the leatherworking guilds in urban Beverley, railing against unfair competition from the countryside. Complaints begin in the 1330s and are common throughout the fourteenth and fifteenth centuries. Leatherworkers in the countryside had advantages over their conservative urban competitors: labour was cheaper; food was cheaper and more readily available in dearths; agricultural by-employments were available; many households involved in leatherworking held or owned land; above all, there were plentiful supplies of water available for the production processes; there were no regulatory guilds in country areas; and production was cheaper because the lack of such guilds allowed for the payment of lower piece-rates.

Other documents refer sporadically to hemp, a herbaceous plant. In and around Hornsea, hemp was grown, it seems, in significant quantities, a do-it-yourself cottage economy crop, an alternative agriculture. Many of the growers were also weavers, using their home-grown fibres, which were 'retted' free of the stalks by soaking in pits in back gardens or in local streams, to manufacture rope, sackcloth and items of stout, coarse clothing.

Hemp appears to have always been a common crop in small crofts on peasant holdings in this area. Labour intensive as it was, it was processed in quantity in the early fourteenth century, before the Black Death, when labour itself was plentiful. Thereafter, in the later fourteenth and fifteenth centuries, judging from the lack of documentary references, it declined somewhat, presumably reflecting the shortage of labour in the post-pandemic world. However, something of a renaissance in its growing and processing took place in the sixteenth and seventeenth centuries, when, prompted by various governmental ordinances, it once again achieved widespread prominence in cropping regimes, if only on a minor scale. Locally this led to a greater emphasis on its growth and commercial potential as a processed material. It was only with enclosure at, in Hornsea's case, the beginning of the nineteenth century, as capitalist economics began to take a grasp on the newly rationalised landscape, that the versatile hemp faded out as a crop in the face of the more highly priced wheat and barley.

Conclusion

By way of summary and conclusion let us join a traveller approaching medieval Hornsea:

He is walking along the western approach from the direction of Seaton in, say, the thirteenth century: crossing into Hornsea, over the parish boundary, marked here by an grey, lichen stained boundary stone. Out of one territory and into the land of another. The grassed and rutted track winds its way between a narrow strip of pastureland – Martla Butts, Mean Piece and Brockhams – and the higher ground, to the left, of the great corrugated arable

113

expanse known as the East Field. No hedges, no fences; just the well-trodden lane separating the one from the other. No barrier between one man's land and the next. The sun is hot, and the sheep and few cattle in the grasslands seek whatever shade can be had. Their watchers – three or four of the older boys, ever alert – sit under an old elm; from the leaf-dappled light, they glance cursorily as the stranger passes and then return to their conversation. Below the green pasture is the mere with its reed fringes rustling dryly in the gentle breeze, and its tangle of willow and alder. Through the tall late summer greenery, now past its best, the occasional glimpse of open water. A useful place to catch fish, eels and wildfowl, and the number of swans and herons is prodigious to behold. Walking on, a gap in the reed-stand affords the traveller a view of a small group of large, long-winged birds, with silvery-grey plumage and swan necks: four cranes stand studiously by the water's edge. And across the mere the hamlet of Southorpe can just be seen, nestling in a hollow close to the far shoreline. Overhead a keening skein of geese home in on the stubbles of the recently harvested corn: despite the gleaners, there are rich pickings still to be had. Now the field is deserted of its human labourers, waiting for the livestock to be turned out to graze and manure before ploughing begins. This year's was a good and plentiful crop, enough for the coming winter and the lean springtime and early summer months that follow. Enough, God willing, to see the families through to the next harvest. Enough also to pay rents and, of course, the tithes owed. The abbot will be pleased. Enough perhaps for some little surplus to be sold at the market. A productive, well-ordered and managed land. The lane twists and turns, as roads do in these parts, avoiding the worst of the obstacles: here and there the imprint of a once boggy patch, caked and cracked; now the outpourings of a spring and its pool of clear, cooling water, surrounded by a luxuriant growth of watercress. Our traveller – let's call him Adam de Thirsk, a monk of St Mary's Abbey in York – stoops and drinks. Onward. Along the wayside the flowers of the harvest field are still to be seen, faded from the heat of these last weeks, past their best: field cow-wheat, corn cockle, rosebay, hawkbit, feverfew, knotweed, mallow, corn buttercup, centaury. A sudden warm gust sends the grass rippling around him, in its oceanic way, rustling and hissing like surf on stones.

Hornsea village is still not yet in sight, hidden by the ridge of higher ground that is the East Field, but its presence is sensed: the occasional shout and the excited bark of a dog is heard, carried along on the breeze; and smoke, from the hearths of as yet unseen houses, spirals lazily upwards. The mere's margin is close now, a small boat drawn up on the thin spit of meadow that separates it from the track. A marsh harrier rises up from the reeded fringe and drifts effortlessly to a huge willow that has collapsed like so many broken sheaves, arching over the still water. The final bend is reached and the road straightens. Westgate comes into view. The beginnings of the village. The street is uneven, mainly grassed, nothing more than a continuation of the road already travelled; but here and there, in the deeper hollows and ruts, it is poorly surfaced with stones gathered from the fields and gravel quarried from the ridge behind the houses. Today the street is dry, but it is often awash with mud and water during the incessant winter rains. Orderly rows of mud-walled and reed-roofed cottages, their outbuildings and, turned by the spade rather than the plough, their vegetable gardens, front the lane to left and right, each holding enclosed by a rough-and-ready willow fence. Private domains in a communal world. Old established, laid out five, six or more generations ago by the zealous Abbot Stephen. People go about their daily round. Familiar and reassuring. Everyday sounds – human and animal – echo between the buildings, wood smoke permeates the air. A dog, hackles rising, and growling all the while, creeps warily towards the stranger, sniffs and, its curiosity satisfied, retreats. Already the stony bulk of the church, rising out of the ridge on which it squarely sits, is visible a few hundred yards ahead, beyond the end of Westgate, framing the view, drawing the eye. Even at this distance, the building exerts a powerful presence: the clustered village properties rest in its shadow, literally and metaphorically. It stands where it is to make all – resident and visitor alike – pay attention. But Brother Adam lingers, passing the time of day with a villager, talking amicably about the past harvest, the weather, happenings in the wider world, the war effort against Scotland and France, rumours of a new tax. An exchange of news and gossip. Presently he moves on; he has important business to transact with the village priest in the Rectory House and the day is not young.

Near Westgate's end the street noticeably widens. The funnel gives out on to a broad open space, grassed and a little uneven in places. Out of the corner of an eye, the traveller registers the stone cross. This is the market place, deserted today of its stalls and booths, of its multitude, of the sights and sounds of market day. Small groups of villagers stand around talking animatedly, as if debating the future of the world; children play; slumberous dogs bask in the sunshine; and one or two pigs are excitedly rooting for ... well, anything. Despite the absence of a market on this day, an animated scene nonetheless. A meeting place, a focal point. But let us not forget the darker side, the pillory and the gallows also, visible symbols of the abbot's reach and rule, oppressive, as some hereabouts would say. Adam quickly takes in the row of twenty or so cottages to his right, with their narrow gardens reaching back almost to the mere's shore. They front the green space before him. Identical in shape and form to those he has already passed, but some are larger – longer, of three or four bays – than their neighbours. These belong to the wealthier tenants, unofficial leaders and opinion-makers in this community, as they are everywhere. Assertive of their rights. Fleetingly, following through on this train of thought, he remembers the matter in hand: if there is to be trouble it will surely come from these people. At the far end of the row, two new cottages are under construction: cruck frames, half loft and mud walls in place, bundles of reeds and hazel rods and a pile of timber ready to finish the job. The population is growing. He notices an alleyway, leading down to the rough ground by the mere, dividing the row into two unequal blocks. Behind one of the cottages three women, a mother and her young daughters, the late afternoon sun burning on their faces and bare arms, thatch a small stack of this year's harvest sheaves, to keep out the weather and so prevent the corn from rotting before it is threshed and ground into flour. The family's safeguard against the privations of the coming winter.

The black-cowled monk turns and slowly crosses the green space. As he does so, a four-wheeled wagon, empty of its load, pulled by two oxen and guided by a young man, comes down into the market place, from the rutted

115

track that leads across the pastures to Hornsea Beck and the coast. Wagoner and cleric glance at each other and nod an unspoken greeting.

Adam makes his way past the church to the Rectory House, his progress silently followed by half-a-dozen pairs of eyes. At the gateway to the rectory enclosure the village priest, William de Melton, later destined to become Archbishop of York, meets him. They exchange a few words, step in and are lost to sight …

… By the time he has transacted his business and once again returned to the market place, the late summer's evening shadows are drifting across the village. A fine evening. The sun is reddening, going down. The moon is coming up the other side, a proper harvest moon, corn-coloured and full. He could hear a distant unrest of rooks, the birds no doubt circling for the evening. The market place is deserted except for a group of five or six children, homeward bound after an evening of foraging in the surrounding countryside. They carry wicker baskets laden with crab apples, wild raspberries, nettles and a variety of herbs: all useful supplements to the household economy.

As the sun sets, we leave Brother Adam on the threshold of his night's lodging.

CHAPTER 4

INTERLUDES

Introduction

The three centuries between 1500 and 1800 saw a transformation of English society and culture, national events prefiguring change at the local level. In the sixteenth century, Henry VIII, in a fit of pique, brought about a realignment of religious affiliations, and the suppression of the monasteries released large new areas of land for the consolidation of new kinds of ownership; a constitutive moment of English absolutism, the unification of England symbolised in the destruction and appropriation of the Roman Church's buildings and lands. In the following century, the autocratic rule of Charles I rocked the country, culminating in revolution and Commonwealth, followed by the reassertion of monarchy in 1660, and yet more upheaval in the 'Glorious Revolution' of 1688. These years also saw the embryonic seeds of agrarian capitalism being sown, to blossom, flourish and become entrenched in the eighteenth and nineteenth centuries.

On another level the transformation began with the rise of rural industries – the expansion of leatherworking in the case of Hornsea – which gradually restructured English society. The everyday lives of individuals, households, neighbourhoods, communities and classes were changed. The pace of life was altered, and interconnections multiplied, horizons expanded and orientations changed. Experiences varied from place to place and person to person, the process was uneven, but however we describe it, there was a massive aggregate effect. The world is what it is today because of what happened in dynamic parts of the world in the sixteenth, seventeenth and eighteenth centuries. East Yorkshire, and with it Hornsea, was one of those parts.

Economic decline and the fall in population that followed the Black Death led to a long period of relative stagnation in Hornsea, as in other parts of the region. In Hornsea's case this was to last until the later part of the eighteenth century. Nevertheless the village maintained its trading function, attracting business from the surrounding countryside.

Population

There is nothing like an even remotely accurate set of statistics from which to construct a population profile for the period 1490-1800. This is particularly so for the first two hundred years, when an absence of source material means that nothing useful can be said. Thereafter, things become clearer. However, extrapolating backwards from the known, the broad downward trend is not in doubt, and represents a continuation of the pattern first identified in the later middle ages, in the aftermath of the mid-fourteenth

117

century demographic crisis discussed in the previous chapter. For the later part of the early modern period, this is supported by an analysis of the entries in the parish baptism and burial registers, which for Hornsea begin in 1654 and are complete from then onwards. To some extent these registers are not without their problems: the earliest entries are few, leading one to suspect that they were by no means consistently or accurately kept, thereby presenting only a partial picture. It is, nevertheless, possible to arrive at very approximate population levels for the place between c.1654 and 1800:

1654	600 (estimated)
1672	590 (estimated from Hearth Tax)
1700	450 (estimated)
1750	220 (estimated)
1801	533 (first national decennial census)

Table 3, below, is based on a study of parish register entries. It presents an analysis of the overall natural increase/decrease in Hornsea's population at ten-year intervals over this time, allowing the general trend to be established.

A number of comments can be made:

- When the registers commence in the mid-seventeenth century the population of Hornsea was still at a low ebb. With the exception of the 1690s there was a nett population loss. High mortality levels were experienced in the 1650s 60s, 70s and 80s: recurrent outbreaks of plague and smallpox. Some of the episodes coincide with mortality crises in other parts of the county and elsewhere in England; other factors resulting in high death rates are likely to have been more localised.

- The last years of the seventeenth and first years of the eighteenth century are characterised by a brief spell of population growth, after which it fell again for the rest of the century. Locally, from 1718 onwards, the following epidemics are known to have occurred, reversing the slight upward trend in population growth of the previous twenty-five years or so and acting as a brake on any hopes of further expansion: 1718-19 typhus; 1720-21 autumnal dysentery and smallpox; 1722 smallpox; 1728 and 1762 general fever (influenza); 1767, 1787, 1792-93 and again in 1798-99 smallpox; 1796 and 1797 whooping cough.

- Climate was a crucial factor in all of this: across eastern England as a whole, the earlier eighteenth century was a time of below average rainfall and stronger than average winds, the later part of the century being colder and wetter than usual. In particular, harvest failures in 1718, 1728 and 1741 resulted in widespread distress – hunger, verging on famine in some

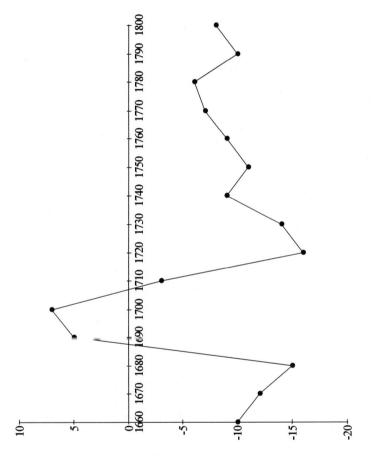

Table 3. Natural increase/decrease in the population of Hornsea, 1660-1800.

parts, was a commonly reported condition of those years[1] – reducing immunity and leaving an already weakened population susceptible to every contagious disease that came along.

- It was not until after 1800 that births began to outstrip deaths and population levels began once again to approach those of the high medieval period.

Lords of the manor

In November 1539 St Mary's Abbey, together with its landholdings, was surrendered to the Crown and four centuries of monastic ownership in Hornsea was obliterated at a stroke. Whilst many such properties were more or less immediately sold on, the manor of Hornsea remained a Crown possession until 1696, administered through the Court of Augmentations. During most of that time it was leased to various tenants, as the following summary makes clear:

- 1539   Crown
            Constable family
- 1597   Moore family
- 1625   Reverted to the Crown
- 1649   Following the Civil War and the establishment of the Commonwealth, ownership passed to Parliament
- 1650-51   Sir Robert Borwick (described as 'Trustee appointed by Parliament')
- 1651-59   William Spencer, Francis Lewis and William Micklay (described as 'Trustees appointed by Parliament')
- 1659-60   William Spencer and William Micklay (described as 'Trustees appointed by Parliament')
- 1660   Reverted to the Crown at the Restoration
- 1662   On the marriage of Charles II to Catherine of Braganza the manor passed to the new queen as

---

[1] As an aside, it is extremely difficult, if not impossible, for us today to appreciate the centrality of the harvest to the well being of the population in pre-modern times. Grain and bread and hunger and the search for food to assuage it are dominant, core images in the early modern period. Most of the population for most of the time were haunted by the fear and threat of famine. Continual hunger, being permanently on the verge of starvation, was the basic experience of most of the population until relatively recently. In 1843, for example, army recruiting officers found it almost impossible to find men who could satisfy even the minimum height requirement. This was a recurrent complaint, which reached its peak in 1914 when 41% of British recruits were rejected as being unfit for military service. Somewhat earlier, in 1904, a report found that one-third of all British children grew up hungry.

part of the marriage settlement. This arrangement appears to have become effective in 1670: between then and 1673 the manor court rolls refer to 'our Sovraigne Ladye the Queene, Ladie of this mannor'

- 1673   Thomas Elliot
- 1674-80   Hugh and Slingsby Bethell
- 1680-84   Slingsby Bethell
- 1684-1759   Acklam family. In 1696 the Crown granted the manor to Hans Willem Bentinck, Earl of Portland; in 1743 his grandson William, Duke of Portland, conveyed the property to Hugh Bethell. The Acklam family continued as tenants
- 1759   Lease surrendered by the Acklam family and thereafter the manor descended through the Bethell family until the twentieth century

Land and people

The disruption in ownership following the dissolution of St Mary's Abbey had little – if any – effect on the rhythms of everyday existence in Hornsea. Life for the population went on very much as it had done over the previous few centuries: the mundane activities of collecting water from well, stream or mere, walking through the village, chatting with a neighbour over a boundary fence, tending flocks and herds, planting and harvesting the fields, being able to see distant landmarks and remembering the myths and stories about them. The economic necessities of 'making a living' took precedence over such concerns as to whom the rent was paid and to whom other dues and services were rendered. All the evidence speaks of a basic, fundamental continuity between the pre- and post-1539 years. This of, course, is not to imply a static, unchanging world. Things did change: organic growth and development, but within a basically medieval framework; this was to endure in all its essentials until the beginning of the nineteenth century.

Continuity and change running in parallel can best be seen in the agricultural economy of the parish. Throughout the sixteenth and seventeenth centuries and into the eighteenth the medieval pattern as described in the previous chapter remained largely in place. Thereafter, until enclosure in the early nineteenth radically transformed the landscape, piecemeal change was the order of the day. Whilst the management of the agricultural system remained broadly within the remit of the manorial court and its officials, the field system itself underwent a certain amount of physical reorganisation from the seventeenth century. Following the depopulation of Northorpe, probably in the earlier seventeenth century, the arable lands of the former hamlet were incorporated into Hornsea's field system. This resulted in a certain amount of reorganisation: the former East and West fields of Hornsea were amalgamated to become West Field, and the land of Northorpe (North Field and South Field) became the new East Field. The boundary between the two fields was approximately on the line of the present-day B1242 Atwick Road. At Hornsea

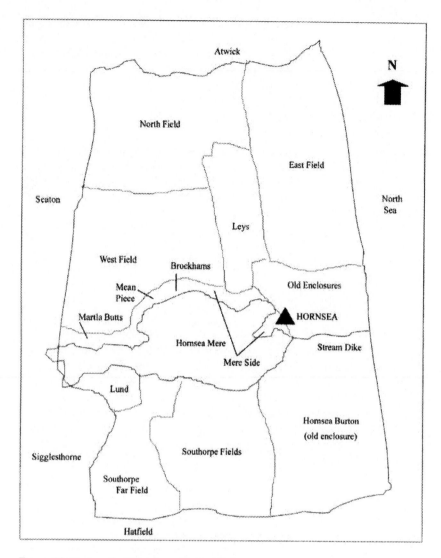

Figure 22. Hornsea in the early modern period.

itself, perhaps the biggest change was the creation of a third arable field sometime around or slightly before 1770. Known as North Field this was not an expansion of the total area under arable cultivation, but a sub-division of the former West Field, creating an entirely separate field in the process. It lay, as the name suggests, in the northern part of the parish, along the boundary with Atwick and to the west of the B1242 road. This act of reorganisation was brought about by the need to compensate landholders in the East Field for progressive land loss due to coastal erosion; the erosion of the cliff line to the north of Hornsea steadily reduced the field area. In 1609 it was said that the cliffs had receded westward by 240 yards/219.45 m since 1547; in 1612 it was reported that land 'lay daily in waste of the sea'; in 1637 it was alleged that 100-200 acres/40-80 ha of East Field had been lost within living memory.

Erosion was a constant problem. There are also many references from the eighteenth century, with annual losses, according to contemporary reporting, averaging between 2-3 yards/1.80-2.70 m. There is of course no way of checking the accuracy of these figures. All that can be said is this: whatever the actual rate of land loss, it was, over time, substantial.

Arable agriculture continued to dominate the local economy during these centuries. At the same time, however, there was a greater emphasis on pasture and livestock rearing than previously, reflecting no doubt the reduced population levels and the consequent inability to work large areas of arable intensively. Zones of permanent pasture appeared in the open fields from the sixteenth century, intermixed with the arable. Other areas of common pasture and meadow received frequent mention in the manorial court rolls and other documents: the Leys and the Tetherings in the West Field, together with between four and seven un-named 'pastures', perhaps a couple of hundred acres/80 ha in all; Chrystals (23 acres/9.30 ha), Holmes (24 acres/9.71 ha) and How Carr (9 acres/3.64 ha) to the east of the village; Brockhams, Martla Butts and Mean Piece between the mere and West Field, around 150 acres/60.70 ha in total; and the 34-acre/13.75 ha Mereside between Hornsea village and the mere. Parcels within some of these areas were apparently enclosed and in separate occupation. In 1650 and again in 1664-67 there are references to eight leys in the Leys, evidently divided between various proprietors. And, in the early eighteenth century, documents refer to individual 'lands' within Chrystals, again suggesting that it was divided, presumably by physical markers, between the proprietors. To the south of the mere, in the territory of the by now depopulated hamlet of Southorpe, extensive areas of pasture are recorded, one historic (the Lund), but others newly converted from the former arable. Here, the 97-acre/39.25 ha Southorpe Far Field became pasture, along with the 70-acre/ 28.32 ha Hold, which lay between the site of the hamlet and the mere. The Hold was first recorded in 1539, suggesting that Southorpe was well on the way to desertion by that date; the first mention of Southorpe Far Field as pasture comes later, in the 1670s. In 1758 there was a proposal to enclose the lands of Southorpe, arable as well as pasture. Ultimately, agreement could not be reached between the proprietors concerned and the attempt failed. This can be seen as an early drive towards creating agricultural efficiency within the parish, prompted perhaps by the parliamentary enclosure movement which was gaining momentum across the East Riding at this time. Southorpe, along with Hornsea, had to wait until the first decade of the nineteenth century before enclosure came about.

There was, however, some early private enclosure within the parish. In about 1663 the open fields and pastures of Hornsea Burton were enclosed by agreement, again no doubt reflecting depopulation within the hamlet. The land was divided between eight individuals: Marmaduke Constable received 103 acres/41.68 ha, William Audas 92 acres/37.23 ha, four others received between 40-70 aces/16.18-28.32 ha, and two between 15-20 aces/6.07-8.09 ha. Only the 8 acre/3.23 ha common was left unenclosed: four owners had equal shares in it and two others had the right to use its pond for the watering of their beasts. After enclosure Hornsea Burton very largely became grassland, providing pasture for cattle and sheep, the area being divided into separately hedged fields. Some of these fields still survive in today's

123

landscape: small rectangular fields, sometimes irregularly-shaped, which contrast with the much more regular and larger fields laid out elsewhere across the parish at the time of parliamentary enclosure in the early nineteenth century.

There is some evidence for increasing diversification throughout the period. This may be characterised as the rise of an alternative agriculture. Certainly, the old staple crops were still grown in quantity: wheat, barley, oats and rye. But, within the traditional agrarian regime new crops made their appearance on a small scale from the seventeenth century onwards. Cabbages, carrots, hemp, rapeseed and flax are all mentioned as being grown, mostly it seems in small acreages on enclosed plots. Turnips also, yielding both tops and roots to feed to cattle, or, when boiled, fed to lambs and poultry. Local documents also mention clover and lucerne, grown as grass substitutes. The increase in both clover and turnips was associated with a surge in dairying in and around Hornsea during the later part of the seventeenth century. From about 1700 potatoes began to make an appearance.

The wider economy

During the seventeenth century the economic base broadened, with the trend increasing in the eighteenth. Although farming remained at the centre of things, the most important dimension of life within the parish, industrial activity, albeit on a small scale, became a significant component within the overall local economy, most of which was connected in one way or another with agriculture. These should be seen as secondary activities, supplementary, undertaken at slack times during the annual agrarian cycle. That said, tanning and leatherworking, whose origins go back into the middle ages, had, by the later seventeenth century, become full-time activities for a small number of people. Leatherworking became an important strand in the local economy at this time. From 1667 the manor court appointed leather feelers and leather tryers to ensure the quality of products. The parish registers and other documents of this period refer to glovers, tanners, cordwainers, curriers, saddlers and skinners. Evidently, a thriving industry was developing. During the seventeenth century a tanyard was located next to the Stream Dike, to the north of Southgate, described in the manor court rolls as 'all that cottage with barns and stables, buildings and other outhouses belonging and adjoining together with the Tanyard, Orchards, Garth and Beckside.' Many leatherworkers also lived in the Southgate area, which must have resembled something of an industrial quarter. The consequent stench, the bad smells hanging over the village, must have been pervasive.

Leatherworking connected back to agriculture. Rape oil was used in the final stages of leather preparation, as a cheaper alternative to olive oil (2s a gallon compared to 3s 8d for Spanish olive oil in the 1620s and 1630s, for example). It is no coincidence to find, therefore, that rape was grown in some quantity during the seventeenth and eighteenth centuries, the seeds then crushed to provide the necessary oil.

The manor court rolls and other documents refer to a range of other, semi-industrial activities taking place at Hornsea during the early modern period:

- *Brewing* References to commercial-scale brewing at Hornsea occur from the 1620s onwards, in the area between Southgate and Mereside, where a malt kiln is recorded in 1625, 1659 and 1708. A malt kiln is also recorded in Eastgate, 'adjoining the pasture called Leys,' in the late 1670s and again in 1795. Another is referred to in 1719, at the corner of Southgate and Football Green.

- *Rope making* Throughout the seventeenth and eighteenth centuries one or two rope makers were trading in the village, in Newbegin and Southgate, using locally grown hemp. Like rape, hemp was grown in increasing quantities at this time, particularly in the late eighteenth century, when the government introduced a bounty of 3d per stone for hemp, as an incentive to greater levels of production. This was due to increased shipbuilding at the time and the consequential rise in demand for rigging, brought about by an expansion of overseas trade. The extent to which this directly affected local rope making production is unknown. However, between about 1750 and 1800, as far as can be determined, the amount of hemp being grown locally more than trebled, from around twenty acres per year to over sixty acres.

- *Brick making* The first recorded reference to a brick and tile yard at Hornsea, on Westgate, comes in 1710; thereafter, documents occasionally mention it through into the early nineteenth century. This is not to suggest an absence of brick making prior to 1710, just that we have no documentary evidence for its presence. As most building work used cobbles at this time, brick making must have been on a very small scale, almost certainly undertaken on a part-time basis. This changed during the later eighteenth century, when more houses began to be constructed in brick (see below).

- *Smithing* Throughout the seventeenth and eighteenth centuries Hornsea had at least one blacksmith operating at any one time, from premises at the Market Place end of Southgate.

- *Milling* There was at least one windmill at Hornsea during the middle ages. By the seventeenth century, two were in use. The manor court rolls for 1659 refer to 'a cottage in Southgate at the beckside and near to the milne house.' A second entry, this time from 1668, mentions a mill 'lying in the Cristill in Hornsey East Field near the beck milne.' This second, wooden-constructed mill was located on the site of the present Elim Lodge, on the east side of Cliff Road. It was destroyed by the hurricane of December 1732, and was replaced some time before 1785 by a brick-built structure on Atwick Road, which continued in use until the beginning of the twentieth century.
A windmill also existed in Hornsea Burton during these centuries.

By the seventeenth century a horse mill was also in use in Hornsea, on Eastgate. In 1670 this is referred to in the manor court rolls as 'the close next to George Robinson and one stable joining upon the horse milne.' Additional detail was provided in 1671: 'William Wallis leaves one horse milne and a barn and a garth called Kilne garth to his son William on condition that Anne his wife shall have half the profit from the said milne.' The reference to 'Kilne garth' seems to indicate that brewing was taking place nearby.

Hearth Tax 1672

The Hearth Tax assessments allow an unusually clear picture of local communities at specific dates in the second half of the seventeenth century. An Act of Parliament first introduced this property tax into England, Wales and Ireland in 1662 (Scotland was not included until 1691), and was part of a series of measures taken by the House of Commons to ensure that the newly restored Charles II could live 'of his own' – that is, that Crown income should be sufficient for the monarch's needs. Under the terms of the legislation, from 25 March 1662

> Every dwelling and other house and edifice, and all lodgings and chambers in the inns of court, inns of chancery, colleges and other societies ... shall be chargeable ... for every fire-hearth and stove within every such house, edifice, chambers and lodgings as aforesaid, the sum of two shillings by the year, to be paid yearly ... by even and equal portions

These 'even and equal portions' were payable at the feasts of Michaelmas (29 September) and Lady Day (25 March), with the first instalment falling due at Michaelmas 1662.

Within this framework, three exempted categories were applied to England and Wales (Ireland had different exemptions, which need not concern us):

- 'No person who by reason of his poverty, or the smallness of his estate is exempted from the usual taxes, payments and contributions towards the church and poor, shall be charged or chargeable with any duties by this act imposed'

- If 'the house wherein any person doth inhabit is not of a greater value than of twenty shillings per annum upon the full improved rent; and that neither the person so inhabiting, nor any other using the same messuage, hath, useth or occupieth any land or tenements of their own or others, of the yearly value of twenty shillings per annum, nor hath any lands, tenements, goods or chattels, of the value of ten pounds in their own possession, or in the possession of any other in trust for them'

- 'This act ... shall not extend to charge any blowing-house, and stamp, furnace, or kiln, or any private oven within any of the houses hereby charged, nor any hearth or stove within the site of any hospital or alms-house for the relief of poor people, whose endowment and revenue doth not exceed in true value the sum of one hundred pounds by the year.'

126

The basis of the act was self-assessment:

> And to the intent that a just account may be had and taken of all the said hearths and stoves by this act intended to be charged, be it enacted … that every owner, or occupier of every such house, edifice, lodgings and chambers, shall respectively within six days after notice given unto him or them … deliver a true and just account in writing under the hands of such owners or occupiers, as aforesaid, of all the said hearths and stoves which are within their several and respective houses, edifices, lodgings and chambers.

Ministers of religion and parish officials were responsible for making assessment lists of the hearths of taxpayers within their area. These were then inspected by the local Justices of the Peace and then enrolled by the Clerk of the Peace, who also provided the exchequer with duplicate copies. The petty constables then had to collect the tax within six days of Michaelmas or Lady Day and forward the monies, along with a list of any defaulters, to the high constable of the hundred within twenty days. The high constable then had ten days in which to pass the receipts and names of defaulters to the county's high sheriff, who, in turn, had another thirty days in which to make his return to the exchequer.

The tax, then, was assessed on the number of hearths in a householder's dwelling, and is comparable with the present-day Council Tax. Nationally, the surviving yearly returns are incomplete. For our purposes let us take the complete 1672 return for Hornsea as an illustration, providing us with a moment-in-time snapshot of the place. Eighty-three households with a total of 145 hearths paid the tax. The statistical breakdown is as follows:

No of hearths	No of dwellings	%
1	44	53.01
2	24	28.92
3	10	12.05
4	3	3.62
5	1	1.20
6	1	1.20

Table 4. Statistical analysis of the 1672 Hearth Tax return for Hornsea.

In addition fourteen households, with one hearth each, were discharged from payment. In all therefore there were ninety-seven households in Hornsea, of which eighty-three (90.72%) paid the tax.

The number of hearths per house is a reasonably accurate indicator of the number of rooms in a dwelling. This can be interpreted as an expression of the prosperity or wealth of the occupier; or, in the case of those exempted, an indicator of their poverty. The abstracted evidence contained in the above table is indicative of a relatively poor community. Over half the taxed properties had only one hearth (53.01%); only twenty-four had two hearths (28.92%), and so on up to one dwelling with six hearths (1.20%). The single house with six hearths – Old Hall in the market place, belonging to the

Acklam family – suggests a tiny resident elite. Furthermore the general prosperity of Hornsea can be gauged by calculating the percentage of properties exempt from payment. Overall fourteen dwellings, 14.37% of the total, did not pay the 1672 Hearth Tax, again suggesting a low level of prosperity.

A second aggregate measure of wealth in Hornsea as a whole is the average number of hearths per dwelling. In 1672 the average for the village was 1.64. This again illustrates the lack of prosperity within the settlement.

Taking the wider perspective for a moment, let us consider the position of Hornsea within the context of north Holderness. The North Division of the Holderness Wapentake (in which Hornsea was located) contained around 7% of the total East Riding population in 1672. In terms of the Hearth Tax it was a cottage-dominated area. Some 90% of households (1,141 households in total, of which 919 were taxed) had only one or two hearths; 8% had three to five; only 1% had six to nine; and 0.6% had ten or more. Hornsea was the largest village in the division, followed by Brandesburton with eighty-five households and Beeford and North Frodingham with eighty-two each. At the other end of the scale, Catfoss had nine and Eske just three households. The only large house was that of Sir Hugh Bethell at Rise, with thirteen hearths. Across the whole division 222 households (19.45%; or nearly one in five) were discharged from payment. If exemption is taken as an index of relative poverty then north Holderness was one of the poorest areas in the East Riding.

The tax provides a guide – no more than that – to the social structure of Hornsea at the time. In general terms, and without corroboration from other sources, the following profile can be suggested: households with one or two hearths would have belonged to labourers, small farmers and artisans; those with three to five hearths would have included the yeomanry, medium farmers and the more prosperous artisans and traders; the gentry and squirearchy would have fallen into the six or more hearths category. As can be seen from the above figures, eighty-two properties had one or two hearths (including those that were exempted from payment). This represents 84.54% of all houses in the village. Fourteen properties had three, four or five hearths (14.43%), and only one had six hearths (1.03%). With four-fifths of the population living in one or two hearth dwellings, the social complexion of the settlement is heavily weighted towards the 'lower' orders. This is also indicative of a poor community. These figures broadly compare with the rest of the East Riding: 82.5% of households had one or two hearths; 13% had three, four or five; 2.7% had six or more; and 0.7% had ten or more.

The Hearth Tax records list heads of households only. Extrapolating to arrive at an overall population figure is fraught with difficulties. Many historians choose to use a multiplier of four or five to arrive at rough-and-ready population levels. Multiplying by these figures gives us 388 and 485 respectively for Hornsea. In the absence of detailed population statistics (which, nationally, only started to be systematically compiled from the beginning of the nineteenth century) all we can confidently say is that the population of Hornsea in 1672 was somewhere around or between these figures.

The built environment

Externally at least, and with the exception of the church, Hornsea possesses no buildings earlier than the seventeenth century. The two oldest properties in the town are Low Hall, in Southgate, and Old Hall, set back on the north side of Market Place. The Acklam family built both in the later part of seventeenth century.

Of the two, Low Hall is the oldest. The origins of the property and its architectural history are obscure. In the 1660s, the manor court rolls indicate that the Acklam family owned three cottages on this site. It seems that the present house is either a remodelling of these cottages or, more probably, a rebuild on the plot. Either way, Peter Acklam was responsible for this change, which seems to have taken place in the mid- to late 1670s. The house was extended in the eighteenth century. Today, the brick and cobble building is rendered and colourwashed, hiding much of its architectural detail. Tall and narrow, it is of two storeys with cellars and attics and topped by a pantile roof, and was originally of four bays. Although much altered internally, it still retains a fine seventeenth century staircase, and three fireplace surrounds with overmantels, each of which originally contained contemporary paintings of a biblical nature. These were still visible in the middle years of the nineteenth century, when Bedell was writing his history of Hornsea. According to his account, they consisted of 'ships – another, Moses striking the rock – and the third, Noah's Ark.'

Low Hall remained in the Acklam family until 1777, when Peter Acklam, the fourth of that name, surrendered 'a Capital Messuage or Mansion House with Stables, outbuildings, orchards, etc, situate in a place called Southgate.' The property subsequently became an inn, known in the early nineteenth century as The Old Hotel, to distinguish it from the New Hotel in Market Place. In 1875, it became a temperance hotel, followed by a change of use to livery stables and 'apartments.' From the earlier twentieth century up to the present, Low Hall has been a private residence.

Another Peter Acklam built Old Hall, in Market Place, some time after 1660, most probably in the 1680s. This Acklam became lord of the manor in 1684. In 1651, Robert Moore sold the adjacent Rectory House to Peter Acklam, who later demolished the property, replacing it with Old Hall. No doubt, the new house was built to reflect Acklam's new-found status. Architecturally, the house clearly shows Dutch influence; at this time, English architecture was infused with Dutch influence, a consequence of exiled Royalists returning from Holland after the Restoration of 1660.

From the outside, the building has altered little over the last three hundred years. It is constructed in red brick with a pantile roof, of three bays and two storeys with attics. On the west side, there is a lower wing of two bays and two storeys. The whole building has shaped gables in the Dutch manner. In plan, the building has a central direct entry into a hall range with projecting cross wings.

As with Low Hall, Old Hall remained in the Acklam family until 1777. In the nineteenth century it became a farmhouse, before reverting to a private dwelling. During the Second World War, Old Hall was used as a prison by

129

Plate 28. Low Hall, Southgate. (Photograph: Stephen Harrison collection)

Free French forces, and then, for a short time in the early 1950s, was home to the embryonic Hornsea Pottery. It is now a private residence.

One further property deserves mention at this point: Corner Cottage and Sunset Cottage, at the corner of Scalby Place and Westgate. Outwardly, this is an earlier eighteenth century cottage, subsequently divided into two separate dwellings. It is a single storey property with attics, constructed from cobblestones, with brick dressings and a pantile roof. The remains of a single cruck blade in the north wall of Sunset Cottage speak of earlier, medieval origins, indicating that the building was once of timber-frame construction.

On the night of 23 December 1732 a violent storm – a 'hurricane' – caused considerable physical damage to Hornsea. In 1786 the Rev William Whytehead, rector of Atwick and curate of Hornsea, using eyewitness accounts, wrote the full story of the gathering and breaking of the storm and its effects on the village:

> … It arose from the Mere in a direction towards the sea, destroying and unroofing 24 houses, 14 barns and other outhouses standing near the market cross, or within 150 yards on each side of it, besides the damage which the church sustained; it blew down the east end of the vicarage house, and took off its roof, and though Mr Gale, the curate, and his numerous small family were then in their beds, not one received the least injury; one of my neighbours tells me that, immediately after the storm, he, the curate, went running over to their house with a young child in his shirt flap, saying, this is all I have left, supposing the others to have been killed. The hurricane, in its progress towards the sea, overturned the windmill, in the field called the Dales, not far from the footpath leading from the church to the beck, and what was very extraordinary, the mill stones were carried 150 yards from the mill by the strength of the wind. Sheets of lead were blown from the church, and wrapped round two sycamore trees, now standing in hall garth. A woman and a child, who were in bed together, in a chamber of one of the unroofed houses, were blown into the street with the bed under them, and received little, if any, bodily harm; a beam was blown from a house on the west side of the street, into the garret window of a house on the other side of the street …

Whytehead infuses an acute, detailed, objective account with a sense of wonder – almost of awe – at the natural and human drama, a feeling that might well have come straight out of the medieval period.

Storm damage resulted in a spate of rebuilding, which began the process of substantially altering the appearance of Hornsea, and which would reach its fulfilment in the next century.

The area around the market place and along the roads leading away from the historic nucleus was intensively developed during the later part of the eighteenth century. Houses and cottages, some with shops, fronted directly on to the streets. Behind were long and narrow rear gardens and orchards, which were increasingly built over with stables, workshops, privies and, in

131

Plate 29. Old Hall, Market Place. (Illustration: Stephen Harrison collection)

Plate 30. Corner Cottage and Sunset Cottage, Scalby Place. (Photograph: Stephen Harrison)

some cases, cottages to sub-let. Cellars may have been a feature of many of the properties around the market place, for example at No. 6. Here, in November 2002, building work exposed a small cobble- and brick-walled cellar of probable late eighteenth century date. As pressure for accommodation increased there was sub-division of some of the larger property plots and cottages. The dimension of plots, and of the buildings within them, showed considerable variation in size. A 'little cottage house' in Westgate, sold in 1760, measured 7½ yards in length by 5 yards in width. Its garden was 19 yards long by 6 yards wide. In Southgate a cottage and garden measuring 12 yards by 6 yards was sold in 1771; a similar Southgate property in 1779 was said to measure exactly half that, 6 yards by 6 yards, indicating that sub-division of plots may have been in progress. A newly built cottage in 1783 at the 'high end of the garden' in Southgate was 12½ yards long by 6 yards wide. The property had two ground floor rooms and two chambers above. Three years later it was sold on 'with free passage through the garth adjoining.'

Property deeds illustrate a gradual change in the nature of holdings around the historic core of the settlement. The original pattern was of a house and/or shop, with garth and stable to the rear. Examples of this are a cottage, garden, orchard and shop on the south side of market place in 1726; another two cottages, also on the south side of market place, with orchards and stables behind in 1739; a house in Newbegin with yard, garden and stable to the rear in 1752; a 'messuage with garth' in Westgate in 1758; a house with 'a plot of ground on the backside in a street called Southgate' in 1760; and in 1777 Low Hall on Southgate was described as 'a capital messuage or Mansion House with stables, outbuildings [and] orchards.' Throughout the later eighteenth century this was gradually giving way to a more concentrated use of the central gardens and orchards, with property converted and sub-divided, and its use generally intensified.

In 1719 a cottage in Southgate was described as lately 'converted into a kilne and reserving the Pigeons chamber with the benefit of the Pigeons and free Liberty of egress through the kilne chamber aforesaid.' A house and garth also in Southgate had acquired a 'limekiln and appurtenances' in 1725. In 1745 another property in Southgate had, in addition to its garden and orchard, a dyehouse, stable and 'other edifices.' A cottage in the market place had a workshop that was formerly a barn, together with a dyehouse 'lately built' at the south end of the garden, in 1753. A brewhouse and cottage were built in the garden of a house in Westgate in 1769. A deed of 1770 refers to 'dwelling houses lately erected' on Mere Walk, between the market place and Fair Place. A bakehouse 'lately erected' in the garden of a cottage in Newbegin is referred to in 1780.

The results of such developments (which continued into the next century) can be seen on the later nineteenth century large-scale Ordnance Survey plans of the town's historic nucleus, where, squeezed and breathless, a maze of yards and passages gave access to cottages, ash-pits and dung-heaps, wash-houses, privies and stables, as well as various industrial workshops and warehouses behind shops and houses fronting the street. This was particularly so to the south of the market place.

134

Plate 31. The later eighteenth century cellar at 6 Market Place.*Top*: detail of brick steps from ground floor and brick and cobble walling. *Bottom left*: general view. *Bottom right*: detail of cellar wall showing cobbled walling and infilling with different sized bricks; the infilling on the right is the presumed site of a coal shute. The floor (still *in situ*) was composed of 'slipping sand', a hard and firm material that keeps relatively dry as water seeps down through it. (Photographs: Stuart Walker)

135

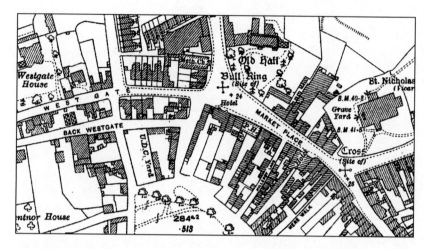

Figure 23. Extract from the 1:2,500 Ordnance Survey plan of Hornsea (1890 edition) showing infilling to the south of Market Place. (Reproduced by courtesy of the Ordnance Survey)

By 1784 there were 128 inhabited properties in Hornsea: forty-six houses and eighty-two cottages. At this time there were around 140 families living in the settlement, implying that a number of dwellings were sub-divided or in multiple occupancy. Using a multiplier of four or five, this would suggest an estimated overall population of between 560 and 700 inhabitants – somewhat higher than both the 1672 Hearth Tax estimates and the first accurate census return of 1801.

Seventeenth and eighteenth century inventories indicate a general pattern for the layout of the more substantial housing in Hornsea. Although precise locations are not given, many of the surviving inventories apparently relate to properties around, and in the immediate vicinity of, Market Place.

At the centre of dwellings was the hall, also known variously as the 'hawle house', forehouse or firehouse, which was sometimes equipped with beds. Henry Jackson, who died in 1677, had such an arrangement, along with a chamber over the hall and a 'street chamber.' The name of the last room suggests that Jackson's hall was not directly on the street frontage. It was quite common to have beds in one or more chambers. The brewer Peter Hall had beds in two parlours. Francis Willson, a tanner, had a bed in his parlour, while a chamber over the buttery was used for storing tallow and other household items rather than for sleeping. In many houses, however, beds were confined to the chambers. The hall was the main living area.

Most inventories mention a kitchen. In many cases there was also specialist storage or working areas for food and drink and other household goods: frequently butteries, sometimes brewhouses, linen stores, oil and tallow houses, mast lofts. Workshops or warehouses were often an integral feature of the house, with stables and sometimes substantial agricultural buildings at the rear. Marmaduke Browne, described as a yeoman at his death in 1692, had a milk house, 'barne on the backside,' a stable with loft over it, a

136

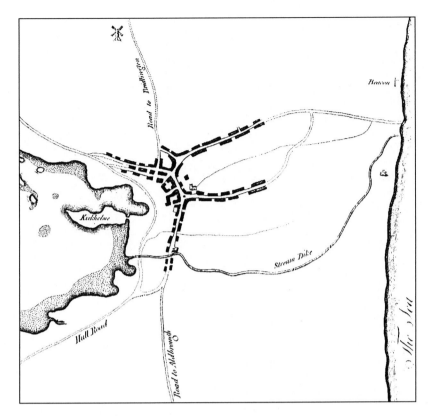

Figure 24. Extract from a 1784 plan of Hornsea showing the extent of the settlement at that date. (Illustration: Stephen Harrison collection)

mast loft over the kitchen, together with agricultural implements and stock 'on the backside of the house.'

Access to workshops and other developments behind houses was gained via passages, sometimes with rooms above them. The inventory of Sarah Carr (1765) mentions a chamber over the entry. The apparently smaller house of William Ketteridge had lofts rather than chambers, one of which was over the entry.

What of the moveable goods contained in these properties? The inventory of the relatively prosperous farmer George Hornby of Southgate, dated 30 October 1728, provides the following listing:

	£	s	d
Imprimis his purse and apparel	7	0	0
It. In the firehouse a dresser with eight dishes of pewter and nine plates, some brass implements, a fir table with frame, four chairs, a little iron range, an iron pot with other implements	3	6	8
It. In the kitchinge and Milke house a table, a milk tub, a churn, some bowls with other implements		13	4

137

	£	s	d
It. In the Chamber a bed with bedding, a kneading tub, two wheels, some wooll with other implements		15	6
It. Two draught beasts, three cows, two stears, two whyes, two half gate stears and two calves	37	10	0
It. Two draught horses, a mare, a foal, a mare five years old and a colt three years old	15	0	0
It. Corn in the barn and stack thrash'd and to thrash and wheat, beans and oates	26	0	0
It. Wheat sowne downe	15	10	0
It. One waine and waine gear, plough and plough geare with foure harrows and other implements of husbandry	5	5	0
It. A pigg and some poultry	1	0	0
It. Some hay in stack	2	10	0
It. Forgotten goods		3	4
	116	8	4

Or the inventory of the less prosperous farmer William Prudhom, dated 19 June 1739:

	£	s	d
Imprimis his purse and apparel	4	11	11
It. Brass and pewter	1	16	8
It. Iron fire vessel		6	9
It. Wooden vessel and earth [ceramic] pots		7	2
It. Bedding and beds	2	10	5
It. Tables, formes, chaires, stooles and cushions		15	9
It. Chests and boxes, and clock		13	4
It. Spinning wheele, Card, Hemp, yarn and other things		9	10
It. Meale, Malt, Beef, Butter and Cheese, and old books	2	5	11
It. Beasts	16	19	4
It. One old horse	1	10	0
It. Oates		17	0
It. Hay		11	0
It. Carts, wheeles and husbandry geare	2	19	7
It. Firefuel and Bees		7	5
It. Dunghill and other old things		9	8
	37	11	9

What is particularly interesting about these inventories – and others of the same century – is the range and quantity of household items owned. Eighteenth century households contained on average many more goods than households a century or more earlier. The same range of seating and table furniture was still present, as was hearth furniture, cooking implements, and pots and pans. The major change was an increased degree of comfort. More pewter vessels were kept; the wooden platters and bowls of a century earlier had largely gone.

Storage items, such as dressers and cupboards, did appear more frequently in the hall. This was a much-changed room. Many halls were without beds, a radical departure from the seventeenth century. They contained tables, chairs and stools, as well as dressers, presses and cupboards, and also a range of new items, such as clocks, looking glasses, bibles and books. Some halls also still continued in the traditional manner with beds present, even though the trend was declining. Even in traditional halls increased standards of material comfort are indicated by the presence of new items (leather-backed chairs, pudding pans, and the like).

With the partial separation of the old hall and sleeping function went a separation between space used for sleeping and that used for storage. Rooms with both beds and stored goods became increasingly rare in the eighteenth century. More rooms were used specifically for storage than in earlier centuries, including the storing of cheese, butter, and various cereals. There are a few references to work upstairs: for example, a (spinning) 'wheel' in the bed chamber of George Hornby's house presumably represents his wife's activities.

The major changes of the eighteenth century compared with the previous one were:

- The development of the hall as seen in the wider range of items found there and the larger number of halls without beds.
- The overall rise in the quantity of material culture within the house.
- The rise of both stored goods and items such as dressers and chests specifically designed for storage.
- The rise of unifunctional rooms at the expense of multifunctional space.

A number of comments can be made on the external appearance of the buildings themselves. Residential accommodation fell into two broad categories: houses, that is, structures with a ground floor and at least one upper storey; and cottages, that is, single storey or one-and-a-half storey properties. As mentioned above, there were forty-six houses and eighty-two cottages in Hornsea in c.1784.

Of the houses, the three most substantial seem to have been: the vicarage, in Newbegin, just beyond the church; Old Hall on the north side of Market Place; and Low Hall in Southgate. The vicarage (demolished in the early nineteenth century and replaced by the present structure on the same site in 1831-32) was described in a 1764 Terrier:

> The Vicarage House is 20 yards long and 6 [yards] broad [60ft/18.30m x 18ft/5.50m], built chiefly with brick and covered with Tyles. The kitchen, four low Rooms which are floored with Brick, except the Dining Room which is floored with Wood, four chambers besides Garretts. There is a large yard in which is a Barn and stable covered with Thatch, an orchard fenced with a Clay wall.

Unfortunately no illustrations appear to exist of this building. The date of the structure is not known. It certainly existed in 1732, when the great storm caused considerable damage to its roof. The overall dimensions and the length to width ratio of 3:1 are reminiscent of a single storey medieval longhouse. At least in origins. If this is the case, then the first floor and garrets must have been added subsequently, perhaps in the sixteenth or seventeenth centuries. Alternatively, a possible context for extending the house may be found in a (partial) rebuilding following the 1732 storm, which allowed the original core to be expanded vertically. Either way, the sources are silent.

Religion

Nonconformity in religion has a long history in Hornsea, going back to the seventeenth century but reaching its zenith in the nineteenth. This section examines the origins of these religious practices.

The first group for whom we have evidence is the Society of Friends (Quakers), whose presence is documented from the 1650s onwards. The founder, George Fox, visited Holderness in 1651, propagating a new religious belief, according to the tenets of the New Testament. His message was simple and unadorned: there was no need for special buildings, that is, churches, in which to hold services; no need for an ordained ministry because all believers were thought of as being in the priesthood; no need for ceremony between fellow human beings; no need for the taking of oaths. As a result, Quakers refused to pay tithes, used to support the established church and clergy, and did not take oaths when giving evidence. These beliefs were to lead supporters into conflict with state and local authority. Until 1682 and the passing of the Act of Toleration, Quakers suffered persecution, harassment and prosecution for their beliefs, regularly receiving prison sentences and the exaction of fines.

The first reference to Quakers in Hornsea occurs in 1656, when Oliver Ketteridge of Hornsea Burton was fined for refusing to take an oath. Three years later, in 1659, he received thirteen weeks imprisonment for refusing to pay the parish clerk's wages. Again, in 1660, he was arrested and imprisoned after attending an illegal Quaker meeting at Sigglesthorne.

The early history of Quakerism in Hornsea, however, is inextricably linked to members of the Acklam family, an important Holderness clan who originally came from Dringhoe, Bewholme and Skipsea, and who became substantial property owners in their adopted place of residence. They were people of substance, to be reckoned with, even, between 1684 and 1759, becoming lords of the manor. The first mention of the family in Hornsea occurs in 1629, when a George Acklam, described as the lord of Bewholme, near Skipsea, is recorded as resident. He was a Royalist sympathiser, who was later to be heavily fined by the Commonwealth for his pro-monarchy beliefs. The Dringhoe Acklams, however, were Parliamentarians, and this branch of the family appear regularly in the Hornsea court rolls from the early 1650s. They were also Quakers.

Peter Acklam of Hornsea, described as a 'dangerous and obstinate and quaking speaker' and 'the chief of the sectaries in the East Riding', is the first Acklam Quaker for whom we have documentary references. He was also a prominent Parliamentarian and had served as a Major in the Civil Wars, most notably at the second siege of Scarborough in 1648. This Acklam was arrested and imprisoned in 1660 for refusing to take the Oath of Allegiance to the recently restored Charles II. He was:

Plate 32. The picturesque irregularity of eighteenth century houses and cottages, intermixed with later properties, on Southgate. (Photograph: Stephen Harrison)

Sent for from his own house by John Bellasis, Governor of Hull, who without cause committed him to the Custody of a Marshall. After two weeks confinement he was had before several Justices who tendered him the Oath of Allegiance and for refusing to swear Committed him to York Castle.

Again, in 1665, he was arrested for holding Quaker meetings at his home – Low Hall, in Southgate; and in 1678 he was prosecuted for non-attendance at church, under the Statute of Absence from National Worship – a fine of £20 per month was imposed for every month of absence from worship at the parish church.

Quakers did not accept the need for burial in consecrated ground. In 1665 Thomas Acklam bought a cottage called Low Close in Southgate. On his death in 1667 he was buried in the garden of this property, as was his wife Anna Maria, who died later in the same year. Thomas bequeathed all his Hornsea properties to his son Peter, who substantially enlarged Low Close, also known as Low Hall, between May and November 1675.

The property was let to George Atkinson with the stipulation that:

> The new garden plot be returned to the use of the said Peter Acklam and Alice his wife, Peter Acklam and Thomas Acklam his sons and Anna Maria his daughter for a burying plot when and as often as they or any of them shall desire the same.

Altogether, between 1667 and 1758, nine Acklams were buried in the garden of Low Hall:

- 1667   Thomas and Anna Maria Acklam, each aged 72 years
- 1690   Peter, son of Thomas Acklam, aged 72 years
- 1692   Alice, wife of Peter Acklam, aged 76 years
- 1699   Thomas, son of Peter Acklam, aged 38 years
- 1700   Anna Maria Acklam, daughter of Peter Acklam junior, aged 12 years
- 1734   Anna Marie Acklam, daughter of Peter and Alice Acklam, aged 68 years
- 1744   Peter Acklam, son of Peter and Alice Acklam, aged 85 years
- 1758   Isabella, wife of Peter Acklam, aged 92 years

Seven of the gravestones still survive.

According to the manor court rolls, on his death in 1760 Peter Acklam

> Did hereby give a cottage in Westgate in Hornsea formerly a parcel of a cottage near adjoining being occupied as a stable with a yard and belonging to John Storr and Issac Smith Both of Owstwick in Holderness and to Robert Milner of Kingston upon Hull their heirs and assignes in Special Trust and Confidence that they shall stand seized and possessed thereof to the Sole Use and benefit of the

People called Quakers forever and that the said premises or a part thereof shall be constantly maintained in due repair for performance of Public Worship by any of the said people so long as may be found Expedient and if the same be found of no use then the Trustees to sell the same and apply the produce thereof for the sole use and Benefit of the people called Quakers belonging Owstwick Monthly Meeting forever.

This property – Quaker Cottage – in Back Westgate became the regular meeting place for Hornsea Quakers until 1818.

The Acklams left Hornsea in 1777. Quakerism continued, with at least two families remaining – the Lamberts and Watsons. With the death of Dinah Lambert in 1818, the sect died out in Hornsea. Quakers were then absent from Hornsea until the 1970s. In 1972, after renovation, Quaker Cottage once again became a place of worship for the local Society of Friends congregation.

Sporadic references from the 1710s to the registering of meeting places for unspecified nonconformist worship probably relate to the Presbyterians. In 1714 George Whitfield registered one such (unidentified) place, as did Charles Bondfield in 1716. There are no specific details. Presbyterians, although very few in number, were active in Hornsea at this time, certainly in the first half of the eighteenth century (see below).

Dissenters of whatever persuasion formed a small minority in the later seventeenth and eighteenth centuries. Visitation records of the Archbishops of York provide a summary of religious affiliation at various dates in the eighteenth century. For example, Archbishop Herring's Visitation of 1743 records that

> There are 133 families in the Parish 4 of which are Dissenters one Popish family, two of the Sect of Quaker and the fourth Presbyterian. We have no Meeting House but one for Quakers. They meet twice a week on Sundays and Thursdays. There are seldom more than 4 or 5 go to the meeting, no Teachers amongst them.

An entry in the Hornsea Register of Burials, dated only to the eighteenth century, records:

> 131 Families in this parish
> 297 Communicants
> No papists, no dissenters except 3 Quakers

Conclusions

The three hundred years that separated 1500 from 1800 saw many changes in Hornsea, as they did across the country as a whole. A time when ordinary people, their homes and their activities become more visible. Although agriculture remained dominant, the economy expanded and diversified. Employment opportunities multiplied and the settlement's population began to slowly grow, both through in-migration and natural increase. This, together with growing levels of prosperity, led to changes in the physical character of Hornsea. Brick and tile houses gradually replaced the traditional cobble and thatch dwellings, and the development of small-scale industries resulted in the construction of commercial buildings. Despite all of this, by the end of the eighteenth century, Hornsea was still firmly locked to the land, a deeply agricultural place. Dramatic change had to wait until the next century.

CHAPTER 5

ONWARD AND UPWARD

Introduction

By the end of the eighteenth century the pattern of streets and lanes that was established during the middle ages still physically bound Hornsea. A population little more than it had been on the eve of the Black Death in the fourteenth century. Church and market place and the rhythms of the annual agricultural cycle dominated the scene, still providing focal points for the everyday pattern of life just as they had for centuries, sustained by people's practices and daily and seasonal routines: 'an agricultural village standing in a little valley, on the bleak coast that hears the German Ocean roar, deep booming, between Hornsea Mere and the sea.' The development of Hornsea during the nineteenth century was a microcosm of the transformation from the rural to the urban. The new century brought new frameworks, new opportunities and new horizons: industrialisation, a burgeoning economy, an ever-expanding Empire, social movement, urban expansion, religious dissent, and the imposition of rules, ordinances and governmental, local and national, controls on an increasingly disciplined society. Change was the keynote. A fundamental restructuring of all aspects of being: social and economic, political and religious, cultural and societal. The rise of the modern. A vast, untidy century of genius. The pace at first was slow, but by the 1870s and 1880s it had gathered momentum, and by 1900 Hornsea had become a very different place. This was the world that we are heirs to.

Victorian Hornsea, like all urban places at the time, was a metaphorical battlefield; segments of the community pitched against each other, combining and re-combining over different issues at different times; fluidity in social, economic, political, religious and cultural issues. Conservatives fought Liberals. Dissenters fought the Church of England. Protestants fought Catholics. The middle classes fought against the upper classes – and both waged war on the lower orders. Workers fought their employers. Protectionists fought against Free Traders. The godly fought against the ungodly. One shopkeeper fought to win the customers of another. All were fighting for the hearts and minds of the people. The battles were waged across newspaper columns, in speeches and meetings, in rallies and processions. Campaigns were also played out in buildings: the pub on one corner, the Nonconformist chapel on another, and the Anglican church on a third.

Population

1801 is a crucial date in attempts to reconstruct population data for individual places. In that year, with the institution of the national decennial census, we have the first-ever accurate population statistics for towns and villages across Great Britain.

After a prolonged period of stagnation, English population growth in general was spectacular during the later eighteenth and throughout the nineteenth centuries; although primarily related to changes in the birth and death rates in the general modernisation of society, it was also connected to increased agricultural production, especially in corn but also in meat, fuelled in turn by massive industrialisation and the rise of the urban industrial working class. Between 1741 and 1801 the population of England and Wales rose from 6m to 8.9m; the following half-century saw growth accelerate to 17.9m; and by 1911 population levels had reached 28.4m. In 1801 20% of the population lived in towns with more than 5,000 inhabitants; by 1851 this proportion had reached 54%, and by 1911 it was around 70%.

At first glance the East Riding appears to be broadly parallel to the above trends: in 1801 24% of its 111,192 population lived in towns of over 5,000 inhabitants, 50% of 220,983 in 1851, and 72% of 392,392 in 1901. These bald figures, however, are somewhat misleading: overwhelmingly, town-dwellers were concentrated in the Municipal Borough of Hull, which, by 1901, accounted for 84% of all the county's population living in towns of more than 5,000 residents. Hornsea never joined the likes of Beverley, Bridlington, Cottingham, Driffield and Hull as one of those urban centres during the nineteenth century; it never achieved a population in excess of 3,000. Although it was fully urban, it was more like Hedon, Market Weighton and Pocklington in terms of its size. Outside Hull, the East Riding was – and remains – a principally rural county.

One of the problems we encounter, when discussing population trends in resorts such as Hornsea, is in differentiating the permanent resident population from the temporary, holidaymaker population. During the summer months temporary visitors swell Hornsea's actual population to varying degrees. When the decennial censuses coincide with the 'season' these temporary visitors artificially inflate the resident population: generally it is not possible to distinguish between the two. During the nineteenth century one census, that taken on 7 June 1841, occurred during the summer months. The effects of a swollen population were tersely recorded on the document: 'More than 50 visitors are included in the return.' Conversely, the return for 1851, taken on 31 March, includes the following statement: 'The reason [for the decline in population] is that visitors had not commenced when the census was taken.' A note on the return for 3 April 1871 records that 'The increased population in the parish of Hornsea with Hornsea Burton is ascribed to it being a favourite resort.' As this census was taken outside the holiday season, we must conclude that it is a general comment relating to the growth of the resident population – that is, that Hornsea was becoming a favoured place for permanent residence.

Between 1801 and 1901 the population of Hornsea grew from 533 to 2,381, a rise of around 350%. Across the century as a whole, growth was uneven: up to 1851 there was a 77% increase; from then up to 1901 the increase was 152%.

In the forty years 1801-41 the population increased from 533 to 953 (1,005 if we include the fifty or so visitors recorded in the 1841 census), with the highest rises occurring in the decades 1801-11 and 1831-41. In 1851 the number had fallen back slightly, to 945. In functional terms, Hornsea was still

146

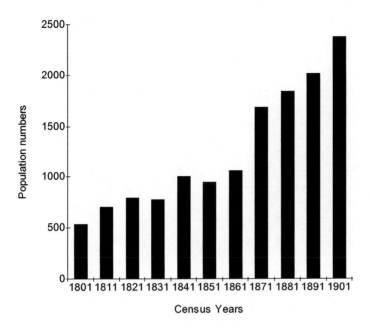

Figure 25. The population of Hornsea 1801-1901.

Note: The 1841 census was compiled on 7 June, that is, during the summer holiday season. Out of a total recorded population in Hornsea on that day (1,005), fifty-two persons were listed as 'visitors.'[1] This number is recorded in the above graph. Subtracting these individuals gives a resident population of 953.

Year	Recorded population	Numerical Change	% change
1801	533	-	-
1811	704	+ 171	24.3
1821	790	+ 86	10.8
1831	780	- 10	1.3
1841	1,005	+ 225	22.4
1851	945	- 60	6.3
1861	1,063	+ 118	11.1
1871	1,685	+ 622	36.9
1881	1,836	+ 151	8.2
1891	2,013	+ 177	8.8
1901	2,381	+ 368	15.4

Table 5. The changing population of Hornsea, 1801-1901

---

[1] Visitor numbers compare favourably with those at Bridlington (60), Cromer (50) and Skegness (44).

147

Year	Recorded population	Persons per square mile	Persons per square kilometre
1801	533	102.50	39.54
1811	704	135.38	52.22
1821	790	151.92	58.60
1831	780	150.00	57.86
1841	1,005	193.27	74.55
1851	945	181.73	70.10
1861	1,063	204.42	78.86
1871	1,685	324.04	125.00
1881	1,836	353.08	136.20
1891	2,013	387.11	149.33
1901	2,381	457.88	176.63

Table 6. The changing density of population, 1801-1901.

very much an agricultural village for the first half of the century, with population growth resulting, very largely, from natural, internal, increases.

The second half of the nineteenth century was a period of rapid population growth in Hornsea, from 953 in 1851 to 2,381 in 1901, with the greatest decennial increase taking place between 1861-71. During those ten years, the population expanded from 1,063 to 1,685, a 36.9% increase. This can be attributed to the coming of the railway in 1864, an event which marked the beginning of Hornsea's development as a desirable dormitory town, chiefly for people from Hull. In the seven years after the opening of the rail link with Hull, the population increased by 58%. From 1864 to 1901, growth was largely fuelled by in-migration, overwhelmingly from Hull, as can be seen from the following table:

Place of birth	1851	1891
Hornsea	410 (43.39%)	894 (37.55%)
Hull	37 (3.91%)	724 (30.41%)
Rest of East Yorkshire	397 (42.01%)	501 (21.04%)
Rest of Yorkshire	45 (4.76%)	167 (7.01%)
Elsewhere	56 (5.93%)	95 (3.99%)
Total	945	2,381

Table 7. Place of birth of Hornsea inhabitants, 1851 and 1891.

Arguably, the development of Hornsea as a dormitory town for Hull was of far greater significance to the place than its development as a seaside resort, as will be referred to later.

It is instructive to compare the growth of Hornsea with its two rival resorts in Holderness: Bridlington, to the north, and Withernsea, to the south. Both were developing rapidly during the nineteenth century, as the following graph makes clear:

148

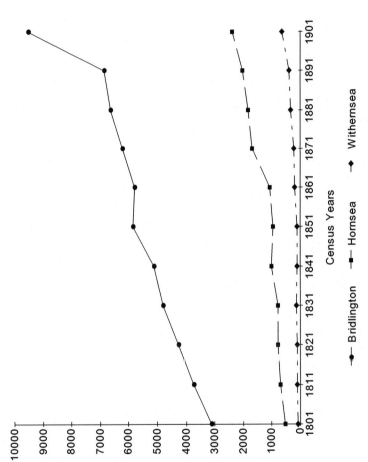

Figure 26. The nineteenth century population growth of Bridlington, Hornsea and Withernsea compared.

The growth of Hornsea and Withernsea is particularly variable. Bridlington, on the other hand, shows a steady rate of increase. What is particularly noteworthy in all three cases is the marked increase in population in the decade following the establishment of rail links with Hull. For Bridlington this happened in 1846, for Withernsea in 1854 and not until 1864 in the case of Hornsea. Following the opening of the railway, the rate of growth in both Withernsea and Hornsea was steady across the rest of the nineteenth century (from 202 to 645 (219%) and 1,063 to 2,381 (124%), respectively). In Bridlington, however, population growth was less pronounced in the 1850s, but thereafter continued steadily (from 5,839 to 9,528, or 63%), increasing dramatically in the last decade of the century, from 6,840 in 1891 to 9,528 ten years later (an increase of 39%).

Reworking the pattern of the land

Writing some forty years after enclosure, Bedell produced a somewhat nostalgic account of the old way of life. His nostalgia was not confined just to the personal, but permeated his view of history. He had no doubt at all that people had been happier with the old system of husbandry. 'There is perceptibly less of heartiness and joviality of manner in this part of Holderness than 30 or 40 years ago', and the reason for this was that the people had lost their common rights:

> The common rights attached to the numerous old cottages gave many a cottager an interest in the commonwealth that cannot be felt now. Small allotments were made on the inclosure in lieu of these common rights, but few of them are now in the occupation of the cottagers.

Enclosure (or 'inclosure' as it was spelt in the eighteenth and early nineteenth centuries) turned the population from a 'bold peasantry' into something resembling 'economic men' and many of the old customs disappeared also. Bedell, with his attachments to an 'adjusted' feudal society, wrote with enthusiasm of the old ways, was sceptical of progress being proclaimed on every side and saw it as a threat to human dignity. Like William Cobbett a generation earlier, he is directly in touch with the rural England of his time but, like Cobbett also, is looking back to a happier country, the old England of his boyhood; Bedell counterpointed agrarian enclosure and its new found confidence with a feeling of loss and melancholy and regret. Here is a flavour of the rhythm and seasonality of life that disappeared with the coming of the modern age:

> Before the inclosure, Whitsun-week was a sort of rustic carnival. The pastures were "broken" (that is, cattle were turned into the fresh grass) on old May-day, but the gaieties took place at Whitsuntide. On Whitsunday, two young girls went round the town to collect flowers. In the evening these were made into a garland at the nowtherd's. Such of the milkmaids as chose it went after milking to the making of the garland, and had "cold posset" and "white cakes." Those who

150

were so inclined took their cake away with them, and it was a common thing to take a piece of white cloth to wrap it up in. On Monday morning, the milkmaid that got first into each pasture (Hornsea and Southorp), received a ribbon, and was called the *Lady* or Queen of that pasture for the rest of the year; and to be first on this occasion some of them would sit up all night, and be in the pasture perhaps by three in the morning. The same day the milkmaids had a dinner at the nowtherd's, before which a fiddler with the two girls carrying the garland, and the *Ladies* of the pasture went round the town and called on each of the young women that was expected at dinner. After dinner they had a dance till milking-time. On returning from Southorp pastures, it was usual to dance for a short time on the Common, near the spot where the cart-road over it entered Lelley-lane. In the evening, there was dancing again. On Wednesday, the married people had an entertainment – in modern times, tea – and there was another dance. On Thursday, the jury had supper. On Saturday, the gaieties were at the highest, and there was a "great dance," commonly kept up late into Sunday morning. The dances took place in a barn prepared for the occasion.

So evocative of communal existence, these customs and more besides were set to disappear from the collective consciousness in the early years of the nineteenth century. The agent of change – fundamental and far-reaching change – was enclosure. But before considering the dynamics of change let us for a moment take a step back and view the agricultural geography of Hornsea on the eve of enclosure.

At the beginning of the new century the parish was still very much medieval in appearance, a mosaic of old enclosures, open field arable land and unenclosed common pastures and meadows. Although the configuration and juxtaposition of individual blocks of arable, pasture and meadow had changed over time, the basic patterning was the same as it had been in, say, the thirteenth or fourteenth centuries. For example, by the late eighteenth century a North field had been added to the existing East and West fields at Hornsea; this had been created not by taking in more land, but through the reorganisation of the existing arable. Also, blocks of pasture were intermingled with the arable. Altogether, a countryside that had evolved out of centuries of do-it-yourself enterprise. An asymmetrical and small-scale landscape of sinuous boundaries, old trees, oddly shaped copses and irregular fields, whose arrangement reflected the natural contours and vegetation.

In 1800 old enclosures, with their irregular boundaries, were scattered across the landscape in discrete blocks, held by individuals and with no communal constraints on their use: to the south of the mere; in the west of the parish; on the sites of the former hamlets of Southorpe and Northorpe; and around and to the east of Hornsea village itself. About 380 acres in total. Beyond these irregular-shaped enclosures lay the arable open fields: North, East and West fields to the north of the mere, and Southorpe fields (also sometimes known as Hither Field) to the south of the mere. About 1,150 acres in all. The arable was still farmed communally, in ridge and furrow strips, largely as it had been since the middle ages.

151

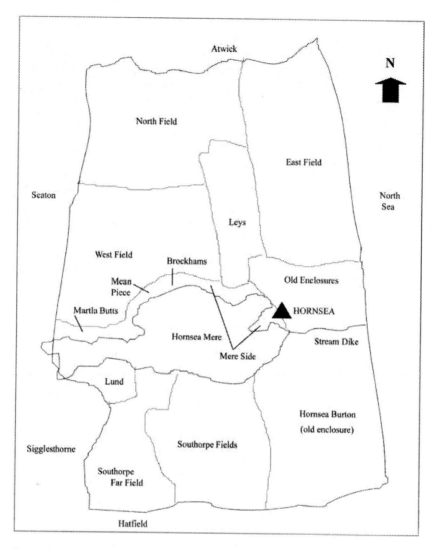

Figure 27. Hornsea on the eve of enclosure in 1809.

Parcels of common meadow and pasture were scattered about the parish: the Tetherings in West field; the Leys, lying on either side of the Atwick road, to the north of the village; between the village and the sea, three common meadows or pastures known as How Carr, Chrystals and Holmes; to the west of the village, between the West field and the mere, and adjacent to Seaton road, Brockhams, which was divided, through custom and use, into three separate parts: from east to west, Mean(y) Piece, Martla Butts, and Brockhams; Southorpe Far Field was an area of pasture that lay along the western boundary of the parish to the south of the mere; the Hold, a small pasture, lay between the old enclosures of the former Southorpe hamlet and the mere. The accumulated total of these areas was in the region of 400 acres. References to individual 'lands' in eighteenth century documents seem to imply that some of these pastures were divided between individual properties.

152

For example, in 1764 the vicar of Hornsea is recorded as having two and four-fifths horse gates in the Leys, representing a four-acre share; somewhat earlier in the same century, references to individual 'lands' in Chrystals also suggests some form of division.

Except for scrub-like alder carr fringing the mere, woodland was noticeable only by its absence. Certainly, small pockets of mixed deciduous woodland and individual trees existed, but in overall terms the landscape was devoid of such features and would have had a windswept appearance. Tree planting became a particular feature of the second half of the nineteenth century.

Finally, in the pre-enclosure parish, settlement was, with few exceptions, concentrated in Hornsea village. This is an important contrast with what was to develop later.

All this was about to change. Enclosure.[2] The process of transforming the 'paternalistic,' and what has been called the 'moral' economy of English agriculture, into a capitalistic economy. A dislocation with the past. A complete transformation of the character and complexion of the countryside, symbolising a process of centralisation and modernisation that had been ongoing in the countryside since the beginning of the eighteenth century. At a meeting on 16 August 1800 the leading landholders in Hornsea – chief among whom were Charlotte Bethell (lady of the manor), Peter Acklam, Cornwell Baron Wilson, Marmaduke Constable, Philip and Catharine Blundell, Robert Croft (vicar of Hornsea), William Whitfield, John Kirkus, Brian Taylor, Thomas Marr, and the Feofees of Hornsea church – agreed to enclose the parish for the 'public Good and the mutual Advantage of all Persons … [because] … the common Pastures, and other Common and Wastelands and Grounds in their Present state are incapable of much Improvement …' Implicit in this statement is the recognition that agricultural practices needed to become more efficient. This was a common thread that lay behind the justification for all English enclosures in the eighteenth and nineteenth centuries. There was a general belief that enclosed land was more productive than common land, and that enclosure would therefore allow productivity to be significantly increased. In the words of the agricultural writer Arthur Young (1741-1820), 'An Act of Enclosure frees the cultivator from the shackles in which he was before manacled' (1808). This meant that the

---

[2] Enclosure was the process whereby any common rights over land were abolished and the land divided between the proprietors, to be held 'in severalty' – that is, in individual ownership unfettered by communal constraints. It did not necessarily imply that the land concerned would be hedged or fenced, although in practice this was the result in the vast majority of cases. Enclosure resulted in the consolidation of landholding, reducing the multitude of small strips into a handful of compact blocks per owner. Enclosure was not new, it had occurred differentially and piecemeal across the country since at least the thirteenth century, but from the eighteenth century the extent and pace accelerated enormously. After 1700 most enclosure was achieved through a parliamentary enclosure act – a cumbersome procedure. No parliament ever initiated enclosure; the initiative came from the owners of land in a parish, and the vast majority of enclosure acts apply to one parish only. Nationally, between 1700 and the second quarter of the nineteenth century, nearly 4,000 acts were passed, enclosing more than eight million acres.

amount of food being produced would increase, thus preventing a rapidly growing population outstripping the ability of agriculture to feed them. For much of his adult life, a leading and eloquent advocate of enclosure, Young[3] is also alluding to the fact that the communal nature of the pre-enclosure system stifled innovation and experimentation; enclosure opened the way for a more balanced and rational pattern of land use and management. In the moral discourse that accompanied enclosure, improved agriculture was upheld as the very hallmark of Western civilisation. Privately owned permanent arable was considered to be not simply an alternative farming system, but an advance in the scale of civilisation. This was made clear in a parliamentary select committee report of 1795, convened to consider means of promoting enclosure:

> The idea of having Lands in Common, it has been justly remarked, is to be derived from that barbarous State of Society, when Men were Strangers to any higher Occupation than those of Hunters or Shepherds, or had only just tasted the Advantages to be reaped from the Cultivation of the Earth.

This theme resonates through the writings of many agricultural commentators. For instance, slightly later in 1835, J.C. Loudon placed open field farming just above the 'economy of savages' in a category called 'barbarian agriculture,' whilst 'the agriculture of science' (that is, enclosure) represented the pinnacle of achievement.

Patriotism also provided a powerful strand in the arguments for improvement. This linked into the threat of food shortages in the contexts of Britain's European adventures and unprecedented population growth at home. Both fuelled national anxieties over food supplies in the long-term. The very process of agricultural improvement became an act of patriotism. In 1861, for example, John Beasley, echoing the earlier thoughts of Arthur Young and others, wrote 'that man who owns or occupies an acre of land, and does not make it produce all it is capable of producing, is an enemy to his country.'

Self-interest was a further motivating force. Rising prices – caused by the French Revolutionary and Napoleonic wars and, later, the Crimean War – made the intensive cultivation of land more profitable, thus encouraging enclosure. The anticipation of higher profits also encouraged farmers to experiment with new crops, new cropping rotations and new livestock breeding methods; this could only be achieved through enclosure, whereby

---

[3] Young was exasperated by the open field system, disliked the circuitous cattle ways that petered out in the fields and pastures, hated the absence of markers and signposts, and yearned for efficient roads that would take agricultural produce to market and open up the village to the wider world. Young the improver lingered with appreciation over a fine crop of waving corn, or a well-ordered farmyard. Towards the end of his life, however, he began to doubt some of the effects of enclosure, particularly the contradictory social and economic consequences: 'I had rather all the commons in England were sunk to the sea, than the poor should in future be treated on enclosing as they have been hitherto.' By most acts of enclosure the poor had been injured, often grossly, and Young imagined the poor man saying, 'All I know is, I had a cow and Parliament took it from me.'

individual farmers had autonomy of action rather than the constraints imposed by communal practices. In short, enclosure and developments in farming practices were the manifestations of shifts in society and attitudes towards wealth and wealth creation, science, technology, progress, land ownership, and rural exclusion.

Accordingly a statement of intent to enclose was attached to the door of Hornsea parish church on three consecutive Sundays: 17, 24 and 31 August 1800:

> Hornsea intended Inclosure
>
> Notice is hereby given that Application is intended to be made to Parliament the next Session for an Act to divide, allot and inclose the open fields, ings, pastures, commons and Waste Grounds in the Township and Parish of Hornsea in the East Riding of the County of York, and for making a compensation in lieu of the Tithes thereof and of the ancient inclosed lands in the said Township
> Dated this 16th August 1800
>
> Jn Lockwood [solicitor]

The same notice of intent was also reproduced as advertisements in the *Hull Packet* and *York Courant* newspapers.

Between September 1800 and the beginning of 1801 regular meetings were held. These addressed a number of preliminary issues: the area of the town fields, the price per oxgang of compensation to be paid, the appointment of commissioners and surveyors. It was agreed that there was:

- eighty-one oxgangs of land in the North, East and West fields. Here the oxgang was calculated at sixteen acres, giving a total of around 1,304 acres;
- 400 acres of permanent pasture and meadow;
- twenty-four oxgangs in the combined Southorpe Far field and Southorpe field. The oxgang here was calculated as equivalent to twenty-four acres, giving a total of 576 acres. The larger size of the Southorpe oxgang is probably a reflection of the more easily worked nature of the land in this area – that is, more land could be ploughed with the ox/horse team per day than to the north of the mere;
- about 300 acres of old enclosure in Hornsea and Southorpe.

Consensus was also achieved on the following:

- that the amount of compensation per oxgang was to be 13s 4d;

- that the enclosure commissioners were to be John Moiser, Peter Jackson and John Lee (for details, see below);

- that the surveyors were to be Samuel Dickinson and Robert Atkinson (for details, see below);

- that the solicitors were to be John Lockwood and Robert Norris.

Even before the enclosure process was fully underway concerns were being expressed by the unpropertied poor of Hornsea – the cottagers and labourers and their families – about the potential loss of their traditional grazing rights. This social and economic class made up the largest group within the settlement (perhaps up to three-quarters of the entire 500-odd population). Among the cottagers and labourers some were craftsmen and tradesmen (blacksmiths, carpenters, cobblers, carriers and publicans) and these and others (although not all) had limited rights to graze animals and collect fuel and other resources on the nearby common pastures and wastes, a use sanctioned by custom and regulated through village by-laws. The range of common produce was in reality large and the uses to which it was put were varied. Shared landuse of commons offered many harvests. They included hazel nuts, herbs for cooking and healing (wild chervil, fennel, mint, wild thyme, marjoram, wild basil, tansy), mushrooms for soups and stews; all manner of young leaves for salads and vegetables (watercress, young hawthorn and nettle, wild sorrel, chicory, salad burnet); crab apples for cider; elderberries, blackberries, raspberries, wild strawberries, rosehips and haws and sloes for jellies, jams and wines; rabbits and hares for stews and for sale. Common rights provided turf for fires, furze, reeds and weeds for fodder and litter. They offered rushes for hats and chair seats, besoms and brooms. Fallen wood was gathered for fires, walking sticks and hurdles, for bowls and spoons. Even loose wool caught on thorn bushes could be gathered and turned into blankets and clothes. Yet, these marginal activities, which from the perspective of the twenty-first century may seem of little consequence, were important – even vital to some – not only for their produce, but also for the reality of having an area under the control of one's own immediate labour. What was being threatened by enclosure was a marginal independence on uncultivated land.

Joseph Lambert highlighted this problem of 'time-hallowed custom' in a letter he wrote, on behalf of the unpropertied, to Joseph Dickinson, one of the to-be enclosure commissioners, on 11 March 1801:

> ... I have presumed to throw some hints before thee, because thou has not been present at all the meetings with thy colleagues and because I thought perhaps thou might not have seen our joint claims which was for all geese, pigs and five sheep free in the average fields for the winter half year and the further stray of such stock as was likely for a cottager to have (say three gates or more). Also that the farmers stocked in common and could not lett any gates prior to the fields being cut and mode of culture altered.
>
> Many who have benefited by the aforesaid privilege to the amount of 30s or 40s annually, for instance some at times have only a flock of geese and a pig then again a sow and her board, sometimes two board and frequently as many as three cows, or a horse and cow or two horses.
>
> There are several of our poor neighbours who keep asses upon the backs of which they hang a sort of pannier into which they gather

stones when the tide is out the greater part of the year for paving, building and for lime, also some who keep a horse and little cart for useful purposes, the little free common with a trifle of help was summer pasturage and the winter they was of great service having had liberty also to cut grass between the lands and the furrows.

This was one of the issues that had to be resolved during the process of enclosure (see below).

Following the standard format in such matters, a petition to enclose Hornsea was presented to the House of Commons on 2 January 1801:

> To the Honourable the Commons of the United Kingdom of Great Britain and Ireland in Parliament Assembled.
>
> The humble Petition of several Proprietors of the open arable fields, meadows, pastures, common and Waste lands hereinafter mentioned.
>
> That within the township of Hornsea in the parish of Hornsea in the East Riding of the County of York there are certain open arable fields, meadows, pastures, common and waste lands which are computed to contain in the whole about two thousand five hundred acres.
>
> That the said open arable fields, meadows, pastures, common and waste lands in their present situation are capable of very little improvement, but that if the same were inclosed and specific shares thereof allotted to the several Proprietors, a considerable benefit would accrue to all the Proprietors interested therein and to the public in general.
>
> Your Petitioners therefore humbly pray that leave may be given to bring into this Honourable House a Bill for effecting the purposes above mentioned subject to such regulations as this Honourable House shall think proper.
>
> And your Petitioners in duty bound shall ever pray &c.

Charlotte Bethell, Peter Acklam, Cornwell Baron Wilson, Marmaduke Constable, and Thomas Marr signed the petition.

Leave was granted for the presentation of a bill. Locally, Richard Bethell, Marmaduke Constable, Peter Acklam, John Newsome, Samuel Frost and Benjamin Bedell were responsible for drafting the proposed legislation during the early months of 1801. Thereafter, the parliamentary process unfolded rapidly and without opposition. The Bill was presented to the House of Commons on Friday 8 May 1801 and received its second reading on Tuesday 12 May; this was followed by the Committee stage on Monday 1 June; on Friday 11 June it went through the third reading and was passed the same day. On Monday 15 June the Bill was presented to the House of Lords, had a second reading the next day, and went through the Committee stage on Wednesday 24 June. The Royal Assent was granted on Saturday 27 June.

The act was entitled:

> An Act for Dividing, allotting, and inclosing, the Open Arable Fields, Meadows, Pastures, Common and Waste Lands, within the Township of Hornsea, in the Parish of Hornsea, in the East Riding of the County of York; and for making a Compensation in lieu of the Tithes thereof, and of ancient inclosed Lands in the same Township.

The preamble to the act stated, in standard formulaic terms, the rationale for the enclosure of Hornsea:

> … And whereas the Lands of the several Proprietors in the said Open Arable Fields, Meadows, and Pastures lie intermixed and dispersed in small Parcels, and the same, as also the said Common and Waste Lands, are in their present state capable of very little (if any) Improvement, and are in general so situated as to render the Cultivation thereof inconvenient and expensive: And although it would be of great Advantage to the said Proprietors and Persons interested, and an improvement of their Property, that the same Open Arable Fields, Meadows, Pastures, Common and Waste Lands, should be divided and inclosed, and specific Shares thereof allotted to the several Persons interested therein …

Essentially the act consisted of a detailed set of rules that were to be followed during the enclosure process. Enclosure commissioners (that is, individuals tasked with ensuring that the process was carried out in accordance with the legislation) and a surveyor were named, their powers specified and their duties listed in considerable detail. A detailed survey was made with a plan of the area to be enclosed. All those owning land and/or common rights submitted written claims to the commissioners, who reviewed the evidence and then accepted, modified or rejected the claims. Then began the physical transformation. New roads and watercourses were laid out and plots of land were awarded to the parish for the digging and quarrying of road-making materials. Instead of the old scattered strip-holdings and common land, landholders were awarded plots of land equal in value to their former strips and common rights. The lord of the manor (in Hornsea's case, the lady of the manor) was awarded extra land in lieu of manorial rights, and sometimes land was awarded to the church and the lay tithe owner in lieu of tithes. Enclosure was expensive and all costs had to be borne by the community involved. Proportionality was the guiding principle – that is, the costs incurred by an individual were in direct relation to the size of that individual's new holding. As the Hornsea act stated:

> That the Owners of the said Open Lands and Grounds hereby directed to be divided and inclosed, and also the Owners of the ancient inclosed Lands herein-before mentioned, shall pay his, her, or their Shares of all the Charges and Expenses preparatory to or

attending the obtaining and passing of this Act, and of surveying and valuing the said ancient inclosed Lands, and settling the Compensation for the Tythes thereof, and surveying, valuing, dividing and allotting the said Lands and Grounds hereby directed to be divided and inclosed, and of setting out, forming, and making the said public Roads, Drains, and Watering Places for Cattle, and of preparing and inrolling the said Award of the said Commissioners, and all other reasonable Expenses and Charges of the said Commissioners and Surveyors, and other proper and necessary Expenses in the Execution of this Act, from Time to Time as the same shall respectively accrue, to such Person or Persons, and in such Proportions and in such Manner, and at such Time or Times, either before or after the Execution of the said Award, as the said Commissioners shall direct or appoint ...

And be it further enacted, That all and every Person and Persons entitled to any of the Allotments to be set out in pursuance of this Act, shall, and they are hereby required, within the Time to be appointed by the said Commissioners, at his, her, or their Charges respectively, to inclose and fence his, her, or their several Allotments in such Manner and Form as shall be ordered and directed by the said Commissioners.

Finally, the commissioners prepared the enclosure award and large-scale plan. These documents provided a detailed written summary and cartographic record of the new layout, giving the locations, acreages and ownership of each plot, the courses of new roads, footpaths and drains, and directions of hedging and fencing and the efficient maintenance of drainage. Together, the award and plan provided the permanent legal record of the enclosure.

As agreed at the preliminary, pre-parliamentary stage, the Hornsea act reaffirmed John Moiser of Huntington near York, Peter Jackson of Riston Grange, Leven, and John Lee of Enholmes (Patrington) and Leconfield Parks, as commissioners to oversee the enclosure process. However before work commenced Moiser withdrew (for unknown reasons; perhaps the travelling distance between York and Hornsea was too great), and was replaced by the Quaker Joseph Dickinson (1746-1823) of Beverley. All three men were experienced in this type of work: during the course of his working life, Dickinson oversaw as many as forty-six East Riding enclosures (active 1766-1817), Lee worked on six (active 1801-29), and Jackson on four (active 1801-20). They also worked on enclosures in adjoining counties. The joint surveyors were Samuel Dickinson (born c.1770; son of the above Joseph Dickinson; also, like his father, a Quaker) of Walkington near Beverley and Robert Atkinson (1771-1814) of Catwick, just a few miles inland from Hornsea. Like the commissioners, both surveyors were experienced in this type of work: Dickinson was responsible for fifteen East Riding enclosure plans (active 1794-1814), and Atkinson for ten (active 1771-1814). The social status ascribed to all was that of 'gentleman'. In essence they made a (not inconsiderable) living from this work, carpet-bagging their services from one enclosure to the next.

Once the act entered the statute books the commissioners could begin their work. The following notice was appended to the door of the parish church on 2 August 1801, and was inserted in the *York Courant* on 3 and 10 August:

> Notice is hereby given that the Commissioners appointed for carrying into Execution an Act of Parliament lately passed entitled "An Act for dividing, allotting and inclosing the Open Arable Fields, Meadows, Pastures, Common and Waste Lands within the Township of Hornsea in the Parish of Hornsea in the East Riding of the County of York and for making a compensation in lieu of the tithes thereof and of Ancient Inclosed Lands in the same Township" do intend to hold their first meeting under the said Act at the House of John Hudson, Innholder, in Hornsea on Wednesday the 19th Instant at 10 o'clock in the Forenoon when and where all persons having or claiming any Estate, Property, Tithes, Ecclesiastical Dues, Right, Title or interest within the Township of Hornsea aforesaid are required by themselves or their Agents to deliver a true and particular account in Writing of their respective Estates and Claims. And at the same meeting it is intended to appoint some Banker or other person with whom the Monies to be received under the said Act shall be deposited for the purposes and according to the directions of the same Act.
>
> And Notice is hereby further given, That the Commissioners will meet at the place aforesaid on Thursday 20th Instant at 8 o'clock in the morning to perambulate the Boundaries of the said Township of Hornsea.
>
> By Order
> John Lockwood
> Robert Norris
> Solicitors

This notice marked the start of the process of change on the ground.

The commissioners held their first meeting on 19 August 1801. Between that date and April 1802 they met on fourteen occasions, extending over twenty-two days.

At the first meeting the commissioners and surveyors took the oath prescribed by the act, prior to starting work on the enclosure:

> I ... do swear (or being one of the People called Quakers, do affirm) That I will faithfully, impartially and honestly, according to the best of my Skill and Judgement, execute and perform the several Powers, Trusts, and Authorities reposed in me as a Commissioner, by virtue of *An Act for dividing, allotting, and inclosing the Open Arable Fields, Meadows, Pastures, Common and Waste Lands, within the*

160

Township of Hornsea, *in the Parish of* Hornsea, *in the East Riding of
the County of* York; *and for making a Compensation in lieu of the
Tithes thereof, and of ancient inclosed Lands in the same Township*,
without Favour or Affection, Prejudice or Malice, to any Person or
Persons whomsoever.

So help me God …

Date	Location	Agenda
19-20 August 1801	New Inn, Hornsea	Receive claims Perambulate the township boundaries
10 September 1801	New Inn, Hornsea	Receive claims
9 October 1801	Tiger Inn, Beverley	Hear objections to claims
2-4 November 1801	New Inn, Hornsea	Hear evidence for and against 'such claims as have been objected to'
19-21 November 1801	New Inn, Hornsea	As above
14-15 December 1801	New Inn, Hornsea	As above
19 December 1801	Tiger Inn, Beverley	Valuation
26 December 1801	Tiger Inn, Beverley	Commissioners signed the list of claims allowed and 'specified such of the objected ones as they proposed to allow and disallow'
5-6 January 1802	Tiger Inn, Beverley	Disallowed claims specified
25-26 January 1802	Tiger Inn, Beverley	As above
30 January 1802	Tiger Inn, Beverley	? (No details available)
3 February 1802	Tiger Inn, Beverley	? (No details available)
10 April 1802	Tiger Inn, Beverley	The claim of William Foster disallowed; ordered to quit the premises he occupied by 12 April 1802
29 April 1802	New Inn, Hornsea	Formal conclusion to proceedings

Table 8. Meetings of the Hornsea enclosure commissioners.

The minutes of this first meeting are of interest:

Be it remembered that at this meeting many of the Proprietors
delivered in their Claims to the Commissioners.

Be it remembered that at this meeting the Proprietors present
unanimously appointed Sir Christopher Sykes Baronet and Robert
Carlile Broadley Esq., Bankers in Beverley, as proper persons in
whose hands the Money to be raised and received under and by
virtue of the Powers of the said Act during the progress of the said
intended Division and Inclosure shall from time to time as often as

161

the same shall amount to the sum of £50 be paid and deposited pursuant to the directions of the said Act.

Be it remembered that the Boundaries of the said Township were perambulated, ascertained and fixed and that the same were staked and marked accordingly except as to that part of Southorpe Pasture in the said Township which adjoins to Land in the Township of Goxhill belonging to Marmaduke Constable Esq.

Enclosure was a potentially disruptive process. In order to safeguard agricultural production in the interim, the meeting also registered the following requirement:

Ordered that the Course of Husbandry to be used in and upon the land and ground by the said Act directed to be divided and inclosed as well with respect to the laying down ploughing following and tilling thereof as the stocking and eating the fallows or stubbles from henceforth until our further Order in that behalf shall be the same as hath heretofore been used and accustomed in the said Township before the passing of the said Act. And that no person or persons shall cut dig take gather or carry away any Underwood, Thorns, Whins, Sods, or Turves in upon or from any part of the open fields, meadows, pastures, common and waste lands intended to be divided and inclosed without our Consent.

This and the second meeting (10 September 1801) were devoted to the receiving of written claims. In all, eighty-four claims, with supporting evidence (no longer surviving), were submitted. The September meeting also concluded unfinished business: 'At this Meeting the Boundary of that part of Southorpe Pasture which adjoins Lands in Goxhill belonging to Marmaduke Constable Esq was staked and marked out.' Whatever the problem – presumably uncertainty over the actual course of the parish boundary on the ground – it had been resolved.

Subsequently an itemised listing of all claims (name of claimant, number of messuages, number of cottages, amount of old enclosure, amount of land in the Leys, number of oxgangs in the open fields, and number of oxgangs in Southorpe Field) was attached to the parish church door.

On 19 September the commissioners ordered that the following notice be inserted in the *Hull Packet* and *York Courant* (21 and 22 September):

Notice is hereby given that a List of Claims is left at the House of John Hudson Innholder in Hornsea for the Inspection of Proprietors and Persons interested and that the Commissioners will hold their next meeting at the Tiger Inn in Beverley on Friday the 9th day of October next to receive any objections in writing to any of such Claims.

What is of particular interest here is the location of the meeting: the Tiger Inn in Beverley, fifteen miles to the west of Hornsea. Why this venue was used is not known. Possibly it was a mechanism for dissuading objections.

At the 9 October meeting the following written objection was received:

> We whose names are herewith subscribed, being respectively Proprietors or Agents of Proprietors of Lands and Tenements at Hornsea in the East Riding of the County of York do severally object to the respective Claims of the several Persons claiming right of Common Stray Average or Pasturage in the open and unenclosed arable fields Meadows Pastures Common and Waste Lands within the township of Hornsea in the Parish of Hornsea in the said Riding (the right of Common in a place called the Mere side only excepted) for or on account of their respective Messuages or Cottages or Sites of Messuages or Cottages or other Hereditaments meaning or purporting to be Messuages or Sites of Messuages or Cottages in Hornsea aforesaid Because the rights so claimed in the said open and unenclosed fields Meadows Pastures Common and Waste Lands (except as aforesaid) are not appurtenant to the said respective Messuages or Cottages or Sites of Messuages or Cottages or other Hereditaments And Because none of such persons are entitled to such Claim by immemorial and uninterrupted Usage or otherwise.

Given under our hands this 9th day of October 1801

Samuel Frost
Jacob Bingham
William Gray
John Galloway
Joseph Wilson

Notwithstanding the protests, the commissioners summarily extinguished common rights. The apologists for enclosure trotted out the argument that continuing to allow free access to natural resources would result in economic disaster, that common usage was inefficient. What the enclosers meant, of course, was economic disaster for them. This was an ideological fiction. The extinguishing of common rights was enshrined in the legal framework that grew up to legitimise the seizure of the commons. The basic assumption was that common rights were 'granted' by some theoretical landowners in the past, and could therefore be just as arbitrarily withdrawn. Just what state of affairs existed before that moment was kept deliberately vague, the landowners seemingly coming into possession of their estates with the mysterious abruptness of Adam's inheritance of Eden. This legal myth made the law not an arbitrator, but an instrument of appropriation. As E.P. Thompson wrote, 'the law pretended that, somewhere in the year dot, the commons were granted by benevolent Saxon or Norman landowners, so that uses were less of a right than by grace … it guarded against the danger that use-rights might be seen as inherent in the users.' (*Customs in Common*, 1990, pp.160-61).

The enclosure process was essentially concluded by 20 March 1802. On that date the commissioners issued the following document, which was pinned to the door of the parish church on the following day:

> We the Commissioners named in an Act of Parliament passed the last session intitled "An Act for dividing, allotting and inclosing the open arable fields, Meadows, Pastures, Commons and Waste Lands within the township of Hornsea, in the parish of Hornsea, in the East Riding of the County of York; and for making a Compensation in lieu of the Tythes thereof, and of ancient inclosed land in the same Township" do hereby and direct that all manner of Tythes and all right of Common and right of Pasturage and average in and upon or payable in respect or arising out of the lands and grounds within the Township of Hornsea aforesaid shall cease, determine and be forever extinguished from the 12th day of April next.
>
> And we do hereby also order that the several persons for whom allotments have been staked out by us in the Township of Hornsea aforesaid shall accept the same, that the allotments in the Pastures, Commons and Waste Lands shall and may be entered upon immediately and ploughed, cultivated and managed as the persons interested therein may think proper and that the allotments in the open fields shall be subject to an offgoing Crop to the respective occupier thereof but that the owners thereof subject thereto shall have liberty and they are thereby authorised to sow Grass Seeds amongst the Corn.
>
> And we do also hereby further order that the fences and ditches of the allotments staked out as aforesaid shall be made in such manner and form as the Surveyors under the said Act have directed in the notice given to the several persons interested therein.
>
> Given under our Hands this 20th day of March 1802
>
> > Joseph Dickinson
> > P. Jackson
> > Jn. Lee

By April 1802 the commissioners had allotted 2,243 acres of land, which included:

- 409 acres in the East Field
- c.240 acres in the North Field
- c.153 acres in the West field
- c.100 acres in the Leys
- 34 acres in Mereside
- 24 acres in Holmes
- 23 acres in Chrystals
- 9 acres in How carr

- 351 acres in the Southorpe Fields
- 94 acres in Southorpe Far Field
- 111 acres in Southorpe Field and Southorpe Pasture.

Altogether sixty-five individuals received land:

Acreages	No. of individuals
< 100 acres	8
50-99 acres	6
20-49 acres	5
10-19 acres	12
10 > acres	32

Table 9. Allocation of land at enclosure.

The largest single allotments were: 340 acres to Philip and Catharine Blundell, owners of the rectorial tithes; 241 acres to Charlotte Bethell, lady of the manor; 215 acres to Marmaduke Constable; 130 acres to Brian Taylor; 110 acres to John Kirkus; 104 acres to Peter Acklam; 103 acres to William Whitfield; 100 acres to Cornwell Wilson; and 68 acres to the vicar. As such 1,401 acres (62.46% of the total allotted) went to just ten individuals. These new holdings were not always awarded as consolidated blocks; sometimes they were distributed around the former common arable and pasture. For example, Charlotte Bethell had parcels of land in the former North field, in the former Southorpe fields, Southorpe Far Field, the Lund, and in the Holmes. Peter Acklam's land was distributed between the former West field, East field, the Leys, and Mereside. On the other hand Philip and Catharine Blundell had their award as a compact block in the former West and North fields. The remaining acreage – 842 acres (just 37.54% of the total area enclosed) – was allotted to fifty-five individuals. These smaller owners of land – having less than 20 acres each – tended to have all their holdings as one discrete block. The smallest award, just twenty square perches (605yds²), went to Thomas Myass, described as a 'yeoman of Hornsea.'

A marked contrast in the size and shape of the allotments along the cliff top compared with those further inland is apparent on the enclosure plan, which shows many long, narrow, east-west aligned strips of land 'extruding from the cliff edge,' allotted to many different owners. This arrangement was a characteristic feature in the enclosure of many Holderness coastal parishes. Presumably this was due to the importance of access to the beach for fishing and for the collection of cobbles and sand for building purposes, although coastal erosion and a wish to share the problem equitably may also have been a consideration. All this land has since been lost to the sea.

The award made provision for a twenty square perch common watering place at Mereside, to the south of the Seaton road. A further two acres between the mere and Southgate, named as Fair Place, was allotted to be held in trust by Richard Bethell, son of Charlotte, as a 'pasture and watering place and for use as a fair ground for the sale of beasts.' On the coast a one-acre plot between the beach and Sea Road was reserved as a common landing ground for boats.

The reorganisation of the parish infrastructure was also addressed in the enclosure award. The existing roads and rights of way were not appropriate for access to the new holdings. A network of new public and private roads and public footpaths came into being. The public roads were:

- Hull Road, leading from Lelley Lane, the continuation of Southgate across the old Southorpe Field, to the boundary with Rolston parish;
- Beverley Road, also known as Seaton Road, leading from the west end of Hornsea village, towards Seaton village and onwards to Beverley;
- Bewholme Road (or Lane), leading north from the Beverley road over the old West and North fields to the Atwick parish boundary;
- Bridlington Road, also known as Atwick Road, leading north from the village over the Leys and the North field to Atwick, Skipsea and onwards to Bridlington;
- Sea Road, a short direct route from the east end of Eastgate (Hornsea village) to the coast.

In addition, two bridle roads were to be laid out: Cliff Road, to be used as a 'private carriage road,' was to run from the north end of Newbegin to the Atwick parish boundary; the other, Fair Road, from the junction of Newbegin and Southgate at the market place, was to run westwards and then northwards to the Fair Ground. The purpose of this thoroughfare was to enable drovers and their beasts to have good access to and from the Fair Ground on market days.

The award stipulated that all the above roads were to be forty feet in width, staked, ditched and bounded out. This was to be the responsibility of all those whose land bordered the routeways.

A further public road, this time twenty feet in width, was laid out from Fair Road to the Hull road beyond the Stream Dike. This route followed the eastern margin of the mere. Three 'private roads' connected the fair ground with Beverley Road, Market Place and with Southorpe Field.

Six public footpaths were also laid out:

- From the south end of Cliff Road to the beach;
- Eastwards from Southgate through Football Green and then northwards to Cliff Lane;
- From the Beverley road to the parish boundary with Seaton;
- Three linked routes to the south of the mere: from the Hull road through Southorpe Field to the boundary with Rolston parish; beside the mere to the Wassand parish boundary; and southwards to the boundary with Goxhill parish.

After enclosure, all the land became private property, that is, not subject to communal use. As the act emphasised:

> That it shall be lawful for the Persons interested in the said Lands and Grounds hereby directed to be divided and inclosed, immediately after the Allotments shall be staked out by, or by the Order of, the said Commissioners, at any Time before the Execution of their Award herein mentioned, by and with the Consent of the

166

Commissioners, to ditch out their several Allotments, and with Quickwood or otherwise, to fence the same in such Manner, and at such Time or Times as the said Commissioners shall think proper, and for that purpose direct; and in case such Ditches, Quicksets, or Fences shall afterwards be wilfully damaged, hurt, or destroyed, or any Crops standing or growing on such Allotments shall be in anywise injured by any Person or Persons whomsoever, the Person or Persons committing the Fact, is and are hereby declared Trespassers, and shall be liable from Time to Time to answer Damages in respect thereof, in like Manner as Damages are recoverable in Actions of Trespass, by the Laws now in being, for Injuries done to Lands.

Even so, and although the land was now in private ownership and could be farmed according to choices made by the individual owner, initial restrictions on land use were imposed by the commissioners. For instance, it was ordered that:

No Sheep or Lambs shall be depastured or kept in any of the said intended Inclosures during the Space of Ten Years from the Execution of the Award of the said Commissioners, unless the Persons respectively depasturing or keeping Sheep or Lambs, do, at their own Expence, effectually guard and fence the young Quickset Hedges on every Side of the Allotment or Allotments in which Sheep or Lambs shall be depastured or kept as aforesaid, so as to prevent any Damage or Injury being done to such Quickset Hedges, or to their Neighbours Crops, by any Sheep or Lambs …

The penalty for infringement was also stipulated:

… if any Person or Persons shall, during such Space of Ten Years, depasture or keep any Sheep or Lambs in any of the said intended Inclosures, unless he, she, or they shall and do at his, her, or their own Expence, so guard and fence as aforesaid, such Person or Persons shall, for every such Offence of which he, she, or they shall be convicted before any One of His Majesty's Justices of the Peace for the East Riding of the County of York (not interested in the Matter in Question), on the Oath or Affirmation of One or more credible Witness or Witnesses, which Oath or Affirmation the said Justice is hereby empowered to administer, forfeit and pay such Penalty or Penalties, Sum or Sums of Money from Time to Time (not exceeding at any One Time the sum of Twenty Pounds) as he the said Justice shall think just and reasonable, to be levied by Distress and Sale of the Goods and Chattels of the Person or Persons so offending, by virtue of a Warrant under the Hand and Seal of such Justice, at any Time within Six Calendar Months next after such Offence committed, rendering the Overplus (if any) on Demand, after deducting the reasonable Charges of such Conviction, Warrant, Distress, and Sale, to the Person or Persons whose Goods and Chattels shall be distrained and sold as aforesaid, which Penalty or Penalties, Sum or Sums of Money, when so recovered, shall be paid to the Person or Persons whose Quickset Hedges or Fences, or Crops, shall be damaged or injured by any such Sheep or Lambs.

The Hornsea enclosure act was passed in 1801. At the beginning of the process the proprietors envisaged that all allotments should be made by 1 January 1802. They were actually set out by 20 March of that year. However, the award was not signed until 1809, fully seven years later. Whilst no Hornsea-specific reasons can be put forward to account for this delay, Jan Crowther, in writing more generally on this question, has suggested the following:

> Since all that remained after the allotments had been made was the drafting of the award and the settling of accounts, the attorney or clerk to the enclosure looks a likely culprit, possibly exaggerating the legal niceties to increase his profit. This was certainly a contemporary view: in 1844 it was alleged in evidence to a Select Committee on Inclosure that 'wherever attorneys have been employed they have increased the disputes for the purposes of keeping the matter in hand'. The degree of inconvenience experienced as a result of delays is difficult to assess. In his evidence to the 1844 Select Committee William Blamire, a tithe commissioner, said that there were:
>
> > Many cases of very great loss and inconvenience resulting from the non-execution of awards; parties acquire no title to their land by the mere direction of an inclosure commissioner to enclose and enjoy in severalty; a party having received that authority has no legal title until the award is regularly executed.

Enclosure, then, substituted smaller, hedged and fenced, individually owned fields in place of the very large open fields and commons. It abolished common rights and all communal regulation of farming. Private initiative and private decision-making and control replaced communal decision-making and control. A society that had formerly worked by co-operation was replaced by one in which the individual owner mattered more than the community. And, the power of the large landowner increased dramatically after enclosure.

During the period c.1740-1850 parish after parish in the East Riding was transformed by enclosure.[4] As enclosure abolished the old working systems associated with open field agriculture, the landscape took on a radically new appearance and meaning. Running along and across the grain of the land, hundreds of miles of new roads and drains were constructed, and thousands of miles of new hedges planted. These features had first been planned on the surveyor's drawing board with pen and ruler before their courses were staked out over the countryside itself. Planned in this way,

---

[4] Locally, Hornsea was very late in enclosing. Of the adjacent parishes, Goxhill was enclosed between 1650-85, Seaton in 1657, Bewholme, in 1740, Atwick in 1772, Sigglesthorne in 1781, and Leven in 1796. Only Rolston was later (1860). Wassand was enclosed at an unknown date.

enclosure is ruled by a sense of linear – in the most literal sense – enclosed space: the new roads within each parish tended to be straight, running between parallel hedges; and the new hedges were straight, with right-angled corners, enclosing square- or rectangular-shaped fields. When seen on a map, there is a marked and immediate contrast between these newly created roads and fields and the much older winding lanes and irregular-shaped closes, paddocks and fields. At enclosure some of the pre-existing roads and lanes ceased to be used, their rutted surfaces added to the newly laid out fields. Even the word 'field' began to change its meaning: before enclosure it normally referred to the huge acreages of open arable land sub-divided into hundreds of un-hedged strips; after enclosure 'field' came to mean, as it does today, a distinct hedged or fenced space of limited size. A uniform and geometric landscape came into being.

These revolutionary transformations changed more than the physical appearance of the countryside. The very fabric of society was altered. In particular, social and economic relations between – and within – the community changed: a new class of farmer came into existence, as did a new class of wage labourer (that is, people who sold their time and skills for a money payment). Co-operation and mutual assistance, both major features of the old system, became a thing of the past. And, as hinted at above, property relations changed: the concept of private property became widespread and entrenched.

The loss of common rights, the rise of the wage labourer, the redefinition of property rights ... Enclosure was symptomatic of a much wider process that was ongoing during the first half of the nineteenth century, whereby an older tradition of radicalism based on an appeal to customary rights gave way to organised political agitation which reflected popular acceptance of social and economic change and a growing consciousness among working people of their class identity, an awareness among workers that their interests were different from, and in tension with, those of the employing and propertied classes. In other words, it was out of processes such as enclosure that the working classes were forged.

The wholesale reorganisation of the landscape brought about by enclosure is, perhaps, nowhere better seen than in the establishment of new farmsteads. Where each farmer's land had previously been scattered amongst the open fields, pasture and meadow, enclosure resulted in the creation of compact farms. For the first time since prehistory each farmer now had all his land at one point in the landscape. Discrete units of production. In many cases the opportunity was taken to relocate from the village and construct new farmhouses and ranges of functional buildings within the boundaries of the new holdings. Farms in the modern sense of the word. In the process hundreds of new farmsteads were created across the face of the landscape, giving the countryside a much more lived in and dynamic appearance. Scattered at intervals across the landscape, tight clusters of buildings at the centre of their fiefdoms. The movement away from existing centres of population brought about – for the first time – the construction of purpose-built, co-ordinated ranges of farm buildings. Prior to enclosure, these had been built, rebuilt and added to in an *ad hoc* manner, sometimes with a construction history extending back over many centuries. Following enclosure, farm design,

169

involving the deliberate arrangement of buildings in a regular and convenient layout (in order to facilitate an integrated flow of processes around the farmyard), became commonplace, aided by the proliferation of pattern books, such as Daniel Garrett's *Designs for Farm Houses etc for the Counties of Yorkshire, Northumberland, Cumberland and the Bishoprick* [sic] *of Durham* (1747), P.F. Robinson's *Designs for Farm Buildings* (1837), G.A. Dean's *On the Construction of Farm Buildings* (1844), or the essays that regularly appeared across the pages of the *Journal of the Royal Agricultural Society of England* throughout the nineteenth century. In East Yorkshire, as in many other areas of England, the new farmsteads were, more often than not, constructed around a central square- or rectangular-shaped foldyard, with adjoining barns, stables, cattle sheds and granaries. The entire complex was in many cases surrounded by a distinctive shelterbelt, planted to protect the inhabitants and buildings from extreme weather conditions.

Following enclosure at Hornsea twenty-five farms came into being. This figure raises some interesting points. First, size of holdings. In tabulated form the holdings break down into the following:

Size (acres)	No. of holdings	Combined acreage	% of holdings	% of total acreage
1-20	5	71	20.00	2.88
21-50	2	88	8.00	3.56
51-100	9	680	36.00	27.51
101-150	5	685	20.00	27.71
151-200	2	388	8.00	15.69
200 +	2	560	8.00	22.65
Totals	**25**	**2472**	**100.00**	**100.00**

Table 10. Size of holdings after enclosure.

Bedell provides details of the agricultural arrangement at Hornsea following enclosure. Of crops and cropping he writes:

> The common course of crops, except on the small quantity of light land, is – after a bare summer fallow, wheat with seeds (clover, &c) to be eaten, or rarely, mown, the next year or two years – then wheat again, followed by oats or beans, and again bare fallow. The substitution of a green fallow for the unprofitable dead fallow is increasing with the increased growth of turnips, which used never to be attempted on the clay; the same cause is producing an increase of the practice of stall-feeding, and the use of linseed cake may be considered as increasing.

> The average production of wheat throughout the parish per acre, may perhaps be stated at about three quarters; the quality in general equal to the average of Yorkshire wheat, or perhaps rather above it, the grains having a clear, fresh-coloured, thin skin – average weight, about 62lb per bushel.

From 1866, with the appearance of the Board of Agriculture's annual agricultural census returns (known as the June Returns), the first systematic collection of such data, it is possible to provide a more rounded picture of the parish's agrarian system. Space precludes a detailed year-on-year analysis, but the return for 1870, for instance, gives this snapshot:

Cropping		
Crop	Acreage	% of total area
Wheat	362	12.56
Barley	308	10.68
Oats	340½	11.79
Beans	65	2.25
Peas	112	3.88
Potatoes	10	0.36
Turnips	570	19.77
Mangolds	63½	2.18
Carrots	5	0.17
Rape	59	2.05
Sugar beet	4	0.15
Total	**1899**	**65.85**
Grassland	985	34.15
Total	**2884**	**100.00**

Table 11. 1870 cropping return for Hornsea.

Stocking	
Livestock	Number
Horses (agricultural)	159
Cows of all ages in milk or calf	231
Cattle:	
< 2 years	162
> 2 years	230
Sheep	1378
Lambs < 1 year	840
Pigs	362
Total agricultural livestock	**3362**

Table 12. 1870 stocking return for Hornsea.

171

Twenty-seven years later, at the height of the great agricultural depression that blighted the English countryside at the tail end of the century, the following data is provided in the annual return:

Cropping		
Crop	**Acreage**	**% of total area**
Wheat	309	10.71
Barley	284	9.85
Oats	290	10.06
Beans	60	2.08
Peas	72	2.50
Potatoes	7	0.24
Turnips	589	20.42
Mangolds	38	1.32
Carrots	8	0.28
Rape	34	1.18
Sugar beet	1	0.03
Total	**1692**	**58.67**
Grassland	1192	41.33
Total	**2884**	**100.00**

Table 13. 1897 cropping return for Hornsea.

Stocking	
Livestock	**Number**
Horses (agricultural)	135
Cows of all ages in milk or calf	259
Cattle: < 2 years	153
> 2 years	261
Sheep	1498
Lambs < 1 year	975
Pigs	392
Total agricultural livestock	**3673**

Table 14. 1897 stocking return for Hornsea.

A comparison of the 1870 and 1897 figures is instructive. Whilst the total productive acreage stayed constant, the amount of grassland increased from 985 acres to 1192 acres, from 34.15% to 41.33% of the cropped area. With it, livestock numbers also grew, from a total of 3362 to 3673. This reflects the greater emphasis placed on the rearing of livestock during the agricultural depression: essentially, whilst also depressed, market prices for livestock remained higher than those for cereals. The changing emphasis can also be seen in the number of working horses present in the parish, from 159 to 135: as arable cultivation decreased, fewer horses were needed to work the land. Fodder crops also increased, whilst the acreage under cereals showed a corresponding reduction. In 1870 wheat, barley and oats accounted for 1010½ acres, or 35.03% of the total area under crops. In 1897, this had reduced to 883 acres, or 30.62% of the overall arable area.

172

The early years of the nineteenth century saw the slow adoption of machinery:

> Within the last two or three years a few wheel ploughs and patent harrows have been introduced, and there is one of Crosskill's patent clod-crushers in the parish, the owner of which (Mr G. Whiting) has also other improved implements. There are two fixed thrashing machines, but most of the thrashing is done by a portable machine, one of which is kept in the parish and let out by the day. Thrashing by the flail is nearly out of use. The [seed] drill is now much used, but a good deal of wheat is yet sown broadcast.

As the century progressed, agricultural machinery became more commonplace. The following is a list of equipment at Trinity House Farm, Hornsea Burton, in 1894, and is fairly typical of what would be found on local farms at the time: 2 wagons, 2 heavy carts, 1 water cart, 1 13-spouted corn drill, 1 3-row press drill, 1 manure drill, 1 6ft Massey Harris binder, 1 grass reaper, 2 Cambridge rollers, 3 JHB iron ploughs, 3 iron scrufflers, 2 sets of iron harrows, 1 turnip cutter, and gear for 6 working horses.

Bedell had this to say about agricultural wages in the years around 1848:

> The labourers here and throughout the East Riding appear to be better off, both in regard to habitations and wages, than those that are heard of in many parts of England. Wages, 2s a day in winter, and 2s 6d in summer, without meat – and with meat, *about* 7s a week in winter, 9s from May-day to Midsummer, and 10s thence to Martinmas. Servants in the house – A foreman, about £25; second man, about £17; £10 or £12 to young men.

In 1874 wage rates for agricultural servants, that is, those who were hired annually and receiving board and lodging as part of their wage, in the Hornsea area were:

> Young foremen £25; experienced foremen £30; young waggoners £18; experienced waggoners £20; strong plough boys from £13 to £15; young maid-of-all-work £9 to £12; housemaids £12 to £14.

At the same time, agricultural labourers were earning 15s per week, rising to around 18s during the harvest period.

By the 1890s agricultural wage rates were roughly the same as twenty years before, reflecting the severe and prolonged downturn in the fortunes of farming during the last decades of the nineteenth century.

A commercialising economy

At the beginning of the nineteenth century agriculture was the staple activity. In 1801 just under 84% of the economically active population were involved in agriculture, either as direct producers (79%) or in related service

173

industries, such as milling, rope making, the manufacture and repair of implements, and the like. Old village crafts had yet to be displaced by the mass produced goods that became ubiquitous in the later part of the century.

New levels of economic specialisation and diversity were taking place during the nineteenth century. Hornsea's economic growth during this time was part of the general transformation of the western world that created an unprecedented level of economic activity and widespread prosperity. Essentially, the process was driven by market forces and was international in character. Increasing personal affluence created increasing demand for goods and services, which, in turn, stimulated the supply of new and improved commodities, as well as extending the network of trade across much of the world. Western Europe, particularly Britain, played a prominent role in this process and many of its manifestations can be seen in the economic history of Hornsea.

Hornsea's changing economic base can be illustrated with three sets of 'moment-in-time' statistics, collected from the census returns of 1801, 1851 and 1891. As a percentage of the economically active population, these figures fully demonstrate the change from an essentially rural – village – community to an urban centre.

Economic activity	1801	1851	1891
Crafts	8.60%	23.75%	28.33%
Domestic servants	1.58%	10.20%	15.13%
Trades	3.90%	14.50%	16.84%
Agricultural workers	72.50%	23.14%	7.82%
Services	1.77%	8.90%	11.75%
Labourers	3.82%	6.33%	4.60%
Professions	0.68%	4.62%	5.91%
Inn-keepers	0.99%	2.15%	2.80%
Independent	1.26%	3.54%	4.26%
Farmers	4.90%	2.00%	1.30%
Clerical workers	-	0.87%	1.26%

Table 15. The changing economic character of Hornsea, 1801-91.

Over the course of the nineteenth century, economic activity increased both in scale and range. In the 1820s there were forty businesses in Hornsea, offering a limited range of goods and services. By the 1890s, when the place was recognisably a town, this had grown to 123, a rise of 307.50%. The following table and graph chart the change in detail:

Economic activity	1823	1840	1848	1867	1879	1892	1901
Architects	-	-	-	-	-	-	1
Attorneys	-	-	-	1	1	3	2
Auctioneers	-	-	-	-	2	1	1
Bakers and confectioners	4	1	1	4	1	3	8
Banks	1	1	1	1	1	3	2
Blacksmiths and farriers	-	3	2	3	3	3	1

174

Boot and shoe makers	6	4	5	7	7	9	6
Brewers and maltsters	-	-	1	-	-	-	-
Bricklayers and plasterers	5	3	1	5	7	4	5
Brickmakers	1	1	-	2	2	1	1
Butchers	4	4	5	4	3	5	4
Carpenters	-	-	4	-	3	3	2
Cattle dealers	-	-	-	1	1	1	1
Corn and coal merchants	-	-	-	-	3	8	3
Corn millers	-	-	-	-	-	1	1
Druggists/chemists	1	2	2	3	4	2	2
Fire and insurance agents	-	-	-	-	1	11	2
Fishmongers	-	-	-	1	1	1	2
Flour dealers	-	-	-	-	-	-	1
Furniture dealers	-	-	-	-	-	-	1
Glass, china and earthenware dealers	-	-	-	-	1	-	-
Greengrocers	-	-	-	1	2	3	-
Grocers and tea dealers	3	10	5	-	3	7	6
Hairdressers	1	1	1	1	1	2	1
Hatters	-	-	1	-	-	-	-
Horse dealers	-	-	-	1	-	-	-
Hosiers and glovers	1	-	-	-	-	-	-
Inn and tavern keepers	3	5	5	6	5	6	7
Ironmongers and hardware dealers	-	-	-	-	2	4	2
Land surveyors	-	-	-	-	-	1	1
Linen and woolen drapers	-	-	1	2	2	6	5
Machine makers	-	-	1	2	2	2	1
Milk dealers	-	-	-	-	-	2	2
Milliners	-	4	-	-	2	14	4
Newsagents	-	-	-	-	-	1	2
Photographers	-	-	-	-	-	-	1
Plumbers, glaziers and painters	2	2	2	2	3	3	3
Rope and twine spinners	1	-	1	-	-	-	-
Saddlers and collar makers	1	2	2	1	1	1	1
Shopkeepers	-	-	-	-	4	1	6
Spirit and wine merchants	-	-	2	2	2	2	2
Stone and marble masons	-	-	-	-	1	1	1
Straw hat manufacturers	-	3	-	-	1	-	-
Surgeons	-	2	-	2	3	2	3
Tailors	2	3	6	4	3	3	2
Timber merchants	-	-	-	1	1	1	1
Tinners and braziers	-	-	1	2	-	-	2
Watch and clock makers	1	1	1	1	3	2	3
Wheelwrights	3	4	-	-	2	-	1
Total	40	56	51	60	84	123	103

Table 16. Nineteenth century economic activity in Hornsea.

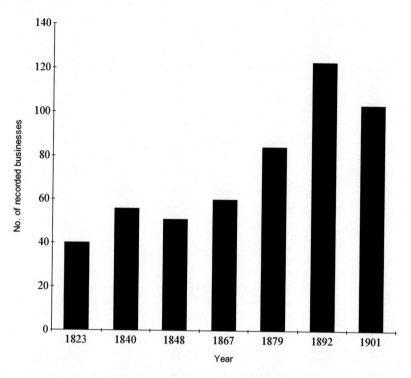

Figure 28. The commercialising economy of Hornsea, 1823-1901.

All the above figures clearly show the shifting economic complexion of Hornsea across the nineteenth century. Up to the 1850s, the place was still a recognisably agricultural settlement set in a deeply rural landscape. In 1801 over 70% of the economically active earned a living from agriculture, as either yearly-employed farm servants or weekly-paid farm labourers. By 1851 this group was in decline; and during the second half of the nineteenth century primary agriculturalists declined further, to under 10% of the overall employed population. Craftsmen accounted for 8.60% of the employed in 1801, mostly deriving their livelihoods from agriculturally related activities, such as blacksmithing and rope making. As the century progressed, craft activities became an important sector of the town's economy. As a group, they also became more diverse, and included tailors, shoemakers, dressmakers and watch and clock makers, serving the needs of the town and those living in the surrounding parishes. In a world of horse-drawn vehicles, blacksmiths, saddlers and wheelwrights featured prominently. Throughout the century, for example, there were up to three blacksmiths, two saddlers and four wheelwrights at any one time. Craftsmen, many selling their products directly to the customer, outnumbered tradesmen: in 1801, 8.60% of those employed were craftsmen, only 3.90% tradesmen; by 1891 these were 28.33% and 16.84% respectively.

In 1801 the most common retailers were butchers, grocers, bakers and confectioners. As the century progressed, more specialized retailers began to make their appearance: greengrocers, fishmongers, wine and spirit merchants, tea dealers, milkmen, coalmen, newsagents. From the 1870s and 1880s shops were increasingly taking over from markets in the sale of perishable goods. For instance, from the late 1860s through to 1901, Hornsea had between four and eight bakers and confectioners, between three and seven grocers and tea dealers, up to five butchers, and up to six general shopkeepers. Also, the expanding volume, variety and cheapness of mass-produced factory goods curtailed the work of some craftsmen-retailers, and increased the sales of those tradesmen who were just shopkeepers. By the 1880s more and more factory-made boots, shoes, clothes and watches were being sold, and new types of shops were making their appearance in Hornsea, reflecting the widening range of goods available and the new tastes of prosperous consumers. Towards the end of the century, with a population of around 2,300, Hornsea had six boot and shoe shops (plus three boot and shoe makers), a newsagent, furniture dealer, photographer, two watch and clock retailers, and six linen and woollen drapers.

The growing complexity and sophistication of Hornsea, with its rising population, can be seen in the wide range of professional services that were located in the town. The growth of resident professionals is a reflection of the changing nature of the settlement through time: in 1801 just 0.68% of the economically active population fell into this category, by 1851 it was 4.62%, and by 1891 it had risen to 5.91%. Apart from the Anglican and nonconformist clergy, there were various teachers, solicitors, medical practitioners, bankers, auctioneers, insurance agents, even an architect. These professional services, an important feature of urban life, were valued not only by the townsfolk themselves but by those country visitors who had legal business to pursue, an insurance policy to arrange, the valuation or sale of property to consider, or perhaps medical problems to deal with.

Although relatively few in number, a small proportion of the total employed population, the professionals were an essential part of the function of the town. As educated people, able to take on many roles, their influence far outweighed their numbers. Also, it needs to be remembered that many other professionals lived in the town but did not work in the place, commuting to Hull on a daily basis.

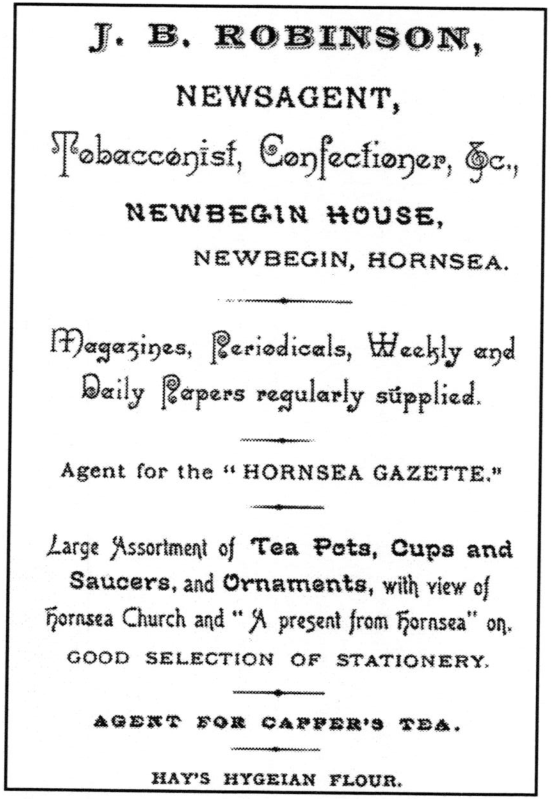

Poulton's Artistic Photographs.

This celebrated series, comprises views of all places of interest in the

UNITED KINGDOM.

They are supplied unmounted, mounted as Opalines, Medallions, Letterweights, and a variety of other artistic designs, most suitable for presents.

A Large Assortment of these Photographs are on sale at all the principal Stationers and Fancy Dealers.

VIEWS OF HORNSEA & DISTRICT

may be obtained from

COOK LAKING,

Stationer, &c., NEWBEGIN, HORNSEA

J. B. ROBINSON,

NEWSAGENT,

Tobacconist, Confectioner, &c.,

NEWBEGIN HOUSE,

NEWBEGIN, HORNSEA.

Magazines, Periodicals, Weekly and Daily Papers regularly supplied.

Agent for the "HORNSEA GAZETTE."

Large Assortment of **Tea Pots, Cups and Saucers, and Ornaments,** with view of Hornsea Church and "A present from Hornsea" on.

GOOD SELECTION OF STATIONERY.

AGENT FOR CAFFER'S TEA.

HAY'S HYGEIAN FLOUR.

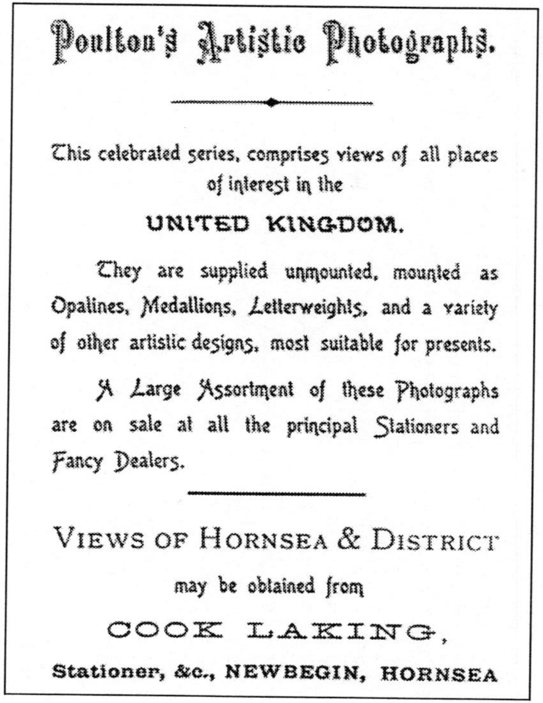

Figure 29. Later nineteenth century advertisements for local shops. (Illustrations: Stephen Harrison collection)

At the beginning of the nineteenth century Hornsea's commercial district was concentrated almost exclusively in Market Place, with many shops occupying the ground floors of otherwise residential accommodation. By the time Bedell wrote his history of Hornsea in 1848, the central shopping zone had extended along Newbegin. From his descriptions it is possible to conclude that a variety of shops and other businesses had opened on both sides of the road, from around the church to the vicinity of the present-day Co-Op supermarket.

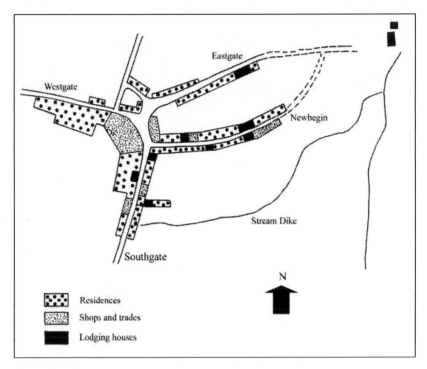

Figure 30. The morphology of Hornsea in 1848. (Compiled from textual information contained in E.W. Bedell (1848), *An Account of Hornsea, in Holderness, in the East Riding of Yorkshire*)

As the town developed during the second half of the century, the number and distribution of shops had increased. By 1900 shops extended all the way along Newbegin to its junction with New Road, and along the southern part of Cliff Road. Shops were also located along Southgate, around its junction with Market Place. In addition, corner shops had sprung up in outlying locations, in the newly-developed residential areas outside the historic core, serving the everyday needs of residents in those areas. Wherever they were situated, most of the shops were small-scale, with frontages of between 12ft and 15ft, and usually converted from two or three storey houses. Shops and residential housing sat side by side, unlike, say, the Promenade in Bridlington or Middle Street South in Driffield, which were almost entirely given over to commercial activity.

Plate 33. 118-128 Newbegin: shops, some with late nineteenth century frontages, converted from eighteenth century residential cottages. (Photograph: Stephen Harrison)

Carrier service

Prior to the coming of the railway, Hornsea was connected to the wider world by carriers. The centrality of the village carrier cannot be overstated. They – usually men, but, occasionally, older women – were generally based in villages and provided important services to local communities: they transported goods from country producers to towns; conveyed fare-paying passengers between destinations, particularly on market days; and acted as shopping agents for villagers. In his 1876 novel *Cripps, the Carrier: a Woodland Tale*, R.D. Blackmore's fictional carrier Zachary Cripps provides an illustration of this activity. At the market he had 'a great host of commissions' to execute for his numerous contacts in the outlying villages he served. He had dealings with 'farmers, butchers, poulterers, hucksters, chandlers and grocers' and the villagers on whose behalf he traded knew that he would 'spend their money quite as gingerly as his own.'

Carriers supplied village shops, bringing stock from the markets and transporting goods which arrived by rail. In these respects, they provided a crucial link with markets, and were key figures in the widening gap between consumer and producer, a gap particularly marked as the importation of foodstuffs grew in importance from the 1870s onwards. Because of the frequency of carrier services, the output of town factories could be sent quickly and cheaply to country districts, contributing to the decline in rural crafts.

Overall, for the villages and hamlets, carrier services provided a most important link with the outside world. They began to decline with the gradual introduction of rural bus services after the First World War. There were, however, a few carriers still operating until the middle of the twentieth century.

180

The number of carriers as listed in the Hornsea trade directory entries remained fairly constant during the course of the nineteenth century, at between two and seven. The number of places served also remained steady, at between two and six. The frequency of services per week also remained constant, except in the 1820s and again in the 1870s and 1880s, when there was a dramatic increase. In both periods, the number of services more than doubled. No explanation has been found for the rise in the 1820s, but the later increase may be associated with the railway and the development of Driffield, some fifteen miles to the north-west, as a regional market centre.

Date	No. of carriers	No. of places served per week	No. of services per week
1823	4	2	12
1840	3	2	5
1867	2	2	3
1879	7	6	11
1892	3	2	5
1901	3	2	5

Table 17. Carrier services to and from Hornsea, 1823-1901.

Up to the 1860s, the carriers looked southwards, connecting Hornsea to the market centres of Beverley and Hull. Throughout the century, the number of services to Hull was the greatest of all the routes travelled. But in the 1870s and 1880s there was a noticeable increase in both the number of carriers and the places served. The geographical spread also extended and was directed to the north of the town, connecting it with the villages of Skipsea and Beeford, and the market town of Driffield. The services to the villages are not easily explained, except in so far as Rose Carr – perhaps Hornsea's most famous carrier – had family connections in Beeford; and Skipsea was on the way to Beeford. At this time Driffield was expanding as a market centre and would be a natural focus for communities in northern Holderness. The rise in services may also be associated with the railway. This appears somewhat paradoxical. Carrier services were not, as might be expected, impeded by the development of the rail network. In fact, the railway provided opportunities for the carrier system to develop, taking goods and people to and from the railway stations. Towards the end of the century, the number of Hornsea carriers diminished, with services to Beverley and Hull only.

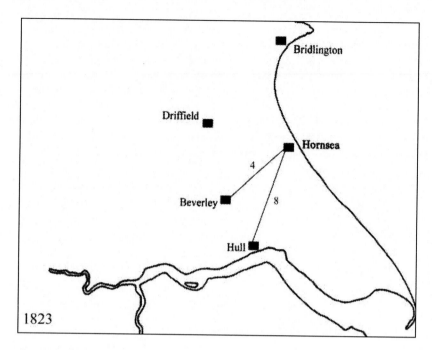

Figure 31. The Hornsea carrier service, 1823.

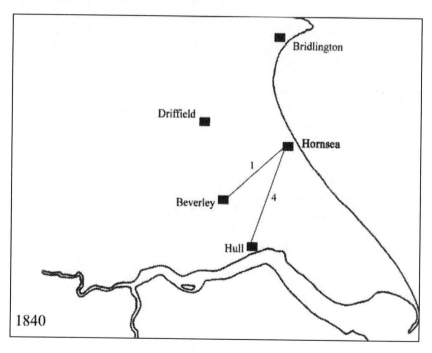

Figure 32. The Hornsea carrier service, 1840.

182

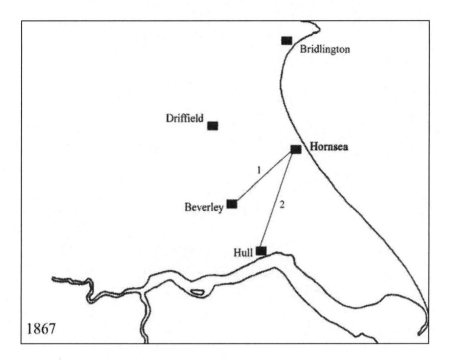

Figure 33. The Hornsea carrier service, 1867.

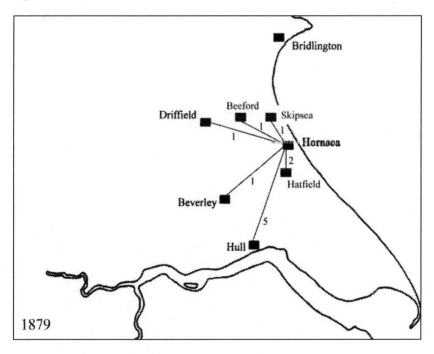

Figure 34. The Hornsea carrier service, 1879.

183

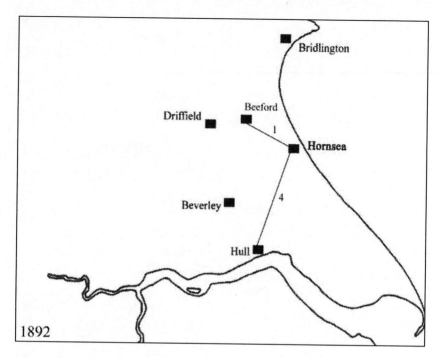

Figure 35. The Hornsea carrier service, 1892.

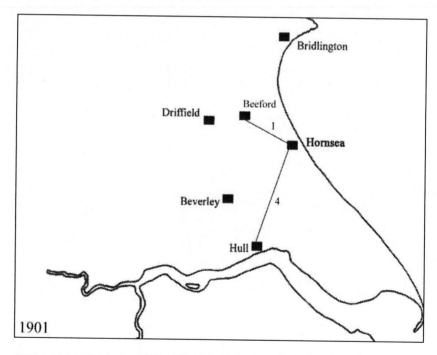

Figure 36. The Hornsea carrier service, 1901.

184

An analysis of the daily frequency of carrier services shows that, as would be expected, most activity took place on market days in Beverley, Driffield and Hull. This reflected the proliferation of shops in these towns and their growing importance as general retail centres for a wide geographical area, as well as a gradual change in the shopping habits of country people. The services on market days indicate an increasing dependence by rural areas upon local centres, a deepening connection between town and country.

Date	Mon	Tues	Wed	Thurs	Fri	Satur	Sun
1823	-	4	-	-	4	4	-
1840	-	2	-	-	1	2	-
1867	-	1	-	-	1	1	-
1879	1	5	-	1	3	1	-
1892	-	3	-	-	2	-	-
1901	-	3	-	-	2	-	-

Table 18. Daily frequency of carrier services to and from Hornsea, 1823-1901.

By the 1920s and 1930s carrier services had decreased dramatically, and by the late 1940s and early 1950s they were a thing of the past, replaced by rural bus services and an increase in motorcar ownership.

Place of polite resort

The built environment everywhere gives a powerful sense of materiality to the idea of history. It invites us to see history not as a simple and straightforward chronological gallop through time, from this point to that point, but rather topographically, a multi-layered reality in which the physical layout of the original settlement – the fields beneath the streets – shapes patterns of subsequent occupancy. It makes us more alert to changes in the idea of public space, to consumer revolutions, to human ecology, and to the competing housing needs of different classes. It preserves the visual evidence of past states of being.

Let us now explore these multi-dimensional meanings as they affected Hornsea during a century of transformation.

A view of Hornsea in the middle years of the nineteenth century – before the coming of the railway – confirms that, though a reasonably prosperous settlement, the place barely extended beyond its medieval bounds, and still presented an overwhelmingly rural aspect. The properties are densely clustered in the market place area, which retained (and even today still has) a medieval sense of enclosure – this in spite of being built over many times. The majority of dwellings – predominantly cottages, but with the occasional house to vary the roofline – were largely of late seventeenth or eighteenth century construction, reflecting - as it did almost everywhere – a major episode of rebuilding during those years. In some cases residential accommodation of an earlier age actually lay encased behind later, more modern (and therefore more aesthetically acceptable) facades. Although of 1860 the scene depicted in this watercolour could be of any date in the first six decades of the century, before the consolidation of Hornsea's position as a seaside and urban centre.

Physically, at least, Hornsea at the beginning of the nineteenth century – indeed, up to the coming of the railway in 1864 – must have resembled many of the present-day nearby villages – Atwick or Skipsea, for example.

Plate 34. A British 'rural idyll'? A prospect of Hornsea in 1860, looking north from the Hull road: sheep and cows graze by the mere, with its fringe of trees and rushes, in high summer; a combination of industry and repose, of realism and idealism. This aesthetically pleasing, 'homely' image clearly reflects the dominant rural idiom favoured by so many painters of the Romantic school (c.1830-70): an intimate portrayal of an English place, a slow-paced, misty, hidden Arcadia lost in the meadows of Little England. (Photograph: Hornsea Museum; from a painting by John Lewis Roberts. Reproduced by courtesy of Stuart Walker))

Between 1801 and 1901 Hornsea's housing stock grew from 133 to 623 properties, a five-fold increase. Physical growth was not steady across the period, but characterised by uneven development. Within this framework, however, the expansion of the built environment was not *ad hoc*: the regulation of space and the uses to which it was put became an increasingly dominant imperative as the century progressed.

Four phases of development can be identified:

1. A steady but unspectacular growth in the first three decades of the century.

2. Slower growth during the 1850s, probably a consequence of the failure of the proposed rail link with Hull to materialise.

3. A most striking increase between c.1860-70, which was triggered by the opening of the railway in 1864, bringing in its wake a period of renewed building activity, establishing Hornsea as a seaside resort on a modest

though reasonably prosperous scale. The coming of the railway also entrenched Hornsea's position as a dormitory town for Hull businessmen and their families. The *Spectator* of 27 September 1873 described the town as '… little more than a marine suburb of Hull.' Outward growth was characterised by piecemeal development, the construction of new roads and houses being determined at any one moment by the nature and sequence of plots coming onto the market for building.

4. After sluggish development in the 1880s, the following decade witnessed another period of sustained growth, which lasted into the twentieth century, and was consequential on further in-migration from, principally, Hull. Piecemeal outward growth is also a characteristic of this phase of development.

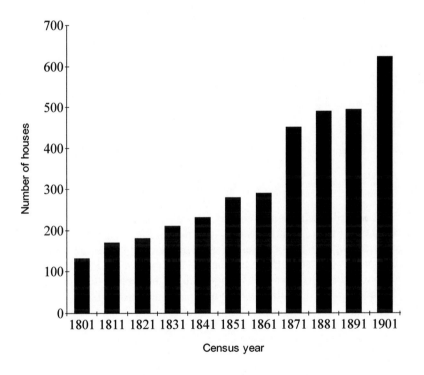

Figure 37. The rate of house building in Hornsea, 1801-1901.

187

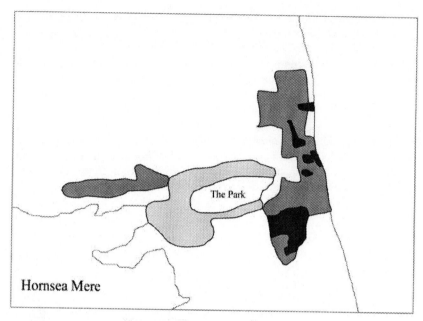

The growth of Hornsea: pre-modern to c.1900

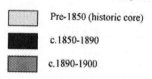

Pre-1850 (historic core)

c.1850-1890

c.1890-1900

Figure 38. The growth of Hornsea: pre-modern to c.1900.

The earlier nineteenth century is characterised by two types of development. Firstly, infilling within the existing street pattern. This was characterised by the construction of small brick-built houses and cottages, much of which was speculative building and lacking unity in design. In the main, tradesmen (often combining workplace on the ground floor with living space above) and the labouring classes occupied these properties.

Examples of infilling include:

- 52 (The Nook) Southgate.

- The vicarage on Newbegin, built in 1831-32 to designs by George Jackson and David Thorpe. This replaced – more or less on the same site – the earlier vicarage as described in the previous chapter. The more evident class-consciousness of the vicar is seen in the new style of vicarage, separated from his parishioners by a cobbled wall and, unlike the previous house, set some way back from the street frontage. A symbolic and physical separation grounded in the new values and sensibilities of a new century and age.

188

- The present Pike and Heron public house on the west side of Market Place, which dates to about the same time as the new vicarage.

- Swiss Terrace, 90-100 Newbegin, built c.1840 by George Goodwin, a Hull merchant, and so-named because of their Swiss-chalet architectural style.

Whilst the general picture for the earlier part of the century is one of infilling and an increasingly overcrowded population upon the central plots around Market Place, Hornsea also acquired some sizeable properties on the roads leading away from the historic core: Eastgate, Southgate, Westgate, and Newbegin. These new developments were initially piecemeal and consisted, in the main, of large detached houses situated in their own grounds. Interestingly, many were built by or for Hull businessmen, beginning a trend that was to intensify as the nineteenth century progressed.

Perhaps the earliest of these substantial houses was Holme Lea (also known as the Lair and Burnside) in Eastgate, originally built around 1800 by William Conway of Hornsea. This property has an interesting structural history. It was enlarged sometime shortly after 1806 by William Whitehead, also of Hornsea, who then sold it to William Gibson, a Hull shipbuilder, in 1819; between then and 1859 it was largely rebuilt by Edward Gibson, William's son; and towards the end of the nineteenth century it was re-fronted. The house still survives, in a prominent position next to the Cottage Hospital. Also of c.1800 is Marine Villa, 102 Newbegin, Hornsea's first seaside villa, built for Thomas Collinson of Hull.

Slightly later, in 1845-46, Hornsea House, later known as The Hall, was built on Eastgate for John Wade (d.1850), to designs by the architect Charles Hutchinson of Hull. The house was later occupied by Wade's son Joseph, who substantially enlarged the property. In the later nineteenth century, Hornsea House, set within six acres of landscaped grounds and well-maintained gardens and screened from public view of a curtain of trees, was the most imposing residence in the town. Following Joseph's death in 1896, the house was bought the following year by Christopher Pickering, a prosperous Hull trawler owner and fish merchant, for £6,000. Today, only the later nineteenth century entrance lodges remain; the house itself was demolished to make way for Hornsea secondary school in the 1950s.

189

Plate 35. Hornsea House in the later nineteenth century. The central block was built in 1845-46 for Hull merchant John Wade. Later, his son, Joseph, almost doubled the size of the property, adding wings and servant accommodation. (Photograph: Stephen Harrison collection)

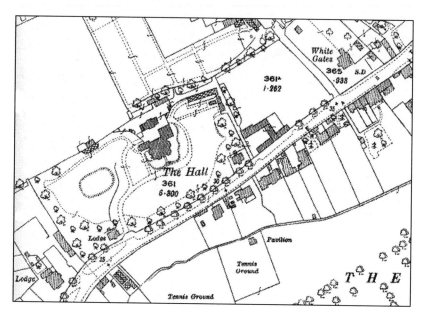

Figure 39. Hornsea House and grounds, Eastgate. (Ordnance Survey 1:2500 map extract, Sheet 197.3, published 1927. Reproduced by courtesy of the Ordnance Survey)

Plate 36. The later nineteenth century gatekeeper's lodge on Eastgate, standing guard over the western entrance to Hornsea House. A highly ornate and public display of wealth and privilege. (Photograph: Stephen Harrison)

By the mid-1840s, apart from limited development on the coast, the built-up area was still largely confined to the historic core. In 1847 Bedell could still write:

> There are three principal streets, one of them skirting the east end of the mere in a semicircular form, and called in different parts of it Westgate, Market-Place, and Southgate … The streets called Newbegin and Eastgate branch from the neighbourhood of the Market-Place towards the sea, uniting about 200 yards before reaching the cliff. There are houses on each side of Newbegin for the first two or three hundred yards, and a few houses in Eastgate, the remainder of the ground between the town and the sea being occupied by arable and pasture closes, over the last two of which there is a pleasant footpath from Newbegin (or Cliff-road) to the sea.

One event is of crucial importance in understanding the development of Hornsea in the second half of the nineteenth century: the opening of the railway in 1864 was the catalyst which triggered a sustained period of urban development that lasted into the early decades of the twentieth century. The impact of railways on the development of seaside resorts in general was noted by the *Times* in August 1860:

> A new town arises on the beach. Marine Terrace, Sea Villas, Prospect Lodges, Belle Vues, hotels, baths, libraries and churches soon accumulate until at length the old borough is completely hidden and can perhaps only be reached by an omnibus.

191

This statement is so true when one looks at the development of Hornsea after the coming of the railway.

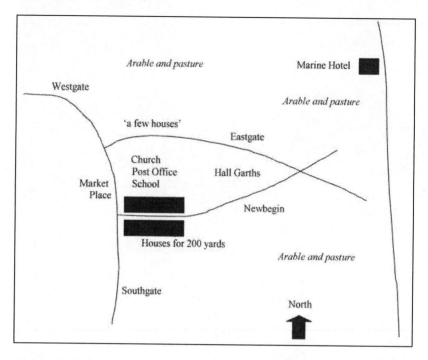

Figure 40. Schematic reconstruction of Hornsea in 1848. (Compiled from textual information contained in E.W. Bedell (1848), *An Account of Hornsea, in Holderness, in the East Riding of Yorkshire*)

In this context it is important to emphasise that the arrival of the railway did not just result in the creation of Hornsea as a holiday destination; it also provided the trigger for the birth of a dormitory town. As early as 1880 it was commented that: 'Since the construction of the railroad from Kingston upon Hull the town has much increased and many persons of business now reside here.' Arguably the development of Hornsea as a dormitory town for Hull was of far greater significance than its function as a seaside resort. It must be remembered that from the mid-nineteenth century to the First World War mass recreation was largely confined to day excursions and outings on Sundays and other national holidays. It was not until after the Second World War that all workers received paid holidays. The improvement in communications between Hornsea and Hull is clearly reflected in the growth of the permanent population. In the pre-railway phase, between 1801 and 1851, the population increased from 533 to 945; by 1901 it had grown to 2,381. The first signs of major population expansion can be detected in the 1871 census, just seven years after the opening of the railway: in the decade 1861-71 the resident population increased by 36.9%, from 1,063 to 1,685. And all of this is reflected in the built environment.

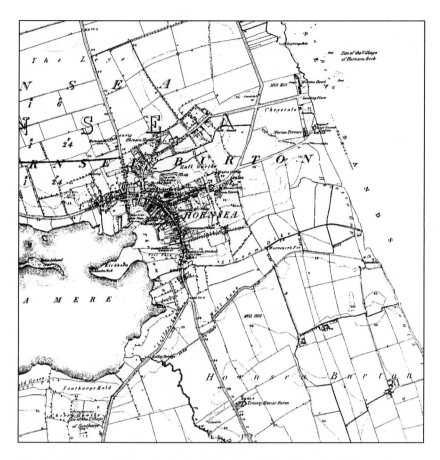

Figure 41. Hornsea in the mid-nineteenth century (Extract from the Ordnance Survey 1:10,560 map Sheet 197; surveyed 1852, published 1854). The old village nucleus is still intact with, as yet, no signs of the extension of building lines out to the coast, despite the presence of the New Road. Only two isolated areas of development can be seen at the coast: Marine Terrace, a block of lodging houses, and the sophisticated Marine Hotel. Hornsea in the pre-railway era is still an agricultural village, but the seeds of change have already been sown.

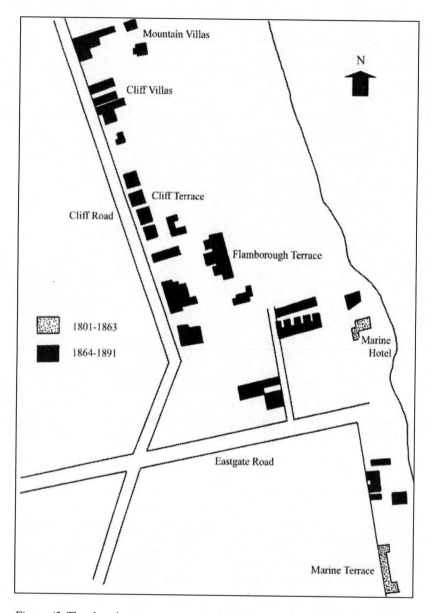

Figure 42. The changing townscape: coastal development before and after the coming of the railway in 1864. (Adapted from Barker, *Hornsea: A Study of a Coastal Town*)

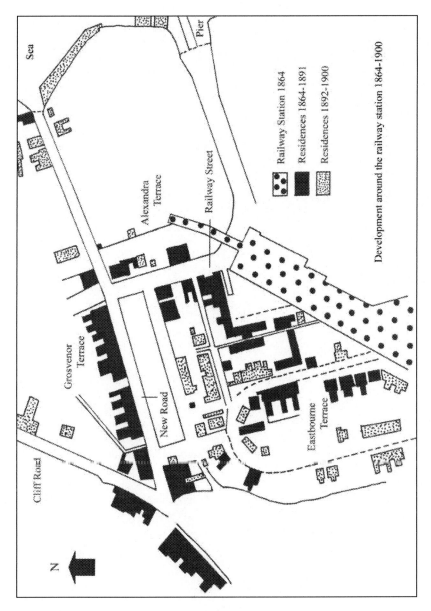

Figure 43. Development around the railway station, 1864-1900. (Adapted from Barker, *Hornsea: A Study of a Coastal Town*)

195

Later Victorian architecture, heavy with the certainties of the age, is still a powerful presence within the town. The urban villa of the nineteenth century, the 'ornamental' villa as it was sometimes called in the builders' copy-books, was a site for historical fantasy. The revolt against what was thought of as the monotony of the Georgian terrace, and the belief that houses should reflect individual tastes, produced a riot of styles, eclectic mixtures of period architecture. Deliberately variegated: some are stylistically early English, others Italian, Gothic or of Chalet type.

Between 1864 and the early 1890s development in Hornsea was concentrated in two areas: around the railway station and New Road, and northwards between Cliff Road and the coast. Bracing sites with good sea views. In both areas several landowners were responsible for laying out new roads and building plots, but many people (usually jobbing builders and speculators), particularly from Hull, were involved in the actual construction of houses.

A broad-based chronology of the developments can be reconstructed:

In 1865 Hull shoemakers Samuel and Thomas Haller bought a ten-acre site on the south side of New Road, which was later to become known as the Grosvenor (or Oval) estate. Here the following properties were built between 1865 and the mid-1870s:

- 4-12 New Road.

- Eastbourne Terrace (8-16 Eastbourne Road).

Until the 1880s development of the Grosvenor estate was slow. In 1881 Alfred Maw of Hull took over the remaining empty plots. Relative inaction followed until 1886. In that year Maw conveyed the site to Hull builder John Emerson, who began a programme of infilling on around ninety still-vacant plots. Perhaps the most notable buildings attributable to Emerson are 18-32 Eastbourne Road, four pairs of three-storey semi-detached houses.

In 1866-68 Hornsea entrepreneur Joseph Armytage Wade purchased a fifty-acre block of land adjoining New Road and southwards along the coast to Stream Dyke. On this narrow strip of land he had constructed:

- 1867: the Alexandra Hotel. 1868: Wilton Terrace.

- 1869: Alexandra Terrace (1-4 Railway Street).

- 1860s-70s: Grosvenor Terrace.

- 1882: Albert Villa (also known as Brampton House), Railway Street.

Plate 37. The Alexandra Hotel, Railway Street. A symmetrical two storey, five bay building in grey brick with round-arched windows to either side of the entrance and outer bay windows. Originally, the building had three storeys plus attics. Built alongside the railway station, the Alexandra was Hornsea's principal hotel. (Photograph: Stephen Harrison)

All told, by about 1890 around seventy houses had been erected on Wade's land.

Also in 1866-68 William Jackson of Hull bought a seventeen-acre plot along Cliff Road, which became known as the Lansdowne estate. Here, apart from Cliff Road itself, the first streets to be laid out were Flamborough Terrace Road (later part of the Esplanade) and Hartley Street, which date to the late 1860s and early 1870s. The most notable houses built at this time include:

- Cliff Villas.

- Carlton Terrace.

- Flamborough Terrace.

- Headland View.

The Lansdowne estate also attracted a number of other builders:

- Elim Lodge, Cliff Road, built by Thomas Keyworth of Hull in 1871.

- Mountain Villa, also on Cliff Road, built by Hull tanner Thomas B. Holmes in the 1880s.

- Cliff Terrace, also by Holmes, dating to the 1880s-90s.

By 1890 this area contained about forty houses.

Plate 38. Brampton House, Railway Street, probably to designs by R.G. Smith: a tall, three storey, three-bay villa in grey brick, with an elaborate stone doorcase; originally, the house had a balustraded parapet. This imposing property was built for John Hunt, a Hull music-hall proprietor, as his permanent residence. (Photographs: Stephen Harrison)

198

Plate 39. Cliff Road. (Photograph: Stephen Harrison)

In 1875 Pierre Henri Martin du Gillon of Sheffield bought fifty-nine acres of land adjoining the cliff edge at Hornsea Burton, then spatially separated from Hornsea proper by arable land and pasture. Inextricably linked to his scheme for the construction of a pleasure pier and commercial harbour (see below), du Gillon had ambitious plans for developing a South Cliff estate here – effectively, a new town complete with church and shops, a place of polite resort, which could be construed as challenging the role of Hornsea proper as a seaside destination. It was to be a further two years before the scheme was publicly unveiled. As the *Hornsea Gazette* reported on 24 March 1877:

> In addition to the laying out of the estate, Mr du Gillon has undertaken to enclose and form a public garden or recreation ground, on the principle of the Spa at Scarborough; and also to erect sea defences of a very substantial character, along the entire frontage of the property. It is intended to apply an area of about 4½ acres, with a frontage to the sea of 400 yards, to the purposes of the public garden; within which, and on the slope of the cliff overlooking the sea, it is intended to erect two blocks of buildings, one to be fitted up as an aquarium, and the other will comprise baths, reading and refreshment rooms. In front of each of the buildings there will be a terrace, covered by a large veranda, and at a higher level than the top of the sea wall, so that in all states of the weather visitors will be enabled to enjoy the sea breeze without any discomfort. The enclosure to be laid out with walks, and planted with shrubs. A band pavilion, ornamental lodges at the entrance gates; and rustic seats placed beside the walks and in other suitable positions. Flights of stone steps will give access to the sands at convenient intervals. A concrete sea wall will extend along the front of the public gardens, which are further to be protected by timber groynes. A concrete breastwork, with groynes, along the rest of the frontage of the estate will afford complete protection from the sea.

An idea of the extent of the proposed work will be best conveyed by mentioning that the estate as laid out will furnish sites for about 500 houses; of which about 100, viz., those on the esplanade, will be first-class residences. Sites are provided for a church, an hotel, and other buildings. There will be upwards of 2¼ miles of roads, mostly 50 feet wide, and the whole estate will be efficiently drained. The sea wall will, along its entire length, form an agreeable marine promenade; and walks are to be formed on the side of the cliff, giving access to the esplanade on the top.

It is interesting to note in passing that this proposal bears a striking similarity to entrepreneur Anthony Bannister's 1854 scheme for a new seaside town further down the coast at Withernsea. Here, with the help of architect Cuthbert Brodrick, an existing coastal village was to be transformed into a pleasure resort through the laying out of a gridded road system, the building of sea walls, promenades, hotels, and socially graded terraced housing; all, like du Gillon's plans, focused on a pier.

The South Cliff Estate did not see the light of day: du Gillon abandoned the scheme when his dream of building a pier collapsed in 1879. Likewise, the scheme at Withernsea, although partially successful in making the transition from paper to bricks and mortar and concrete, did not, in the end, live up to expectations.

During the last decades of the nineteenth century several new streets were laid out at the coast: Victoria Avenue, near the Marine Hotel; Carlton Avenue; Carrington Avenue; Clifford Street; and Belvedere Park. Of this time architecturally noteworthy houses include 59-69 Eastgate, 4-14 Esplanade, and 1-8 Victoria Avenue.

Throughout the later years of Victoria's reign infilling continued within the historic core of Hornsea and new buildings expanded the fringes of the town to north, south and west, into what today we would call green belt areas. Notable examples include:

- 1862-74: Bank Terrace, Mill Lane, off Rolston Road.

- About 1865: terraced cottages known as Ocean Terrace and Welbourne Terrace, to the rear of Southgate.

- About 1865: Westgate House, Westgate.

- About 1866: 26-28 Westgate (formerly Firbank House).

- 1868: Suffolk Terrace on Seaton Road.

- 1878-79: the first three houses in Northumberland Avenue, off Leys Lane.

- Late 1870s: Ventnor House in Westgate (27 Westgate; now known as Grebe House).

- 1890-1900: terraces of smaller houses constructed in Mill Lane, Mount Pleasant and Eastgate View.

- 1895: St Bede's College, Atwick Road.

- About 1900: a long terrace of small houses built in Marlborough Avenue, off Rolston Road.

Houses built during the second half of the nineteenth century are characterised by considerable variety of style, size and materials. They range from small cottages to large villas; stand singly or in pairs, short rows or long terraces; and are constructed from red, yellow, white or pink brick. Considerable numbers have brick or wood bay windows to ground and first floors, and some have attics or full second floors. A small number of properties have towers or pinnacles. Others have stone dressings or are faced with decorative tiles. Decorative brick- and woodwork is a distinctive feature of the more substantial properties.

It was not all new building. As well as the construction of new houses, some existing dwellings were remodelled during the century, reflecting changing tastes and the concept of modernity. A good example is the present 65 and 66 Southgate. Now two houses, it was originally built as one dwelling in the late seventeenth or early eighteenth century. During the mid-nineteenth century it was divided into two dwellings and 'modernised.' Further remodelling took place in the later twentieth century.

Plate 40. Market Place Hornsea at the end of the nineteenth century. (Photograph: Alan Avery collection)

201

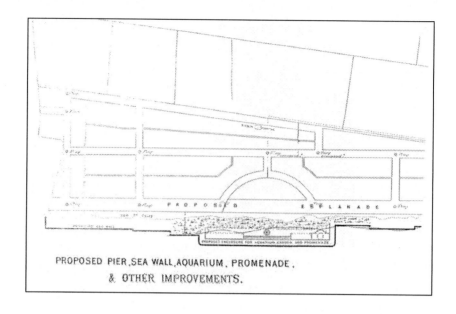

PROPOSED PIER, SEA WALL, AQUARIUM, PROMENADE,
& OTHER IMPROVEMENTS.

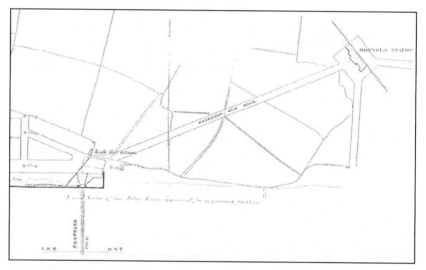

Figure 44. Outline plan produced to accompany du Gillon's grandiose scheme for the South Cliff estate with integrated pier and promenade; the plan also shows the relationship of the development to Hornsea railway station, a mile or so to the north, together with the projected means of approach. Originally, the proposal allowed for the construction of 218 houses, lying in four rows parallel to the cliff edge. Building plots were to be sold at between 5s and 12s per yard, according to the position of the plot within the development; plots on the sea front, with their expansive vistas, were more expensive than those further inland. Later, it was intended to increase the number of houses to around 500. A church was to be built at the southern end of the estate. Fronting the sea, a promenade, garden and aquarium were envisaged. The scheme never got beyond the drawing board, collapsing amid financial difficulties. The land was to remain undeveloped until the twentieth century. (Stephen Harrison collection)

202

Architects of nineteenth century Hornsea

George Jackson and David Thorpe
- Vicarage, Newbegin, 1831-32.

Charles Hutchinson
- Hornsea House, Eastgate, 1845-46 (now demolished).

Rawlins Gould
- Railway station, 1864.
- Station House, 1864.

Joseph Wright
- Primitive Methodist chapel, Market Place, 1864.

William Hawe
- Westgate House, Westgate, 1866.

R.G. Smith
- Alexandra Hotel, Railway Street, 1867.
- Brampton House, 1872-73.

J.K. James
- Wesleyan church, Newbegin, 1870.
- Wesleyan church hall, Newbegin, 1875.

Samuel Musgrave
- United Reformed church, New Road, 1872-74.

R.G. Smith and F.S. Brodrick
- Police station, Newbegin, 1879.

Table 19. Architects of nineteenth century Hornsea.

Plate 41. Rows of tightly packed terrace housing were built around the railway station, sometimes arranged along curving streets. Each dwelling has a narrow street frontage and is very tall in height, usually of three storeys. In the Marlborough Avenue and Alexandra Road area, one is reminded of the narrow streets of terraced housing that can be found in industrial towns across Britain. This may be a reflection of their late date, from c.1864 into the early years of the twentieth century, and their use as desirable residences for commuters. (Photographs: Stephen Harrison)

Plate 42. Houses in the New Road, Albert Avenue and Esplanade areas are large, with densities that are much lower than those in the immediate vicinity of the railway station, although the date of development is the same. These were once the houses of wealthy individuals. (Photographs: Stephen Harrison)

From clay to bricks and tiles: producing the built environment

Plate 43. Earlier nineteenth century bricks forming a boundary wall in Scalby Place. The bricks themselves: handwrought, hand fired, varying in colour, texture and shape. Rugged good looks. Tactile, textured and grainy. Craft material. Growing old gracefully, maturing and improving with the passage of time. (Photograph: Stephen Harrison)

During the earlier part of the nineteenth century Hornsea seems to have had only one brick and tile making business operating at any one time, serving the needs of the village and immediate district. Essentially, this was small-scale production, reflecting the low demand for such products at this time. The Ordnance Survey 1:10560 scale map of 1854 depicts a brick and tile yard well to the south of the village, on the cliff edge in Hornsea Burton.

Although brick and tile was used, cobbles collected from the beach and dug out of the boulder clay around the village formed the main building material. In most buildings brick was used sparingly, for dressings, detailing and tucked gables. A feature of the older parts of the town is the use of cobbles for garden and other boundary walls.

In the nineteenth century, the lord of the manor issued licences allowing local people to collect building material from the beach:

For every ton of stone or cobbles	3d
For every ton of gravel	2d
For every ton of sand	2d

From the early 1860s this began to change. Exploiting the seemingly endless local supplies of clay, Hornsea's brick and tile works were responsible for providing many of the materials needed by the town's building trade throughout the second half of the nineteenth century. In 1861 Joseph Armytage Wade established a brickmaking yard near Hornsea Bridge, between the Hull and Rolston roads (with, from 1864, a siding connecting the works with the newly-opened Hull to Hornsea railway). In doing this, he was

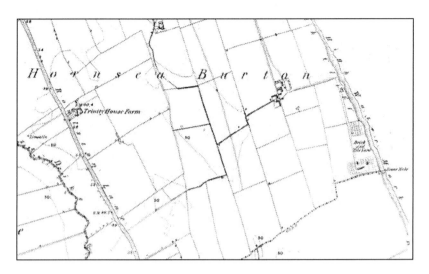

Figure 45. The earlier nineteenth century brick and tile yard in Hornsea Burton. (Ordnance Survey 1:10560 map extract, Sheet 197, surveyed 1852, published 1854. Reproduced by courtesy of the Ordnance Survey)

Plate 44. A later eighteenth century cottage in Eastgate. This one storey house with attics was constructed from cobbles with the use of brick kept to a minimum. (Photograph: Stephen Harrison)

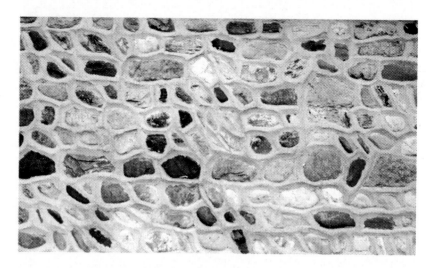

Plate 45. Before the second half of the nineteenth century, cobbles formed the main building material. Cobbles were collected from the beach and transported in panniers – large wicker baskets – slung on either side of the back of a horse or donkey. In 1801 Joseph Lambert, a Hornsea weaver, wrote:

> There are several of our poor neighbours who keep asses upon the back of which they hang a sort of pannier into which they gather stones when the tide is out the greater part of the year for paving, building and for lime in great quantities.

The first documentary reference to a pannier man in Hornsea occurs in 1609. The practice continued into the 1920s. (Photograph: Stephen Harrison)

anticipating the upsurge in demand for bricks and tiles that was likely to occur with the construction of the projected railway and the rise in house building following its arrival. After what appears to have been a shaky start, perhaps verging on near collapse, the business was fully operational by 1868, when it became known as the Hornsea Brick and Tile Company. Between the 1860s and 1873 Wade's company came to have a monopoly on the manufacture of bricks, tiles and drainage pipes in Hornsea.

In 1873 the rival Hornsea Steam Brick and Tile Works was formed, operating from premises off Seaton Road, to the west of the present Suffolk Terrace. Wade's company proved too dominant and the second enterprise was short-lived, closing in 1881. A major contributory factor to its demise was the high wages offered to employees: £30 to £40 per year, more than double that of agricultural workers. Sales of products could not sustain such a high wage bill indefinitely, leading to bankruptcy.

During the second half of the nineteenth century the Hornsea Brick and Tile Company reigned supreme, becoming the only large-scale industrial business in the town and a major source of employment. Wade even provided a row of cottages for employees, known, appropriately enough, as Brickyard Cottages (now 36-48 Marlborough Avenue). The bricks, tiles and pipes manufactured by the company built Hornsea, not only above ground but below as well, with the sewage and foul water drainage systems.

Plate 46. Joseph Armytage Wade (1817-96), a man unto himself. Joseph Armytage Wade was born at Ferrybridge in the West Riding of Yorkshire on 4 April 1817. At the age of three the family moved to Hull, where his father Abraham (1783-1853) and uncle co-owned a timber yard. He first appeared on the local scene in 1853 when he inherited Hornsea House in Eastgate, together with other 'messuages, lands, tenements and hereditaments situate at Hornsea,' from his father who also bequeathed him a half-share in the family's thriving timber business in Hull. Shortly afterwards Wade became a resident of Hornsea and for the next thirty and more years he was a dominant and dominating figure in the affairs of the town, so much so that he came to be known as the 'King of Hornsea.' This title was not bestowed in recognition of any benign qualities he possessed; rather, it referred to his autocratic and despotic style, a brusque, overbearing and self-righteous manner which on many occasions enraged local sensibilities and destroyed much goodwill that he might otherwise have enjoyed. From a reading of contemporary accounts – even when discounting the obvious anti-Wade bias of the *Hornsea Gazette* – there is no doubt that he was a thoroughly awkward and difficult character; a complicated and contradictory individual. His bombastic manner and overbearing attitudes – he would do what he wanted, no matter what the opposition – and his predilection for introducing vitriolic personal attacks into his arguments made him many enemies in Hornsea, not least during his time on the Local Board of Health and during his attempts to provide a pier for the town. His religion, Methodism, and politics, Liberal, alienated him from the predominantly Anglican and Tory upper and middle classes that were potentially his allies and supporters. His power base within the local community lay, not surprisingly given his religious and political affiliations, in the town's working classes. Beneath all the bluster, awkwardness and studied offensiveness a vulnerable social conscience lay concealed. His philanthropic gestures, in both Hornsea and Hull, earned him the accolade 'Poor Man's Friend.' Although self-aggrandising as it undoubtedly was, his philanthropy was caused by a genuine concern for those less fortunate than himself. Over the years many letters of appreciation and support for his charitable endeavours appeared in the pages of the *Hornsea Gazette*. This from 1872 is representative: ' ... sarcastic letters will not alter the good opinion of those who have known Mr Wade for years in deeds as well as words. If sickness overtakes a poor man's family, or adversity, who is always the first to give relief? Why, Mr Wade.'

With a remarkable talent for upsetting people, making life difficult for those whom he perceived as getting in his way and obstructing his various schemes, Wade was endlessly gossiped about, in every tone from awe to contempt.

Joseph Armytage Wade died on 3 March 1896 and was buried four days later in Hornsea churchyard.

There can be little doubt that Wade and his supporters and the antagonism that they generated acted as a serious impediment to Hornsea achieving its potential as a seaside resort in the middle and later decades of the nineteenth century. Arguably, had it not been for this, Hornsea could have gone on to rival Bridlington's position as the premier resort on this stretch of coast. In the fifteen or so years following Wade's death, however, the town made great strides forward in promoting itself as a holiday destination: for instance, the railway line was converted to double track, and the Floral Hall, Imperial Hydro Hotel, a promenade and a sea wall were all built. This is not to deny the contribution made by Wade in laying some of the foundations which enabled the town to make progress in the years leading up to the First World War, such as bringing the railway in the first place and, whilst chairman of the Local Board of Health, in promoting sewage and water schemes for the benefit of resident and visitor alike.

Plate 47. The Hornsea Brick and Tile Company premises between the Hull and Rolston roads in the later nineteenth century. The five-sailed windmill was used to power the hauling of clay wagons from the clay pit to the production areas. (Photograph: Stephen Harrison collection)

Plate 48. The bricks that made Hornsea. (Photograph: Stephen Harrison collection)

210

Of the company's products, the most innovative was the Patent Interlocking Roof Tile, developed around 1872 by Wade and his partner John Cherry. Resembling fish scales, and known as Acorn Tiles, examples can still be seen on buildings in and around Hornsea, most notably adorning 31 New Road and, slightly further afield, at Ellerby, on the roof of St James' church.

Plate 49. The interlocking roof tiles developed by Joseph Armytage Wade and his partner John Cherry. (Photograph: Stephen Harrison)

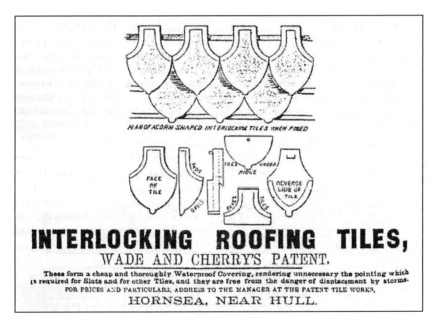

Figure 46. Promotional material for the interlocking roof tiles. (Illustration: Stephen Harrison collection)

Plate 50. Interlocking tiles embellishing the façade of 31 New Road. (Photograph: Stephen Harrison)

> Alice had been to the seaside once in her life and had come to the general conclusion that wherever you go to the English coast you find a number of bathing machines in the sea, some children digging in the sand, then a row of lodging houses and behind them a railway station.
>
> Lewis Carroll, *Alice's Adventures in Wonderland* (1865, p.48)

The eighteenth century saw a revolution in taste. With changing aesthetics the seaside became an attractive tourist destination. It was the sands that put Hornsea on the map. When sea bathing became a fashionable pastime in the late eighteenth century Hornsea began to attract summer visitors. Apart from the beach, the gentle countryside, spacious vistas and rich woodland of this part of Holderness made up the kind of landscape enjoyed by the Georgians; bathing could be interspersed with expeditions in search of the picturesque and visits to local country houses, such as Burton Constable and Rise Park. It did not matter if the sea was far from warm on this coast; sea bathing and the drinking of sea water ('taking the waters') in the early days was, after all, undertaken for medicinal and therapeutic reasons rather than pleasure.

The attractions of Hornsea were offset by the difficulty of getting there. Until the coming of the railway Hornsea was frequented entirely by East Riding people, which, in effect, meant a mixture of the county's gentry and the more prosperous citizens of Hull. As a result, the nineteenth century history of Hornsea falls into two sections, before and after the railway: two-thirds of a century of modest growth as an old-fashioned agricultural village where a small clientele built houses or passed the summer; and a far quicker blossoming into a full-scale seaside resort in the 1870s and 1880s, boosted by the 1871 Bank Holiday Act and the institution of a week's annual holiday in the coalfields of West Yorkshire and the Midlands. After the coming of the railway the old core remained; along the seafront were hotels, lodging houses and the occasional holiday homes of the more prosperous, all of the most agreeable, unpretentious character.

The mass tourism that transformed Blackpool or Margate or Scarborough made no mark here. Popular though Hornsea was, it was on a small scale.

The analytical tool for a discussion of the origins, development and changing fortunes of Hornsea as a seaside resort is provided by R.W. Butler's resort cycle model.[5] Butler's model proposed an evolutionary cycle, consisting of several life-stages, for the history of seaside resorts and areas. The actual cyclical model is based on the 'product life-cycle', where tourism is viewed as the product, and visitor numbers considered a substitute for sales. From this starting point Butler sees the model as explaining the evolution and potential decay of tourist destination areas over a long period of time.

---

[5] Butler, R.W., 1982. The concept of a tourism area cycle of evolution: implications for management of tourism resources. *Canadian Geographer* 24.1: 5-12.

The cycle of evolution has six sequential stages:

1. *Exploration.* This first stage is characterised by small visitor numbers and lack of tourist provision.

2. *Involvement.* Following on fairly quickly from 1, the local community responds by providing some limited, basic facilities.

3. *Development.* There is a rapid take-off in visitor numbers; the local community responds with the development of additional tourist facilities.

4. *Consolidation.* Tourism has become a major element in the local economy; many visitor facilities are available.

5. *Stagnation.* Visitor numbers peak as capacity levels are reached. Although the resort now has a well-established image, it is no longer a fashionable destination.

6. *Post-stagnation.* Five possibilities face the resort at this stage in its evolutionary cycle:

    6.1 Rejuvenation.
    6.2 Steady growth.
    6.3 Stability.
    6.4 Marked decline.
    6.5 Catastrophic decline.

This section is concerned with an exploration of stages 1 to 4 in the evolutionary cycle (see Table 20, below, for a summary); stages 5 and 6 will be considered in the next chapter.

The embryonic origins of Hornsea as seaside resort can be traced back to the later eighteenth century. Paradoxically, though, the early beginnings were centred on the chalybeate springs around the mere rather than on the seaside itself. 'Taking the waters' – that is, the drinking of mineral spring water – for medicinal purposes became a popular national pastime for the more mobile leisured upper and middle classes who were prepared to endure the often long and, given the state of most roads at the time, uncomfortable journeys in the pursuit of health. Hornsea, albeit at a lowly level, joined the ranks of such places as Bath and Scarborough as a spa, attracting the well-to-do who were intent on 'taking the cure' as offered by the liberal drinking of chalybeate spring water. The habit of the wealthy and leisured classes going to a domestic spa to drink health-giving mineral waters was reinforced during the French Revolutionary and Napoleonic wars in the later eighteenth and early nineteenth centuries, when continental Europe was closed to English visitors. Perhaps it was this factor that provided the impetus for the development of Hornsea's springs. Sea bathing, also initially for health purposes, was a natural corollary of this trend, which in turn led to the rise of the recreational seaside holiday.

Hornsea had three chalybeate springs: near Bewholme Lane; between Westgate and the mere; and on the coast, near the site of what, after 1837, was

Stage	Dates	Summary
1. Exploration	Late C18	• Chalybeate springs exploited • Limited accommodation for visitors: lodgings to be had in inns and private houses; some inhabitants supplement their income by providing rooms for visitors • Limited public transport to and from Hornsea
2. Involvement	c.1800-1850	• Beginning of sea bathing • Provision of bathing machines • Annual races on the beach • Dancing Rooms open • First lodging houses and hotel appear • First appearance of full-time lodging house keepers • Limited public transport to and from Hornsea
3. Development	c.1850-1870	• Hull to Hornsea railway opens • Visitor numbers increase • More lodging houses and second hotel • Assembly Room and Public Rooms open
4. Consolidation	c.1870-1920	• Visitor numbers increase further • More lodging houses • Pier constructed • Promenade constructed • Musical promenades begin • Annual Hornsea Regatta and Aquatic Sports begin • Library opens • Mere opens for boating and fishing • Tennis Club opens • Cinema opens

Table 20. Summary of Butler's resort cycle model (Stages 1-4) as applied to Hornsea.

to become the Marine Hotel. Of these the most important was the one between Westgate and the mere, whose precise site is now lost. In 1778 it was referred to as 'a Spring of a Vitriolic Quality nearly as strong as Scarborough Spaw.' In the early nineteenth century this spring belonged to Stephen Linskin, who vigorously promoted it as Hornsea's premier watering hole:

A shallow well for the convenience of visitors taking the cure was dug out some four feet square and three feet deep with a channel of brick for the outflow to the Mere a few yards away ... In attendance during the season was an elderly lady who, with a tin cup attached to a wooden handle, ladled the water out of the well. She then filled a horn drinking cup and handed it to the 'clergy, nobility and gentry' who after paying her a trifle took their prescribed dose.

In 1825 Linskin sold the spring to the Constable family of Wassand Hall. By the time of the sale a brick shelter, complete with doorway and windows, had been constructed around the spring. Until its backfilling in about 1870, the spring was leased, visitors paying a small charge to enter the enclosure and drink the water.

Perhaps it was the efficacious quality of the water from this spring that John Hudson, landlord of the nearby New Inn, was advertising in the summer of 1816. In the *Hull Advertiser* Hudson begged

> ... leave to recommend the HORNSEA CHALYBEATE LIMESTONE SPAW to public attention; the water of which has been analysed by a Professional Gentleman, and is highly recommended as useful for all the purposes in which Chalybeate waters are generally employed; such as Chronic Weaknesses of the Stomach, and Organs of Digestion, and general debility; and particularly Scrofulous Complaints of every description when unaccompanied by fever.

By the 1830s and 1840s Hornsea's chalybeate springs were falling into disuse. They no longer attracted the patronage of a wealthy and leisured clientele, who were now finding their pleasures at the coast. Instead they were serving humble locals, many of whom believed that the spring water could cure simple ailments such as sores and coughs.

Although the chalybeate springs initially attracted visitors to Hornsea – mainly from Hull, but, in lesser numbers, from further afield as well – it was the supposed curative qualities of sea bathing that led directly to the development of the resort. From the later eighteenth century visitors intent on taking to the sea became a frequent sight during the summer months, including the Reverend George Lambert of Hull who went 'there to spend a few days and bathe' in 1798.

Sea bathing drew heavily on the traditions associated with 'taking the waters' at spas, and played an important role in the development of sea bathing on the English coast. In the early days, Hornsea, like other seaside resorts, was referred to as a 'watering place'; visitors bathed in the water and drank, but it was salt water rather than chalybeate spring water that was considered the panacea for all manner of complaints. John Hudson's advertisement quoted earlier also made mention of the virtues of salt water bathing: 'Independently of the advantages Hornsea possesses for SEA BATHING John Hudson has fitted up a WARM SEA WATER BATH, with the use of which Ladies and Gentlemen may be accommodated at an hour's notice.' The provision of a warm seawater bath is indicative of rising amenity standards in the early nineteenth century. For those who wished, it meant that cold bathing in the open sea could be spurned now that coal was widely available for furnaces to heat water.

The bathing ritual itself was closely modelled on the practices of the spas. It was the search for better health that first persuaded people to take up sea bathing. The medical profession advised bathers to dip before 10am so that the cold waters would invigorate the constitution for the rest of the day. Bathers rarely swam. Instead they were dipped under the waves as if they were taking a medicinal bath. 'Dippers' were employed to submerge bathers into the 'healing brine.'

Up until the middle years of the nineteenth century it was customary for men and boys to bathe naked; wearing a bathing costume was considered effeminate. Males also thought that clothing would prevent them from obtaining the full benefits of having saline water next to their skin. Women and girls, however, usually wore flannel gowns when in the sea. 'Promiscuous bathing' was also the norm, that is, both sexes normally bathing in the same section of sea. It must be remembered, though, that in the early years of resort development visitor numbers were small, so bathers were not crowded together. What was acceptable in the eighteenth century came under increasing attack in the nineteenth. This coincided with a shift in emphasis from sea bathing for therapeutic reasons to swimming for leisure. With this changed circumstance, and with increasing numbers of people visiting coastal areas, nude bathing was no longer considered acceptable in the presence of ladies and children. As early as 1800 the *Observer* denounced nude bathing:

> The indecency of numerous naked men bathing in the sea close to the ladies bathing machines, and under the windows of the principal houses at most of the watering places has long been complained of, but in general has not been … redressed.

Complaints about nude sea bathing steadily grew. Evangelicals, who regarded nudity and mixed bathing as immoral, along with other moral salvationists, made increasingly vociferous calls for the segregation of the sexes on the beaches of England. Bowing to moral indignation and mounting pressure, as mass tourism to the seaside became a reality during the middle and later years of the nineteenth century, byelaws were enacted by resort after resort to enforce segregation and regulate behaviour. It is perhaps no coincidence that Hornsea's own byelaw came into force in 1864 – the year the railway opened the town to the potentials of mass tourism. The invention of specially designed 'bathing dress' in the 1890s meant that the sexes could henceforth indulge in mixed bathing with propriety.

Bathing machines were introduced to English resorts during the second half of the eighteenth century. In them bathers could change and then be transported down to the sea. In reality they were little more than huts on wheels, which were hauled up and down the foreshore by bathing attendants – 'dippers' – or horses according to the state of the tide. There are sporadic references to between two and twenty bathing machines variously operating at Hornsea during the first forty or so years of the nineteenth century; more thereafter. In the 1850s it was reported that:

217

The upper margins of the beach, covered only by the highest tides, is loose, heavy sand, strewn with hardened lumps of clay, fatiguing to walk upon; but grows firmer as you approach the water. The wheels of the bathing-machines have broad wooden tires to prevent their sinking.

Plate 51. Bathing machines at Bridlington in the early nineteenth century. Bathers were dipped under the waves by attendants. (From George Walker, *The Costume of Yorkshire*, 1814; Stephen Harrison collection)

Documentary references to lodging houses and hotels in Hornsea during the earlier part of the nineteenth century are not plentiful. The overall impression though, despite one or two adverse comments, is of gradual evolution in the provision of visitor accommodation. White's 1831 *directory* stated that 'there are many good and economical lodgings for numerous visitors.' In 1835 Sir George Head wrote that Hornsea had become 'a principal place of resort as a watering-place for the citizens of Hull and the inhabitants of the surrounding country.' Yet the place was not to his liking. He complained about 'the inferior style of accommodation,' where those who visited Hornsea had to seek lodgings in small cottages in the old village because there were only two inns, both of which were no more than 'ordinary public houses.' The situation seems to have improved shortly after Head's visit, for White's *directory* of 1840 informs us that Hornsea was 'A small but pleasant town and bathing place which since 1831 has been considerably improved and enlarged owing to its popularity as a bathing place.'

Writing in 1848 Edward Bedell, the historian of Hornsea, stated that 'there are several most comfortable and well-conducted inns and several lodging houses have been built of late years.' He also identified a growing occupational trend towards the appearance of full-time lodging house keepers:

> Until within the last ten or fifteen years, lodgings at Hornsea were
> principally let by people depending on their ordinary occupations or

218

resources and having rooms to spare. Of late, however, the number of those who depend on their success in letting lodgings for remuneration for the higher rent they pay, and outlay for furniture, has greatly increased, and consequently an indifferent *season* occasions considerable disappointment [emphasis in original].

He also quoted some of the prices charged:

Lodgings vary in price from £3 or £4 a-week, down to 10s or 12s, or less. The exclusive use of a house, or the occupation of part of a house, with one or two sitting-rooms, plainly furnished but clean, kitchen, and four or five beds, may be had from about £2 to £3 a-week.

White's 1867 *directory* mentions Hornsea's increasing attraction as a resort and the consequential growth in accommodation for visitors: 'a pleasant town and fashionable bathing place ... [where] ... many comfortable lodging houses have been built within the last few years, both in the town and on the sea shore, for the accommodation of the numerous visitors who resort hither in the bathing season.'

Yet even as late as the early 1870s complaints could still occasionally be heard. A visitor, writing in the 27 September 1873 issue of the *Spectator* was clearly unimpressed: there were no cabs at the railway station, two hotels near the sea front were temporarily closed, and he had difficulty in finding lodgings.

During the first thirty years of the nineteenth century there appear to have been four hotels – in reality, little more than coaching inns – in Hornsea:

- Hare and Hounds (renamed Rose and Crown by 1840) in Market Place.

- Prince of Wales (renamed the Victoria Inn by 1840 and the Victoria Hotel by 1848) in Market Place.

- Straker's Hotel (renamed the New Hotel by 1872; the Pike and Heron since the 1980s) in Market Place.

- Old Hotel (Low Hall), also known as Heslop's Inn, in Southgate.

In June 1837 the first Marine Hotel joined them. As the *Hull Advertiser* commented at the time: 'The *growing importance of this Watering Place* has induced Daniel Jameson to open an Establishment called the Marine Hotel – Good stabling and coach house' (emphasis added). The L-shaped building stood in an isolated position at the seaward end of Eastgate, surrounded by 'pastures and arable fields' and connected to the settlement by an un-made lane. Its position was also strategic, capitalising both on a nearby chalybeate spring and the sea.

Figure 47. The Marine Hotel in 1843. (Stephen Harrison collection)

Figure 48. The Marine Hotel in 1845. (Stephen Harrison collection)

The opening of the hotel was an important event: it marked the real beginnings of Hornsea's development as a seaside resort and its transition from village to town. Solid, substantial and brick-built, the Marine Hotel also marked the onset of a change in the physical appearance of Hornsea.

In 1842 Thomas Cunnington of Hull bought the Marine Hotel. Cunnington is credited with popularising Hornsea as a resort over the following decade. The following year the hotel was enlarged to provide more accommodation and a refreshment pavilion, connected to the hotel by a subterranean passage through the cliffs, was built on the adjoining beach. The

220

hotel was designed to attract a 'superior' clientele, as the following publicity advertisement of June 1843 makes clear:

> The situation of the MARINE HOTEL may well challenge comparison with any similar Establishment on the Northern and Eastern Coasts of England. Located in a salubrious Neighbourhood; commanding delightful views of the German Ocean from the romantic Cliff on which it is built; and abounding with attractions in the inviting character of the surrounding scenery; it possesses all the elements that can be supposed essential to tempt the worn-out and weary sojourner in large Towns to exchange for a time his city dwelling for the beauties and the breezes of Landscape and of Sea.

> Private suites of Apartments, replete with comfort and elegantly furnished, can be engaged. A *Table d'Hote* daily, where the Epicure and *Bon Vivant* may gratify his taste upon economising principles. A Coffee-room, where Refreshments, consisting of Luncheons, Coffee, Tea, Sandwiches, &c., of every kind, may be had at the *lowest possible charges*. Thus, every endeavour has been made to suit the varied wants and circumstances of Visitors.

> LOCK-UP STABLING – BATHS, HOT, COLD AND
> MEDICATED
> *METROPOLITAN AND PROVINCIAL PAPERS*

> Arrangements have been completed by which Passengers arriving in Hull by the Morning Train at Fifteen Minutes past Eight a.m., and the Afternoon Train at Four p.m., are conveyed direct from the Station to the MARINE HOTEL, HORNSEA, in about Two Hours.

> Conveyances also daily from Beverley to Hornsea, and shortly from Bridlington – thus enabling Visitors from Hull to Bridlington, if they choose, to pass a day or two at Hornsea.

At around the same time, the out-of season charges were: 'Terms for the months of May, June, October and November, Two guineas per week, including Board, Sitting and Bed Room. Children, 7 shillings to 10 shillings. Male Servants, 21 shillings. Female Servants, 18 shillings.' These figures clearly reflect the hotel's intention of attracting the more well to do visitors.

The Marine Hotel was demolished in 1874. The reason for this is unclear: some accounts mention a fire gutting the building, others that the threat from coastal erosion was the reason for its demolition. What seems to have happened is this: the building was severely damaged by fire and not immediately rebuilt because of the threat from coastal erosion. However, a second Marine Hotel was in existence by 1880, on a slightly more inland site. This was a much smaller building than its predecessor, apparently more like a farmhouse than a hotel in appearance. It had whitewashed walls, a pantiled roof and a range of outbuildings – stables etc – on the west side. This, too, was destroyed by fire at the end of the nineteenth century and replaced by the

Plate 52. The third Marine Hotel. (Photograph: Stephen Harrison)

present Marine Hotel, a brick and tile building with half-timbering and tile-hung gables.

A second hotel opened in 1867: The Alexandra, near the railway station. The hotel was named after Princess Alexandra of Denmark, the wife of Edward, Prince of Wales (later Edward VII). The Alexandra had twenty-two bedrooms, four reception rooms, a billiard room and smoking room, but only one bathroom. There was also a restaurant and coffee room, both of which were open to residents, passers-by and 'excursionists.'

In 1887 the Hornsea Mere and Hotels Company leased The Alexandra. This company also rented Hornsea Mere from the Strickland-Constable family, turning it into a leisure attraction for visitors. The Hornsea Mere and Hotels Company, whose directors included William Bethell of Rise Park, Captain Miller of Kilnwick Hall, and Alfred Maw and Charles Forster of Hornsea, with Henry Strickland-Constable of Wassand Hall as chairman, formed in 1885 'to acquire for a term the exclusive right of Fishing, Boating and Skating on the greater portion of the magnificent Lake known as Hornsea Mere and to Purchase and carry on The Alexandra Hotel at Hornsea.' They also wished to buy ten houses in the adjacent Wilton Terrace, which would then be used to extend the hotel.

The company began with high hopes and grandiose ambitions, but these quickly faded. Evidently, there was little support for the scheme within Hornsea. This prompted a plaintive letter from Alfred Maw, published in the *Hornsea Gazette* on 12 December 1865:

> ... it is heartrending to me and most discouraging and wearing to some of the Directors ... I almost blush for all my fellow townsmen who have any interest at stake in the place and who have not given their support to the undertaking ... It now rests entirely with the Hornsea people to support the scheme or not ...

They did not. Interestingly, most of the opposition to the scheme was orchestrated by a small, but powerful and influential group of middle class residents, incomers and natives alike, who were hostile to any attempt to develop the town as a tourist destination. They did not want their tranquillity disturbed by hordes of working class 'excursionists.' Exclusivity was their aim. This is a pattern we see repeated on many occasions during the nineteenth century, when looking at the development of Hornsea as a seaside resort. In the face of indifference and outright hostility, the company's backers modified their plans: instead of buying the Alexandra, they would lease it, and Henry Strickland-Constable agreed to reduce the rent on the mere. The plan to purchase ten houses in Wilton Terrace was abandoned.

The mere, with new access roads and jetties, opened to the public on 2 March 1886 for fishing and boating. However, later that year, on 21 July, an accident occurred on the mere: Louis Henderson, the company's boatman, fell into the water and was drowned. This tragedy shook public confidence and cast gloom over the company's activities, which was only somewhat alleviated by the opening of the Alexandra, re-branded as the Mere Hotel, on 21 August, after a long delay caused by the lack of capital with which to refurbish the premises.

In 1887, in an attempt to increase visitor numbers to the mere, a refreshment room was opened on Kirkholme point. This building is still used as a café. 1887 saw a second fatal accident on the mere, when, on 18 July, a Mrs Ann Stephenson fell from a boat and was drowned. As with the previous episode, this did nothing to instil confidence in would-be visitors and resulted in fewer attendances than the company anticipated.

From the very start the Hornsea Mere and Hotel Company was under-capitalised, leading to major financial difficulties and, ultimately, causing its collapse. On 6 September 1887 the shareholders were told that the company had lost £3 14s 6d on its mere business and that the hotel was £283 10s 7d in debt. Matters did not improve over the next eighteen months. At the next shareholders' meeting on 16 March 1889 those present were told that total losses since the company started trading amounted to £823 1s 2d. They also heard that £400 was still owed to Alfred Maw, who had provided furnishings and fittings for the Mere Hotel, and that £300 was still outstanding on the purchase of boats and other equipment used by the mere side of the business.

On 18 May 1889, as the business continued to slip towards the precipice, the company announced that the Mere Hotel had been sub-let to a Miss MacDonald, who would operate independently of the Hornsea Mere and Hotels Company. By the early twentieth century the hotel had reverted to its original name.

Maw and his associates henceforth traded as the Hornsea Mere Company. Although increased numbers of events took place on the mere in 1889, the season was, through a combination of poor attendance and bad weather, very poor. And the debts continued to mount.

An emergency shareholders' meeting was held in early February of the following year. This meeting decided that the company should cease trading: 'that it has been proved to the satisfaction of this meeting that the Company cannot, by reason of its liabilities, continue in business and that it is advisable to wind up the same, and accordingly that the Company be wound up voluntarily.' The Hornsea Mere Company ceased to exist on 28 February 1890. Later that year, on 9 May, the company's property, including thirty-seven assorted pleasure boats, chandlery and seats, was auctioned. Much was bought by James Holmes, former boatman to the company, who took over the boat hiring and fishing businesses and refreshment room.

After Holmes took over the business, leisure use of the mere was strictly controlled by the Strickland-Constable family. For fishing:

> All licensees agree to be bound by the following conditions: To pay £5 5s per year in advance; the license to date from the day taken out. To fish or troll for pike only. To use not more than one rod and one line at one time. To take no pike less than 22 inches in length. To show all fish, and have it weighed on landing. To land only on Kirkholme Point at the place appointed. To fish only in that portion of the Mere known as the Eastern portion, viz: to the East of the boundary line. Fishing for bait not allowed on any condition. Any fish not pike caught whilst fishing to be given up on landing. Close season: from the 15th of March to the 15th of June (both days inclusive).

To boat on the mere:

> Persons may put on their own boats at the following rates: 15ft in length and under, £3 per year; over 15ft and under 20ft, £4 per year; over 20ft, £5 per year. All money to be paid in advance. To boat in that portion of the Mere known as the Eastern portion, viz: to the East of the boundary line. The year for boating commences on the 1st day of March, and closes on the last day of February, the year following. A small reduction from the above rates for boating is made to persons not residing in Hornsea. Boats may be hired by the hour, day, or week.

Holmes ran the business successfully up to the First World War, closing down when the mere became a flying boat base for the Royal Naval Air Service. The enterprise was restarted after 1919 and continued throughout the inter-war years.

Most visitors to Hornsea stayed in lodging houses. The number of lodging houses available varied considerably across the nineteenth century, reflecting the changing popularity of the place as a seaside resort:

1831	*White's Directory*	4 lodging houses
1840	*White's Directory*	28 lodging houses
1846	*White's Directory*	69 lodging houses
1851	*White's Directory*	70 lodging houses
1857	*Kelly's Directory*	7 lodging houses
1858	*White's Directory*	49 lodging houses
1867	*White's Directory*	46 lodging houses
1872	*Kelly's Directory*	25 lodging houses
1879	*Kelly's Directory*	28 lodging houses
1889	*Kelly's Directory*	30 lodging houses
1892	*Bulmer's Directory*	55 lodging houses
1897	*Kelly's Directory*	68 lodging houses

However, when we consult the lists appearing in the *Hornsea Gazette* from the 1860s onwards we find that the number of lodging houses is consistently higher: for example, in 1869 there were 95 lodging houses, 125 in 1870, 97 in 1875, 68 in 1880, 97 in 1890 and 110 in 1900. The discrepancy can be explained. The number of lodging houses appearing in the various directories relates to those providing full-time accommodation, whilst the higher numbers reported in the newspaper relate to both full-time and part-time lodging housekeepers.

How many visitors came to Hornsea? Where did they come from? For the second half of the nineteenth century, the *Hornsea Gazette* printed week-by-week lists of visitors and where they came from. It would be tedious to present a week-by-week summary of seasonal visitors for the entire second half of the century. Instead, figures for the second week of August, arguably the busiest week in terms of summer visitors, for the period 1870-1900 are given in graph form, which can be used to identify broad trends.

In the first decade after the coming of the railway, visitor numbers increased year on year. From the mid-1870s through to the late 1880s, there was a steady decrease in numbers, reaching their lowest point in 1880-82. This would suggest a decline in the popularity of the resort. Weather played a contributory role in this downturn; these years saw a series of wet and cool summers. The lack of amenities, an absence of visitor attractions, were also factors. Interestingly visitor numbers to Bridlington, twelve miles up the coast, increased during this period. This reflects the greater numbers of attractions available for the diversion of holidaymakers. Hornsea was loosing out.

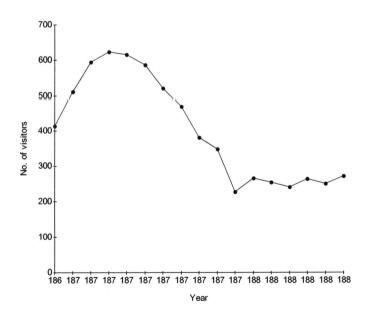

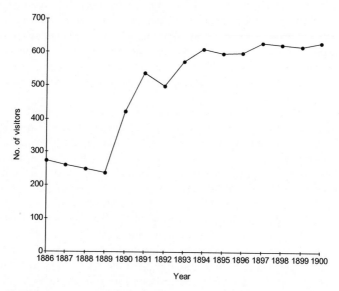

Figure 49. Visitors to Hornsea during the second week of August: 1869-1900. (Source: *Hornsea Gazette*)

Thereafter, until the end of the century (indeed, up until the First World War), numbers steadily increased once again. Rising numbers are directly associated with increasing provision of amenities for tourists (see below).

Where did the visitors come from? Again, the *Hornsea Gazette* is of use: alongside their names, the paper printed their place of permanent residence. The catchment area is fairly restricted, emphasising Hornsea's role as a purely regional holiday centre. As a detailed and random illustration, let us take the week ending 27 July 1889:

Location	Number	%
Hull	271	63.91
East Riding	24	5.66
North Riding	6	1.42
West Riding	60	14.15
NE Midlands	18	4.24
Rest of Britain	44	10.38
Elsewhere	1	0.24
Total	**424**	**100.00**

Table 21. Geographical origins of visitors to Hornsea for the week ending 27 July 1889.

The above figures and geographical spread are typical for the whole of the second half of the nineteenth century. Most visitors to Hornsea came from Yorkshire. Not only that, but from within the county most holidaymakers hailed from Hull – earning Hornsea the epithet 'Hull-by-the-Sea.' Throughout

226

the period under review, between 60% and 70% of all visitors came from Hull alone, a further 20% from the rest of Yorkshire, and the remainder from elsewhere. Hornsea's appeal was firmly regional, not national.

With the growth of Hornsea as seaside resort, the question of providing diversions for the increasing number of seasonal visitors came to the fore. The lack of such amenities was to be a recurrent theme throughout the second half of the nineteenth century. This editorial comment from the *Hornsea* Gazette of 2 October 1869 will serve as an example:

> That Hornsea has considerably improved during the last three or four years cannot be disputed. The indications of this improvement are too numerous and too evident on every side to need pointing out. There are, however, many ways in which its prosperity may be still further increased; and the success which has attended previous efforts in this direction, should have the effect of stimulating us to renewed exertion, as it must assuredly remove some of the difficulties which have hitherto obstructed our progress. One thing is certain, it will never do for us to stand still and be content with what has already been accomplished. Neither should we resist the carrying out of any reasonable project for improvement which may at any time be proposed; or obstinately shut our eyes to the advantages which may be secured by assisting its development. In either case we may rest assured that Hornsea, instead of rising in public estimation, would inevitably decline.

> We have many powerful competitors for public favour, and when we remember that Scarborough "The Queen of watering-places," as well as other less pretentious towns on the east coast, possess more accommodation and greater variety of entertainment and amusement than we can offer our visitors, it is a source of satisfaction to find that Hornsea is surely, though slowly, gaining ground in the opinion of those who periodically spend a portion of the year at the seaside.

Or the following anonymous letter (simply signed 'A Visitor'), which appeared in the 7 June 1879 edition of the same paper and is typical:

> … Some little time ago I had an invitation to spend a few days at Hornsea. Knowing nothing of the place, except that it was located about three-quarters of a mile from the sea, I quite naturally referred to the latest directory [1879 *Post Office Directory*]. There I found the little village was elaborately described. It told me of a beautiful and extensive lake, covering several hundred acres of ground, with a circumference of about five miles, the banks of which formed a beautiful promenade; it was also stored with fresh water fish, and interspersed with small well-wooded islands. From the information I thus received I thought I would travel about 80 miles to visit this delightful spot, being assured I should enjoy myself. When I arrived I began to interrogate my friends about the privilege of visitors with respect to the lake. I suppose we can have a boat and go fishing on

the lake? No, it is private property, and neither fishing nor boating is allowed. That was the first blight of the hopes of my enjoyment. But that is not all; being beautifully moonlight, I thought I should take a walk round this beautiful lake, but that also I could not get. Certainly the walk along Beverley-road was something approaching what I expected, and was very enjoyable, but the question is, could not this be improved? I think Hornsea owns some small portion of the philanthropic humanity, and I for one among the many that visit this pretty place should be pleased to hear of those with power and influence trying to improve the facilities afforded for pastime and recreative enjoyment. I think the difficulty of gaining access to the pleasures the lake affords for the few might be met if some private company could engage a portion of it nearest the Market-place, and there form a landing place for the boats; and the same company, by making reasonably charges for boating and fishing, would be able to afford to be responsible for all damages to the aforesaid private property. After receiving this information about the lake, other places of pastime generally found at the sea-side were asked about. Have you any aquarium here? No. Have you any promenade here? No, but they have of late commenced to build a pier, which I admit greatly improves the beautifully wild beach. But this is not enough. Still more might be done. I did not at all find it nice walking on the heavy sand and unless I walked very near the water I found it heavy indeed; so I had to walk by the water's edge, and unexpectedly a large wave came swelling along and I got a wetting. I should have liked to have gone on the sea, but it was too rough. This I think might be met by building a landing for the boats jutting out into the sea. I also think that a beautiful fore-shore road might be made along the beach. I also found to my astonishment that there was not either a skating rink or public bowling green, no museum, public library, nor public gardens; in fact, nothing could I find of interest in the whole place. Why cannot something be attempted to make Hornsea more attractive to the inhabitants of the large towns within such close proximity? In my opinion, sir, Hornsea, in a very few years, might become one of the most beautiful watering-places on the Yorkshire coast. Why cannot the Public Rooms (so-called) be made into a library and reading-rooms, and the Templars' Hall, or Hope of Hornsea, be converted into a small museum and art gallery, or something to advantage? And that too, I am sure, at a small expense …

Indirectly both the editorial comment and letter draw attention to the main obstacle facing Hornsea's efficient development as a seaside resort: the absence of a single promoting body. Much of the development that took place was fragmented and *ad hoc*. This contrasted significantly with places like Scarborough, where a private syndicate headed by the Cliff Bridge Company was responsible for provide a systematic suite of visitor facilities and amenities. The seeds of Hornsea's failure to become a premier east coast resort can be found in this lack of overall direction.

A lack of unity and purpose is nowhere better seen than in the fiasco that was Hornsea's pier. Or, as it nearly turned out, two piers. As mentioned earlier (see chapter 3) there was a functional pier – effectively a harbour – at Hornsea Beck from the thirteenth to at least the later sixteenth century, which was used by local fishermen and merchants. Sometime between 1558 and 1609 it was destroyed by storms, and never rebuilt, owing to the high costs involved. Over two hundred years had to pass before a replacement was conceived of.

The construction of a pier primarily, but not entirely, for leisure activities was much discussed in the 1860s and 1870s. The unfolding story of Hornsea's pleasure pier is one of ambition, jealousy, vision outstripping resources and the unpredictability of the weather. It is also a tale of petty rivalries, intrigue and the self-interestedness of two men, each with at least one eye to future, posthumous glory: the intensely egotistical Joseph Armytage Wade, adored or execrated in equal measure by the folk of Hornsea, a man with an unshakeable, if not always very judicious, belief in his own myth; and the ever-more ambitious Pierre Henri Martin du Gillon, often cast as the hero in this particular saga. Both were outsiders who settled in Hornsea – Wade permanently, du Gillon more ephemerally – and who, in the name of progress (and profit), ruffled the innate conservatism of the place with their schemes and intrigues. Ultimately it is a narrative of failure.

Here, then, is a tale of two piers: a (hi)story of muddle, self-interest, image-building, indifference, dogged by hesitation and uncertainty.

In 1865 Joseph Armytage Wade formed the Hornsea Pier Company and obtained a Board of Trade licence giving permission for the company to construct a pier within five years. However, beyond driving ten piles in to the foreshore at the end of New Road to gauge the strength of the current and the stability of the sand, nothing further was done. The operation was suspended when a storm destroyed the pile-driving engine. Like some avenue of prehistoric standing stones, the timber piles stood forlornly on the foreshore for many years, christened by irreverent and increasingly sceptical locals as the 'Ten Virgins.' A testament to the vagaries of weather and tide and the high costs and potential dangers involved in the undertaking of complex engineering works on this unstable and unpredictable coast.

In late 1869 a series of letters and editorials in the *Hornsea Gazette* called for more activity on the part of the moribund pier company. Renewed interest in the scheme needs to be seen in the context of resort rivalry between Hornsea and, just a few miles down the coast, Withernsea; in 1869 it was announced that Withernsea was to have a pleasure pier. The race to attract visitors was on. The following give a flavour of the debate. An opening letter from Thomas Haller was printed in the 18 September 1869 edition, sounding the first discordant notes in what, over the next few years, was destined to become a mounting scale of disillusionment:

> The Government having put a stop to the taking of gravel and shingle off the beach from Spurn to Hornsea, thereby depriving many poor men of employment, who have all their lives obtained their livelihood from this occupation along the coast, and the railways from Hornsea and Withernsea of a large source of revenue, I think it

behoves the inhabitants of these places, and especially the shareholders of the Hornsea Railway, if they ever mean to get a dividend, to bestir themselves, and do something to increase the traffic on the line; and I think one means of doing this will be to build a pier, which would do for a promenade as well as for the landing of passengers from the pleasure boats and the steam packets, which would frequently run from Bridlington if there was a pier to land at. It would also be available for the landing of fish, which I have no doubt would be done to a large extent, as there is a line of rails belonging to Mr Wade laid down from the station to the sea side, which could be carried on to some part of the pier, and the fish put at once from the vessel on to the trucks, and sent off at once to the best market. I believe, some time ago a prospectus of a pier company was issued, if so, I think now is the time to proceed with it, and to obtain estimates for the amount required to fully complete the same, and for the contractor to be bound to carry out his contract for the sum stated, taking care that there should be no extras. Sir, I think if this was done there would be no fear but the amount required would be soon subscribed. I have heard within the last day or two that a movement is on foot to build a pier at Withernsea, which I have no doubt will be carried out. I say again that the inhabitants of Hornsea, and especially the shareholders of the railway, should bestir themselves.

This was followed up with an editorial comment in the 2 October issue:

It appears to us that the time has come when a strenuous effort should be made for the furtherance of some scheme for the erection of a pier, and which we believe would benefit Hornsea more than anything that has yet been attempted. Our readers are aware that a Pier Company has for some years been in existence, but, alas! As yet it has shown but few symptoms of vitality, and a notice of the meeting of the directors once a year is the only intimation the public receive that such a company is in being. The advantages that would accrue to Hornsea if this idea were perfected are self-evident. In addition to providing an agreeable promenade for visitors, and thereby most probably increasing their number, the fishing trade would be developed by the conveniences it would afford for the landing of cargoes, and in this way employment might be found for many whose occupation has recently been interfered with by the order of the Board of Trade prohibiting the collection of gravel on the beach. It would also greatly facilitate the launching of the lifeboat, a work which we believe would be very difficult of accomplishment under present circumstances in stormy weather.

It is to be regretted that the efforts which have hitherto been made for the establishment of a Pier Company, have met with so feeble a response from the general public. We should have thought that the shareholders in the railway would have seen that this project is calculated, more than any other, to develop the resources of their line, and thus hasten the period when the traffic shall become sufficiently remunerative to induce the North Eastern Company to complete the terms on which the line was transferred to them, and by which they undertake to guarantee a dividend of 4 per cent to the holders of Hornsea stock. The growth of the traffic is so slow that it is manifest to everyone that, unless some special attraction be provided at this end of the line, the period when this happy consummation shall be arrived at must be long deferred.

… The erection of a Pier could scarcely fail to be self remunerative, and bring a fair return to those who may be enterprising enough to invest their money in its construction. Let the existing Company bestir itself, or it will find that some other organisation will be springing up to supersede and carry off the honour and profit which it might certainly have gained if it had carried out its designs.

Two weeks later (16 October) the paper printed a letter from W.H. Officer:

During the summer we have heard a great deal about the desirability of having a pier at Hornsea, and I have looked week after week for some statement from the Pier Company – I suppose there is one – as to how matters stand in reference to the project. There cannot be any doubt that the erecting of a pier would give a great impetus to the prosperity of Hornsea. I do not think it would yield an adequate return for the capital expended, as a commercial undertaking, but the increase in the value of property, and the increase in the trade of the town, would yield a good return for the money invested, if the shares were taken up by the owners of property and those interested in the trade.

Still nothing happened. Almost two years later, in March 1871, after obtaining a renewal of the Board of Trade licence, Wade informed his shareholders that work would begin in earnest later that year. As the *Hornsea Gazette* reported on 11 March:

The application to the Board of Trade for an extension of time for the construction of a pier at this place … has been granted, and the provisional order of the Board has been lodged with the Clerk of the Peace, at Beverley. J.A. Wade, Esq., the chairman of the company, when alluding to the subject, told the shareholders, who met at the office of the company on Monday evening, that the work ought to be commenced during the present year. He thought a pier would be very beneficial to the town generally, and at the same time would have the effect of materially increasing the receipts from the railway. It would provide a convenience for the landing of fish, and he had no doubt, from the nearness of Hornsea to the fishing grounds in the North Sea, that it would be largely used for this purpose.

Words followed by inactivity.

Two months later, on 13 May, the *Hornsea Gazette* printed the following letter, simply signed 'A Casual':

> I have again come to Hornsea for a temporary visit, and regret to find that nothing is being done towards the building of a pier, which is one of the best projects for promoting the interests of your pleasant and attractive little watering place. I am under the impression that I read in your paper some months ago, that in order to retain the privilege granted by the Board of Trade to the Hornsea Pier Company, it would be necessary for them to commence the work in the present year. If this be really a correct statement of the position, the directors should bestir themselves at once. With the improved prospects of the railway, and the very satisfactory increase in the population, as shewn by the census returns, the difficulties which existed when the company was formed should be to some extent diminished, and I am greatly surprised at the lethargy of the promoters of the company and the tradesmen of the town.

For a further four years nothing much happened. Then, in early 1875, Wade met with Pierre Henri Martin du Gillon, a dynamic, free wheeling French-born entrepreneur from Sheffield, who had recently bought land in Hornsea Burton. He planned to develop this land for residential building; he also wished to construct a pier and adjoining harbour complex. However, the scheme had one important obstacle to overcome: Wade owned the land between the railway station and du Gillon's site. In order to provide an access road for visitors, du Gillon would need to buy a strip of land from Wade. Protracted negotiations were opened, during which, du Gillon was later to claim, Wade tried to undermine the scheme by equivocation. Eventually, after offering him a stake in the new pier, du Gillon assumed that he had got Wade's verbal agreement to sell a strip of land for the new road and co-operate in the building of the pier.

In August 1875, on the basis of the supposed arrangement, du Gillon drew up Articles of Agreement:

> Articles of agreement under seal, made the   day of   1875, between Joseph Armitage Wade, in the County of York, esquire, of the one part, and Pierre Henri Martin du Gillon, of Sheffield, in the said county, gentleman, of the other part.

> Witness that for the mutual considerations herein appearing, and for the mutual advantages to be derived by the several parties hereto as owners of various lands situate within the parish of Hornsea, it is hereby agreed between the said parties hereto as follows, that is to say: 1. The said Pierre Henri Martin du Gillon, shall have the right after the signing of this agreement, to make, construct, and use, along and across the lands of the said Joseph Armitage Wade, situate at Hornsea aforesaid, a foot, horse, and carriage way, of the width of 50 feet at the top, with good drains

therein, in accordance with the plan hereunto annexed, and do all things necessary or convenient for making such road and drains in a substantial manner. 2. The said Joseph Armitage Wade, shall at any time after the completion of such road as aforesaid, when requested in writing by the said Pierre Henri Martin du Gillon, do and concur in all things necessary for dedicating such road to the public. 3. The said Joseph Armitage Wade, shall render to the said Pierre Henri Martin du Gillon, all moral support towards obtaining a Board of Trade order authorising the projection of the pier, contemplated by the said Pierre Henri Martin du Gillon, at Hornsea Burton corner, in the parish of Hornsea aforesaid, and upon completion of such pier, shall at the request and expense of the proprietors thereof, assure to them the right to use for all purposes, the private railway siding belonging to the said Joseph Armitage Wade, at Hornsea, aforesaid, subject to the claims (if any) of the North Eastern Railway Company, and concurrently with the use of such siding by the said Joseph Armitage Wade. 4. The said Pierre Henri Martin du Gillon, shall without delay apply for such Board of Trade order as aforesaid. 5. If the said pier be not constructed within three years after the date of the obtaining of such Board of Trade order, the said Joseph Armitage Wade, shall after such three years have the right to use such road as aforesaid, without any payment. 6. In case the said Joseph Armitage Wade shall make use of the said road for building purposes, in any other event than that provided for by clause 5, whether before or after the said road shall have been dedicated to the public he shall pay to the said Pierre Henri Martin du Gillon the sum of £500 as a contribution to the expenses of such road, and he shall at any time acquire full rights of user of such road by such payment of £500.

In essence, then, Wade was being asked to provide:
- land for a road from the railway station to the pier,

- £500 towards the building of the road if he – Wade – began to use it in developing his land adjacent to the route, provided the pier was built within three years of the signing of the agreement, and

- "all moral support" to du Gillon in obtaining the necessary Board of Trade order for the building of the pier.

Wade was unwilling to sign the Articles of Agreement and from that point onwards relations between the two men soured rapidly, beginning an ineffable sequence of entries and exits belonging more to music hall farce. Tempers became frayed and over the coming months harsh words were exchanged. In early October 1875 negotiations were broken off completely. The joint venture was doomed. Wade's initial enthusiasm had cooled to the point of freezing. Why? Wade's ostensible reason was that du Gillon was unwilling to provide guarantees that the pier would actually be built and that the new road would be to a sufficiently high standard of workmanship. Although no direct evidence is available, it seems more likely that his agreement was made on an impulse following public criticism of his inaction.

When it became clear that du Gillon was actively progressing the project, Wade became jealous. As the self-styled 'King of Hornsea' he was not prepared to play a secondary role. In a spirit of rivalrous resentment, he simply took his bat and ball away.

In December 1875 the increasingly acrimonious debate between the two men further escalated when du Gillon, clearly exasperated by the lack of progress, applied to parliament for an act to allow the compulsory purchase of land belonging to Wade for the construction of a road to the proposed pier. Hornsea's principal landowners supported the application: the Bethells of Rise and the Strickland-Constables of Wassand. This might have been a straightforward procedure but for the fact that the proposal also impinged on the Local Board of Health's sewage disposal facilities. Wade's response was immediate. He called an extraordinary meeting of the Local Board of Health, of which he was chairman, for 18 December. The report of the meeting, which appeared in the *Hornsea Gazette* of 25 December, is of some interest (not least for the insight it provides into the character of Wade and of local politics at this time, as well as background information on the pier project and the dissension between the two promoters) and worth quoting almost in full:

> On Saturday evening last, a special meeting of the [Hornsea Local Board] was held in the National School-room, at eight o'clock, for the purpose of determining on an answer to be given in reply to a notice served on the Clerk by the Hornsea Pier Company [that is, the Hornsea Pier, Promenade and General Improvement Company] of their intention to acquire certain lands and drainage works the property of the Board. Present: Messrs Gallaway, Hornsey, Pearson, Roxby, Stork, and Wade (Chairman); the Law Clerk (Mr Eldridge), and the Surveyor (Mr Geo. Wade).

> The CHAIRMAN having read the notice convening the meeting, stated that the meeting had been called because the answer had to be forwarded by the 21st. The solicitors for the Bill wrote that application had been made in Parliament for powers to acquire land, &c, in which the Board was interested, for the purpose of constructing a pier, sea wall, &c. The plans and sections had been deposited with the Parish Clerk, and the Board was asked for their assent or dissent, or to state whether they intended to remain neutral. The Chairman said that it would be very wrong to throw any obstacle in the way of the project, but the Board was bound to see that the property of the ratepayers did not pass out of their hands without sufficient guarantees being given that their interests would not suffer … He might state that he was applied to to assist in the projected improvement, as he should have been most happy to do, although he did not approve of the place where the pier was to be constructed. The party promoting the undertaking was interested in that locality, but, however that might be, the pier could not fail to do much good, and he promised, subsequent to it being made, that he would give land for a wide road from the Terminal Station to the pier foot. He had been surprised to find that they were seeking compulsory powers

234

to take his land, and they need not be surprised if he disliked the cutting up of his fields without some guarantee that the pier would be made. If the pier were made, the company should have the road, but they wanted to get it without guaranteeing the erection of the pier. The promoter also objected to his (Mr Wade's) interference with the fixing of the tolls to be charged for admission to the pier, but he felt that these might be made too high, and the utility of the pier limited, he was justified in seeking some guarantee on this point before giving the road. However, if the promoters intended to carry out works so as to benefit the community, he would not be found unfriendly, as, moreover, he should benefit perhaps more than anyone else. It puzzled him beyond measure to understand why the promoters had adopted so expensive a course as they had done ... The company proposed to obtain powers over the Board's [sewage] settling pits, outfall, &c, but although it was possible that they did not wish to take the control of these out of the hands of the Board, yet by applying to Parliament they might obtain such great powers that it was necessary for the Board to be watchful.

The CLERK stated that the company proposed to take the underground sewers and settling pits, and to divert the road leading from Bank Terrace to the sea. Unless guarantees were given, this might prejudice the Board considerably, and the only way to secure a position whereby favourable terms might be obtained, was by expressing dissent. If the Board resolved to do this, a special meeting would have to be convened, and notice thereof given in the paper circulating in the district. At this meeting a clear majority of the Board would have to decide what steps should be taken upon its expression of dissent. Subsequently, the Chairman of the Board, as chairman of the local authority, would have to convene a ratepayers' meeting on receiving a requisition signed by 20 ratepayers, who would, however, have to guarantee any costs that might be incurred, and it would be for the meeting to decide on the steps to be taken. A poll could be demanded at the meeting, and it would have to be taken by voting papers.

The CHAIRMAN explained the plans to the members, stating that he had approved the greater part; but he pointed out that several objections he had made had not been removed.

The CLERK said the question of repairs, and of the cleansing of the cesspools, should be considered before the company got hold of them. Another thing, if these works went out of their power, who would repair the outfall? If the company got an Act of Parliament they might fill up the drains.

The CHAIRMAN thought the Board should be in a position to watch, and there was no way of attaining this other than by expressing dissent. There was no way of keeping a man right like having power over him.

235

Mr ROXBY remarked that, should the scheme be carried out, the benefit would be very great.

Mr HORNSEY said the Hull Trinity House thought very lightly of the scheme.

The CHAIRMAN said everyone interested would have to take care that the promoter did not get to their blind side. He would have done so with him (Mr Wade), had he closed with his first offer.

Mr HORNSEY thought it very hard that when a man did not wish to give up his land, he should be made.

The CHAIRMAN remarked that Parliament would never grant powers to acquire land which was not necessary.

The CLERK said that if the Board stated in reply that they should remain neutral, they would put themselves out of court, whilst if they expressed dissent, they would go to the ratepayers, and the decision as to future action would rest with them.

The CHAIRMAN said it would have been better if the promoter had come to the Board, and said, I want to acquire this land, what guarantees do you want? He might yet do this, and an amicable arrangement be come to.

Mr GALLAWAY moved "That in answer to the notice requesting the assent, dissent, or neutrality of the Local Board, served on the Board by the proposed Hornsea Pier Company, for the purpose of acquiring the Board's settling pits, certain sewerage works, or the diversion of the road leading from the Hornsea Bridge Station to the sea, that this Board return the answer of Dissent."

The CHAIRMAN wished it to be understood that this action was not necessarily dictated by any feeling hostile to the project, but as securing to themselves the power to make terms advantageous to the ratepayers.

Mr ROXBY thought "dissent" a somewhat strong term.

The CLERK said it was the only way by which the ratepayers would have an opportunity of saying what should be done, and he thought it would be wrong not to afford them such opportunity.

Mr ROXBY seconded the motion, and it was carried unanimously.

Clearly stung by Wade's 'blind side' comment, an indignant reply from du Gillon appeared in the *Hornsea Gazette* of 1 January 1876. His response is important for the light it throws on the negotiations between the two men:

Sir - I shall feel obliged if you can find space in your next issue for this somewhat lengthy summary of my negotiations with Mr Wade in reference to the intended Hornsea Pier. Had the Chairman of the Local Board simply acted as such, at their last meeting on Saturday, the 18th inst., I should have kept silent. It is, however, time to let the public know the real merits of the case when a man taking an ungenerous advantage of his official position, divulges certain private negotiations, gives an incorrect account of the said negotiations, and ends in the most unjustifiable manner by saying of an absent stranger "Every one interested would have to take care that the promoter did not get on their blind side. He would have done so with him (Mr Wade) had he closed with his first offer." What a kind, temperate, gentlemanly way this is of speaking of a person whom he stated at our last interview, and before witnesses, had throughout treated him with courtesy and consideration. This is the man, moreover, who repeatedly told the Local Board that he was not unfriendly towards us. Your readers will probably think with me, that this is a rather original method of showing friendliness. Upon one point let me try the arduous duty of disabusing Mr Wade. I did not find it difficult to get on what he elegantly calls his "blind side,: nothing of the sort; the only difficulty I had to contend with during my wearisome negotiations with him was to find the side on which he is not blind. For the man who cannot even see his own interest, or that of a community he has so long kept under his tutelage, must be stone blind indeed! Mr Wade's interests and mine were and are identical, except as to magnitude. Everyone in Hornsea knows which of us has most at stake. Seven years ago I went over to Hornsea with some friends with the intention of inaugurating the very scheme now in question. By now, the place might have doubled in size, and Mr Wade's land quadrupled in value. What hindered us from taking active steps? Nothing but the fear of Mr Wade's opposition. Everywhere in the neighbourhood we heard but one stereotyped opinion; people said – but no, I stop for fear of giving pain to a most sensitive gentle nature. Has not the Chairman of the Local Board a right to expect that I should spare his feelings? If you doubt it, reader, refer to the delicate manner in which he spoke of me on the 18th inst. Mr Wade says it "puzzled him beyond measure to understand why the promoters had adopted so expensive a course as they had done." Is he really puzzled about it? How refreshing it is to come across so innocent a nature. Did it not strike Mr Wade that the promoters, unlike himself, were so burdened with their wealth that they could think of no other way of getting rid of some portion of it than by the help of Parliament? On this point, however, I will oblige Mr Wade by giving him a straightforward answer, and thus enlighten the public upon my doings since April last.

For six whole months subsequent to that date Mr Wade kept me dancing most respectful attendance on him with reference to the proposed Hornsea Pier. I wrote to him letters without number, which he generally had the politeness not to answer; made appointments with him which oftener than not he did not keep. However, I will freely admit that when we did meet, he was profuse in excuses, and apologies, and made good use of all the small arts so much in favour with gentlemen of that calibre when they do not want to give a decided yes or no, but prefer tiring you out after the fashion most approved by the followers of good Izaak Walton. In this way time was beautifully wasted; the period appointed for a formal application to the Board of Trade or to Parliament was fast approaching, without anything tangible being done. I therefore gave Mr Wade a fortnight's notice that the engineer, Mr Robinson, and myself would call on him on Friday, August the 20th; also that we should expect a decisive answer from him on that day, in the absence of which we would break off further negotiations. Three days before the appointed time I wrote reminding Mr Wade of the hour and day agreed upon for our interview. On that day Mr Robinson came down from London, I from Sheffield, and we proceeded to Mr Wade's offices in Hull. We were received by him in a most extraordinary way, he pretended that he did not know we were coming; then that he had forgotten it, afterwards that he was so busy that he really could not see us, and much more to the same effect. He cooled down, however, when he found we were not to be shaken off quite so easily, and gave us some thirty minutes of his valuable time. During that half-hour we apparently did more real business than in the whole of the previous months. Certain heads of agreement were then settled upon, we each taking a copy of it in writing, and Mr Wade, after reading his own copy several times, promised that if I would get my solicitors to draw up the agreement in legal phraseology he would sign it. The crucial point with Mr Wade was that we should, by taking a circuitous route, so avoid the bog that the new road, leading from the terminal station to the pier, should offer good building sites on both sides. From previous conversations we had anticipated this point, so Messrs Villiers & Cherry had begun that very afternoon to bore the ground in question. The engineer and myself spent the whole of the next forenoon with them. The result of our borings was most unfortunate, proving conclusively to all of us that the narrowness of the strip of sound land between the bog and the sea was such that it would not admit of a road which would give Mr Wade the advantages he had stipulated for. We therefore telegraphed him to meet us at the Bridge Station that afternoon, at 6.30; this he did, and we all, i.e. Messrs Wade, Robinson, and myself, proceeded to the offices at the brickyard. I will not weary your readers by describing all that took place; suffice it to say that after an interview of nearly three hours, Mr Wade agreed that the road should go in a straight line as shown in the Parliamentary plans now deposited with the parish clerk, and that he would abide in toto by the agreement entered into the previous evening. Before finally parting I said "Now Mr Wade, please read your memorandum over again, and say decisively, before these gentlemen, whether you will sign a legal agreement wholly drawn up in accordance with it, for I am tired of getting legal documents prepared which you scarcely even look at." Mr Wade smiled, read his memorandum carefully aloud, and said "I will sign it." I replied "You will," to which he said "Yes, I will, and now the matter is settled" ...

During the last week of March 1876 a House of Commons Select Committee reviewed du Gillon's proposed bill. A (partial) transcript of the two-day proceedings, containing important information not only on the compulsory purchase application, but also on coastal erosion and the wider economic advantage of having a pier at Hornsea, is given below:

The consideration of this bill came before the House of Commons Select Committee on Tuesday [28 March]. The committee, presided over by Sir John St Aubyn, Bart., consisted of Earl Percy, Mr R. Plunkett, Mr Bell, and Mr A. Bonham Carter, referee.

Mr Pember, Q.C., and Mr Ledgard (instructed by Mr Rees, agent for Messrs Watson & Son, solicitors, Hull) appeared for the promoters of the bill; Mr McIntyre, Q.C. (instructed by Messrs Frankish & Buchanan, agents for Messrs Lightfoot, Earnshaw & Frankish, solicitors, Hull) appeared for Mr J.A. Wade; and Mr McMillan (instructed by Messrs Frankish & Buchanan, agents for Messrs Eldridge & Stephenson, solicitors, Hull) appeared for Mr G.A. Potts.

Mr Pember, in opening the case, stated that Hornsea was a watering place on the coast of Yorkshire, to the north-east of Hull. By the bill it was proposed to erect a pier, commencing near high water, and running out for 370 yards; a road commencing near Hornsea Station, a tramway line along the road, terminating near the pier, another road, and a sea wall or embankment. The reclamation scheme involved in these works would prove highly beneficial to a large tract of country lying to the westward of the Hull and Hornsea Railway. The reclamation and pier scheme hung together, and the scheme was large in its usefulness and complete in its different parts. The sea up to 1852 had gained 132 yards; since 1852, 43 yards; and, since July last, absolutely eight yards. Since July the sea had got rid of a bank of sand that was a sort of protection, and has nothing to obstruct its onward course except the peak composed of the same loose material that had already been overcome by the sea. When this peak was swept away, then the land behind would be annihilated. He commented on the unsuccessful attempts of Mr Wade to erect fences with the view of accumulating a bank of sand for the protection of his property. All that remained of these fences were the ruined stumps, and practically Mr Wade had not done a particle of good. The sea wall would cost £10,000 of the £40,000 capital it was proposed to raise for the works. This scheme would have the effect of a reclamation scheme, and the ordinary practice allowed in these cases was that the promoters, in return for the money they lay out in

239

reclamation schemes, should be allowed compensation. Now the promoters by this scheme would be doing a very great deal for Mr Wade's and others land, and were they to be made an exception to the ordinary rule? All his clients asked was that in return for the money they were going to expend, and which would reclaim the land on the west as well as on the east of the sea wall belonging to Mr Wade, was that they be allowed to take the land on the east, amounting to 19 acres, leaving to Mr Wade, the 40 acres of land on the west, with its enhanced value and its guaranteed safety – land which will be lost to him inevitably in the course of a few months. The inhabitants of Hornsea were unanimously in favour of the scheme. It would improve the amenity of the place, give an impetus to its buildings, and conduce considerably to its general trade and prosperity. The herring trade of Hull would be largely benefited by the erection of this pier at Hornsea. At present the boats have to beat along the sea coast to Hull with their cargoes, and, this being the most difficult part of the voyage, a loss of two or three days is invariably experienced. Were this pier erected the boats would be able to land their cargoes here, and the fish would be carried direct to Hull by train. The market value of the fish by this quick transit was enormous. At present the Hull herring trade reached about 200,000 lasts, each last containing 10,000 herrings. The difference of the value of the last by the fish reaching the market a couple of days sooner was said to be £10 a last. The greatly increased value of the Hull herring trade, which depended on this pier, would from this be easily seen, and might in a few years amount alone to several millions of money. He concluded by taking a number of objections to the petitions of Mr Wade and Mr Potts, the objectors, reminding the committee that the land they required they proposed to obtain by compulsory purchase; they did not want it as a mere gift.

Mr W.F. Bethell, of Rise Park, Lord of the Manor of Hornsea, gave evidence in support of the bill, and stated that the works proposed by the bill would have a most beneficial effect upon the prosperity of Hornsea. There was a great necessity for a sea-wall to prevent the inroads of the sea.

Mr H.S. Constable, of Wassand Hall, considered the scheme would be beneficial to Hornsea, and that a sea-wall was quite necessary. The proposed works would prove a great benefit and advantage to visitors and all parties in Hornsea, and every one he had spoken to about it was of the same opinion. He owned about half the property in the parish.

Mr John Heslop, farmer and owner of house property, had resided in Hornsea upwards of fifty years, and had filled all the parochial and local offices. He considered the plan would be a great advantage to Hornsea. The townspeople were very sorry the bill was opposed. If something were not done as a defence against the sea the land

240

beyond to the westward would be flooded. He did not know it was in the power of the promoters, if they got the bill, merely to make the road across the town to Mr du Gillon's land, and leave the rest. He did not know how many acres of Mr Wade's land the promoters proposed to take.

Mr Marshall Harrison, one of the principal hotel keepers, and farmer, at Hornsea, gave evidence to the effect that the scheme would be a great advantage to Hornsea. He had no doubt if the bill were passed it would be carried out. The scheme would benefit Mr du Gillon, but it would benefit the public more.

Mr C.F. Shackles, a solicitor practising at Hull and residing at Hornsea. He said if the road across Mr Wade's land were made, the sea wall must be made, otherwise it would be throwing money away; and he imagined that if twenty acres of that land were taken under the Lands Clauses Act from Mr Wade, it would be a very good thing for him; he would not have the opportunity again. The outlay which the promoters would have to make in making the road across Mr Wade's land, and the sea wall, was such that they thought they were entitled to be recouped by any increased value for such portion of the land as was capable of being sold; a large portion was incapable of being built on.

At this point the committee adjourned. When it reconvened the next day it continued hearing witness testimony:

John Banyard, Chief-Officer of the Coastguard-station at Hornsea, gave evidence to the effect that from his knowledge of the tides, and the extent of the encroachments already made by the water, the proposed works would prove of incalculable benefit to Hornsea in arresting the further destructive progress of the sea, and at the same time would afford a protecting screen to the lands of several owners whose property now stood in jeopardy. He had seen water on Mr Potts' land.

In cross-examination by Mr McIntyre, he said so far as he knew it did not much matter where the pier was so long as there was a pier at all. He had no doubt a pier there would tend to increase the fishing boats belonging to Hornsea.
Re-examined: He was an independent witness and did not represent any person. The pier would undoubtedly be a great advantage.

Mr Ansell, a member of the Town Council at Hull, and a large owner of fishing vessels, examined by Mr Ledgard, said if the boats were able to land at Hornsea, coming from the Dogger Bank, it would be a saving of 40 miles in the present voyage to Hull. That would be of great importance from a marketable point of view. If conveniences for the fishing trade were established at Hornsea they would be largely taken advantage of by the Hull trade. Hornsea would act as a sort of depot for Hull, and from which fresh supplies of fish could be obtained every morning. The effect of this pier would he believed be the revival of the live cod trade. It was also essential to the herring trade that the fish should land quickly. If they were landed at Hornsea, as they would be at this proposed pier, the herrings would be worth £10, £15 and upwards per last more than if they were landed on the following day. Were the herrings landed at Hornsea a large continental trade would be developed.

Mr Robinson, C[ivil] *E*[ngineer], the engineer for the bill, said the sea had encroached on the foreshore 132 yards since 1801. He described the engineering details of the works, which he held were absolutely necessary for the protection of the foreshore. The object of the tramway was to convey fish and other traffic from the Pier to Hornsea Station. It was run from the pier head to the station, and was the only route for connecting by tramway the railway station and the pier head. The railway company favoured the junction of the tramway at their station. Road No. 1 was for the use of passengers going to and from the pier and Hornsea station. The probable cost of the sea wall he had estimated at £9,000. The total length of the sea wall was 814 yards. Unless this sea wall was erected and the protection afforded which it would necessarily give, the outlet of the sewage works would be washed away in course of time.

Cross-examined by Mr McIntyre: Do you know of any pier scheme where such a quantity of land has been taken as is proposed by you? – I do not know of any other of a like nature.

At the conclusion of this witness's evidence the room was cleared …

Wednesday 29 March was a sultry spring day in the capital, the kind so beloved by novelists: when violence is in the air, the tightened nerve snaps, and a cause is lost. The shadows were lengthening when the committee reassembled and the chairman delivered the verdict. The Hornsea Local Board's argument that the '… powers, rights, privileges and interests of the Board and the ratepayers' would be prejudiced by du Gillon's scheme won the day. The compulsory purchase application was refused. Costs were applied for on behalf of the bill's opponents, but this application, too, was disallowed.

The above is a very partial and biased rendition of the evidence from the two-day hearing. The partisanship of the editor of the *Hornsea Gazette* is clearly evident. The selective nature of the material his readers are presented with is very much in favour of du Gillon – as it is throughout the entire Hornsea Pier saga. In reality the select committee hearing generated over 400 pages of densely handwritten evidence. From a close reading of the unpublished minutes it is obvious, one, that the select committee was even-handed in its approach, taking pains to hear a range of evidence from both sides, and, two, that the *Hornsea Gazette*, although what it published was accurate, chose only to print those extracts that were prejudicial to the interests of Wade, as he was later to point out.

Locally the select committee's decision caused a furore. Letters of the outraged variety piled up on the editor's desk at the *Hornsea Gazette*. The first of these to be printed appeared in the paper's 1 April edition and set the tone, lambasting and criticising the negativism of Wade and blaming him for the failure of du Gillon's scheme:

> I see by the newspapers that the hopes which recently cheered and inspirited those of your inhabitants who understand how the interests of the town can best be advanced, have been ruthlessly stamped out. This is a serious blow to the place, and inflicts upon every inhabitant and property owner the loss of benefits that would have accrued from an increased number of visitors, from expanded trade, and from the enhanced value of all real estate; whilst, at the same time, it points unmistakably to the fact that capitalists seeking to promote any great work at Hornsea may expect the most bitter opposition and obstruction, unless they are prepared to sink their individuality altogether, and to place themselves at the mercy of others. This latter is, in my opinion, the most serious aspect of the whole question and the result of the last attempt to benefit the place will, for a very long time, deter any similar movement, or increase its difficulties. Your inhabitants may therefore now fold their hands; and pay heavy rates for public works, the greatest benefits of which they will never reap; and allow those rival watering-places which are not burdened with public benefactors to pass them in the race.
>
> I am utterly dumfounded by Mr Wade's action in this matter, for to him, and to him alone, is the frustration of this scheme due. He has tried for years to launch a pier company of his own, but it has been amply demonstrated that sufficient capital is not to be obtained for the company of which he is or was the promoter; and one would have thought, if he had the welfare of Hornsea as much at heart as he asserts, that he would have welcomed and assisted the late scheme which was of a more comprehensive and beneficial nature than the old company ever conceived. However, if Mr Wade cannot launch a pier company of his own, he can *prevent* others succeeding where he has failed, and this may probably be a source of satisfaction to him; but if he supposes that the rejection of the Pier Bill will bring him any nearer to allying *his* name with the providing a pier, I think he will be very much mistaken, as the distrust and mortification engendered in the breast of those who would have helped to forward such a work, will prevent them assisting anything of the kind for a long time to come.
>
> With Mr du Gillon, and the other promoters of the bill, I would express the most profound sympathy. They have throughout evinced a disposition to remove obstacles by conciliation, and displayed a desire to meet the wishes of the public, so far as practicable; but they

have been unfortunate in their choice of a locality. At a great expense they have learnt that the only influence which can be allowed to launch a great work at Hornsea, is that which displayed such genius in the construction of the railway that it cost double the amount originally estimated; and which managed it with such consummate ability that impecuniosity supervened, and an alien company had to be called in.

The party of progress has been defeated, but defeated where victory is but a reproach; and its members must strive that those individuals who betray the highest standards of the town, and destroy its future, shall be excluded from every post of honour or dignity in the place.
SENTINEL

In the next week's paper a letter from Lightfoot, Earnshaw and Frankish, solicitors, was printed in defence of Wade:

Referring to the leading article in your issue of last week, we cannot help expressing our great surprise at it, as the manifest object of it was to induce your readers to believe that the pier part of the Bill was thrown out at Mr Wade's instance; whereas you must well know, from having been in the committee room when the Bill was on, and from the contents of Mr Wade's petition, which were read by Mr du Gillon's counsel, that not one word was contained in it in opposition to the *pier*, and the correspondence between Messrs Watson and ourselves, which the counsel read and put in evidence, confirmed this.

Mr Wade instructed us from the first that, although in his opinion, and as was palpable, the proposed pier site was the worst possible for Hornsea, and the effect of it would be to throw back, for years, all other building land near Hornsea, yet, as he had been unable to carry out his own pier scheme, it would not be right to oppose Mr du Gillon's; and, as you must well know, we carried out his instructions to the letter; and having been present in the committee-room and heard the evidence, you cannot well be ignorant of the real reason why the committee, without hearing the case of the opponents, threw out the entire Bill.

This brought the following rejoinder from the editor:

Our correspondents appear anxious to relieve Mr Wade from the odium he has incurred by opposing the late improvement scheme: and we willingly afford them the opportunity. They express surprise at the tenor of our leading article of last week, and assert that Mr Wade did not oppose *the pier*. But the article in question does not contain any such allegation. It is, nevertheless, undeniable that by the Hornsea Pier Bill powers were sought to construct a pier; and that the Hornsea Pier Bill was opposed by Mr Wade before the committee of

244

the House of Commons; that the Hornsea Pier Bill was rejected; and that "the pier" will not now be made. We acknowledge that we are not expert in splitting hairs, and must confess that we are unable to discern where we have overstepped the boundaries of legitimate criticism.

In the last paragraph of our correspondent's letter, certain disastrous consequences are enumerated as likely, in the opinion of Mr Wade, to have resulted from the construction of "the pier" on the proposed pier site. Instead of adducing them in support of their assertion that Mr Wade did *not* oppose the pier, it would have been, in our opinion, more logical to adduce them as *an excuse for his opposition*.

The same issue also contained a letter from du Gillon:

> ... Our DICTATOR [that is, Joseph Armytage Wade] has given us another slap in the face, and hopes we will meekly present to him the other cheek. No!

The collapse of du Gillon's bill and the anti-Wade letters which appeared in the *Hornsea Gazette* drew an angry reply from Wade, attacking in particular the *Hornsea Gazette's* coverage of the parliamentary proceedings. This was printed in the issue of 15 April:

> Permit me to ask, for the benefit of those of your readers who have not entirely shut both eyes and ears to reason on the subject of Mr Du Gillon's bill:
>
> How it was that Mr Du Gillon himself did not venture to appear as a witness on behalf of it? Was he afraid of the truth being pumped out of him on cross-examination?
>
> What prevented Mr Butler, whose disposition may without lack of charity be supposed to have been sufficiently stimulated by his arbitration with the Local Board?
>
> And above all, Mr Editor, what kept you back from discharging the duty you must have so strongly felt, and from displaying before the Committee the marvellous ingenuity you have shown in the columns of your newspaper? If Hornsea has really lost an opportunity of getting a pier and a sea-wall, has it not been from the incomprehensible failure at the critical moment of yourself, the promoter, and the phalanx of your own contributors who presented not their evidence but their amiable faces to the committee?
>
> How was it that not one of your witnesses, beside the Engineer and Mr Shackles, would own that they knew anything about the Bill? Nor even whether it guaranteed pier or sea wall, or was only a Bill for getting hold of 45 acres of land, or as much as the Committee would grant, for speculation?

How was it that Mr Shackles failed to convince the Committee that it was right to alienate one man's land for another man's benefit?

What wholesome dread prevented every one of your champions from taking so much as a single share in Mr Du Gillon's Company?

Why have you not published the evidence *as it was given before the Committee*, Mr Du Gillon's parliamentary agents having printed it, and a copy of it having been furnished to you by Mr Eldridge? Did you not publish your own version instead? Was the reason for this extraordinary course the fear that as Mr Du Gillon's friends had by their evidence convinced the Committee that this was not a Bill for the making of a pier, but for getting hold of other people's land, so the true version of what his witnesses said would convince your readers of the rottenness of the whole scheme?

Will you venture to assert that there is one atom of truth in the statement that the chairman of the parliamentary committee said he was *sorry* that the preamble was not proved. If he were *sorry*, would it not have been absurd on his part summarily to dismiss the Bill, without ever giving Mr Du Gillon leave to construct the pier, although neither I nor Mr Potts wished to hinder him from making a pier if he really intended it; and without even waiting to hear what we had to say against the scheme?

Are you not aware that if Mr du Gillon wished *bona fide* to make a pier, he had no need to bring a bill into Parliament for it; that the only things which required the sanction of an act of Parliament were the compulsory purchase of land, the levying of tolls on the *public* road, the power to interfere with the Board's drains and road, and the power to alter the course of the stream dyke, and the right of "jurisdiction upon the beach?"

Did you not try to prevent the Local Board from doing its duty to the ratepayers in opposing the attempt to obtain these unheard-of powers?

Did you not suppress the acknowledgement made by Mr Du Gillon's counsel in his speech before the committee that the Local Board was in the right, and that he had conceded what it required?

Are you not aware that if Mr Du Gillon's attempt had succeeded, he could have prevented any one else making a pier for five years to come?

Can you cite any similar instances of powers sought by act of Parliament to interfere with the rights of property, and of the local authorities, and of the public, and to hold for so long a period as five years the right (which necessarily bars others) to construct a pier?

246

Do you yourself believe one word you have written on this subject from the first? Do you think it seemly in any one assuming to hold a very exalted position to engage in an agitation in favour of a scheme for enabling one person to get hold of the property of another, with whom he is notoriously at variance, no matter whether a jury have to assess its value or not?

Are you not aware that if I had really wished to oppose the erection of a pier, *per se*, I could easily have thrown out this bill upon "standing orders?"

When you have answered the foregoing questions relating to the so-called Pier Bill, I will ask you a few more …

The editor sought fit to add his own rejoinder:

Mr Wade has thought fit in the above petulant letter to cast upon us imputations which it is quite unnecessary for us to rebut, and he is quite welcome to any advantage he may anticipate from our silence. He should know that we write only in accordance with our belief; but it appears next to impossible to convince Mr Wade that any person can be conscientious when holding opinions differing from his own. It is somewhat remarkable too, that he should speak so confidently as to the contents of the *Gazette*, when he at the same time declares he is not in the habit of wasting his time upon it.

A new company was then formed by du Gillon: the Hornsea Pier, Promenade and General Improvement Company Limited. The *Hornsea Gazette* of 8 July 1876 reported the inaugural meeting of the new company:

A meeting of gentlemen interested in the construction of a pier at Hornsea was held in the Public Rooms on Tuesday evening [4 July], when Mr Alfred Maw was called upon to preside, and Mr Henry Robinson, C[ivil] E[ngineer], of London, attended to furnish information on the engineering details.

The CHAIRMAN said the meeting was held with the object of devising the best means for providing a pier and making other improvements on the foreshore that were universally acknowledged to be necessary to the prosperity of the place. It was contemplated to form a company to carry out the proposed work. He had waited upon several gentlemen in the neighbourhood to ascertain the amount of support likely to be accorded to such a scheme, and he was gratified to say that he met with very liberal encouragement; so much so that he felt assured they should be enabled to carry out the scheme successfully.

247

Mr DU GILLON said he had been induced by the sympathy which had been manifested towards himself on the failure of the late pier scheme, to combine with others in another endeavour to provide a pier. The late scheme failed through its opponents impressing the parliamentary committee with the idea that there was no company, but simply an attempt by one individual to "grab" the land of another proprietor. Those present knew well enough that the land in question was comparatively useless, or would be so very shortly; but of this the committee were not fully aware. In support of the present project, while here a short time ago for the benefit of his health, he had in five days succeeded in obtaining a subscription list amounting to between £6000 and £7000, and the number of intending shareholders at the present time was about thirty. With the object of diminishing the expenses he proposed to place at the disposal of the company all the plans and surveys which he had been obliged to provide for the previous scheme; and he had also guaranteed the cost of the preliminary legal proceedings over and above five per cent on the shares subscribed. All the land required for the pier and its approaches, belonging to him, he should give to the company free of charge; further, he should be prepared, as soon as permission was obtained for the construction of the pier, to commence, at his own expense, improvements on his estate, south of the site proposed for the pier, which were estimated to cost considerably over £20,000. Those improvements included the making of a sea wall from the foot of the pier for nearly a mile along the front of his land, surmounted by a promenade, with the building of an aquarium, and other works which must prove attractive. It would be seen, therefore, that the construction of a pier was not all that depended upon their deliberations tonight. The sea defence he proposed in front of his land would be a wall of solid material 9 feet thick, backed up to the boulder clay; and the engineer proposed to continue this wall some little distance to the north of the pier, so as to protect it. With respect to the communications between the pier and the railway stations, it was thought better in the present movement to confine themselves strictly to the making of a pier, seeing the ill success of the previous scheme, and leave this matter to the development of events. He had no doubt they concurred with him in believing that something would have to be done for the protection of the outfall of the town's sewers, and it would then be time enough to consider how and by whom that land should be protected. As to the probability of remuneration to the company, he might remark that he only knew of one pier, that at Scarborough, on the north cliff, which did not pay, and that was caused by superior attractions having been previously provided on the south, as well as owing to the workmanship or some of the materials of the pier having proved deficient in quality, thereby requiring a constant and heavy outlay in repairs. The circumstances at Hornsea would be somewhat different, and while he had no desire to hold the expectation that at the first there would be anything like a return of 25 per cent, but he really believed that the improvements on his own estate would serve as a feeder to the pier, and he had no wish to conceal the belief that his land would also be improved by the making of the pier, for he felt confident the advantages would be mutual; and with the proximity of Hull with its large population, and the probability of the development of the fish traffic, he thought there was sufficient ground to look for a reasonable return on the outlay from the first. As soon as the pier was assured he should begin with his own improvements, while for any services or advantages he could render the company he sought no remuneration, and it should be distinctly understood that no "promotion" expenses would be incurred. They should remember also that the present time was most favourable for the execution of the work, as there was no doubt that from the state of the iron trade contracts could be obtained much lower than would have been the case only a short time ago. He then quoted from the returns of several pier companies, showing dividends varying from 3½ to 15 per cent, and argued that from local causes the capital required in the present case would be much less than was usually needed in schemes of a similar character. The capital already promised was sufficient to construct a pier extending so far in to the sea that there would be 2ft. 3in. of water at shore end of pier at high water spring tides, increasing to 19ft. 6in. at the end of the body of pier; and supposing the head were built there would be at the extreme end 21ft. 6in. He suggested that it might be worthy of consideration by the company whether they should carry out the entire work, or at the commencement to do a portion, and complete it when a sufficient amount of capital should be subscribed.

Mr ROBINSON C.E., then explained the proposed project, and confirmed the statements made by the previous speaker. On the subject of cost, he said a pier 26 feet wide and 780 feet long (which would give 8 feet depth of water at the head at low water spring tides) with a head beyond 100 ft. square, and giving an additional area of 10,000 square feet, might be constructed for £11,000 to £12,000. In this estimate he included the sea defence and all other works necessary for the pier itself, but he did not include any buildings on the head. These might be plain or ornamental, and would vary in cost accordingly. The position fixed for the pier was a very favourable one, because at that point the dip of the beach was greater, and consequently there would be a given depth of water at a shorter distance from the cliff. He believed that a saving of 15 per cent at least would be effected if the pier were made at once, in consequence of the depressed state of the iron trade, and said he knew of contracts having been made 30 per cent lower than a couple of years ago. His estimate was made on the assumption that the work would be carried out at once; if delayed, the circumstances might not be so favourable. His idea was that a sound and substantial pier was desired, and that it was not intended to spend money on gimcracks.
Several drawings, plans and photographs were submitted by Mr Robinson, in which the gentlemen present appeared to take

249

considerable interest, and the inquiries they made respecting them were very courteously answered by him.

After some consideration the following resolution was moved by Mr HESLOP, seconded by Mr JAMES, and carried unanimously: "That it is desirable to form a company for the purpose of making a pier and other improvements in Hornsea, to be called the Hornsea Pier, Promenade, and General Improvement Company, Limited."

Mr C.J. TODD then read over the Memorandum and Articles of Association of the company, which had been prepared; after which, Mr HARRISON moved and Mr W.H. BODEN seconded their adoption, which was carried unanimously.

The articles of association were then signed by several of the gentlemen present, and it was understood that they would be forwarded to London on the following day for registration, which course we have since been informed has been adopted.

In the same issue, an editorial comment applauded the formation of the new company – and, at the same time, could not resist taking a side-swipe at Wade:

Our readers will no doubt rejoice with us to find that there is yet some possibility of a pier being constructed at Hornsea ... A company is being formed for this purpose, and although the new scheme is not so extensive as the one previously proposed, we feel sure that its realization would produce almost universal satisfaction in the town and neighbourhood. The previous scheme was rejected by the House of Commons in consequence at the extent of land sought to be acquired for the improved communication with the two railway stations, the owners of such land being unwilling to dispose of it, and having on this ground opposed the project. Although we regard the original scheme as being more comprehensive, and better calculated to have promoted the general interests of Hornsea, we consider the promoters of the project now under consideration have exercised a wise discretion in confining themselves for the present, to the construction of a pier – and a pier only – under the impression that when that is accomplished the necessity for other improvements will become so manifest as to render it more than probable that the public sympathies will soon become enlisted in its favour. The statement that about one-third of the required capital has already been subscribed, or promised, is the best indication of the appreciative feeling with which the new Pier scheme is thus far entertained, and we heartily wish the company complete success.

A prospectus was issued in late July 1876 with a proposed capital of £20,000, issued in £10 shares. A board of nine directors was established (du Gillon as chairman; A. Maw of Hornsea and Hull; B.L. Wells of Hornsea and

Hull; J. King James of Hornsea and Hull; W.M. Jackson of Hull; W. Carr of Hull and Hornsea; J. Heslop of Hornsea; W.H. Carter of Hornsea; and J.G. Payne of Benningholme Hall and Hull), and solicitors (Watson and Son and C. James Todd, both of Hull) and bankers (the London and Yorkshire Bank) appointed. The aim was to construct not only a pleasure pier, but also two roads, a tramway, a protective sea wall, and a commercial harbour and associated facilities alongside the pier. As the prospectus stated:

> This Company has been formed to provide the favourite Watering Place of Hornsea with a Pier, and other such improvements as may from time to time be decided upon …

> The Pier will be constructed to serve as a commodious and ornamental promenade, and will be provided with those facilities for recreation which have made similar piers at other watering places remunerative.

> Suitable arrangements will be made and proper appliances provided to land fish. This will supply a long-felt want, and afford a considerable source of income. To accommodate this traffic, the Pier will be made much wider than the generality, affording ample room for a separate road-way if found necessary, which can be railed off, as at Southport, from the promenade portion of the structure. At the present time, the fishing fleets from the river Humber take their cargoes to Grimsby or Hull for carriage by rail to London and the Midland counties. There is always a liability to interruption and delay, by reason of unfavourable winds retarding the smacks getting into the Humber. If means for landing fish at all tides is provided at Hornsea, it has been ascertained that the smacks will make use of it to a very considerable extent, as it would at times save as much as two days in going up the Humber and as much in returning. It has also been ascertained that the fishing-boats along the coast will largely use the Pier for landing their fish, the finest fishing-grounds of the neighbourhood being in close proximity to Hornsea.

> The landing of fish at the Pier will form a source of attraction and amusement to inland visitors, as has been found to be the case at Margate, Whitby, and other places, where they frequent the piers at the times when the fish is being landed.

> The Pier will also much increase the facilities for boating, which are at present of a very limited character.

> The balance sheet of the various Pier Companies such as Hastings, Blackpool, Southport, Morecambe, and Eastbourne, show profits varying from 5 to 15 per cent, on the capital expended. The conditions under which the proposed Pier will be erected, are equally if not more favourable to success than at many other places where piers pay well. For instance the fish traffic, although but slightly

increasing the cost of the Pier, will yield a large profit; again, from natural local circumstances, the capital to be expended on the proposed Pier will not be half the average cost of the five piers already named, which is above £25,000 …

By the following year du Gillon had become evermore ambitious: he envisaged nothing less than an entire new town – the South Cliff estate – focused on the pier, as described earlier in this chapter.

Meanwhile, on 4 November 1876 the Hornsea Pier, Promenade and General Improvement Company gave public notice that they were applying for a Board of Trade licence to construct a pier. This news spurred Wade to renewed activity. Just fourteen days later, the Hornsea Pier Company gave similar notice, their permission of 1871 having lapsed under the five-year rule. The *Hornsea Gazette* chose not to make serious comment on this somewhat ludicrous state of affairs until early in the following year. In March 1877, during the Local Board election campaign (in which Wade was standing for re-election), an editorial in the paper (24 March) undertook a comprehensive, wholly negative (but with more than a little truth), assessment of Wade's performance in Hornsea affairs, both on and off the Local Board. Nonetheless, it does provide interesting comment and perspective, as this extract indicates:

We write from conviction, after many years of close observation of Hornsea matters, and not by the inspiration of the Pier and Promenade Company, nor of any individual or body of individuals; and we must not be supposed to pledge in any way the Pier and Promenade Company when we say that we do not see any other course open to that company but to oppose Mr Wade before the House of Commons, as the very idea of two piers at Hornsea is simply absurd. It must be evident to any thinking person that the only result of two companies being entrusted with the requisite powers to construct a pier must be that one will nullify the other, and we shall be, if possible, further from the desired end than when the original company had the whole field to itself. Further, unless assured that Mr Wade's scheme has received a fair proportion of financial support, we are warranted in assuming that if he were successful in obtaining the sole power for his company, it would remain in the same state of stagnation which has characterised it for so many years; had he been able to secure such financial support and assistance, the pier would doubtless have been built long before this; but as he has so conspicuously failed in what is the real difficulty with which he has to cope, we think he would display more consideration for the welfare of the town in which he is so deeply interested, were he to cease his antagonism, and allow the new company the opportunity of showing whether they can supply this great public need.

… He appears to think that the new scheme is based on personal antagonism to himself; but in this he is egregiously mistaken. It was only after ten years of weary waiting for his company to carry out the work, that a new organisation sprang into existence; and when it has been clearly shown that the mismanagement of the Hornsea Railway during Mr Wade's chairmanship had not been forgotten by the investing public, and that, consequently, there was little or no hope of his ever being able to raise the requisite capital. For ourselves, during nearly all those years, we cordially supported Mr Wade's endeavours to procure a pier, and it was only from a sense of public duty that we forsook the advocacy of his company when its impotence had become so evident, and when a project was brought forward possessing more elements of success.

Whenever Mr Wade's vanity prompts him not only to think but even openly to avow that he, and he alone, can compass Hornsea's development, let him call to mind that the new company has made much greater strides in a few months than his own company did during ten years, and the strange delusion may possibly, to some extent, be dissipated; and he may then ask himself whether he is not chiefly responsible for the comparative stagnation which has hitherto reigned in Hornsea. Mr Wade may be excused for attaching such undue importance to his own personality, but we may be pardoned expressing the opinion that if he ceased to surround himself with subordinates ill-fitted to assist him he might perhaps attain a juster appreciation of his own powers, and his public conduct might be more tolerant and less injurious, not only to his own interests, both socially and pecuniary, but also to the general well-being of Hornsea, for which on all occasions he never fails to proclaim himself to be so extremely anxious.

Predictably a legal wrangle ensued, with each company petitioning against the proposals of the other. A head-on collision was looming just around the corner. Throughout the first half of 1877, both companies held regular meetings in the town at which the benefits and reasonableness of their respective proposals were rehearsed and the claims of the rival group were denigrated and lambasted. All this was fully (and, at times, gleefully) reported in the *Hornsea* Gazette. Claim and counter-claim filled the air and the columns of the town's newspaper. Matters were finally brought to a conclusion in July, when the two claimants appeared before a select committee of the House of Commons. After hearing submissions, arguments, claim and counter-claim, the chairman delivered his verdict. A stark – and somewhat unusual – choice was on offer. Either each party agree to the construction of the other's pier or permission for the building of one pier only would be granted. As neither du Gillon nor Wade could be certain of victory, they agreed to the compromise. So, Hornsea was potentially to have two piers: a north pier built by Wade and a southern one built by du Gillon, separated by a mere 800 yards of beach. On this basis separate parliamentary legislation was passed on 6 July 1877 for the Hornsea Pier (North) and Hornsea Pier (South).

Pierre du Gillon was first to begin. Within a month he had signed contracts for the building of sea defences to either side of the pier's site and for the construction of the proposed harbour. Hoping to more effectively

253

stamp his mark on Hornsea he took up residence in the town,[6] no doubt also doing so in order to keep a watchful eye on his rival. From the outset the work was severely under capitalised. This was compounded in November 1877 by a storm, when machinery and other equipment were destroyed and building materials washed away. The project never recovered from this setback.

After a further eighteen months of desultory activity, du Gillon was ready to admit defeat. In his capacity as chairman, he called an extraordinary general meeting of the Hornsea Pier, Promenade and General Improvement Company for 1 May 1879. At that meeting, the company was declared bankrupt and wound up. Failure was attributed to the high litigation costs incurred in the battle with Wade's rival company. As the *Hornsea Gazette* reported two days later:

> The notice convening the meeting having been read, the CHAIRMAN [du Gillon] introduced the business by stating that they had been called together to consider a recommendation from the directors that the company be wound up. The directors had come to this determination unanimously, after carefully considering the responsibilities and liabilities of the company, and it remained for the shareholders to consider whether they would confirm and adopt such recommendation. He expressed his regret that the company was not in a position to carry out its original object, and read a statement of the liabilities of the company as far as they could at present be definitely ascertained. He concluded by formally moving a resolution to the effect that the company be wound up voluntarily, and that Mr Charles F. Shackles be the liquidator.
>
> Mr W. DYSON, JUN., expressed his concurrence with the directors, and believing that it was to the interest of the shareholders that the affairs of the company be wound up with as little delay as possible, he seconded the motion.
>
> Mr B.L. WELLS said he and his co-directors made the recommendation with some regret, but they believed that it was the most prudent course to take. A considerable amount of money had been expended, but he thought the directors could scarcely be blamed for that; it had been forced upon them by the circumstances in which they had been placed, and their money had mostly gone in law. He believed, however, that most of them had taken shares from a desire to secure a pier, rather than from the expectation of a direct pecuniary return, and they had this consolation that while they had not succeeded in carrying out their own scheme, their action had contributed very materially towards securing the pier now being constructed by another company. The shareholders had already paid two calls, and he believed a third would meet all the liabilities of the company.

---

[6] In 1878 he was elected to the Local Board of Health (of which Wade was chairman); he was also an active committee member of the Hornsea Regatta.

After some further consideration, the resolution was put to the meeting and carried unanimously.

Mr WELLS then said as this was the last occasion on which they should meet together, he wished to move a vote of thanks to Mr du Gillon for his honourable and indefatigable conduct as chairman of the company. He had often been placed in trying circumstances, but had manifested throughout a desire to promote the interests of the shareholders.

The motion have been seconded by Mr MARSHALL HARRISON, was carried unanimously.

Mr DU GILLON, in replying, said it was particularly gratifying to him to receive their vote of thanks thus unanimously passed, more especially as winding-up meetings were not usually those at which directors received kindly expressions from their fellow shareholders. He had met them in that very room at the formation of the company, a perfect stranger, still having the reputation of being a successful man; they had now had time to try and prove him, and he had evidently gone through the trying ordeal to their satisfaction. Their vote of thanks, under these circumstances, greatly relieved his mind, and would enable him to bear-up with more equanimity against the company's want of complete success, for after all, they had now got a pier at Hornsea, and that was their main purpose in becoming shareholders in this company. He concluded by again expressing his thanks.

The proceedings then terminated.

Soon afterwards du Gillon left Hornsea.[7]

The failure of du Gillon prompted Wade – in triumphalist tone (and rather prematurely as it turned out) – to pen a letter to the *Hornsea Gazette* (24 May 1879):

My attention having been called to the report of the meeting of the Hornsea Pier, Promenade &c. Co., which appeared in your issue of the 3rd inst., I have for the first time read it this morning. Had not the subject been so grave a one as the waste of some thousands of pounds in gratifying an unfriendly feeling, I should have looked upon the report as an excellent joke. To spend some thousands in attempting to prevent a Company from obtaining parliamentary authority to construct a pier, and in other litigious ways during two Sessions to hinder that work, is a mode of promoting the construction

---

[7] In 1881 he was working as a shipbuilder in Falmouth, Cornwall; later he moved back to the West Riding to teach French.

more ludicrous than any which ever yet appeared in *Punch*. However, I am glad that the friends whom you have so energetically urged forward are pleased with their expenditure, and as they now acknowledge that the pier which has been constructed will benefit them. I beg to suggest that they also spend an equal sum in substantial and valuable shares to help it forward, for it cannot be properly carried out unless a larger proportion of the share capital be taken up.

Wade's Hornsea Pier Company started work on the north pier in the summer of 1878. Like du Gillon, Wade also suffered from the under capitalisation of his project. At the company's March 1879 annual general meeting, he complained that the 'long period of apathy on the part of Hornsea people and the severe and vexatious opposition in Parliament and of the opposition from people outside Hornsea' had resulted in many fewer subscriptions than anticipated. In all, working capital was just £8,700. It is clear that public confidence in both schemes had been shaken by the much-publicised enmity between the two rivals. At the same meeting Wade also announced that, in an effort to save costs, the length of the pier was to be reduced from 1,145 ft to 1,085 ft.

By August 1879 the project architect – Eugenius Birch (who had designed the piers at Blackpool, Brighton, Margate, and Scarborough, among others) – and contractors – Bergheim and Company – were petitioning the courts for the liquidation of the pier company over unpaid bills. Somewhat characteristically Wade lodged a counter suit, claiming shoddy workmanship. Whilst the conflicting claims were addressed, another company – De Fontaine and Company – completed work on the pier. At its 1880 annual general meeting the scale of the financial problem facing the pier company became evident: it owed £3,500 in legal costs and had debts of around £35,000 over and above the monies raised by subscription.

In May 1880, owing to the continued financial difficulties of the pier company, De Fontaine applied to the Chancery Division for a restraining order preventing Wade and his fellow directors from taking possession of the completed structure. This application was successful, and the court appointed a receiver and manager.

Although the pier was completed by the summer of 1880 it did not open to the public that year. However, on August Bank Holiday Monday, the Hornsea Regatta committee were allowed to use the pier as a vantage point for the judging of races.

On the night of Thursday/Friday 28/29 October 1880 fate dealt another blow to the pier. For a week and more previously, a large number of vessels had been lying wind-bound in the Humber estuary. On the morning of the twenty-eighth the wind shifted to a gentle southwesterly breeze, which prompted the shipping to continue with their voyages. All day vessels plied northwards along the Holderness coast. At around 7pm the wind veered to the east-north-east and within a short time increased to a 'perfect hurricane.' Mike Sewell captures the suddenness when he writes:

In the North Sea it was the swift onslaught of the storm which caught everyone unawares, and vessels had no time to run for shelter. The ships under sail (the majority) had little chance to take precautions before the storm overwhelmed them. The force of the wind carried away sails and rigging while, on the east coast, with the wind coming from the east-north-east, ships were driven helplessly towards the shore. Many ships tried to anchor. But again, the force of the storm upon the ships' hulls caused the anchors to drag or the cables to snap. To make matters worse, visibility was severely restricted by torrential rain, sleet and hail.

From the perspective of the shoreline at Hornsea, the *Hull Packet* provides a contemporary view of the 'Great Storm':

Hundreds hurried from their houses to the beach. The night was pitch dark, but by the aid of a few feeble lights here and there, it could be seen that the waves were running mountains high, whilst boiling surf was being thrown up to the beach far and wide. The bell of the lifeboat house was rung and the men hurried to their duty but for some time it was impossible to get horses for the purpose of bringing the lifeboat on to the scene. Although six powerful horses were obtained and a start was effected very little progress was made, however, the animals being unable to face the wind. Torrents of rain were also falling and the sand was being blown in all directions. The result was that the attempt to get the boat to the beach was given up in despair. If it could have been taken there, it is declared there would have been insuperable difficulties in launching it on account of the huge breakers. Rockets were sent up and in one instance a line was thrown across a vessel but it did not appear to be of much use to those on board. It is stated that a vessel in the offing was burning lights as a signal of distress. These lights suddenly disappeared. It could not be ascertained what became of the ship. Later on the pier attendant went to put the light at the head of the pier but he could not walk upright. Whilst creeping along one of his hands suddenly slipped into space and he found that a large portion of the pier had been destroyed.

The brig *Earl of Derby* had caused the destruction of the seaward end of the pier. With a crew of nine she was sailing in ballast from Le Havre to Seaham, County Durham, and, after spending 27 October sheltering in the Humber estuary, had resumed her voyage on the next morning. The vessel was struck by the storm off Skipsea, half-a-dozen miles to the north of Hornsea, and her sails were blown away. Out of control, the brig was then blown towards the shore. The *Hull Packet* takes up the narrative:

Plate 53. A rare photograph showing damage to Hornsea Pier after the 'Great Storm' of October 1880. (Photograph: Stephen Harrison collection)

The vessel was driving before the storm on her beam ends. The captain ordered both anchors to be got ready to let go, but the gale blowing so hard the order was countermanded and it was deemed best to run in shore, so as to save life. Orders were given to look out for a red and green light, the ship being in broken water became altogether unmanageable. Shortly after Hornsea Pier was seen on the port bow and the man at the wheel put the helm hard-a-port. The vessel did not answer to her helm and the waves dashed her against the pier.

The *Earl of Derby* was repeatedly buffeted against the pier, becoming entwined within its supporting legs. As the ship crashed against the pier, a jumble of timber and twisted ironwork rained down on the stricken vessel, dismasting her and destroying the captain's cabin. Amidst the mounting chaos and confusion, the mate and three crew members managed to scramble on to the pier and the safety of land. A little later several pier legs gave way, freeing the vessel, which afterwards ran aground near the outflow of the Stream Dike, where coastguards using lifelines took off the remaining crew.

With the coming dawn, the damage to the pier became evident: around 250 ft of the seaward end had been damaged. With the approval of the receiver this section was demolished and the remaining length repaired as necessary. With limited finances available, repairs were slow, but the pier finally opened to the public on Saturday 6 August 1881. The pier remained open until the end of September; thereafter, it was open annually between Whit Monday and the end of September. Despite attempts from 1885 onwards to increase public use by the holding of regular weekly promenade concerts, the pier was never a popular visitor attraction – except on the annual Regatta Day, when the structure was used as a viewing platform for the boat races. On these occasions, according to the *Hornsea Gazette*, between 2,500 and 4,000 people would pass through the pier turnstiles; usually, however, numbers were in the low hundreds. Beyond the turnstiles, the attractions – booths selling

Plate 54. Hornsea Pier looking towards the town, 1890s. (Photograph: Stephen Harrison collection)

shrimps, teas and such like – were clearly insufficient to tempt visitors to parting with their entrance fees. Income from admissions was always modest, and went towards repaying the company's outstanding (and substantial) debts and towards maintaining the pier in a safe condition. It never made a profit, and, for its entire life, remained in the hands of the receiver.

Income was evidently insufficient to meet maintenance costs, for, by 1890, there were calls for the pier to be closed on safety grounds. The *Hornsea Gazette* of 1 March 1890 carried a short piece on that year's annual general meeting of the pier company, reporting that 'the Chairman [that is, Wade] strongly commented upon the unfair practice of residents and others forcing an entrance to the pier when closed, many of whom systematically withheld their support during the season when open to the public.'

Notwithstanding the calls for its closure, and despite dwindling admissions revenue, the pier struggled on for another seven years. Wade died in March 1896, and the following year the Hornsea Pier Company was finally wound up. This event sealed the fate of the pier, the structure that Wade had intended as his epitaph. The pier was sold to Ellis and Tattersall of Manchester, who planned its demolition. The new owners kept the pier open until the end of the 1897 summer season. The structures timberwork was auctioned on 28 October 1897. Ironically, Richard Wade, Sons and Company of Hull purchased much of this; this firm had been headed by Joseph Armytage Wade from 1853 until his death, and at the time of the auction was in the hands of his younger brother John Edward.

The pier was dismantled to beach level during the winter of 1897-98. Most of the piles were left *in situ*; two of these were recovered during the 1970s and can now be seen on the sea front and in the Memorial Gardens, New Road. The entrance pavilion survived the general demolition, but was taken down during the interwar years.

259

Towards the end of the nineteenth century, it is clear that great efforts were being made to attract visitors to Hornsea. A promenade was constructed along the North Cliff in 1890, described in the following terms:

> The promenade is the chief rendezvous of both residents and visitors. It consists of a broad gravel walk, on top of the cliffs; seats, shelters, and flowerbeds adding to its comfort and appearance. A bandstand is in the centre, from which it is expected the newly-formed Hornsea Brass Band will add to the general enjoyment.

A private syndicate was responsible for establishing the Promenade Gardens in 1897, later renamed the Victoria Gardens. These were taken over by Hornsea Urban District Council in 1905.

'All change, please'

A rail link between Hull and Hornsea was first proposed in the 1840s. In 1846 George Hudson's York and North Midland Railway Company obtained an enabling act (The York and North Midland (East Riding Branches) No. II Act), which allowed for the construction of a branch line to Hornsea. The new line, part of the existing Hull and Selby Railway, was to leave the Hull to Bridlington line at Leconfield and, after following a somewhat tortuous route through Holderness, was to terminate beside Atwick Road, a few hundred yards south of the windmill. The Hull to Hornsea railway never progressed beyond the planning stage. Hudson's inglorious financial collapse in 1849 and the opposition of many Holderness landowners to the proposed route caused the scheme to be abandoned. A second attempt in 1853 also ended in failure.

A further eighteen years would pass before Hornsea acquired a rail link. In the meantime, the failure of the 1846 and 1853 schemes placed Hornsea at a serious disadvantage. With the opening of the Hull to Bridlington line in 1846, the Bridlington to Filey line in the following year, and the Hull to Withernsea line in 1854, these three places (Bridlington and Filey more so than Withernsea) began to quickly develop as seaside resorts. Effective transport was an essential concomitant to the development of coastal holiday destinations. As far as the east coast is concerned, the race was already more or less won by the time Hornsea appeared even on the start line.

The prime mover in bringing the railway to Hornsea was, yet again, Joseph Armytage Wade. Local tradition has it that sometime around 1858, whilst travelling on horseback between Hornsea and Hull, Wade was waylaid by a common thief and relieved of his purse and other belongings. His resolve to provide a rail link to the town, thus ensuring a safe means of travel through the badlands of Holderness, supposedly grew out of this experience. However that may be, he waited at least three years before publicly unveiling his proposal. As Mike Sewell has pointed out, it is more likely that the already wealthy Wade

> … saw investment in the railway as an opportunity to increase his riches. The profits would not only come from owning shares in the

260

railway company, but also from speculating in land, particularly at Hornsea, where the price of building land would be expected to rise. In addition, Wade no doubt realised that he would be able to sell timber to both the railway company and also to builders at Hornsea.

The motive behind the construction of the railway was purely financial, whatever Wade's personal ambitions were. By linking into the developing regional network through Hull it was anticipated that the new service would, as well as bringing other benefits to the area, provide direct, cross-country access to Hornsea from the heavily populated industrial areas of West Yorkshire and the midland counties.

A public meeting to discuss the project was called for the evening of 7 October 1861.[8] The National School on Mereside was packed: local landowners, farmers, businessmen, and the more middling sort. From the floor, Wade was elected to chair the meeting. He then made a lengthy speech, which extolled the virtues of his scheme, 'principally that it would be cheap, at less than £50,000.' Getting into his stride, he went on with his sales pitch, emphasising the great benefits that would accrue from a rail link:

> A railway would provide Hornsea with a link not only to Hull, but also to the great cities of the country. Hornsea, which had sunk from its former position as a favourite and fashionable watering place, would experience a great revival. Not only would visitors flock there, it would be attractive for people to come and live there, with a consequent rise in the value of building land. Farmers would be able to send their produce out more easily and the movement of coal and fertiliser would be quicker and simpler. Wade emphasised that, owing to the flatness of the landscape, the building of the line would be without difficulty.

Something for everyone. A tempting prospect for would-be investors.

The meeting was clearly enthused by what it heard. So much so that by the evening's end some £3,000 worth of shares had been applied for. This was in addition to the £19,000 Wade had already been promised by family, friends and business associates. A meeting in Withernwick the following week produced an equally receptive outcome. After two false dawns it looked as though Hornsea's time had come at long last.

However, potential trouble loomed later that month. On 23 October a well-attended public meeting at Leven, some half-a-dozen miles to the west of Hornsea, discussed the possibility of a rail link between Beverley and Hornsea. Nothing conclusive came out of this meeting, but Wade was sufficiently anxious not to let the initiative slip out of his hands that he successfully petitioned the Mayor of Hull to convene a public meeting to

---

[8] This meeting is important in another respect. It marked the beginning of a nearly thirty-year association by Wade in the public affairs of the town. In 1864 he was a founder member of the Hornsea Local Board of Health, serving as its chairman 1864-73 and again between 1874-89. Between 1872-83 he was a churchwarden. In 1880 he helped to found the Hornsea and District Liberal Club, becoming its first president. And in 1884 he was elected the first chairman of the Hornsea School Board.

discuss his scheme. At the ensuing meeting on 30 October Wade's proposal received a favourable response from the audience, the majority of whom were drawn from Hull's prosperous business and mercantile communities. The outcome of this meeting was decisive. It persuaded Wade and his backers to go ahead and form the Hull and Hornsea Railway Company. The first meeting of the provisional directors took place in Hull on 13 November. Wade was elected chairman, most probably because he was the major shareholder in the fledgling company. His co-directors were: William Wright, a landed proprietor at Sigglesthorne, who also owned a seed crushing mill in Hull; Benjamin Haworth, a Hull Banker (also with local connections, administering an estate at Rolston on behalf of his wife); and Thomas Haller, Thomas Sykes and Edward Broosheft, all Hull businessmen. Although the idea of a railway was enthusiastically supported in Hornsea, it is interesting to note that, with the exception of Wade, none of his fellow directors had any real or direct connection with the town; an example of venture capital from the regional centre speculating to accumulate. No doubt prompted by his involvement with the railway, Haller, in particular, would go on to buy, at cheap prices, significant amounts of land in Hornsea for house-building. Another instance of speculating to accumulate.

Figure 50. Emblem of the Hull and Hornsea Railway Company. (Stephen Harrison collection)

In early 1862 Lord Hotham of South Dalton promoted the railway in parliament, introducing the Hull and Hornsea Railway Bill. After a smooth passage through the parliamentary process, the bill received Royal Assent on 30 June 1862. With this, the Hull and Hornsea Railway Company became a legal entity, with an authorised capital of £70,000 in £10 shares and powers to borrow a further £23,000. As we shall see, the financial underpinning of the new company was woefully inadequate, grossly underestimated, leading to severe problems over the next few years.

On Wednesday 8 October 1862, with due ceremony, Joseph Armytage Wade cut the first turf on the site of what was to become the Hornsea railway terminus, in sight and sound of the sea – also, incidentally, on land owned by Wade, which he had sold to his railway company for £288 per acre. This event marked the beginning of construction, a task contracted to S and T Crawshaw of Askham Bryan, near York; they were engaged to construct the line, but not the station premises and other buildings associated with it, for £26,287 18s.

Work proceeded apace throughout the rest of 1862 and into the following year, with the confident expectation that the line would be opened to traffic on 1 July 1863. Problems, however, began to appear, slowing progress considerably. In particular, an embankment between Hornsea Bridge and the terminus station became a major frustration, exacerbated by having to cross low-lying and marshy ground. The engineering difficulties were compounded by the demand of Richard Bethell of Rise Park that arches be built through the embankment to allow access to his land on either side of the line. A viaduct rather than an embankment became the preferred solution. This greatly added to the cost and, inevitably, put the work behind schedule. The timescale slipped. The 1st of July came and went. In August, tenders were accepted for building the stations, with the contracts being awarded to J.T.R. Robinson, who was to build the Hornsea terminus station for £2,534, and to Hockney and Liggins, who were to build the remainder – Sutton, Swine, Skirlaugh, Ellerby, Marton, Whitedale, Sigglesthorne, Goxhill and Hornsea Bridge – at a total cost of £3,000.

By mid-March 1864 the S and T Crawshaw had completed their work – after a fashion, as we shall see. On 21 March, a Board of Trade Inspector accessed the line. His inspection was favourable, and the directors decided to open the railway at short notice, on Easter Monday, although building work on the stations was far from complete; nor were the goods sidings at the stations ready for use. Creditors were also demanding payment for outstanding invoices. The company was already in financial difficulties. Later in the following year, as debts mounted, the shareholders authorised the raising of an additional £50,000 in shares and the borrowing of a further £16,600.

On 28 March – Easter Monday (not a public holiday until 1871) – 1864, just one week after the Board of Trade inspection, the line opened. The *Hull Packet* reported the event:

> The long wished for day has at length arrived. The Hull and Hornsea railway is now open to the public. On Monday last the first train started from the Wilmington Station – the arrangements to run from

Paragon Street ... being not yet completed, at noon and was well filled with passengers, despite the miserable weather which prevailed. The station and every spot adjacent, was crowded with spectators anxious to witness the departure of the train and as it moved slowly away they cheered lustily. A band in one of the fore carriages played merrily, and everything was indicative of gladness at the completion of an enterprise which will undoubtedly prove very advantageous to several hitherto more progressive towns, to which the absence of railway communication has certainly been detrimental. Everything went smoothly and the train arrived at its destination in safety at one o'clock, amidst the great cheering of the enormous crowd which had gathered together, and which seemed to be the whole population of Hornsea. During its travel it was greeted every now and then with loud cheering which burst from the lungs of small groups of gazers stood by the cottages near the rail. On Mr Wade, chairman of the company, the other directors, the secretary, engineers, contractors etc alighting, the applause was loud and prolonged. When the approbation had subsided, Mr Wade addressed the assembly and declared the Hull and Hornsea Railway to be open (loud applause and firing). He hoped that it might be the means of affording hundreds of thousands of people that means of recreation and enjoyment which it placed within their reach (cheers). He had the greatest faith in the success of the line. Mr Wade concluded by asking the crowd to give his brother directors, the engineer and the secretary, and others who had worked zealously, three hearty cheers. This request having been duly complied with, a procession headed by the band, walked to the chairman's house. The town was profusely adorned with flags, banners and devices bearing suitable mottoes and everybody seemed to keep the day as a holiday. Evidence of rejoicing was not wanting, neither were good wishes. Mr Wade fearful that he should not receive enough good wishes wished himself one. In a transparency exhibited directly over the front entrance of Mr Wade's house was the following sentence, "Prosperity to the Chairman and Company of the Hull and Hornsea Railway." Several trains ran to and fro during the day, and when the last train arrived at Hornsea no accident of any kind had happened.

The railway was constructed as a single-track line, although sufficient land had been purchased for the laying of a double-track system; this had to wait until the beginning of the twentieth century. In an effort to minimise costs, the Hull and Hornsea Railway Company did not own any rolling stock, which was leased from the North Eastern Railway. Initially, three trains a day ran in each direction: 8.00am, 2.30pm and 6.00pm from Hull and 8.50am, 4.00pm and 7.30pm from Hornsea. Trains called at all stations except Goxhill, which was only open on Hull market days. The single fare between Hull and Hornsea was 2s first class, 1s 6d second class and 1s third class. The return tariff was one-and-a-half times the single ticket. Season tickets were also available, with a discount for Hornsea residents. Also, in an effort to promote the development of the town, 'Parties building at Hornsea are to have free

Plate 55. The railway station of 1864, built to designs by Rawlins Gould of York. This is a flamboyant architectural composition: a symmetrical single storey building, of fifteen bays with a five-bay extension on the west side, in red brick with sandstone dressings and a hipped slate roof with moulded eaves cornice. The central five bays, the entrance to the station, break forward to form a loggia of five open round-headed arches with moulded bases and imposts and projecting key stones; the central opening is flanked by rusticated pilasters supporting a low pediment. A central double-leaf six-panel door under a fanlight with radial glazing in a round-headed opening with a projecting key block, gave access to the station concourse. Built to impress, a highly visible statement of confidence and future prospects, Hornsea station was intended as the showpiece of the line, costing nearly as much to build as all the other stations on the line put together. It was the only station to have a refreshment room and bar, and the First Class waiting room was embellished with a marble fireplace. As befitting his status and surroundings, the Hornsea stationmaster, provided with a suitably lavish station house (lower left photograph, extreme right), was the most highly paid on the line; so, too, was the chief porter. The railway station closed in 1964 and this building has since been successfully converted to housing. (Photographs: Stephen Harrison)

265

passes during the erection of their buildings, the class to be determined by the description of the property'. Goods and livestock were transported at between ½d and 5d per mile.

The railway clearly boosted the popularity of the resort. By 1870 there were seven trains each weekday in both directions and one on Sundays; an extra train ran on Sundays during the summer months from the mid-1870s. In 1890 there were nine trains each way on weekdays and three on Sundays. In addition, special excursions ran during the season.

The opening of the railway brought rapid and easy communication between Hull and Hornsea and the coast. The short distance from Hull – a travel time of around 40 minutes – encouraged residential holiday visitors, day visitors and, more importantly for Hornsea's expansion as an urban centre, the relocation of Hull businessmen and their families to the resort. All of these factors resulted in the rapid development of Hornsea between 1864 and the 1890s, both as a holiday destination and as a burgeoning residential centre.

However, as far as the railway itself was concerned, matters were not that straightforward. Shortly after the line opened, a long-running dispute with the Holderness Drainage Commissioners began. The Commissioners alleged that the bridges over both the Holderness Drain and the Lambwath Stream had been wrongly built and that they were impeding effective drainage, with potentially disastrous results. The railway company strenuously denied this charge. A court case ensued. In 1865 the Drainage Commissioners obtained an injunction obliging the company to modify the bridges in question. There were also problems with the main contractor, S and T Crawshaw, who was contracted to maintain the line for one year after its opening. As the first anniversary approached, it was clear that the line was in an unsatisfactory condition: trackside fencing and hedging was in a poor state; ballast on the track was insufficient; brickwork was coming loose; and station yards lacked their gravelled surfaces. The company refused to accept the line. S and T Crawshaw, who were owed £10,000, claimed that their work had been in accordance with the specifications detailed in the contract. Another dispute was looming. In an effort to keep costs to a minimum, to build the railway as cheaply as possible, corners had been cut.

Altogether, the first year of operation was a near disaster. Passenger numbers were reasonable, but not as great as expected. Most passenger traffic originated in Hull; despite extensive advertising in West Yorkshire and the Midlands, with their huge urban conurbations, passenger numbers from these areas were negligible. Goods traffic was also low. Seemingly, farmers had been put off using the railway for the export of produce and the import of agricultural supplies because of the incomplete state of station yards and goods sidings.

By April 1865, the company had made a nett profit of just £1,629. Huge debts were outstanding, including that to the Crawshaws. Essentially, the railway company had massively underestimated the cost of the project. For instance: contractor's costs had escalated to £58,000 from the original £26,287 18s; the purchase of land, originally estimated at £9,500, had risen to £21,000; the building of stations, originally costed at £5,534, had more than doubled to £11,330. And, the construction of the viaduct at Hornsea Bridge had cost £8,497. In essence, total costs had nearly doubled, from an original estimate of £68,000 to an actual £122,000. From the very inception of the project, the company was debilitatingly undercapitalised. This sorry state of affairs can be attributed to a number of inter-related factors: the inexperience of Wade and his fellow directors; the absence of an accountant; the absence of a land valuer (the company had paid excessive prices for the land it acquired – here, it should be noted, that Wade himself, along with other directors, sold land to the company. A case of profiteering); and the original contracts had been allowed to run over budget.

However, in the summer of 1865 salvation of a kind seemed within grasp. An extensive deposit of gravel had been discovered on company-owned land near to the goods yard at Hornsea Bridge. At this time, the West Dock (later, re-named the Albert Dock) at Hull was under construction and large quantities of gravel were needed. The company concluded an agreement to supply 50,000 tons of this material at 1s 8½d per ton. Facilities were needed for the extraction, storage and shipment of the gravel. In return for providing these, S and T Crawshaw had their maintenance contract terminated. In addition, they also agreed to have payment of monies owed to them deferred to a later date.

This did not stem the growing levels of indebtedness. Lower than anticipated passenger traffic. Lower than expected freight traffic. Creditors clamouring for payment. The situation could not continue indefinitely. The end was nearing for the Hull and Hornsea Railway. During the summer of 1865, Wade began negotiations with the North Eastern Railway Company, hoping that he could persuade its directors to lease the terminally ill line. This proved unacceptable to the NER board of directors, who wanted to subsume the line within their system. By December 1865 negotiations were completed. The NER would take over the Hull and Hornsea Railway, along with the company's debts – some £80,000 by this time. Before this could happen, enabling legislation was required: accordingly, a bill began its passage through parliament.

Meanwhile, the company's position was becoming ever more untenable. Some creditors had waited long enough for payment. Just before Christmas 1865, bailiffs, acting on behalf of a group of creditors, seized the company's moveable assets along the entire length of the system. Instead of assigning specific items to individual creditors, the property was put on public sale on 28 December. Thomas Liggins, a partner in the company responsible for building all the stations on the line (except the Hornsea terminus), and which was still owed monies by the railway company, purchased all the items. Liggins then offered to lease the property back to the company on condition that they paid him £90 immediately and then £8 per month until July 1866, when the outstanding balance would be due. Wade and his fellow directors had no option other than to agree to these terms. Liggins, it should be noted, would have been fully aware of the impending amalgamation of the line, which was scheduled for July. If all went according to plan, the money owed to his company would be paid by the NER as part of the amalgamation agreement.

A further blow was struck in February 1866, when the company's bankers refused to honour cheques drawn on its account. As a result, the company secretary had all cash taken at stations sent directly to him, in order that he could pay all pressing invoices and, thus, keep the company out of bankruptcy until the amalgamation became effective. Desperate measures.

Later that month, on the 22nd, a shareholders meeting was told the obvious: that the company was failing, had, indeed, more or less failed; that levels of both passenger and goods traffic had not come up to expectations. That new investors had failed to materialise – at this point, the company had £50,000 in un-issued shares. That income was insufficient to keep the company afloat. Shareholders also heard of the talks with the North Eastern Railway Company, which would be discussed at a special meeting in April. For their part, shareholders were critical of the directors and the way in which they had (mis)managed the company's affairs.

On 13 April 1866 an extraordinary meeting of shareholders was convened, which approved the directors recommendation that the company be taken over by the North Eastern Railway Company. After due parliamentary process, royal assent was given to the enabling legislation on 16 July 1866. On this day, the Hull and Hornsea Railway Company ceased to exist. After amalgamation, the line quickly settled down to become a minor country branch of the mighty NER; its future more secure than it had been as an independent operation. The Hull and Hornsea branch was run by the NER until nationalisation in 1947, when it became part of British Railways. The line finally closed in 1964, falling victim, as so many other rural routes did, to Dr Beeching's rationalisation of the rail network.

The Civic Project

Hornsea's urban infrastructure developed slowly during the nineteenth century. Up to 1864, parish affairs were conducted by the Vestry, which appointed all village officials, such as overseers of highways and the poor, policemen, and churchwardens. Moves to establish a Local Board of Health, under the provisions of the 1848 Public Health Act and the 1858 Local Government Act, began in late November 1863. On the 13th of that month a poorly attended meeting was held in the National School to discuss a petition, signed by twenty-two ratepayers, and already presented to the Privy Council, that a Local Board of Health for Hornsea be formed. Joseph Armytage Wade was elected chairman for the evening. Arguments for and against. The debate crystallised around the costs that a Local Board would entail, on whether any potential improvements to living conditions could justify the extra financial burden that would be imposed on local ratepayers. At the end of the evening a vote was taken: on a show of hands, thirty-nine voted in favour of the proposal, thirty-one against. To many of those present, this was a narrow and unconvincing margin. Opposition to the outcome was vocal. As he was entitled to do, Thomas Cunnington, owner of the Marine Hotel, demanded that a paper poll be carried out. Wade had to agree, and set a deadline of 28 December for the return of ballot papers. This time the result was not in doubt: 181 in favour, 67 against. Even so, opponents to the setting up of a Local Board alleged improper practices – vote rigging, gerrymandering. A Home Office inspector was called in: his enquiry upheld the validity of the ballot.

On 5 May 1864 a meeting of ratepayers was held at the National School to formally establish the Hornsea Local Board of Health. The meeting elected twelve members: Joseph Armytage Wade, Richard Marshall, William Hodgson, James Ruff, Thomas Green, Edward Bennett, Thomas Pearson, Richard Hornsey, Samuel Simpson, John Warcup, Henry Walker, and William Stork.

The first meeting of the Board took place on 3 July 1864, at which Joseph Wade was unanimously elected chairman – with the exception of 1873-74, a post he was to hold until 1876. Committees were formed to oversee water supplies, drainage and sewerage, street lighting and, later, burial of the dead.

The first task of the Board was to draw up a list of bye-laws. This was completed by February 1865 and approved by the Home Office in May of that year. Altogether, 184 bye-laws became enforceable, relating to both the urban area and the seaside resort, and covering such matters as:

- The regulation of hackney carriages, horses, mules, asses, and pleasure boats. If plying for hire, all of these had to be licensed, and drivers and boatmen had to wear an official badge. In an attempt to prevent the spread of disease, carriages were forbidden to 'carry any dead body, or any person labouring under any infectious fever or disease or any offensive matter or thing'.

- The regulation of slaughterhouses through licencing and the enforcement of basic standards of hygiene.

- The setting out of minimum standards for the upkeep of lodging houses: floors had to be swept every day and washed at least once a week, all walls and ceilings had to be limewashed at least twice a year, and there had to be one privy or water closet for every twenty lodgers (although smaller lodging houses were allowed to share privies).

- The prevention of nuisances and the removal of refuse. Residents were required to remove 'any animal or vegetable matter, fish, offal, ordure, blood, bones, manure, shells, broken glass, china or earthenware, soil, stones, rubbish, dust, ashes, house refuse, waste refuse, or runnings from any manufactory, or any offensive or noxious matter whatever'.

- Regulating the width of all new streets and laying down what materials could be used in the construction of new buildings; new houses had to be properly ventilated and drained.

- Regulations to minimise fire hazards.

- The regulation of public sea bathing. There were to be separate male and female bathing areas, at least 200 yards apart, and boats had to remain at least 200 yards away from bathing areas. Men were allowed to bathe naked before 8am; after that time, males over 12 years of age had to wear bathing costume, except when using bathing machines. Females over 10 years of age had to wear a bathing dress at all times and they were not permitted to bathe from the beach after 8am – instead, they had to use bathing machines.

As Hornsea grew and as it became increasingly popular as a holiday destination, the inadequacy of the existing drainage and sewerage system became more and more apparent. In 1873 the Board agreed a drainage and sewerage plan. Five miles of pipes and sewers were to be laid, with an outfall at the low water mark of the spring tides. A sewerage works was to be constructed on Hodgson's Field, approximately on the site of the present pumping station. Wade's Hornsea Brick and Tile Company was awarded the contract to provide bricks and pipes for the work, the first of many conflicts of interest that arose during his time on the Board. After considerable disruption across the town, the scheme was completed in 1875, at a cost of £9,652. Financing this project was beyond Hornsea's means, so a government loan was obtained; this was to be repaid in thirty years by a terminal annuity.

Wade's business involvement in the scheme caused something of a stir. A Mr C.F. Shackles, a Hull solicitor and Hornsea resident, put a letter before the Board alleging misconduct over the awarding of the contract for bricks and pipes to the Hornsea Brick and Tile Company. The letter stated that 'the chairman [that is, Wade] had been interested in the same and was therefore disqualified from holding office.' In the face of this 'most insulting, unjustifiable and vexatious letter', the Board rallied to Wade's defence, claiming no misconduct, and even going so far as to ask the Local Government Board in London for an enquiry. No enquiry was deemed necessary, and there the matter rested; although a certain degree of mistrust and suspicion lingered within some sections of the Hornsea community.

At the same time as the drainage and sewerage system was under construction, the Board was also examining ways of providing clean drinking water to the town, to replace the often fetid and polluted water supplies, with all their health hazards, drawn from wells and streams. As it happened, freshwater had been found in a borehole at Wade's brickyard on Rolston Road, and in November 1873 he offered this supply to the Local Board, on condition that he could take sufficient water for his manufacturing processes. But, a couple of months later he suddenly withdrew the offer, stating that 'the gift has been treated with scorn and every annoyance has been thrown upon me, that it was possible to throw upon me.' Evidently, his motives caused suspicion. Instead the Board purchased a 200-gallon water cart, which toured the streets selling fresh water at ½d per four gallons. The water, incidentally, came from Wade's borehole.

It was not until a waterworks was constructed on Atwick Road in 1878, at a cost of £10,000, that piped water became available to the town, giving the inhabitants their first supply of consistently unpolluted drinking water. Indeed, as the *Hornsea Gazette*, referring to a report that had appeared in the *Sanitary Record*, commented at the end of December 1877, ' the Hornsea authorities are not proceeding any too soon with their waterworks, for … [the] pump water is not fit to drink.' For those who could not afford to have piped water to their homes, standpipes were provided at strategically placed locations across the town: in Southgate, Market Place, Bank Street (then known as Golden Square), and Newbegin.

In 1884 the Local Board purchased two acres of land in Southgate for £1,000. At the time, this plot was occupied by the White House and a range of farm buildings, which were subsequently demolished to make way for the town's new cemetery. The cemetery opened in 1885. Somewhat unusually, two lodges fronted the cemetery: a mortuary chapel to the right of the entrance gates, and a boardroom and office, to be used by the Local Board, to the left. These two buildings cost £300. The cemetery was used until the 1950s, when the then urban district council purchased a site for the Edenfield burial ground in Marlborough Avenue.

In 1894 Hornsea District Council came into being, replacing the Local Board of Health.

Plate 56. Southgate cemetery: the left lodge used by the Hornsea Local Board of Health as a boardroom and office. In front of the building are the remains of a medieval cross; according to local tradition this limestone cross (the cross head now missing) on its stepped and chamfered base once stood in Market Place, where it marked the site of the weekly Thursday market. (Photograph: Stephen Harrison)

Institutions and Societies

The church, chapels, various benevolent societies, and numerous cultural and recreational societies and clubs were at the centre of Hornsea social life during the nineteenth century, especially during the period 1850-1900. Education, 'improvement' and self-help were very much promoted in Victorian Hornsea, characteristics that go towards defining the urban nature of the place. The developing social scene can be seen in the following chronological listing:

271

- 1856   Oddfellows' Lodge formed.
- 1840s   Hornsea Reading and Conversation Society formed.
- 1856   Hornsea Brass Band formed.
- 1859   Hornsea Cricket Club formed.
- 1862   Branch of the Druids formed.
- 1863   *Hornsea Gazette* began publication.
- 1864   Hornsea company of the East Yorkshire Artillery Volunteers formed.
- 1870   Hornsea Floral and Horticultural Society formed.
- 1872   Lending Library established.
- 1873   Lodge of British Workmen formed. Temperance Society formed.
- 1874   Hornsea Vocal Society formed.
- 1875   Freemasons' Lodge formed.
- 1876   Annual Hornsea Regatta and Aquatic Sports began.
- 1879   Hornsea and East Holderness Cricket Club formed. Hornsea Tennis Club formed.
- 1880   Hornsea Liberal Club formed.
- 1882   Hornsea Choral Association formed.
- 1880s   Hornsea Cycling Club formed.
- 1899   Hornsea Football Club formed.

Theatre going was also a feature of town life; and visiting circuses, fairs and other attractions provided regular entertainment for the less sophisticated inhabitants.

The Community on parade

Although there are sporadic references to Quakers and Presbyterians from the seventeenth century onwards, it is not until the 1770s that nonconformity in religion took hold in Hornsea. The later eighteenth and first half of the nineteenth centuries were a time of religious revival in the place. In the face of Anglican neglect and an Anglican clergy frequently perceived as distant and socially superior, nonconformity flourished and the fires of old dissent were rekindled. The position of the Anglican church was insecure: between 1721 and 1831 there was no resident vicar in Hornsea and the parish was under the charge of a curate; the church fabric was badly damaged during the hurricane of 23 December 1732 and was not completely repaired and restored until 1868.

For a place of its size, Hornsea was well endowed with a range of nonconformist churches during the nineteenth century. The strength and confidence of nonconformity, as well as its chronological development, can be gauged from the following catalogue, which charts the building and rebuilding of its outwardly visible manifestations:

- 1808   Independent (Congregational) Chapel (Bethesda Chapel), Southgate.
- 1814   Wesleyan Methodist Chapel, Back Southgate.

272

- 1836   Primitive Methodist Chapel, Westgate.
- 1864   Primitive Methodist Chapel rebuilt in Market Place.
- 1870   Wesleyan Methodist Chapel rebuilt in Newbegin.
- 1872   United Reformed Church, New Road; built to replace the Independent chapel in Southgate
- 1881   Salvation Army presence in the town.

Evangelism sought to transform both the heart and conditions of social existence. A social malaise was diagnosed and Methodism, in particular, advanced a unique and powerful cure for the

> Thousands who had sunk to a level of monotony unbroken from year to year, except by fairs, racehorses and fox-hunting. [They] found in … soul-stirring preaching, services, fervent prayer meetings, lively class meetings and hearty singing … a life, freedom and a joy to which they had been strangers … They feel at home there as they do not in the parish church.

By and large, Methodism appealed mostly to the poor and dispossessed, and found a ready constituency in both the developing urban centres and countryside alike. It message attracted people who were caught between a passing traditional order and a developing society, giving them responsibilities and opportunities.

In line with the national movement, the history of Methodism in Hornsea is one of splits and factions, preachers competing for the hearts and minds of its adherents. Having said that, Methodism was a vibrant cultural component within the developing town, and with its emphasis on activities throughout the week – religious, educational and social – dominated the lives of many residents. Whilst appealing primarily to the working and lower middle classes, a number of Hornsea's leading figures were part of the various congregations that developed, contributing to the building and rebuilding of the town's chapels.

Methodism had modest beginnings in Hornsea. A small congregation formed sometime between 1770 and 1780, attached to the Patrington Circuit. The first meetings were held in Low Hall, Southgate, and then in a nearby granary. In 1814 a chapel, capable of holding 250 people, was built on Back Southgate, on the corner with Chambers Lane. This chapel, reflecting the increasing congregation and an accumulation of funds, conformed to Wesley's own strictures that 'all preaching houses be built plain and decent; but not more expensive than is absolutely necessary.'

In 1834 Hornsea was detached from the Patrington Circuit and became the head of a newly formed Hornsea Circuit, reflecting the growing importance of the place as a Methodist centre.

The Back Southgate building served as a place of worship until the Trinity Chapel was constructed on Newbegin in 1870, to designs by J.K. James of Hull, at a cost of £1,500. Unlike the austere, older chapel, the new building was elaborate in its architectural detailing: red brick with stone dressings, lancet windows, and a columned porch with ornately carved

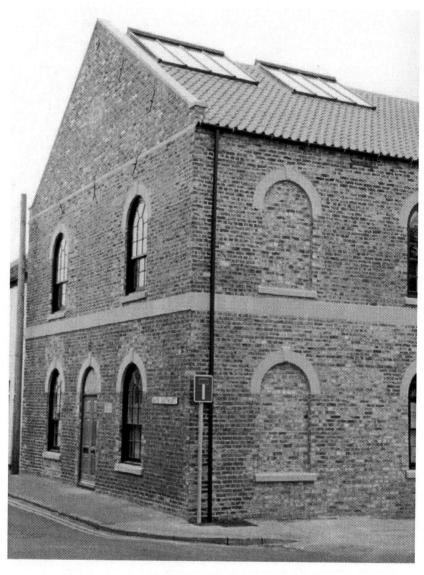

Plate 57. The first Wesleyan Methodist chapel in Back Southgate. A plain, simple brick building with pedimented façade, round-headed windows, and stone dressings. After 1870, when a new chapel was opened, the building was put to various uses: in the 1880s and 1890s it served as the barracks of The Salvation Army. When the Hornsea Salvation Army disbanded, Joseph Armytage Wade bought it for use as the headquarters of the Hornsea and District Liberal Association. (Photograph: Stephen Harrison)

capitals. With seating for 600 people, the new accommodation reflected the growing population of Hornsea in the years after the opening of the railway and the place's growing status as a dormitory town. The new chapel was also located prominently within the town, on a main thoroughfare connecting the urban centre with the seaside. The rationale behind the new building was recorded in the *Hornsea Gazette* of 7 August 1869, in a report covering the laying of the foundation stone for the chapel:

[The] present chapel was built in the year 1814. At that time it was generally thought that very quiet and retired situations were the most suitable for Methodist chapels, and the Hornsea chapel was built in such an obscure place that some of our Wesleyan friends from a distance can spend a few weeks here without finding the chapel. Since the railway was opened the population of Hornsea has increased, and we have found some difficulty in accommodating the visitors who do find the chapel, generally having to divide families by placing them in different pews, one here and another there, that it became very desirable to obtain a more commodious chapel where we could set apart ten or twelve pews for the use of visitors during their stay in Hornsea. The circuit being numerically small and comparatively poor, we learnt with great regret that the whole of the watering-places fund, raised by the Rev W.M. Punshoo, was appropriated, and we began to fear that a long time would elapse before we could realize the object we had at heart. Encouraged by the heartiness of our esteemed superintendent, the Rev A. Lockyer, we determined at any rate to secure a suitable site of land for our chapel, and having done so we laid our case before the quarterly meeting, held December 28th 1868, who gave their consent to the purchase of the land we had on offer, named trustees, and appointed a committee to take such steps as they thought best for raising the money to pay for the land and make arrangements for building as soon as they saw a fair prospect for doing so. This committee called a meeting of their friends on the 10th February last and at that meeting £230 10s was promised. We determined to thoroughly canvas the circuit for help, and if possible to go before the May District Meeting for leave to apply to the chapel building committee for their consent to erect a new chapel. At a meeting held on the 9th of April, our subscription having realized £344 10s 1d, we thought we might proceed, and secured the services of Mr J.K. James, as architect; took all necessary steps, and having had no drawbacks, we thankfully report that our subscription list up to this day amounts to £745 10s 1d which sum does not include a grant of £50 and a loan of £120, without interest, from the chapel building committee. We have received substantial help from many of our friends in Hull and elsewhere, and hope to raise about £100 more in subscriptions; and then, with the proceeds of this day and the opening services, we shall be able to open our chapel with no other debt than the £120 lent by the chapel building committee. The friends in the circuit a short time ago paid the remaining debt of £200 off our present chapel, so that the whole amount it may realise will go towards paying for the new chapel. The total outlay for chapel, schools, classrooms, and furnishing will be about £1,600. The whole nett income of the chapel to go towards the support of the ministry in the circuit.

The opening ceremony took place on 30 June 1870.

Later, in 1875, schoolrooms were built beside the new chapel, also to designs by J.K. James.

Primitive Methodism arrived in Hornsea in 1821, following a split in the movement some ten years earlier. The Primitives sought to 'restore the original simplicity of Methodist doctrine, devotedness of life, and fervour of worship, and to introduce some new principles, such as camp meetings and female preaching.' To many, the simplicity and spiritual fervour of the Primitives, sometimes called 'Ranters' or 'Camp-Meeting Methodists,' seemed to herald the renaissance of a Methodist golden age that had died with John Wesley in 1791.

A small local community was formed in 1821, attached to the Driffield Circuit, following a visit to the area by William Clowes, one of the joint founders of the movement, who was systematically preaching his way through the East and North Ridings of Yorkshire with a number of followers. His revivalist message clearly caught the imagination of people in Hornsea. Meeting at first in a barn, a 'room' in 1824, a 'building' in 1833 and a house in 1835, Primitive numbers had sufficiently increased by 1835 for a chapel to be built in Westgate (now demolished; on the site of Melbourne House), with a minister's house (Clowes House; now 'Coningsby') in Back Westgate.

The success of Primitive Methodism in Hornsea is clearly seen in Market Place. Here, in 1864, a new chapel capable of seating 400 worshippers was built, to designs by Joseph Wright of Hull, and costing £1,000. This is an impressive, Italianate building in red brick with stone dressings, and a flight of broad steps leading to a wide, round-arched entrance. At the same time, the congregation was detached from the Driffield Circuit and the new chapel became the head of a newly formed Hornsea Market Place Circuit. A schoolroom was added to the rear of the chapel in 1897. The chapel remained in use by Methodist congregations until 1983. After that date, the building was put to various uses, most recently as a Pentecostal church.

The expansion of Methodism coincided with a revival of older established dissenting groups. The opening of the Independent (Congregational) chapel (Bethesda Chapel) on Southgate in 1808 – Hornsea's first purpose-built nonconformist place of worship – may have resulted from this process and, certainly, must be seen in the context of the more general religious developments taking place in Hornsea at this time. The origins of the Independents in Hornsea can be traced to the missionary efforts of members of the Fish Street Chapel in Hull, particularly those of the Rev George Lambert, who first visited the place in 1798 to take advantage of the sea bathing for medicinal purposes. He and fellow evangelists were appalled at the 'desolate district of Holderness' when they visited 'Hornsea, Skipsea, Beeford, Lissett, Frodingham, Bonwick, Colden, Welwick, Bewholme, Brandesburton, Leven, Coniston, Swine, Ottringham, Patrington, Long Riston, Winterton, and Foston.' In these places:

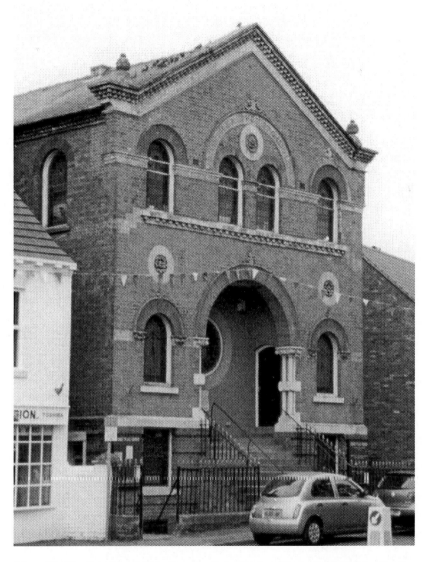

Plate 58. The Primitive Methodist chapel in Market Place. (Photograph: Stephen Harrison)

We see not the hells and gin-palaces and brothels of the Metropolis; but fornication abounds; the village green is the scene of many a brutal conflict; the village ale-house resounds with the 'song of the drunkard,' ribaldry, and blasphemy. On the Sabbath, after the villager has shown his respect to the squire and clergyman, repeated his responses to the Liturgy, and heard a discourse on moral duty, he sports on the green undisturbed.

The area was ripe for conversion 'on account of the ignorant, neglected, and degraded state of its inhabitants.' This is the context for the Fish Street chapel's Holderness Mission.

Lambert recorded the beginnings of the Independents in Hornsea. During his 1798 visit, he stayed in the cottage of John Scaife on Newbegin, opposite the parish church. Here he preached to a small group of people:

> The attempt was made and for a short time attendance was given but by the force of prejudice, unbelief, enmity to the gospel and persecution these messengers of mercy were obliged to desist for a time. But God who hears the prayers of his people was pleased in Mercy to open the heart of one of the inhabitants to receive Jesus by faith who soon after opened his house as a temporary place of worship.

The 'house' referred to was John Scaife's home. By 1807, through the efforts of visiting missionaries from the Fish Street chapel, enough converts had been made for a chapel to be built in Southgate. Lambert was present at the opening ceremony on 23 June 1808:

> After preaching the lecture last night, and rising soon after four o'clock this morning, I went to Hornsea to the opening of a new place of worship. Preached in the forenoon from Hag. ii, 9, with great pleasure and liberty. Brother Arundel spoke in the afternoon from Jacob's Vision, Genesis xxviii, 10-22; and Brother Hobson in the evening from Psalms. xxvii, 4; but as I had to return in the evening, I did not stay until the last service. It is a peculiar pleasure, and has a promising aspect, to see so many tents [that is, chapels] set up for God, as is the case at present; and it gives me peculiar satisfaction to have seen it at Hornsea.

By the late 1860s the congregation had outgrown the accommodation. Plans were laid to build a new church. Land was bought on New Road from Joseph Armytage Wade for £290, and in 1870 a committee was formed to raise the estimated £2,600 construction costs. The architect Samuel Musgrave of Hull was commissioned to design the new 500-seat building, which opened with great ceremony and some drama in July 1874. As the *Hornsea Gazette* records:

> An eloquent and powerful sermon was preached by the Rev Mellor but as he expounded on his text, a storm that had been threatening for some little time, burst over the town, the lightning which was very vivid, lighting up the whole building and being succeeded by loud peals of thunder, to the evident alarm and disquietude of several in the congregation. Dr Mellor however continued his discourse and in the midst of the awful storm, his undaunted bearing allayed in no small degree the fears of those who were listening to him.

Plate 59. The Independent chapel on Southgate, built in 1808 at a cost of £465; subsequently enlarged, with a burial ground added in about 1847. After 1874, when the new chapel in New Road opened, this building was taken over by the Independent Order of the Good Templars, a temperance organisation from Hull, and converted into a lodge room and lecture hall. In the late nineteenth and early twentieth centuries it was used for dances and concerts. In 1911 it became the parish hall for St Nicholas' church. The building is now unused. (Photograph: Stephen Harrison)

This was followed by a celebratory meal. The *Hornsea Gazette* again:

> On adjourning to the tents to partake of a cold collation it was found that the rain had penetrated through the canvas and done serious mischief to the viands. While the friends were partaking of the good things provided for them, the rain again fell very heavily and it was found necessary to resort to the protection of umbrellas which of course prevented the full enjoyment of this part of the proceedings, but the utmost good humour prevailed.

Built of white brick with red brick and stone dressings, the new church was an imposing Gothic structure with a nave, two shallow transepts and a tall south-west tower topped by an octagonal spire. This building was severely damaged by fire in 1968 and subsequently remodelled. In 1972 the church became part of the United Reformed Church, an affiliation which continues up to the present.

The Salvation Army, a missionary movement with a military style, formed by William and Catherine Booth in 1878 (out of the Christian Revival Associated, founded 1865), had a noisy presence in the town from the late 1880s, attracting adherents from, especially, the lower working classes, who had been largely untouched by Methodism or any of the other religious groupings. The poor, more especially the so-called undeserving poor, the 'submerged tenth', formed a natural constituency:

> We believe that God has given us a mission to the throngs in the great thoroughfare roaming about on the Sabbath day and all other days, thoroughly unconcerned about death, judgement and eternity … our experience tells us that although their aversions to Chapels and Churches is as strong as can well be conceived, they will nevertheless eagerly listen to any speaker who will, with ordinary ability, in a loving and earnest manner set before them the truths of the Bible in the open air.

The message was simple: poverty was the Devil's weapon, driving men to drink and women on to the streets; some men and women were pointed towards eternal damnation by the circumstances in which they were born and lived. Souls had to be saved. With uniforms and military ranks, playing martial music which disrupted the quiet Sundays of the streets in which they proselytised, services were turned into circuses, interrupted by frequent cries of joy, the shaking of tambourines, the banging of drums and the playing of accordions. But it worked. Men and women who would not normally consider entering church or chapel were prepared to listen to rousing sermons when delivered in a theatrical, music hall style. The Salvation Army – described in turn as ridiculous, heroic, subversive, pious, heretical, noble and duplicitous – drew crowds and made converts, much to the dismay of the upper and middle classes.

Plate 60. The United Reformed Church on New Road. (Photograph: Stephen Harrison)

Taking the gospel to the people who wanted it least but who, in their view, needed it the most the 'Hallelujah Army' met at various locations in Hornsea: first in the public rooms on Newbegin; then, from 1881, in the Temperance Hall on Southgate; and, from 1883 to the end of the century, in Back Southgate, in the former Wesleyan chapel. The Salvation Army had disappeared from Hornsea by the beginning of the twentieth century, disbanded through lack of support.

One further revivalist group needs mention: the Salvation Soldiers, not to be confused with The Salvation Army, with which there was no connection. In the summer or autumn of 1881 a Thomas Thompson arrived in Hornsea and founded a company of the Salvation Soldiers, with missionary aims similar to The Salvation Army. Thompson soon attracted a following, parading his company through the streets to the accompaniment of loud music. He rented the former Independent chapel in Southgate, renaming it 'The Temple.' In imitation of the revival organisation he bestowed 'military titles' on his chief supporters, giving himself the rank of Major.

As might be expected, tensions quickly developed between the two rival groups, competing as they were for the hearts and minds of the same small pool of supporters – in essence, the dispossessed. According to the Rev Edmund Tew, vicar of Hornsea between 1872 and 1897, a 'regular fight' between the two organisations took place in the streets. In late 1881 the Hornsea Local Board of Health considered a petition, signed by around ninety people, complaining about the activities of the Salvation Soldiers and the noise made by their band, calling for a ban on their outdoor activities. After due deliberation, the Board decided to maintain the *status quo*, largely because it was thought that the Salvation Soldiers 'had the right idea, as they were opposed to drink.'

Things were not as they seemed, though. Matters came to a head in February 1882 when Thompson was arrested at Paragon Station in Hull. He was not who he claimed to be. In fact, he was a deserter from the army, having gone absent without leave from the Life Guards, then stationed in London, on 1 June 1880. Apparently, the police were tipped-off after he had been recognised in and around Hornsea by a groom employed by Frederick Strickland-Constable of Wassand Hall. Furthermore, Thomas Thompson was an alias; his real name was Thomas Scott. After a court-martial he was sentenced to a term of military imprisonment. The Hornsea supporters of Thompson/Scott rallied round, raising money to buy him out of the army. Once again, Tew: '… the poor farm johnnies and others who he had deluded clubbed together their shillings to buy him out of the Service – thinking he would be speedily restored to them.'

Whilst he was indisposed, the rumbustious Rose Carr, a Hornsea carrier and horse dealer, took charge of the Salvation Soldiers, promoting herself from lieutenant to captain. Carr, an ex-Primitive Methodist, has been described as a 'muscular Christian' and a 'hell-fire preacher with all the zeal of a convert.' She also had to deal with the debts left in the wake of Thompson/Scott's departure, so much so that in September 1882 she inserted a notice in the *Hornsea Gazette*, distancing the group from their former leader:

MAJOR THOMAS SCOTT THOMSON is in NO WAY CONNECTED with the SALVATION SOLDIERS, in Southgate, Hornsea, and they will not hold themselves responsible for any Debt or Debts he may contract.

'Major Thompson' arrived back in Hornsea on 23 October 1882. Unlikely as it seems, he was met by a group of enthusiastic and welcoming supporters, who then noisily paraded through the streets.

Following his return, Rose Carr was unwilling to relinquish control of the Salvation Soldiers. A struggle for power and authority ensued, precipitating a split in the movement: Carr's 'division' was based at 'The Temple', whilst Thompson's contingent operated out of a lodging house run by Hannah Moore at 4 Marine Terrace. With The Salvation Army, there were now three rival groups in the town, all trying to attract converts and all in direct competition with each other. As Edmund Tew commented, '… for a short time three different companies paraded the village, all professing to be doing the same work, yet all hating and hated by each other.'

Shortly after his return, Thompson/Scott borrowed £14 from one of his supporters and then absconded. According to Tew, still posing as a clergyman, he went to Manchester, where he died. The Salvation Soldiers subsequently disbanded. Rose Carr rejoined the Primitive Methodist congregation, as did many of the movement's former supporters.

Having dealt with the detail, we need to go back to 1851. The Religious Census of that year provides a glimpse of the community at prayer on one specific day: Sunday 30 March – the same day as the decennial census was taken. Although it is now well recognised that the returns of this ecclesiastical census need to be treated with extreme caution, the record does nevertheless provide a useful, if somewhat flawed and open to conjecture, snapshot of the extent of church attendance in Hornsea at mid-century. The returns are listed below.

Let us take a closer look at the data. On the morning of 30 March 292 people attended worship, or 30.89% of the recorded population. If we add Sunday School attendance, then 362 individuals, or 38.30% of the overall population, were involved in some kind of religious activity. Of all those at worship in the morning the parish church had the greatest proportion of attendees, 100 adults plus 70 Sunday School scholars (46.96% of all those involved in some form of worship). This was because of the Church of England requirement that pupils at the National School should also attend services. Although there was no Anglican service, the largest proportion of the town's population worshipped in the evening: 488 people, or 51.64% of the parish. Turning our attention to the various nonconformist groups, we find that 192 people, or 65.75% of all those participating in services, attended morning worship. Chapel attendance in the afternoon was 118, representing just 12.48% of the parish population. It was in the evening that the full strength of nonconformity becomes apparent: 360 adults, plus 128 Sunday School scholars, giving a total of 488 attendees, or just over half of the total parish population.

283

Denomination	Morning	Afternoon	Evening
Anglican			
Adults	100	-	-
Sunday School	70	-	-
Primitive Methodist	29	118	110
Adults	-	-	128
Sunday School			
Wesleyan Methodist	56	-	110
Adults	-	-	-
Sunday School			
Independent			
Adults	107	-	140
Sunday School	-	-	-
Total	**362**	**118**	**488**

Table 22. 1851 Ecclesiastical Census returns for Hornsea.

In 1851 the parish population was 945. A total of 868 religious attendances on Sunday 30 March 1851 were recorded, representing 91.85% of the total population. This aggregate figure takes no account of individuals who attended on more than one occasion.

Conclusion

By the closing years of the nineteenth century, Hornsea was recognisably a town and bustling east coast holiday destination. As well as providing a range of seaside attractions and diversions, the place also had everything we associate with an urban centre: high density housing in a variety of styles and finishes, shops, street lighting, piped water, sanitation systems, gas works, a police station, church and a whole range of nonconformist chapels and meeting places, road and rail networks to the wider world, a weekly newspaper, a library, an urban district council, and much more besides. Over the course of the century, but more particularly from the 1860s onwards, the place had been transformed beyond recognition.

Even after allowing for ulterior motives and gross self-interestedness, it is undeniable that Joseph Armytage Wade and a small, shifting group of associates, most of whom were incomers from Hull, drove much of the change. Their schemes and intrigues were not always successful, often, like the railway and pier fiascos, doomed to failure: cases of vision sometimes outstripping resources. Opposition was plentiful, coming from the older, more established residents, from those who, with nostalgia and not a little regret, looked back to earlier times when the pace of life was more settled, more secure, a time when routines and rhythms were in harness with the natural world. Lamenting a lost world and seemingly having little control over the increasing complexity of life under Victoria and her bureaucratic, far-reaching governments, many objected to the articulate, educated middle class incomers packing committees, riding roughshod over local sensibilities, and through force of argument and, sometimes, sheer bloody mindedness, taking Hornsea into uncharted territory. Overall, though, the changes – the provision of clean drinking water, an effective sewage system, gas and electric lighting, and so on – resulted in enormous benefits for the population at large, taking Hornsea into the modern world. By 1900 – despite the upsets, despite the clash of personalities, despite the failures, despite the bluster, despite the tantrums – Hornsea was more than well placed to meet the challenges and opportunities of the new century, to effectively build on the achievements of the previous forty or so years.

CHAPTER 6

DAYS OF OUR LIVES

Introduction

By 1900, during the final months of late Victorian England, Hornsea was in a good position to meet the opportunities and challenges of the new century. The twentieth century opened amid scenes of wild and unruly rejoicing. At Hornsea – as almost everywhere else – the insouciant delight in the new century, as yet unburdened by forebodings or forewarnings, was expressed in an excited display of fireworks, the pealing of bells, and noisy exuberance. With the celebrations, this was the moment when the modern world, our world, began: the motorcar and aeroplane, the beginnings of modern medicine, modern political parties, the modern welfare state, and all the other wonders and atrocities, boredoms and bewilderments of the twentieth century. As the fireworks soared skyward and the church bells rang out, the people were looking to the future.

The town's heyday as a seaside resort was in the years leading up to the First World War: the long, hot, frivolous Edwardian summers, the last long garden party of privilege and class. Golden years. The world on holiday. Wing-collars and straw boaters. Crinoline and croquet. A time when, in one last great show of strength, national identity and pride coalesced around the British Navy, the Empire, glory, power, the superiority of the white race, and the right to rule colonies. A time when package holidays were unknown and when instead of personal CD players and iPods on the beach there were performances by pierrots. A time when peace and prosperity were confidently expected to go on indefinitely. But for those who could read it, the writing was on the wall. The hedonistic spirit of those confident and tranquil years came to a precipitate and shocking end in 1914. Hornsea immediately succumbed to war fever. Amid the holiday bustle, pandemonium broke loose on Bank Holiday Monday, 3 August, with panic buying of food and newspapers. On both that day and the next large crowds gathered in front of the police station where mobilisation orders had been posted. Territorials and reservists, already in uniform, were taking leave of their wives and families and preparing to depart. 'Suppressed excitement was everywhere in the air.' An air of expectation and a sense of anguished foreknowledge of the sacrifice to come clung to the town. News was circulating that Germany, acting in defiance of Britain's ultimatum, had invaded Belgium. Britain was at war. Not for one hundred years, since Napoleon, had there been such a mad rush to war. Four long years of unrelenting carnage and destruction – *the war to end all wars*, and the very worst, until the one that came after – shattered the entrenched certainties of the old order. Four long years when all conversations in Hornsea – when all conversations everywhere – dwelt on life or death, victory or defeat, national survival or national extinction. And for four long years the seaside resort was on hold, the town and beach left to its permanent inhabitants. Things would never be the same again.

After 1918, in the glorious and dreadful turmoil of necessary re-creation, life began anew. In the melancholy aftermath, tempered by 'the myth of the lost generation' and an understandably all-pervasive cult of the dead, an up-beat post-war spirit filled the air. But for many the benefits of victory proved ellusive. At home, as it was around the globe, the 1920s and 1930s proved to be eerie decades of uncertainty, new battlegrounds. The chill wind of economic depression, an ever-widening spiral of unemployment, hunger, poverty and desperation for millions, social trauma, the threat of revolution: the atmospherics of a world on the brink of catastrophe.

On the international stage things were no better. The looming inevitability of another catastrophe, the world slowly descending into violence and rawness: the darkening menace of Hitler and the totalitarian nightmare of Nazism, the League of Nations' ineffectiveness as an arbiter of international disputes and its inability to achieve disarmament and check the rise of military aggression in Germany, Italy and Japan, civil war in Spain, the iniquitous non-intervention pact, and false hopes of peace. Mounting tension. War was coming in an undefinable way, a gathering storm collecting over Europe that would, once again, bring chaos and tragedy to millions of people. A coming apocalypse that had already enjoyed rehearsals in Germany, Spain, China and Abyssinia. And all the while the 1933 hit song 'Stormy Weather' could be heard playing in the background, in retrospect an unintended anthem to an uncertain decade. Such was the way of things until 1939.

The mounting spiral of tension was broken only by the Second World War and the bright, shining future that was confidently expected to follow. 1945, the People's Peace and 'fair shares for all' heralded the dawn of a brave new (if at times brittle) world: the beginnings of a vastly different landscape rising from the devastation, not just the contours but the perspective also. After the miseries of the 1920s, 1930s and 1940s, prosperity was on the horizon, within grasp. A changed world, new opportunities to be had. Hope of future betterment. A new monarch, a new beginning. A line had been drawn. Macmillan's contemporary but subsequently much overworked phrase 'You've never had it so good' echoes down the generations. The 1950s:a time when everyone knew who they were and where they were. But change was perceptible and palpable: in the gloom of a wrecked economy, fuel shortages and wintry cold, people began to dream the American dream. As that decade gave way to the 1960s and then the 1970s, the impingement of all things American on the British artistic, cultural, social and economic scene grew daily. The new world replacing the old. Americanisation and commercialisation. The 1980s and 1990s were times of change, both at home and abroad: times of boom and bust, times of much uncertainty, times of growing international instability. In many ways the history of post-war Hornsea mirrors that of Britain at large.

Population

The upward demographic trend identified in the second half of the nineteenth century continued into the twentieth. Between 1901 and 2001 the town's population rose from 2,381 to an estimated 8,500, a 257% increase.

Year	Recorded population	Numerical change	% change
1901	2,381	-	-
1911	3,024	+ 643	27.00%
1921	4,279	+ 1,255	41.50%
1931	4,450	+ 171	3.99%
1941	No data	-	-
1951	5,324	+ 874	19.60%
1961	5,955	+ 631	11.80%
1971	7,031	+ 1,076	18.06%
1981	7,301	+ 270	3.84%
1991	7,934	+ 633	8.67%
2001	8,500 (est.)	+ 566 (est.)	7.13% (est.)

Table 23. The changing population of Hornsea, 1901-2001.

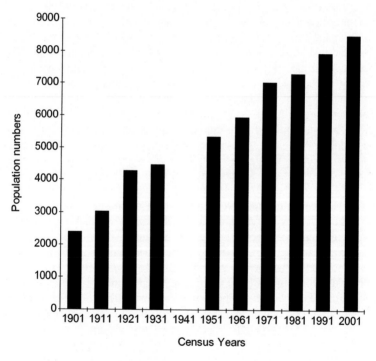

Figure 51. The population of Hornsea, 1901-2001.

Note: 1. There was no census in 1941.
2. The 2001 population figure is an estimate. The census data for this year included the whole of North Holderness Ward (a total population of 9,731).

288

Year	Recorded population	Persons per square mile	Persons per square kilometre
1901	2,381	457.88	176.63
1911	3,024	581.54	224.33
1921	4,279	822.88	317.43
1931	4,450	855.77	330.12
1941	No census because of Second World War		
1951	5,324	1023.85	394.95
1961	5,955	1145.19	441.76
1971	7,031	1352.11	521.59
1981	7,301	1404.04	541.62
1991	7,934	1525.77	588.57
2001	8,500	1634.61	630.56

Table 24. The changing density of population, 1901-2001.

1891 to 1921 was a period of dramatic growth, when the town's population more than doubled, from 2,012 to 4,279, reaching a maximum decennial increase of 41.5% between 1911-21. This may be a reflection of the growth of population and industry on Humberside more generally: Hull reached its highest rate of economic development prior to the First World War, and it seems that outward migration from the place was at its highest during periods of economic prosperity. The 1920s was a period of general expansion, but the growth of dormitory towns such as Hornsea suffered a check in expansion towards the end of the decade, largely as a result of the general economic situation. The rate of increase at Hornsea recovered during the later 1930s. This trend is reflected in the net balance of migration into and out of Hull between 1922 and 1930:

1922	-324	1927	-784
1923	-2,088	1928	-657
1924	-1,936	1929	+4,263
1925	-4,150	1930	+5,203
1926	-2,882		

Between 1931-51 the population of Hornsea increased by 19%, from 4,450 to 5,324, and in the following decade, 1951-61, by 11% to 5,955, which was 5% above the national average. Although the railway closed in 1964, growth has continued up to the present: between 1961-71 to 7,031, 1971-81 to 7,301, 1981-91 to 7,934, and 1991-2001 to an estimated 8,500. Overall, in the fifty years between 1951 and 2001, the population of the town expanded by around 3,176, or 59.6%.

Over the last fifty years immigrants to Hornsea have been drawn very largely from two well-defined groups: the retired, and those commuting to Hull. The attraction of seaside resorts, such as Hornsea, as centres for retirement began in the 1930s. Since that time, the in-migration of the elderly has resulted in an unbalanced age structure. Today, around 35% of the population is over pensionable age. Similarly, whilst there is a healthy balance

289

of population below the age of fifteen years, there is a noticeable gap in the 15-40 years age group, reflecting the national demographic trend.

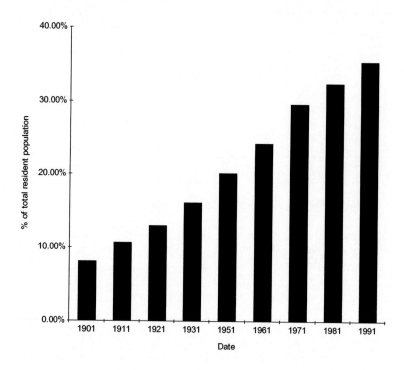

Figure 52. The changing age structure of Hornsea, 1901-99: % of resident population over 60 years of age.

The twentieth century development of the town as a residential centre can be traced through its changing age structure. In 1901 Hornsea was still expanding through internal increases in its population, whilst at the same time attracting relatively young immigrants. At this date, only 8% of the population was over the age of sixty years. The age structure identified here is not unlike that of an early industrial town: a broad base of people below 30 years of age, tapering very rapidly into the older age groups. The age structure in 1931 shows a very significant change, a bulging of numbers in the middle-aged group: 16% of the population is over 60 years of age, whilst the number of people below the age of fifteen shows a relative decline. Clearly, the rate of natural increase has fallen, whilst the in-comers are relatively older. Twenty years later, in 1951, the true dormitory seaside town age structure has been achieved, and has changed very little since then. Older people, seeking a suitable place to retire to, have moved into Hornsea. This group also consists of middle aged people bringing relatively young families with them, who, in most cases, move out of the town when they reach adult age, seeking employment opportunities elsewhere. In this way a gap develops in the 15-40 year age group, and the proportion of people in the older age groups is perpetuated.

Two other factors are worth mentioning here. Because of the in-migration of executives, commuters and so on, Hornsea is very definitely a town of private, owner-occupied housing. Secondly, the town, along with Bridlington, has one of the lowest ratios of individuals to houses in the East Riding: less than three people per household. This reflects the greater numbers of retired people and bungalows in the town.

Hornsea Mere and the First World War

In July 1915 Hornsea Mere was commandeered by the Royal Naval Air Service (RNAS) as a flying boat sub-station, under the operational command of RNAS Killingholme, on the Humber estuary. The mere was chosen because it provided a good, enclosed stretch of water suitable for the take-off and landing of seaplanes. Shore-based facilities were constructed on Kirkholme Point; these were not completed until 1918, by which time the RNAS had become part of the newly established Royal Air Force. In his detailed 2001 study of RNAS Hornsea Mere, Geoff Simmons had this to say about the layout of the station:

Entry to the base was by an unadopted road from Queen's Gardens, with the guardhouse located to the left of the gateway into the site. Known latterly as the Bungalow and the RSPB Reserve Information Hut, this building survived until 1999. To the other side of the entrance, there were several buildings, presumably on the sites where concrete bases can still be seen today; these are thought to have been the men's hut and the first aid hut. The power house still stands as the large concrete building near the café. Two Bessoneau hangars stood on the area that is now the Putting Green, with two slipways to the mere edge. There was a wooden pigeon loft alongside the mere, beyond the Putting Green. To the west, along Kirkholme Point, was the concrete compass platform; further west still, almost at the end of the Point, was a small brick building, possibly the detonator store or magazine. Several boathouses [were located] along the southern shore, between the permanent buildings and the entrance. Today, a boathouse exists between the café and the mere edge that may be of the period.

Also, the present-day café, built originally as a refreshment room in 1887 by the Hornsea Mere and Hotels Company as part of their development of the mere for leisure purposes, was converted to workshops.

The purpose of the base was to provide anti-submarine and general patrols off the Yorkshire coast. Initially, the station was equipped with Baby Sopwith and Short 184 aircraft: the Sopwith was a single-seat fighter-scout aircraft, capable of carrying a single 16lb bomb when on anti-submarine patrols; the Short 184 was a two-seater, armed with a 14-inch torpedo. After the formation of the Royal Air Force in 1918, the base was also provided with land aircraft – Airco DH6s and, later, Airco DH9s – which were dispersed to temporary landing grounds at Atwick, Owthorne and Greenland Top. These were also used for anti-submarine work.

Plate 61. Boating on Hornsea Mere in the 1960s. (Photograph: Alan Avery collection)

In 1918, the station had a complement of 141 personnel: 28 officers, 9 warrant officers and non-commissioned officers above the rank of corporal, 3 corporals, 80 rank and file, and 21 women, most of whom were billeted at various addresses in the town. In addition to twelve seaplanes, the base was also equipped with a range of motor vehicles (a heavy tender, light tender, motorcycle and sidecar, and a workshop trailer).

RAF Hornsea Mere closed in March 1919; shortly afterwards, the mere reverted to its pre-war use as a recreational area, with James Holmes re-opening his boat-hire and fishing business. Nearly ninety years on, the mere still attracts leisure users in great numbers.

Seaside developments

A visitor to Hornsea in the years leading up to the First World War could only marvel at the changes that had taken place over the previous fifty years: new terraces and villas sprawled outwards from around the railway station; on the cliffs new promenades or parades had been constructed; and besides lodging houses there were many new and handsome houses for residents. And, of course, as a reminder of earlier aspirations, the truncated remains of the pier.

In the last chapter, R.W. Butler's resort cycle model, Stages 1 to 4, was advanced as a means of analysing the development of Hornsea in the nineteenth century. To pick up on this theme, Stage 4, that of consolidation, continued into the twentieth century, up to around 1920. This was followed by a period of stagnation, which lasted to about 1950. From that date, up to the present, the town has gone through a phase of post-stagnation, characterised by a degree of stability and even recovery, although the character of the place is very different from sixty years and more ago. All through the twentieth

Plate 62. A summer's day at Hornsea in the early twentieth century. The social chaos of the seaside: working class trippers from the industrial West Yorkshire and north Midlands mingling with middle and upper class professionals and the more genteel sort. During these years, particularly in the inter-war period, day-trippers, encouraged by cheap rail travel and day excursions, came to dominate the local holiday scene. (Photograph: Stephen Harrison collection)

Plate 63. Hornsea Parade after the high tides and storms of March 1906. (Photograph: Stephen Harrison collection)

Plate 64. Hornsea Parade 1907, looking north. (Photograph: Stephen Harrison collection)

Plate 65. Hornsea Parade 1910, looking north. (Photograph: Stephen Harrison collection)

Plate 66. Hornsea Parade during the inter-war years, looking south. (Photograph: Alan Avery collection)

Plate 67. Hornsea Parade in the 1970s, looking south. (Photograph: Alan Avery collection)

century, though, Hornsea's potential as a seaside resort was severely hampered by the lack of effective road links to the main centres of population in northern England. It is instructive to consider the very different trajectory of the town compared with that of, say, Bridlington. Bridlington prospered greatly because of its good road links, Hornsea suffered because of their absence.

Table 25, below, summarises Hornsea's development as a seaside resort from 1900 to the present.

Stage	Dates	Summary
4. Consolidation	1900-c.1920	<ul><li>Hull to Hornsea railway upgraded to double track</li><li>Construction of sea walls and promenades</li><li>Floral Hall built</li><li>Imperial Hydro Hotel built</li><li>Tennis courts laid out</li><li>Golf course laid out</li><li>Roundabouts and swings on the beach</li></ul>
5. Stagnation	c.1920-1950	<ul><li>Decline in number of lodging houses</li><li>Overall decline in number of visitors</li><li>Change from residential holidaymakers to day-trippers</li></ul>
6. Post-stagnation: Stability	c.1950-present	<ul><li>Hornsea Pottery opened</li><li>Closure of railway</li><li>Growth of coach excursions to the town</li><li>Growth in number and size of caravan parks</li><li>Hornsea Freeport shopping village established</li><li>Hornsea Leisure Centre opened</li><li>Amusement arcades on sea front</li><li>Small zoo opened</li><li>Increase in number of car parks</li></ul>

Table 25. Summary of Butler's resort cycle model (Stages 4, 5 and 6) as applied to Hornsea.

In March 1906 a violent storm severely damaged the promenade and timber coastal defences. This resulted in the Urban District Council constructing three new groynes and a 700ft-long sea wall in 1906-1907. The

297

Plate 68. Modern sea defences. (Photograph: Stephen Harrison)

sea wall was extended in 1923, by 400ft on the north side and 1,240ft on the south; and in 1930, it was continued still further southwards, across Hornsea Gap to Hornsea Burton. The sea wall became an attractive and popular promenading area, greatly enhancing the attractiveness of the coastal frontage. More recently, the coastal defences have been strengthened yet again, this time by the careful dumping of massive boulders on the beach, immediately below the promenade.

Plate 69. Hornsea's north beach sometime during the inter-war years. (Photograph: Alan Avery Collection)

The years before the First World War saw further developments aimed at consolidating Hornsea's position as a seaside resort, many of which also directly benefited the town's permanent residents. As if to herald the dawn of a new age, films were first shown in the public rooms in 1900.

1908 saw the opening of tennis courts by the mere and the relocation of the golf course from Hall Garth to a more extensive site outside the southern limits of the town, on Rolston Road; the course was upgraded from nine to eighteen holes. A new clubhouse was also built on the site to replace the Newbegin premises. The Floral Hall was constructed in the Victoria Gardens in 1913. In 1914, not an auspicious time for new businesses, the Imperial Hydro Hotel opened. These years also saw a steady decline in the number of lodging houses, 82 in 1905 down to 42 in 1913, reflecting the beginnings of a change in the pattern of holidaymaking.

Inevitably, with the world recovering from one catastrophic conflagration and waiting to be engulfed by the next, the inter-war years were not good ones for Hornsea. Attempts were made to infuse the place with that Edwardian spirit which had prevailed up to the eve of war. But, putting the clock back to the other side of the war, picking up the pieces and carrying on as before, was simply not an option. Times, moods, tastes and expectations had changed, were still changing. Hornsea did its best in the circumstances.

In 1921, the former steam laundry in Cliff Road was converted into a cinema, the Victoria Picture Theatre, and in 1925 the Star Picture Theatre opened in the former public rooms. However, the town, even during the busy holiday season, could not support two cinemas, and the Victoria Picture Theatre closed in 1928. The Victoria Gardens and the Floral Hall were extended in 1928, and there were fairground rides on the beach at this time.

Cheap rail excursions to Hornsea in the 1920s and 30s attracted many short-stay visitors, individuals and families staying for a week or less, and, more especially, day excursionists. The number of lodging houses declined even further, to thirty in 1925 and only five in 1937. This reflected the change in holiday patterns between 1918 and 1939. Hornsea was becoming a destination for day-trippers. At the same time, for those staying longer, caravans were replacing lodging houses and hotels as the preferred choice of accommodation, a trend that has continued up to the present.

Following the Second World War, day-trippers were the main visitors. The post-war years also saw caravans replacing lodging houses as the main form of accommodation: by 1967 there were only nineteen lodging houses/boarding houses in the town, whilst the number of caravans approached 750. Today, over 80% of all holiday accommodation in the town is provided by caravans, which is far above the national average for seaside resorts. After 1945 most visitors arrived by road, in private cars or coaches. In 1960, a survey by K.L. Mayoh found that 80% of visitors to Hornsea were day-trippers, and that 50% arrived by car and only 25% by rail. As in the nineteenth century, most visitors came from elsewhere in Yorkshire, 40% from Hull and another 40% from the populous districts of the West Riding. A similar survey carried out at Whitsun 1963, this time by K.G. Barker, demonstrated that 40% of all day-trippers came from within a radius of twenty-five miles of Hornsea, the majority, once again, coming from Hull. These trends have continued through to the present.

The years since 1945 have been better. The decline of the earlier part of the twentieth century was halted and then reversed. The last fifty years have been ones of recovery, stability and even progress. In the 1950s, 1960s and again in recent years, the sea wall has been strengthened and, in the last ten years, the promenade area visually and commercially enhanced. Entertainments for visitors have included amusement arcades, a boating lake, a roller-skating rink, a small zoo, and Go-Kart track. With the post-war growth in motorcar ownership, additional car parks have been established close to the sea front.

The movement of people into Hornsea during the holiday season is considerable: during the 1960s and 1970s it was estimated that the population of the town was increased by over 3,000 at peak periods. In the late 1990s, particularly on Bank Holidays and at peak times during the summer holiday period, the number of day visitors to Hornsea can exceed 2,000 people, filling the car parks and crowding the sea front areas; and then, perhaps, going on to make the short journey to Hornsea Freeport. At the same time, the town centre, apart from traffic making its way to and from the coast, can be quite, largely given over to the permanent residents.

In many ways Hornsea differed from the normal run of seaside resorts during the twentieth century. This difference was expressed physically, in the spatial patterning of the place: there was a marked segregation between the holiday resort area and the town centre surrounded by residential areas. A further distinguishing difference can be seen in the intermingling of private houses with boarding houses, cafes and the like, which normally make up the entire sea frontage, which is largely absent in other coastal resorts (as in the area to the north of the harbour at nearby Bridlington, for instance). These differences can be explained as the result of historical circumstances: as Hornsea only developed as a holiday resort in the second half of the

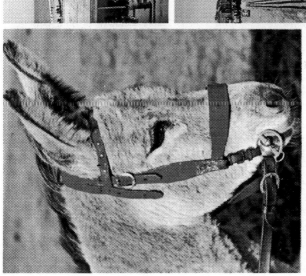

HORNSEA

Plate 70. A postcard from Hornsea, 1970s-style. (Photograph: Alan Avery collection)

Plate 71. At the seaside: views of Hornsea, 2005. (Photographs: Stephen Harrison)

Plate 72. Life on the edge: holiday caravans. (Photograph: Stephen Harrison)

nineteenth century and was then expanding as a dormitory town for Hull, there has been relatively little opportunity for the holiday industry to gain a dominant position within the place.

Throughout the twentieth century resort development continued the pattern established in the previous century. As already mentioned, the distribution of holiday facilities shows a clear avoidance of the town core and residential areas. Today, along the coast we can instantly recognise a holiday area consisting of cafes, gift shops, amusement halls, games areas, hotels, boarding houses, car parks, promenade and beach: a narrow, concentrated zone stretching along the seashore, rarely extending inland more than a few hundred metres. To both north and south there are a number of caravan parks, distinctive in the landscape because of their size. These developed from the 1930s onwards, with increased provision from the 1960s. The caravans form an unbroken coating along the coast extending away from the town, often sited almost to the cliff edge. In an area of coastal erosion, the establishment of caravan parks is a profitable exploitation of land, if only in the short-term. In such areas, permanent development, such as housing, is full of risk; and, for the farmer, the agricultural potential is reduced year on year through loss of land.

Housing

By 1900 Hornsea had grown well beyond its village status of a hundred years earlier to become a small town. The agricultural functions of the place were now of minor significance. To many contemporaries the 'resort' had become the economic force driving the town's expansion. Marus, for instance, hinted at the contrast between 'old and new' in 1906: 'Hornsea consists of an ancient inland village or little town and a cluster of villas and lodging houses on the shore.' But this was only part of the story. Throughout the twentieth century Hornsea continued to expand as a residential centre, mainly as a result of out-migration from Hull, particularly between 1900 and 1940. During this

303

period there was a certain amount of infilling around the railway station, but the main focus for residential building was along the coast and adjacent to Cliff Road. The inter-war years also saw the lateral expansion of the town along the main north and south arterial approaches; a tide of brick flowed steadily outward, south, covering fields along the Rolston and Hull roads as speculators erected hundreds of new homes. These developments were characterised by the construction of uniformly designed housing estates. Tracts of what we would now call 'green belt' were swallowed up in the 1920s and 1930s, catering for the younger generations of men and women who saw their identities as increasingly urban – whether through choice or necessity – and who were inclined to see the acres of new homes and fresh tarmac roads as symbols of progress, prosperity and happiness. The bungalow dominated the 1950s and 1960s – a type of development that distinguished seaside resorts in general during those decades. More recently mixed housing estates and limited infilling within the historic core have taken place. In contrast to earlier times, much of the recent development has resulted from Hornsea's favoured position as a retirement centre, especially for people from the West Riding of Yorkshire. Today, around 30% of the town's resident population are above retirement age.

Before the above themes are explored in more detail two further points should be borne in mind. Firstly, the twentieth century saw a profound shift in the tenure of property towards owner-occupation: a mass market for home ownership was created, transcending class boundaries. By the 1930s a regular salary or wage of around £200 per year was widely regarded as adequate security for a mortgage which might involve repayments of as little as 9s a week, well within the reach of skilled workers. Mortgage repayments of £1 per week bought a standard three-bedroom £650 house, while earnings of £300-£500 per year (teachers, bank officials, Executive Class civil servants and lower paid professionals generally) would have comfortably bought substantial semis or even detached houses of £1,000 or more. In 1910 building societies advanced £9m on mortgages nationally, in 1938 the figure was £21m, in 1960 it was £560m, and in 1980 it had reached £9002m. During the twentieth century the housing revolution profoundly affected the lives of millions of people. Secondly, compared with the diversity and vibrancy of much nineteenth century building, the houses of the twentieth century (with few exceptions, and those mainly from the earlier part of the century) have a depressing uniformity of design and style.

The physical expansion of Hornsea was fuelled by the continued growth of the resident population: not organic growth, but through in-migration. Two main periods of growth can be isolated:

- Between 1901 and 1931 the population rose from 2,381 to 4,450, with the greatest decennial increase, from 3,024 to 4,279 (41.50%), occurring in the years 1911-21.

- 1950s onwards: between 1951 and 1997 Hornsea's population grew from 5,324 to c.8,500, with the greatest decennial increase, from 5,955 to 7,031 (18.06%), taking place between 1961-71.

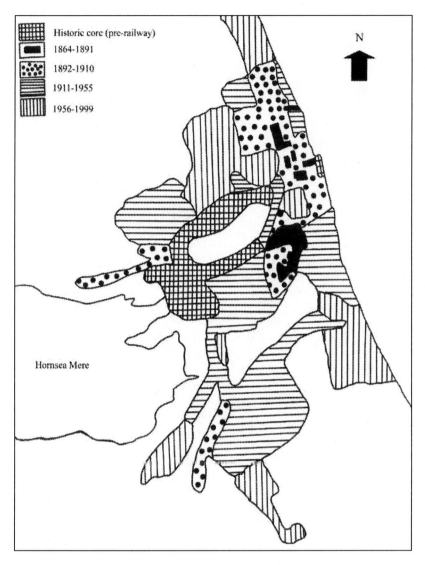

Figure 53. The Growth of Hornsea. (Adapted from Barker, *Hornsea: A Study of a Coastal Town*)

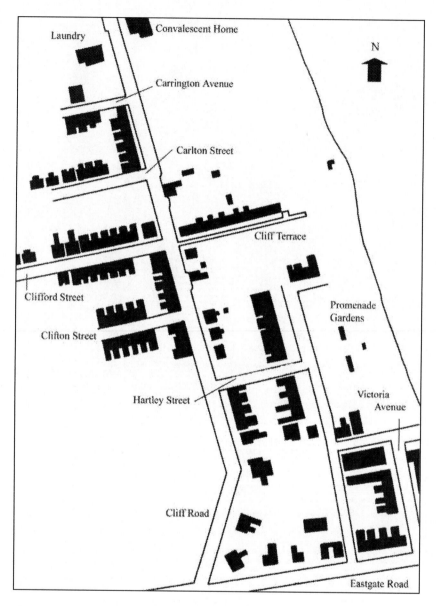

Figure 54. Coastal development, 1900-1914. (Adapted from Barker, *Hornsea: A Study of a Coastal Town*)

Infilling took place in and around the existing street pattern between 1908 and 1925. This included building between New Road and Eastgate, which effectively united the two areas of resort development. Clifton Street and Westbourne Road also date from these years.

Social housing made its appearance in Hornsea in 1920. The urban district council (UDC) had first discussed the provision of council housing in 1914, when it was decided to borrow £1,450 for the erection of eight 'workmen's dwellings' on council-owned land at Mereside. The First World War intervened and the plan was shelved for the duration of the conflict. However, on 4 November 1918, just days before the war ended, the UDC returned to the issue. The sudden end of the war pushed unfinished business to the top of the agenda. At their next meeting on 2 December it was resolved that the provision of 'dwellings for the working class' was urgent and councillors agreed to purchase three acres of land to the north of Football Green from John Witty, at a cost of £800, for the development. A.R. Roberts was appointed architect and by January 1919 a plan for the building of thirty-four houses, later reduced to thirty-two, at a cost of £450 each, together with roads and services, was agreed. The bulk of the properties were to be constructed around an oval green, to be known as Southgate Gardens. Financefor the project was obtained from the Local Government Board, repayable over eighty years, at an annual interest rate of 5.5%. Rents were initially fixed at £16 per year, exclusive of rates.

Bolstered by the gradual extension of local authority powers in the fields of health, housing and sanitation that had occurred during the Great War, and supported by Lloyd George's call for 'Homes Fit for Heroes' and the raised expectations that this engendered, the decision has to be seen as a response to the inadequacy of working class housing in Hornsea in the early years of the twentieth century. Although not widespread locally, particular problems included overcrowding, poor sanitation and the poor physical condition of many of the town's older residential buildings. Such ramshackle housing was badly lit, with few windows. Often the walls were exposed brick or roughcast, with no wallpaper. Space was at a premium, leading to a lack of privacy; and pots and pans and other kitchen utensils would be hung up on the walls. There was an absence of through circulation, and the first thing that would have struck the modern visitor was the smell. In the days before perfumed soap and deodorants, the smell of body odour was pervasive; cooking smells lingered constantly; and the smell of urine and worse would float through the air. The interiors would often be damp, as washing was hung up to dry indoors. Infectious disease and bad health were other major problems associated with these living conditions. Respiratory diseases were a problem. Poor sanitation, especially the use of chamber pots and outside earth closets, encouraged disease. Infections which passed by contagion spread like wildfire in such conditions. Improvements in the housing of the working class were needed, with decent standards at an affordable rent the priority. The provision of social housing in Hornsea played a small part in the bold new vision which stressed not only the ability of state power to transform society and economy, but also its moral obligation to do so for the benefit of all. It has to be said, though, that the provision of housing and other welfare measures was also, in part, a response by the state to militate against social unrest and to

307

diffuse the quasi-revolutionary undercurrents that the government and others detected in the volatile post-war years. Upper and middle class notions of duty tinged with panic.

Building work began in early 1920. The houses were constructed in batches, and all contracts were put out to tender. The UDC minutes refer to the following tradesmen: James Taylor of Anlaby Common (builder), R. White and Son (builder), R. Orwin (carpenter and joiner), R.P. Loten (plumber), C. Thompson (painter), and E.P. Dixon and Son (fences and trees). The first six dwellings were erected on an extension of King Street. At a meeting on 30 March councillors discussed the next batch of houses to be built. After lengthy discussions it was agreed that there should be some variation in design. Following national guidelines on the construction of council housing, as recommended by the Tudor Walters Report (1918: *Report of the Departmental Committee on Questions of Building Construction in Connection with the Provision of Dwellings for the Working Classes in England, Wales and Scotland*) and subsequently issued in manual form by the Ministry of Health to accompany the 1919 Housing and Town Planning Act, and which established council housing as we know it, the UDC agreed that there were to be three basic forms at Southgate Gardens: houses with (1) living room, scullery and two bedrooms; (2) living room, scullery and three bedrooms; and (3) two living rooms, scullery and three bedrooms. Every house was to have an internal WC and coal store off the back lobby, a well-ventilated larder, and a bath in either a bathroom or scullery. The scullery was to contain a glazed sink fitted with hot and cold water, a draining board, a gas copper, and, if the tenant wished to hire one, a gas cooker. Floor space ranged between 950 sq. ft. and 1,400 sq. ft., the latter size comparing more than favourably with many middle class detached houses of the time. The dwellings were relatively long and narrow, giving 'better opportunity for lighting and ventilating thoroughly all parts of the house.' Front gardens were also considered necessary, as were good- sized plots to the rear. The layout was to be in terraces of three to six dwellings each. The UDC also gave attention to the overall layout of the estate, creating in effect a 'garden village.' Again, this followed national recommendations:

By so planning the lines of the roads and disposing the spaces and the buildings as to develop the beauty of vista, arrangement and proportion, attractiveness may be added to the dwellings at little or no extra cost. Good exterior design in harmony with the surroundings and adapted to the site should be secured ... By the choice of suitable local materials, and the adoption of simple lines and good proportion and groupings of buildings, with well-considered variation in design and in the treatment of prominent parts, good appearance may be secured within the limits required by due economy. Eighty years on, these principles can still be seen in Southgate Gardens.

The first houses were completed in the summer of 1920 and by the spring of the following year twenty-three properties were occupied; the remainder were completed by the end of the summer of 1921. The Southgate Gardens properties are among the first professionally designed examples of mass housing built in the country.

Plate 73. Southgate Gardens. Whatever we may think today about the housing standards set in the 1920s and 1930s they represented a major improvement on what had existed before, and most council tenants were glad and grateful that the state provided this most elemental human need. Functionality is a key word in the provision of local authority housing. (Photograph: Stephen Harrison)

The 1920s also saw the southward expansion of the town. By 1925 houses had been built on Rolston Road and near Marlborough Avenue on the Edenfield estate. Demand was high. Houses and building plots were sold from marquee tents. Residents of new streets often endured months of wheel ruts and mud as they waited for paving, sewers, and lights. In Hornsea (as it was nationwide), the inter-war semi, with its half-timbering and bay windows, was historicist in appearance. It was in the period of post-war reconstruction that 'old (or early) English' established itself as the dominant idiom in domestic architecture, covering the broadest spectrum of housing classes. The inter-war house was an avatar of modernisation, marking the arrival of the labour-saving, servant-less home. But it was marketed in a variety of Arcadian styles. 'Fine example of a modern house built in such a manner that it has the appearance of age' runs the caption to the frontispiece of P.A. Barrow's *The House Desirable* (1929).

Prefabricated wooden bungalows had also appeared for the first time in Hornsea – in Strawberry Gardens. The bungalow (the 'bangla' of Bengal) was first developed as an Anglo-Indian house in the nineteenth century, making its first appearance in England in 1869. At first a type of residence exclusive to the upper classes, it became very popular with the English middle classes during the inter-war period. Bungalows – 'not over-costly to build, less expensive to furnish, and easy to run' – combining the advantage of modernity with a rural-romantic 'cottage' image made them especially attractive at this time.

By the outbreak of the Second World War building had begun on Hull Road, and the first wooden bungalows had been erected in Pasture Road; others followed them in Mill Lane (Hornsea Burton Road). Given the financially unfavourable climate during the war, along with labour and material shortages, house building virtually ceased for the duration of the conflict. It commenced with renewed vigour after 1945, much of it on the south side of the town, in Hornsea Burton, with lesser amounts on the north

Plate 74. Inter-war bungalow. (Photograph: Stephen Harrison)

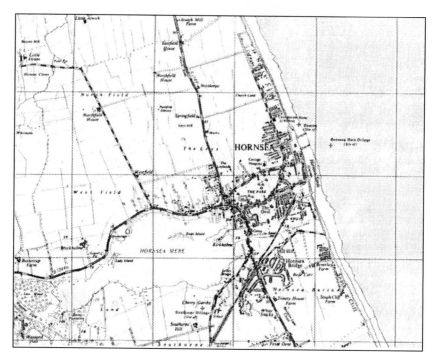

Figure 55. Hornsea in the 1930s. (Reproduced courtesy of the Ordnance Survey)

Plate 75. Recent (2001) infilling on the west side of Market Place. In the nineteenth century this site was occupied by Joseph Armytage Wade's farm; later, until the above development, there was a petrol station on the plot. (Photograph: Stephen Harrison)

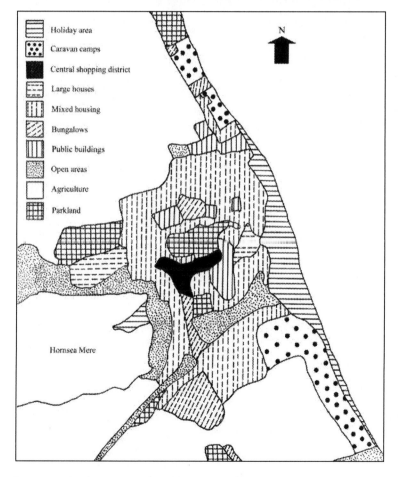

Figure 56. The character of twentieth century Hornsea. (Adapted from Barker, *Hornsea: A Study of a Coastal Town*)

311

side, off Eastgate. On the south side a large council estate was begun in 1946; and the Tranmere Park, Lindale Avenue and Greenacre Park estates were all built in the early 1960s. On the north side of the town, the Ashcourt Drive estate, off Eastgate, was in process of development from 1966 onwards. In more recent years, building programmes have included two large estates: Trinity Fields, off Rolston Road, and, on the west side of the town, the Cheyne Garth estate. Off Cliff Road, Sandpiper Court, a partnership development between the District Council and housing associations, was completed in 1994. More recently still, redevelopment and infilling has taken place within the historic core around Market Place and Newbegin.

Ups and Downs: the Economy

Hornsea has never had a tradition of industry or manufacturing. During the nineteenth century, those who had hoped for industrial development following in the wake of the railway were to be disappointed: the only real industry was that associated with the manufacture of bricks and tiles. By the end of the century, there was, it is true, a gas works, laundry and corn mill, but these were relatively insignificant in providing employment or in generating and redistributing income.

During the twentieth century, the only industrial development was Hornsea Pottery, becoming by far the town's major employer. From small beginnings in the late 1940s the business expanded to become a key national player in the manufacture of mass-produced pottery, sold not only across the length and breadth of Great Britain but even reaching foreign markets as well. For more than two decades in the later twentieth century, the trademark 'Hornsea Pottery' became synonymous with the town itself; while it lasted, a local success story, of which the town was – and is – justifiably proud.

In 1949, already having holiday connections with the town, brothers Desmond and Colin Rawson moved to Hornsea from Cleckheaton, in the West Riding of Hornsea. Desmond, originally trained as a textile designer, had taken up clay modelling whilst recovering from an injury sustained in active service during the Second World War. His younger brother Colin had been introduced to clay during his National Service in the RAF, making anatomical models for the Nursing Orderly training centre at Moreton-in-Marsh, Gloucestershire.

The business began in a small way, producing moulded plaster models of Toby jugs and animals to sell to holidaymakers, from 4 Victoria Avenue, which was also their home. They moved production to Old Hall, Market Place, in 1951. Over the next couple of years the business expanded and the workforce increased to forty employees, quickly outgrowing the available space at Old Hall. In 1954, Desmond moved his family to the former vicarage at Ulrome, seven miles to the north of Hornsea; here, the coach house was brought into service as an additional production centre. Expansion was rapid. By this date, sixty-four people were working for them, making them the largest employer in Hornsea. On 6 March 1954 the business became a private limited company, the Hornsea Pottery Company Ltd, with an issued share capital of 11,500 shares at £1 each. At the same time, a retail shop was opened in Hornsea, and a sales force – Rapier Sales – established to market an ever-

HORNSEA POTTERY

is now well known throughout the British Isles. There
will be someone in your
Home Town selling our
wares.

Whether you have ever
purchased a piece of
Hornsea Pottery or not,
we will be pleased to show
you round the factory.

The Directors and Staff

join in wishing you a

Happy Hornsea Holiday

When you return home, remember to look for
this Trade Mark in your local Pottery
shop. It is your assurance of
quality and good value.

HORNSEA POTTERY CO. LTD.

EDENFIELD WORKS · MARLBOROUGH AVE · HORNSEA
YORKSHIRE

London Office   Northern Office

50 NAPIER HOUSE   5 and 9 MARKET PLACE
24-27 HIGH HOLBORN, W.C.I   HORNSEA

Figure 57. A 1950s advertisement for Hornsea Pottery. (Illustration: Stephen Harrison collection)

increasing range of products nationwide. The business continued to flourish and the lack of space for further expansion was becoming a problem, a brake on further development.

In July 1954, with financial help from retired local businessman Philip Clappison, the pottery moved to Marlborough Avenue, on to the 28-acre Edenfield site, which had been, appropriately enough, part of Joseph Armytage Wade's brick and tile works in the later nineteenth century. After restoring the buildings, used as a piggery for many years, production was under way by 1955. At around this time, guided tours of the factory were started, proving over the years to be a major tourist attraction and a welcome boost for Hornsea more generally.

The range of products increased to include Toby and other character jugs, posy bowls, cruets, ornamental clogs and boots, ashtrays, vases, egg-cups, animals, figurines, and tableware. These items set the range for all future design development, which over the years expanded to include kitchenware and ovenware. Interestingly, many of the pieces produced at Hornsea took inspiration from the coastal setting – for example, the 'Pebble' vase and the 'Coastline' range of tableware.

Over the next twenty years Hornsea Pottery experienced exceptional growth. By the early 1970s the company was employing 250 people and producing over three million items per year, selling to both national and international markets. Visitors to the Edenfield works, now with a leisure complex, were around one million per year. In more ways than one, the Hornsea works had reached capacity.

A decision was taken to look for an additional factory site, with two criteria to be met: that it must be a coastal location and in a landscape that could provide extensive leisure facilities for visitors. Potential sites in Cornwall, Blackpool and as far away as Ireland and Malta were looked at. The eventual choice was across the Pennines, at Lancaster, which had the further advantage in that it was far enough away from Hornsea to avoid direct competition with the parent pottery. The Lancaster factory, with its associated leisure facilities, was officially opened in May 1976, and immediately proved popular with the visiting public.

During the 1970s Hornsea Pottery continued to go from strength to strength. By the end of the decade, the combined workforce at Hornsea and Lancaster had reached 460, and plans were in place to extend the Lancaster factory. And, by 1981 there were 700 people employed by the company. Expansion had been rapid by any standards. Success brought takeover approaches, the most notable of which was from the Wedgewood Company in 1976. All were rejected. As a further consequence of success, this period also saw active collaboration with overseas pottery manufacturers, particularly in Sweden, Portugal and Corfu.

The 1980s, by contrast, were not good. The start of the decade saw a general recession in the pottery industry, leading to redundancies at both Hornsea and Lancaster in 1981. Over the next couple of years, attempts to restructure and revive the business were put in place, including the design of new products. This failed to turn the company around, and receivers were appointed in mid-April 1984. Simply put, Hornsea Pottery fell victim to its own success. And that success, understandably so in many ways, led to over-ambitious plans. After going into receivership the company continued to trade, but went through five changes of ownership during the 1980s and 1990s. All the time, despite the introduction of new product ranges, the business was steadily, inexorably failing. In 1995, the leisure complex on the Edenfield site was sold, becoming Hornsea Freeport and offering a wide range of shopping facilities, including factory outlets, together with leisure areas. Crisis point was reached in April 2000, when, for the last time, administrative receivers were called in, and most of the workforce made redundant. Attempts

314

to find a buyer were unsuccessful: Hornsea Pottery ceased trading. Later that year, the company's assets were sold off.

As an enterprise Hornsea Pottery may no longer exist, but its products, ornamental and functional, its brand, its legacy, continue to adorn millions of homes. A fitting testament to a much loved and, in its time, most successful institution.

Apart from Hornsea Pottery, the town has never had a solid, large-scale industrial base, caused in large part by its geographical isolation and lack of good transport links to the rest of the north of England. In the later 1960s a small, light industrial estate was established in Cliff Road, to be followed in the 1980s by a second, this time off Rolston Road. Both were used by a range of local businesses, and have never grown beyond their original limits.

Most find employment outside the town. For example, a 1958 survey showed that Hornsea had a total economically active population of 1,930. Of these, 45% of the male working population and 25% of the female working population had employment outside the town. Of the 900 or so males working elsewhere, 31.5% had employment in Hull, with the remainder working in the other larger East Riding centres, such as Beverley and Driffield. When the rail link with Hull closed in 1964 fears for the long-term future of Hornsea as a dormitory town for Hull workers were raised by many. However, bus services and, increasingly, the motorcar filled the void; and, since then, the town has expanded further, with more people working in Hull. In 1999-2000, 54% of the working male and 30% of the working female population had employment elsewhere. Of these, 42% of males and 20% of females worked in Hull. What figures such as these effectively demonstrate is the overall weakness of Hornsea as an employer of its own population, with a general lack of employment opportunities other than in the retail sector and seasonally in the holiday industry.

In more general terms too, the proximity of Hull, only twenty miles away, has dominated economic development in Hornsea. Due to the dominance of Hull and, to a lesser extent, Beverley, much of Hornsea's trade is purely local, and this has limited the growth of the retail sector in the town. The range of shops is small, really no more than those necessary for the servicing of everyday needs; and this is somewhat strange for a place with, today, over 8,000 inhabitants. In particular, there is a complete absence of department stores, chain stores such as Boots and Woolworths, and large supermarkets, such as Tesco and Somerfield. Instead, small and local shops – bakers, fruit stores, confectioners, hairdressers, stationers and the like – form the basis of the shopping district. Having said that, though, it is refreshing in these days of cloned high streets to find a central shopping district that has retained its individuality and character. It seems, therefore, that the importance of Hull and Beverley as shopping centres for the residents of Hornsea has been sufficiently powerful to prevent the development of a wide range of shopping facilities, especially in relation to luxury goods, in the town.

Also, as referred to elsewhere in this chapter, shops and other businesses connected with servicing the needs of visitors are located in sea front areas, with the shops in Newbegin and around Market Place depending very little on holidaymakers for their trade. This observation highlights the

Plate 76. Hornsea's central shopping districts: Newbegin (*Upper*) and Market Place (*Lower*). (Photographs: Stephen Harrison)

Plate 77. The former lifeboat station in Burton Road, used since 1974 as Hornsea's town Hall. (Photograph: Stephen Harrison)

dichotomy between residential Hornsea and resort Hornsea, which has been such a feature in the history of the town since the mid-nineteenth century. The advent of Hornsea Freeport in 1995, a self-contained shopping village on the former Hornsea Pottery site, has done nothing to break down this contrast, arguably accentuating it.

Local government

In 1894 Hornsea Urban District Council replaced the Hornsea Local Board of Health. Until 1905, the UDC used the former local board's offices at the cemetery in Southgate, but in that year they transferred to the public rooms in Newbegin. The council bought the pubic rooms in 1920, and remained there until 1927, when Elim Lodge, Cliff Road, was purchased for use as a town hall. In 1974 Hornsea became part of the Holderness district of the newly created Humberside County Council. As part of the change, Hornsea Town Council came into being. This body had twelve elected members, and the powers and duties of a parish council. The former lifeboat station in Burton Road became the new town hall.

317

Plate 78. Hornsea, August 2005. The sea that people like to be beside. Despite the less than perfect weather, the beach is fairly busy. The sun is around from time to time, but the wind is brusque and chivvying, catching you unawares with its bite, as it often does on the Holderness coast. Being British, holidaymakers have come prepared. An intrepid few have ventured into bikinis or trunks, but most are in t-shirts, shorts or jeans, mostly in fashionable greens or beiges. Red, blue and yellow fleeces, not to mention swimsuits and towels, are everywhere. Gulls scavenge on the beach for leftovers from our throwaway society. The sea is featureless, a blank canvas, gunmetal grey. Clouds move swiftly across its surface. (Photograph: Stephen Harrison)

In 1996, following a further change in the structure of local government, Hornsea became part of the new unitary East Riding of Yorkshire Council, which opened offices in the former police station in Newbegin.

Conclusion

The twentieth century saw major changes in the character of Hornsea. For the first few years after 1900, the place was connected to its later nineteenth century past, still a popular holiday destination. But from the 1920s and 30s onwards Hornsea was marching to a different rhythm. Throughout the inter-war and post-war years, with their insistent modernity, the holidaymakers still came, but in ever-decreasing numbers. Hornsea had lost some of its magnetism. The glory days were over. The pattern of holidaying was changing too. The hotels and boarding houses were becoming less popular, replaced by caravans. And for many Hornsea was only a daytrip away. Yet the reminders of the previous century, which forged the spirit and character of the place, are everywhere and constant, in the architecture of its public and residential buildings, in the reuse of the former railway station, and in the public parks and gardens and promenades, etched indelibly, physically, in the townscape and in the collective consciousness. An arresting display of the past. Culturally resonant real estate, the dimming glow of a once golden age. It is made all the more vivid because Hornsea did not experience at first hand the rain of high explosives from the sky during the second great conflict, which in so many places eradicated much of the old and paved the way for regeneration and new directions. The tension between the past and present is palpable in early twenty-first century Hornsea.

A HORNSEA CHRONOLOGY

1086	*Domesday Book*: the first documentary reference to Hornsea. First mention also of Hornsea Burton and Southorpe.
	Following the rebellion of Morcar, William I grants Hornsea to Drew de Bevrère.
1087	Hornsea transferred to Odo, Count of Aumale, following the flight of de Bevrère.
c.1088	Manor of Hornsea granted by Odo, Count of Aumale, to the abbot and abbey of St Mary, York. This event probably triggered the replanning of the settlement; indeed, the direct physical origins of modern-day Hornsea can be dated to this period.
1198	First documentary reference to Northorpe.
	By 1228 Hornsea Beck functioning as a port.
1257	Monday market begins.
1275	Annual fair on or about 6 December begins.
1358	Annual fair from 31 July to 2 August begins.
1423	Church status changed from rectory to vicarage.
c.1520	Pier at Hornsea Beck in state of disrepair.
1539	Following dissolution of St Mary's abbey the manor of Hornsea becomes crown property.
1549	Pier at Hornsea Beck rebuilt.
1609	Pier at Hornsea Beck once again in state of disrepair; seemingly, it was not repaired after this date.
By 1650	Southorpe hamlet deserted.

c.1663	Enclosure of Hornsea Burton.
1665	First mention of Quakers in Hornsea.
c.1670	Low Hall, Southgate, built by Peter Acklam.
1680s	Old Hall, Market Place, built by Peter Acklam.
	By 1697 Hornsea Burton hamlet lost to coastal erosion.
	By c.1700 Hamlet of Northorpe deserted.
1711	First Quaker meeting house licensed.
1732	Major storm causes severe structural damage to village.
	By 1785 Hornsea Beck hamlet lost to coastal erosion.
1801	Bill introduced into Parliament to enclose the parish. Act dated 11 June 1801.
1808	Congregational chapel built in Southgate.
1809	Enclosure award enrolled November 1809.
	Following the enclosure of the parish, the 'Town Meeting' was established to take over from the Manor Court. Its functions were: the levying of poor rates, highway and police rates, and, from 1859, the appointing of assessors for the collection of property tax and income tax.
Pre-1811	Assembly Room in existence.
1814	Wesleyan Methodist chapel built at the corner of Back Southgate and Chambers Lane.
1819	Congregational day school opens.
c.1820	Religious Free Library established at 8 Market Place.
1821	Daily Hull-Hornsea coach service commences.
1829	Methodist day school opens.
	Second daily Hull-Hornsea coach service commences.
1830	Coast Guard station built on cliff-top, to the east of Marine Terrace.

1835	Primitive Methodist chapel built in Westgate (on site of Melbourne House).
1837	Hornsea joins Skirlaugh Poor Law Union.
	Marine Hotel opens.
1842	Hornsea Reading Society established.
1845	National School opens on Mereside; Methodist day school closes.
	North aisle of St Nicholas' church restored.
1846	In response to the growing popularity of the place, the Marine Hotel is enlarged to provide 200 bedrooms.
	Plan to establish a rail link between Hull and Hornsea proposed by the York and North Midland Railway Company; did not materialise.
1848	Policeman appointed at Hornsea, with responsibility also for Atwick, Seaton and Sigglesthorne.
1853	Visit of Charlotte Bronte.
1856	A town brass band formed.
1862	Joseph Armytage Wade establishes the Hull and Hornsea Railway Company.
	Victoria Lodge of the Ancient Order of Druids established (Friendly Society).
1863	Foundation stone of the Hornsea Terminal railway station is laid.
	Hornsea Gazette commences publication.
1864	Hull to Hornsea railway opens to traffic.
	Local Government Act adopted in Hornsea and a Local Board of twelve elected members is formed. Committees: Burial and Sanitary; Waterworks; Highways; and Lighting.
	New Primitive Methodist chapel built in Market Place.
	Lifeboat house built on the shore between New Road and Sands Lane.

East Yorkshire Artillery Volunteers formed at Hornsea.

Hornsea Gas Light and Coke Company formed, with gasworks near Hornsea Bridge railway station.

1866	Owing to financial difficulties, the Hull and Hornsea Railway Company taken over by the North East Railway Company.

J.A. Wade establishes the Hornsea Pier Company and obtains a Board of Trade order to construct a pier within five years.

Restoration of St Nicholas' church.

1867   Hornsea Cricket Club formed. Annual Cricket Week established.

1868   Hornsea and East Holderness Cricket Club formed.

Brick and tile works established by J.A. Wade on land between Hull Road and Rolston Road.

1869   East Yorkshire Artillery Volunteers Brass Band formed.

Assembly Room and Public Rooms built in Newbegin by the Hornsea Public Rooms Company Ltd.

First steps taken to protect coast from erosion.

1870   Hornsea Floral and Horticultural Society formed; annual shows held each June until 1914.

Alexandra Hotel built.

Musical Promenades instituted; held each holiday season in the grounds of the Alexandra Hotel and on the North Cliff.

New Wesleyan Methodist chapel – Trinity Chapel – built in Newbegin.

Lansdowne Gas Company formed – rival to Hornsea Gas Light and Coke Company – with gasworks on Hartley Street and a gasholder on the site of what became Granville Court (mainly to supply the Lansdowne Estate).

The building of Grosvenor Estate near the railway station begins.

The building of Lansdowne Estate, around Cliff Lane (Cliff Road) and the Esplanade, begins.

1871   Board of Trade licence for construction of pier lapses; Wade renews his option for a further five years.

1872   Building of new Congregational chapel in New Road commences.

Opening of a lending library in Public Rooms, Newbegin.

1873   Branch of the United Order of British Workmen formed (Friendly Society).

Second brick and tile works established: Hornsea Steam Brick and Tile Works, to the north of Seaton Road.

1874   New Congregational chapel opens in New Road. Old chapel building is taken over by the Independent Order of the Good Templars (a Temperance organisation) from Hull and converted into a lodge room and lecture hall – the Hope of Hornsea Lodge.

Pierre Henri Martin du Gillon proposes rival pier company – the Hornsea Pier, Promenade and Improvement Company.

Hornsea Vocal Society formed.

Existing Marine Hotel demolished because of coastal erosion; present Marine Hotel built on a slightly reduced scale.

1875   Deep drainage system laid through the town's main streets at a cost of £9,000.

Coast Guard station becomes uninhabitable because of coastal erosion; new cottages for coast guard personnel built in Cliff Lane (now 6-11 Cliff Road).

Alexandra Lodge of Freemasons formed.

1876   Hornsea Regatta and Aquatic Sports established; an annual event held every August Bank Holiday Monday until 1914.

du Gillon obtains Board of Trade licence to construct a pier, two roads, a tramway, and a sea wall. Associated with this du Gillon also has plans to construct a new town in Hornsea Burton.

1877	Rival pier bids discussed by a House of Commons committee – result: if both pier companies agreed, two bills would be passed, but if they disagreed one bill would be introduced into Parliament. Wade and du Gillon agreed (Wade = north pier; du Gillon = south pier).
	Electric lighting introduced (June).
	Work starts on du Gillon's pier and sea wall (August).
	Storm destroys du Gillon's work (November).
1878	Waterworks opens at Leys Hill, Atwick Road, bringing piped water to the homes of those who could afford the service; for the rest, standpipes, or 'Town Pumps,' were provided in Newbegin, Southgate, Market Place, and Golden Square (now Bank Street).
	Work commences on Wade's north pier.
1879	New police station opens in Newbegin.
	Lifeboat House sold and a larger one built at the corner of Eastbourne Road and Burton Road.
	Ladies Tennis Club formed.
	du Gillon's pier company declared bankrupt (April).
	Wade's pier completed – 1,072 ft in length.
	Violent storm destroys 322 ft at the seaward end of the pier (October); this section never rebuilt.
1880	Visit of HRH Alfred, Duke of Edinburgh (16 August).
1881	Hornsea Stream Brick and Tile Works closes.
	Salvation Army presence in the town.
1882	Hornsea Choral Association formed.
1884	Hornsea School Board established.
1885	New cemetery opened on land off Southgate.
	Waterworks extended and improved.
	Police Station opens in Market Place.

Parish Room built near the church, in Newbegin.

Hornsea Mere and Hotels Company formed (June).

In association with the Victoria Hospital for Sick Children, Hull, a convalescent home opens in Cliff Road.

1887	Hornsea Mere and Hotels Company open refreshment rooms on Kirkholme Point, Hornsea Mere.
1890	Hornsea Mere opens for public boating and fishing.
1895	Hornsea Urban District Council formed.
1896	Death of Joseph Armytage Wade (3 March).
1897	Pier dismantled.
1898	Jubilee Gardens open (commemorating Queen Victoria's Diamond Jubilee). Includes tennis courts, a bowling green and formal flower gardens. Funded by public subscriptions.
	Hornsea Golf Club founded (with 9-hole course in Hall Garth and clubhouse in Newbegin).
1899	Alexandra Lodge built for the Alexandra Lodge of Freemasons.
	Hornsea Associated Football Club formed.
	Hartley Street gasworks ceases production.
1900	An additional track for the Hull to Hornsea railway laid – now a double track system.
	Hornsea Volunteer Rocket Life Saving Brigade formed.
	Star Cinema opens in the Assembly Rooms.
	United Cricket Club formed (from the amalgamation of the Hornsea Cricket Club and the Hornsea and East Holderness Cricket Club).
1901	*Hornsea Gazette* ceases publication.
	Hornsea Telegraph commences publication.
	Town pavements laid (stone flags) to replace the gravelled and cobbled footways.

1902	Fire Brigade established, with a station in Market Place.
1906	Storm severely damages sea defences.
1907	700 ft-long sea wall constructed following storm damage of the previous year.
1907	Church Institute in Newbegin opens. Replaces the Parish Room of 1887.
1908	New 18-hole golf course opens on land adjacent to Rolston Road.
	Christian Scientists begin to meet in the town.
	Sir James Reckitt of Hull provides a holiday home for the Port of Hull Society in Cliff Road.
	Hull Guild of Brave Poor Things provides a holiday home in Alexandra Road; moves to a new building in New Road c.1910; closed by 1973.
1909	Mereside school enlarged.
1910	*Hornsea Guardian* commences publication.
1913	Floral Hall built.
1914	Imperial Hydro Hotel (later the Granville Court) on the Esplanade opens.
1915	Temporary Royal Naval Air Service (from 1918, Royal Air Force) floatplane station established on Kirkholme Point, Hornsea Mere.
1919	Royal Air Force floatplane station on Kirkholme Point decommissioned.
	Hall Garth bought by Hornsea Urban District Council; opens as a public park in 1920.
1920	First council houses built at Hornsea (off King Street).
1921	Hornsea Ex-Servicemen's Club founded. Victoria Picture Theatre opens in Cliff Road.
1923	The War Memorial Cottage Hospital, Eastgate, opens.

Sea wall lengthened by 450 ft on the north side and 1,240 ft on the south.

1924   Lifeboat withdrawn; the lifeboat house becomes the fire station.

1926   East Yorkshire Motor Services commence regular bus service to Hornsea from various locations in the East Riding.

1927   Elim Lodge, Cliff Road, bought for a town hall; closes in 1974, when town hall transfers to the former lifeboat station in Burton Road.

1928   Roman Catholic parish of Hornsea created.

Victoria Gardens and Floral Hall enlarged.

1930   A branch county library opens in Elim Lodge.

Sea wall constructed southwards across Hornsea Gap to Hornsea Burton.

1934   *Hornsea Recorder* commences publication.

1935   New school for all school age children except infants opens in Newbegin, following closure of the Church of England infants' school in Westgate. Infants continued to use the Mereside building.

Jehovah's Witnesses begin to meet in the town.

1938   Wakefield Corporation builds a 'camp school' on Hull Road.

1948   After nationalisation of the industry, Hornsea gasworks passes to North Eastern Gas Board.

1950   East Riding County Council buys Ravenswood, 12 Cliff Road, for use as a children's home; closes 1980.

1953   Urban District Council buys site for Edenfield cemetery in Marlborough Avenue.

1955   Hornsea Pottery Company established.

1956   Roman Catholic Church of the Sacred Heart built in Southgate.

1958	County secondary school opens in Eastgate (on site of the former Hornsea House).
1959	Newbegin school enlarged to accommodate infants.
1964	Hull to Hornsea railway closes.
1965	New fire station in Southgate opens.
1966	Civic Society formed.
1967	East Riding County Council builds the Willows old people's home in Newbegin; closes in 1997 and the property is subsequently demolished.
1969	Hornsea conservation area established.
1970	Convalescent home of Victoria Hospital for Sick Children, Hull, closes.
1973	County nursery school opens in the grounds of the primary school in Newbegin.
	New police station and court house built in Parva Road. The old police station converted to offices for Holderness District Council.
1974	Town Council established with twelve elected members, with the powers and duties of a parish council. Former lifeboat station in Burton Road becomes town hall.
1975	New library opens in Newbegin on site of the former Public Rooms.
1977	Hornsea becomes part of Holderness Borough.
1978	The North Holderness Museum of Village Life opens in Newbegin (in the former Burns Farm).
1981	Hornsea twinned with La Grande-Motte.
1982	An edition of the weekly *Holderness Gazette*, published at Withernsea, commences as a new *Hornsea Gazette*.
1987	*Hornsea and District Post* commences publication.
1990	Imperial Hydro Hotel (Granville Court) demolished following fire.

1995	Hornsea Freeport shopping village opens.
1996	Administratively, Hornsea becomes part of the new East Riding unitary authority.
	Hornsea Leisure Centre opens.
2000	Hornsea Pottery closes.

BIBLIOGRAPHY

1. Primary Sources

Beverley Library, Local Studies Collection

Census returns, 1841-1901 (microfilm).
East Riding of Yorkshire newspapers (microfilm; for listing, see below).
Miscellaneous papers relating to Hornsea (for individual items, see below).

Borthwick Institute of Historical Research, University of York

Cause papers.
Tithe award and map.
Wills and probate inventories.
Visitation records.

East Riding of Yorkshire Archives and Records Service, Beverley

AP/3/54	Hornsea enclosure act, 1801.
DDX564	Hornsea Manor records.
LBHO	Hornsea Local Board records, 1872-96.
LDHO	Hornsea Urban District Council records, 1895-1974.
PE30	St Nicholas church, Hornsea, parish records, 1654-1967.
PE30/10	Hornsea Manor Court Roll, 1623-1768.
PE30/11	Hornsea Manor Court Roll, 1769-1816.
RDB(C6)	Hornsea enclosure map, 1809.
UDHO/1/1	Hornsea Urban District Council minutes.
DDQR	Quaker records.
MF2	Nonconformist records (microfilm).
MRP	Nonconformist records.
MRQ	Nonconformist records.
QDE	Land Tax records.
QS	Quarter Session records.

House of Commons Library, London

Papers relating to Hornsea Pier.

Hull Library, Local Studies Collection

Miscellaneous papers relating to the 1801 enclosure of Hornsea.

331

Public Record Office, London

AIR1	RAF records.
E179	Lay subsidy rolls and other taxation records.
HO129/523/2	Ecclesiastical Census, 1851.
RAIL	Railway records.

University of Hull, Brynmor Jones Library

BTO/1	Hornsea Pier Construction, Maintenance and Regulation Board of Trade. Order, 1866.
BTO/2	Hornsea Pier Board of Trade Order, 1871.
CSR/26/45	Hornsea Pier Bill, 1876.
DDCC	Chichester-Constable family of Burton Constable Hall papers.
DDX298	Miscellaneous documents relating to Hornsea Pier, 1875-1974.

2. British Parliamentary Papers

1835	XXXV	*First Report of the Poor Law Commission.*
1836	XXIX, pt.1	*Second Report of the Poor Law Commission.*
1837	XXXI	*Third Report of the Poor Law Commission.*
1837-38	XXVIII	*Fourth Report of the Poor Law Commission.*
1843	XII	Royal Commission. *Employment of Women and Children in Agriculture: Reports of Special Assistant Poor Law Commissioners.*
1852-53	LXXXIX	*Census of Religious Worship, 1851.*
1867-68	XVII	Royal Commission. *Employment of Children, Young Persons and Women in Agriculture.* First Report.
1868-69	XIII	Royal Commission. *Employment of Children, Young Persons and Women in Agriculture.* Second Report.
1870	XIII	Royal Commission. *Employment of Children, Young Persons and Women in Agriculture.* Third and Fourth Reports.

1882	XIV, XV	Royal Commission. *Depressed Condition of Agricultural Interests.*
1894	XVI	Royal Commission. *Agricultural Depression.*
1895	XVII	Royal Commission. *Agricultural Depression.*
1896	XVII	Royal Commission. *Agricultural Depression.*

3. Printed Sources

A. Books on Hornsea

Anon., 1908. *Illustrated Guide to Hornsea.* Hornsea: *Hornsea Guardian.*

Anon., 1983. *Hornsea School 1958-1983.* Hornsea: Hornsea School.

Anon., 1988. *St. Nicholas' Church, Hornsea, September 1988: 1000 years and beyond.* Hornsea: St Nicholas' Church.

Bedell, E.W., 1848. *An Account of Hornsea, in Holderness, in the East Riding of Yorkshire.* Hull: William Stephenson.

du Gillon, P.H.M., 1876. *An abridged history of the Hornsea pier negotiations, prior to the application being made to Parliament: a series of letters reprinted from the "Hornsea Gazette".* Hull: Montgomery and Sons.

Fretwell, A.T.K., 1894. *Illustrated Guide to Hornsea and the Surrounding District.* Hull: A.T.K. Fretwell.

Heath, P., 1964. *Medieval Clerical Accounts.* York: Borthwick Institute of Historical Research (= St. Anthony's Hall Publications No.26).

Heckford, B. [compiled by B. Jakes], 1998. *Hornsea Pottery, 1949-89 – its people, processes and products.* Hornsea: Hornsea Pottery Collectors and Research Society.

Hobson, J.E., 1974. *A Sketch of Hornsea.* No place of publication or publisher listed. Reprinted in 1984 as *A Sketch of Hornsea, parts I and II.* Hull: Malet Lambert Local History Reprints, extra volumes, 61 and 62.

Hobson, J.E., 2002. *A Sketch of Hornsea.* Hornsea: The North Holderness Museum of Village Life. A revised and edited edition of Hobson 1974 by M. Sewell and F. Hobson.

Hornsea Urban District Council, c.1928. *Official guide to Hornsea, with historical and descriptive text and photographs by Frederick Lord.* British (Publicity) Association.

Humberside County Council, 1982. *The Anglian Cemetery at Hornsea.* Beverley: Humberside Archaeology Unit Information Sheet 11.

Lord, F., 1902. *A popular illustrated handbook of Hornsea.* Hornsea: Frederick Lord.

Lord, F., 1907. *Story of Hornsea Parish Church.* Hornsea.

Lord, F., 1985. *Bygone Hornsea.* Hull: Malet Lambert Local History Reprints Extra Volume 79. (This is a reprint of six articles by Lord that first appeared in the *Hull News* in December 1904).

Markham, J., 1981. *Rose Carr, a remarkable Hornsea character*. Hornsea: The North Holderness Museum of Village Life (= Hornsea Museum Publications No.2).

Sewell, M., 1996. *Joseph Armytage Wade, 1817-1896: The King of Hornsea*. Hornsea: The North Holderness Museum of Village Life.

Sewell, M. (comp.), 1999. *Hornsea Essays. Aspects of the History of Hornsea and North Holderness*. Hornsea: privately published by the author. Edited collection of papers; see individual entries under sections B and F, below.

Sewell, M. (comp.), 2000. *Hornsea Essays 2. More Aspects of the History of Hornsea and North Holderness*. Hornsea: privately published by the author. Edited collection of papers; see individual entries under sections B and F, below.

Sewell, M. (comp.), 2002. *Hornsea Essays 3. Further Aspects of the History of Hornsea and North Holderness*. Hornsea: privately published by the author. Edited collection of papers; see individual entries under sections B and F, below.

Sheppard, T., 1893. *An Illustrated Guide to Hornsea and the Surrounding District with Map and Plan*. Hull: A.T.K. Fretwell.

Sheppard, T., 1912. *The Lost Towns of the Yorkshire Coast*. London: A. Brown & Sons. Facsimile reprint issued by Mr. Pye Books, Howden, in 1986.

Smith, M. (ed.), 1993. *Hornsea a century ago. The town and its people in the 1890s*. Beverley: Highgate Publications Ltd.

Southwell, G.L. (comp.), 1983. *Hornsea in old picture postcards*. Zaltbommel: Netherlands, European Library.

Southwell, G.L. (comp.), 1995. *Hornsea*. Stroud: The Chalford Publishing Company.

Walker, F., 1996. *Faces and Places in Hornsea and Holderness*. Cherry Burton: Hutton Press.

Walker, J.E.S., 1995. *The Home Front: Hornsea and Holderness in the Second World War*. Hornsea: North Holderness Museum of Village Life.

B.   Articles and papers on Hornsea

Allison, K.J., 2002. Hornsea. In G.H.R. Kent (ed.), *VCH Yorkshire East Riding, Volume VII: The Middle and North Divisions of Holderness Wapentake*, pp. 273-295. Oxford: Oxford University Press for London University Institute of Historical Research.

Anon., 1925. A chapter in the history of Hornsea: George Fox and the Holderness Quakers. *Hull Daily Mail*, 10 September 1925.

Armstrong, A.L., 1923. On two bone points from Hornsea, East Yorkshire. *Man: a monthly record of anthropological science* 83 (March 1923): 49-50.

Coyle, P., 2003. From Kiln to Table. *Yorkshire Journal* 43 (Winter 2003): 54-63.

English Nature 1951 and 1983. *Hornsea Mere* [Site of Special Scientific Interest designation].

Head, R., 1997. The Anglo-Saxon cemetery at Hornsea. *East Riding Archaeologist* 9 (1997): 10-65.

Lamplugh, G.W., 1925. Well section near Hornsea. *Transactions of the Hull Geological Society* 6(5) (1922-25).

Robinson, J.F., 1906. T. Petch, BA, BSc (Lond.). *Transactions of the Hull Scientific and Field Naturalists' Club* 3 (1903-1906): 182-183.

Read, C.H., 1923. On two bone harpoons from Hornsea, East Yorkshire. *Man: a monthly record of anthropological science* 13(4) (April 1923): 49-

Royal Anthropological Institute, 1923. Bone Harpoons from Holderness, E. Yorks: being the report of a committee of the Council of the Royal Anthropological Institute. *Man: a monthly record of anthropological science* 13(4) (April 1923): 49-50.

Sewell, M., 1999a. Hornsea Pier 1880-1897. In M. Sewell (comp.), *Hornsea Essays. Aspects of the History of Hornsea and North Holderness*: 3-4.

Sewell, M., 1999b. Rose Carr and the Salvation Soldiers. In M. Sewell (comp.), *Hornsea Essays. Aspects of the History of Hornsea and North Holderness*: 9-12.

Sewell, M., 1999c. The Hornsea Mere and Hotels Company 1885-1890. In M. Sewell (comp.), *Hornsea Essays. Aspects of the History of Hornsea and North Holderness*: 15-22.

Sewell, M., 1999d. A Description of the Coast at Hornsea in 1858. In M. Sewell (comp.), *Hornsea Essays. Aspects of the History of Hornsea and North Holderness*: 29-30.

Sewell, M., 1999e. Hornsea's Medieval Religious Guilds. In M. Sewell (comp.), *Hornsea Essays. Aspects of the History of Hornsea and North Holderness*: 31-36.

Sewell, M., 2000a. Payment by Results – The Problem of School Truancy in the 1890s. In M. Sewell (comp.), *Hornsea Essays 2. More Aspects of the History of Hornsea and North Holderness*: 2.

Sewell, M., 2000b. The Great Storm of 1880. In M. Sewell (comp.), *Hornsea Essays 2. More Aspects of the History of Hornsea and North Holderness*: 3-7.

Sewell, M., 2000c. The Hull and Hornsea Railway Company 1861-1866. In M. Sewell (comp.), *Hornsea Essays 2. More Aspects of the History of Hornsea and North Holderness*: 20-29.

Sewell, M., 2000d. Civil Defence Incidents in the Hornsea Area During the Second World War. In M. Sewell (comp.), *Hornsea Essays 2. More Aspects of the History of Hornsea and North Holderness*: 30-33.

Sewell, M., 2000e. Hornsea Beck. In M. Sewell (comp.), *Hornsea Essays 2. More Aspects of the History of Hornsea and North Holderness*: 33-36.

Sewell, M., 2002a. The Roundheads in Hornsea, A Reappraisal. In M. Sewell (comp.), *Hornsea Essays 3. Further Aspects of the History of Hornsea and North Holderness*: 31-33.

Sewell, M., 2002b. Hornsea's First Council Houses. In M. Sewell (comp.), *Hornsea Essays 3. Further Aspects of the History of Hornsea and North Holderness*: 34-36.

Sewell, M., 2002c. Four Royal Jubilees [Queen Victoria's Golden Jubilee, 1887; Queen Victoria's Diamond Jubilee, 1897; King George V's Silver Jubilee, 1935; and Queen Elizabeth II's Silver Jubilee, 1977]. In

M. Sewell (comp.), *Hornsea Essays 3. Further Aspects of the History of Hornsea and North Holderness*: 37-40.

Sheppard, T., 1898. Notes on a large pair of antlers of the red deer (*Cervus elaphas*) from the peat at Hornsea. *Transactions of the Hull Scientific and Field Naturalists' Club* 1: 22-23.

Sheppard, T., 1900a. Geological Rambles in East Yorkshire. Withernsea to Hornsea. *Leeds Mercury Weekly Supplement*, 29 September 1900.

Sheppard, T., 1900b. Geological Rambles in East Yorkshire. Hornsea to Bridlington. *Leeds Mercury Weekly Supplement*, 12 October 1900.

Sheppard, T., 1906. On a section in the Post-Glacial deposit at Hornsea. *Naturalist* (December 1906): 420-424.

Sheppard, T., 1907. On a Section in a Post-Glacial Lacustrine Deposit at Hornsea. *British Association Annual Report*.

Sheppard, T., 1908. Hornsea: Its Mere and Coastline. *Naturalist* (August1908): 302-310.

Sheppard, T., 1912. Coast Changes at Hornsea. *Naturalist* (April 1912): 114-120.

Sheppard, T., 1913a. An Old Plan of Hornsea Mere. *Naturalist* (February1913): 89.

Sheppard, T., 1913b. Coast Changes at Hornsea. *Naturalist* (February 1913): 99.

Sheppard, T., 1913c. Anglo-Saxon Remains at Hornsea. *Hull Museums Publication* 95 (July 1913): 15-16.

Sheppard, T., 1913d. The Hornsea Token. *Hull Museums Publication* 95 (July 1913): 16-18.

Sheppard, T., 1913e. An Anglo-Saxon cemetery at Hornsea. *Hull Museums Publication* 97 (September 1913): 258-272. Reprinted from *Transactions of the Hull Scientific and Field Naturalists' Club* 4(5): 258-272.

Sheppard, T., 1922a. Red Deer Antlers from the Peat near Hornsea. *Hull Museums Publication* 131 (March 1922): 22.

Sheppard, T., 1922b. Harpoons under the peat in Holderness. *Nature* (2 December 1922):

Sheppard, T., 1923a. The Maglemose Harpoons. *Man: a monthly record of anthropological science* 13(5) (May 1923): 80.

Sheppard, T., 1923b. The Maglemose Harpoons. *Naturalist* (May 1923): 169-178.

Sheppard, T., 1923c. The Holderness Harpoons. *Naturalist* (June 1923): 219-220.

Sheppard, T., 1923d. Maglemose Again. *Naturalist* (December 1923): 391.

Sheppard, T., 1930. Maglemose Harpoons. *Naturalist* (May 1930): 193-194.

Simmons, G., 2001. Royal Naval Air Service Hornsea Mere. *East Yorkshire Historian* 2 (2001): 80-86.

Sitch, B., 1991. A possible chariot burial at Hornsea, North Humberside. *East Riding Archaeological Society Newsletter* 36: 12-17.

Sitch, B., 1991-92. A possible chariot burial at Hornsea. *East Yorkshire Local History Society Bulletin* 45 (Winter 1991-92): 23-26.

Tibbles, J., 1997. An Archaeological Watching Brief at the Granville Court Site in 1995. *East Riding Archaeologist* 9: 61-63.

C. Essays, theses and dissertations on Hornsea

Barker, K.G., c.1968. *Hornsea: a study of a coastal town.* Unpublished University of Durham BA dissertation. Copy in Local Studies Library, Beverley Library.

Mayoh, K.L., 1961. *A Comparative Study of Resorts on the Coast of Holderness.* Unpublished University of Hull MA thesis.

Santaniello, J., 1992. *English villages in the middle ages shrank or became deserted for many different reasons. Analyse these reasons as they affected settlement in your area, with examples. Discuss the evidence for the existence and later desertion of one village.* Unpublished essay for the BA degree in Regional and Local History, University of Hull. Contains discussion of Southorpe deserted village.

Shackles, B., 1974. *Hornsea in the nineteenth century. Its growth as a resort.* Unpublished thesis for the Diploma of History (Scheme C, Local History), University of London.

D. Unpublished material on Hornsea

Harrison, S., 2001. *An Archaeological Watching Brief at 49 Market Place, Hornsea, East Riding of Yorkshire, HU18 1AP.* Unpublished Client Report. Document prepared on behalf of JP Developers Ltd; copy held in the SMR Office, Humber Archaeology Partnership, Hull.

Lonsdale, M.J. (comp.), n.d. *Hornsea in the 1850s* [and] *North Holderness villages in the 1850s and 1860s through the eyes of the Beverley Guardian.* Transcripts of newspaper articles; copy in the Local Studies Library, Beverley Library.

Loten, R.A. n.d. *A History of Hornsea (Wesleyan) Methodism.* Typescript copy (4pp); copy held by the Local Studies Library, Beverley Library.

Park, G.R., n.d. *Wade of Hornsea and Wood Hall and Brantingham Thorpe.* Manuscript notes (5pp); copy held by the Local Studies Library, Beverley Library.

Rycraft, A. (trans.), n.d. *Accounts of the vicar of Hornsea, 1488 and 1491* [English medieval documents, items 11 and 12]. Facsimile copies and translations; copies held in the Brynmor Jones Library, University of Hull.

Sharp, W., 1993. *Wade's Hornsea.* Typescript booklet (49pp); copy held by the Local Studies Library, Beverley Library.

E. Directories (in chronological order)

Baines, E., 1823. *History, Directory and Gazetteer of the County of York.*

White, W., 1840. *History, Gazetteer and Directory of the East and North Ridings of Yorkshire.*

Sheahan, J.J. and Whellan, T., 1855. *History and Topography of the City of York and the East Riding of Yorkshire.*

White, W., 1867. *Directory of the East Riding of Yorkshire.*

Post Office, 1872 and subsequent editions. *Post Office* (later *Kelly's*) *Directory of Yorkshire: North and East Ridings with the City of York.*

Bulmer, T. & Co., 1892. *History, Topography and Directory of East Yorkshire.*

F.   Books containing material on Hornsea

English, B., 1979. *The Lords of Holderness 1086-1260. A Study in Feudal Society.* Oxford: Oxford University Press for the University of Hull.

Pevsner, N. with Neave, D., 1995. *The Buildings of England, Yorkshire: York and the East Riding.* London: Penguin Books. The Hornsea entry is on pages 477-83.

Poulson, G., 1840. *The History and Antiquities of the Seigniory of Holderness, in the East Riding of the County of York.* 2 volumes. Hull: Robert Brown (volume 1) and Thomas Topping (volume 2). The chapter on Hornsea is to be found in volume 1: 314-340.

Gilbertson, D.D., 1984. *Late Quaternary Environments and Man in Holderness.* Oxford: British Archaeological Reports (= BAR British Series 134).

G.   *Articles and papers containing material on Hornsea*

Armstrong, A.L., 1923. The Maglemose remains of Holderness and the Baltic counterparts. *Proceedings of the Prehistoric Society of East Anglia* 4: 57-70.

Clark, J.G.D. and Godwin, H., 1956. A Maglemosian Site at Brandesburton, Holderness, Yorkshire. *Proceedings of the Prehistoric Society* 22 (1956): 6-22 (Discussion of the discoveries in 1905 and 1932 of Mesolithic bone points from Hornsea).

Loughlin, N. and Miller, K.R. (ed.), 1979. Hornsea. In *A Survey of Archaeological Sites in Humberside.* Beverley: Humberside Libraries and Amenities: 54-55.

Sewell, M., 1999f. Ancient Crosses of North Holderness. In M. Sewell (comp.), *Hornsea Essays. Aspects of the History of Hornsea and North Holderness*: 5-8.

Sewell, M., 1999g. Archbishop Herring's Visitation of 1743. A Snapshot of Religious Life in North Holderness. In M. Sewell, *Hornsea Essays. Aspects of the History of Hornsea and North Holderness*: 23-28.

Sewell, M., 1999h. Military Activity in North Holderness, 1793-1802. In M. Sewell, *Hornsea Essays. Aspects of the History of Hornsea and North Holderness*: 36-40.

Sewell, M., 2000f. The North Holderness Volunteer Infantry 1803-1808. In M. Sewell (comp.), *Hornsea Essays 2. More Aspects of the History of Hornsea and North Holderness*: 15-19.

Sewell, M., 2000g. The Hearth Tax of 1672. In M. Sewell (comp.), *Hornsea Essays 2. More Aspects of the History of Hornsea and North Holderness*: 37-40.

Sewell, M., 2002d. John Paul Jones off the Holderness Coast, 1779. In M. Sewell (comp.), *Hornsea Essays 3. Further Aspects of the History of Hornsea and North Holderness*: 2-5.

Sewell, M., 2002e. The Religious Census of 1851. In M. Sewell (comp.), *Hornsea Essays 3. Further Aspects of the History of Hornsea and North Holderness*: 5-12.

Sewell, M., 2002f. The Constables of Wassand. A Brief History. In M. Sewell (comp.), *Hornsea Essays 3. Further Aspects of the History of Hornsea and North Holderness*: 12-18.

Sewell, M., 2002g. Crime and Punishment in North Holderness in the Early 1880s. In M. Sewell (comp.), *Hornsea Essays 3. Further Aspects of the History of Hornsea and North Holderness*: 18-24.

Sheppard, T., 1913. Our German Ancestors: Being an Account of the Anglo-Saxon Remains Found in East Yorkshire. *Transactions of the Hull Scientific and Field Naturalists' Club* 4 (1913): 299-300. Reprinted as *Hull Museums Publication* 117 (March 1919).

4. Newspapers

Beverley Guardian 1856 to date
Bridlington Free Press 1859 to date
Driffield Times 1860 to date
East Riding Chronicle and Driffield Express 1872-1917
Eastern Morning News 1864-1929
Hornsea Gazette 1869-1901
Hornsea Guardian 1910
Hornsea Recorder 1934
Hull Advertiser 1794-1867
Hull Courant 1746-59
Hull Daily Mail 1885 to date
Hull News 1852-1901
Hull Packet 1787-1886
Hull Times 1857-1984
York Courant 1725-1848
York Herald 1790-1889
Yorkshire Gazette 1819-1954
Yorkshire Post 1866 to date

5. Hornsea Working Papers (HWP)

The Hornsea Working Papers began as a drawing together of data and drafts of early chapters for this volume. They quickly became the 'building blocks' for the book and a device for the handling and organisation of both ideas and material. Many of the HWPs were revisited several times and went through numerous revisions. They were never intended for wide publication; however, electronic copies will be deposited in the Beverley Local Studies library. A complete list of papers is as follows:

HWP1	A Hornsea bibliography
HWP2	Descriptions of Hornsea
HWP3	Geology and topography
HWP4	Morphology of Hornsea

INDEX

343

Royal Air Force, 291, 315, 327
Royal Naval Air Service, 224, 291, 327
St Bede's College, 201
St Mary's Abbey, 3, 77, 80-3, 87, 89-90, 96, 102, 110, 114, 120-1, 320
St Nicholas' church, 84, 87, 93-5, 279, 322-3
Salvation Army, 273-4, 280, 282-3, 325
Salvation Soldiers, 282-3
Sandpiper Court, 312
Sands Lane, 110, 322
Scalby Place, 85, 131, 133, 206
School Board, 261, 325
      National, 234, 261, 268-9, 283, 322, 328-9
      secondary, 189, 329
      Sunday, 283-4
Sea Road, 166
Seaton, 12, 22, 41-2, 48-9, 51, 54, 59, 62, 69, 80, 85-6, 92, 104, 106, 110-11, 113, 122, 152, 166, 169, 322
Seaton Road, 165, 200, 324
Sheppard, Thomas, 33, 37-9, 53, 63-4, 68, 105
Sigglesthorne, 42, 48, 51, 54, 59, 69, 86, 92, 97, 106, 108, 122, 140, 152, 169, 262-3, 322
Skipsea, 37, 39, 76, 140, 166, 181, 183, 186, 257, 276
Society of Friends, 140, 143
South Cliff Estate, 199-200, 202, 252
Southgate, 82, 85-6, 93, 96-7, 124-5, 129-30, 137, 139, 141, 166, 179, 188-9, 191-2, 200-1, 219, 270-4, 278-9, 282, 318, 321, 325, 329
Southgate Gardens, 307, 308-9
Southorpe, 12, 24, 69, 72, 74, 91-3, 97-100, 106, 108, 114, 122-3, 151-2, 155, 162, 165-6, 320
spa, 214-6
Star Picture Theatre, 299, 326
Station House, 203
Straker's Hotel, 219
Strawberry Gardens, 309
Stream Dike, 42, 48, 51, 54, 59, 69, 97-8, 101-2, 105, 107-8, 111, 122, 124, 137, 152, 166, 179, 258
Suffolk Terrace, 200, 208
Sunset Cottage, 131, 133
Swan Island, 26
Swiss Terrace, 189
Tetherings, The, 123, 152
Temperance Hall, 282
Tranmere Park, 312
Trinity Chapel, 273, 323
Trinity Fields, 312
Tower House, 96
United Reformed church, 203, 273, 280-1
Ventnor House, 200
Vestry, 268